EUROPEAN OTHERS

Difference Incorporated

Roderick A. Ferguson and Grace Kyungwon Hong, series editors

European Others

QUEERING ETHNICITY IN POSTNATIONAL EUROPE

Fatima El-Tayeb

Difference Incorporated

University of Minnesota Press
Minneapolis
London

Portions of the Introduction were previously published as "'The Forces of Creolization': Colorblindness and Visible Minorities in the New Europe," in *The Creolization of Theory*, ed. Françoise Lionnet and Shu-mei Shih (Durham, N.C.: Duke University Press, 2010). Parts of chapter 1 were previously published as "'The Birth of a European Public': Migration, Postnationality, and Race in the Uniting of Europe," *American Quarterly* 60, no. 3 (2008): 865–69. Portions of chapter 2 were published as "Blackness and Its (Queer) Discontents," in *Remapping Black Germany*, ed. Tobias Nagl and Sara Lennox (Amherst: University of Massachusetts Press, forthcoming).

Published by the University of Minnesota Press
111 Third Avenue South, Suite 290
Minneapolis, MN 55401–2520
http://www.upress.umn.edu

Library of Congress Cataloging-in-Publication Data

El-Tayeb, Fatima.
European others : queering ethnicity in postnational Europe / Fatima El-Tayeb.
    p. cm. — (Difference incorporated)
Includes bibliographical references and index.
ISBN 978-0-8166-7015-4 (hc : alk. paper)
ISBN 978-0-8166-7016-1 (pb : alk. paper)
  1. Group identity—Europe. 2. National characteristics, European. 3. Ethnicity—Europe. 4. Race discrimination—Europe. I. Title.
HM753.E48 2011
305.3089'0094—dc22

2011013605

In memoriam Hermann Etzold

CONTENTS

ACKNOWLEDGMENTS

First, my gratitude and admiration to the artists and activists who inspired this study, for their dedication, vision, and perseverance. A particular thanks to Peggy Piesche, Beldan Sezen, Olumide Popoola, Jay Haime, Anne Krul, Sook Ahn, Marlon Reina, Barbara Endres, Donna Muller, Astrid Kusser, and Massimo Perinelli.

This book's transnational, interdisciplinary, and intersectional perspective was fundamentally shaped by the unique intellectual community created at the University of California, San Diego by friends and colleagues like Yen Espiritu, Nayan Shah, Daniel Widener, Takashi Fujitani, Rosemary George, Luis Alvarez, Ross Frank, Jody Blanco, Shelley Streeby, and Curtis Marez, whose feedback was essential.

My sincere appreciation also goes to UCSD's amazing community of student activists who continue to be a major source of inspiration.

A special thanks for their indispensable insights, support, and friendship to Lisa Lowe, Angelina Maccarone, Lisa Yoneyama, Sara Johnson, Kimberly Vinall, Jin-Kyung Lee, Dennis Childs, Luis Martin-Cabrera, Grace Hong, and Tara Javidi.

A number of grants were instrumental in allowing me to finish this project: Amherst College's Copeland Fellowship, for hospitality while in Amherst and beyond (I am especially grateful to Christian Rogowski and Sara Lennox); a scholar-in-residence position at the University of Tennessee in Knoxville (many thanks to Stephanie Ohnesorg and Carolyn Hodges); a UCSD Career Development Grant and UCLA's Mellon Fellowship "Cultures in Transnational Perspective," initiated by Françoise Lionnet and Shu-mei Shih, who are an inspiration in every regard. Many thanks to them and the "mellow felons," in particular Alessandra di Maio.

Finally, my gratitude to my editors, Roderick A. Ferguson and Richard Morrison.

Theorizing Urban Minority Communities in Postnational Europe

Indeed, it seemed to me that haunting was precisely the domain of turmoil and trouble, that moment (of however long duration) when things are not in their assigned places, when the cracks and rigging are exposed, when the people who are meant to be invisible show up without any sign of leaving, when disturbed feelings cannot be put away, when something else, something different from before, seems like it must be done. It is this sociopolitical-psychological state to which haunting referred.

—AVERY GORDON, *Ghostly Matters*

If minor formations become method and theory, then new analytics will be brought to the foreground that creolize the universalisms we live with today from the bottom up and from the inside out.

—SHU-MEI SHIH AND FRANÇOISE LIONNET,
The Creolization of Theory

Fawaka, Merhaba, Conta Bai, Hoe Gaat Het?

In the summer of 2007, amidst continuing discussions of Islam, migration, "black schools,"[1] and Dutch culture, media in the Netherlands presented their audience with what they deemed a brand new phenomenon: *straattaal,* or street slang, a new youth language spoken on the streets of cities across the country. Attempting an authoritative definition, the liberal Christian newspaper *Trouw* declared: "*Straattaal*—the Dutch version of the American slang—originates in multicultural youth groups (particularly in Damsko, Amsterdam) and includes words from among others English/American, Sranantongo [a Surinamese language], and Moroccan" (Pronk 2007).[2] Reporting from a community meeting devoted to *straattaal*, the *Trouw* journalist proceeded to give various examples of this "secret language" spoken primarily by *allochton* youths—including the multilingual greeting heading this section, using terms from Sranantongo, Arabic, Papiamento, and Dutch respectively, and roughly translating to "What's up, welcome, how are you?"—before ending her piece speculating whether this new hybrid code hinders or facilitates the integration of those speaking it (for the most part Dutch citizens of color).

This book will pick up a number of the questions arising in the Dutch discussion, putting them in a larger and in some respects quite different context. Rather than as a new phenomenon or a sign of the "Americanization" of Dutch youngsters, I see *straattaal* and other local variations of these "multiethnolects" (Wiese 2009, 782) all across Europe as symptomatic of a process long in the making, namely the emergence of multicultural minority communities in continental European urban centers characterized by the ambiguous and precarious living conditions of its inhabitants.[3] Migrants and their contested ability to adapt to European societies have been at the center of public and policy debates since their massive postwar arrival in the 1950s, but paradoxically, these debates have seen little change over the last five decades—their focus often is still on the moment of arrival and "what if" scenarios: namely, what happens to Europe if these people stay (see, e.g., Schramma 2001)? Half a century later, it should seem fairly obvious that the vast majority of migrants did stay and that the face of Europe has changed accordingly. The logical conclusion however, that they are by now as European as those worrying about them, is rarely drawn, prevented by an often unspoken, but nonetheless seemingly very precise, racialized understanding of proper Europeanness that continues to exclude certain migrants and their descendants.[4]

As a result, over the last twenty years, metropolises across the continent witnessed the emergence of new networks based on the experiences of an increasingly younger, ethnically diverse urban population confronted with contradictory projections, demands, and ascriptions with regard to national and ethnic identifications often in stark contrast to their complex lived realities. In response to the specific forms of exclusion and marginalization it faces, the second and third generation of migrants frequently draws on and transforms modes of resistance and analysis originating outside of Europe and circulated in transnational discourses of diaspora, ranging from hip-hop culture to women of color feminism.[5] *European Others* explores the emergence of these minority cultures and the new kinds of political movements they generated by mirroring their creative creolization in using an innovative theoretical lens that draws on a variety of methodologies; critical race theory, queer of color critique, Caribbean créolité; usually not applied to Europe. It is a book thus that addresses issues of race, identity, and resistance, focusing on a group largely invisible in popular as well as academic discourses, namely Europeans of color.

The terms "of color" and "Europe" require some clarification and as both are central to my study, I will do my best to be exact in my use. However, my definition of "Europeans of color" does not claim any scientific precision. Though racializations always pretend to name natural, unchanging, obvious facts, they are always ambiguous, shifting, and unstable. This is hidden by what Étienne Balibar calls the "fictive ethnicity" on which all nation states are built:

> No nation possesses an ethnic basis naturally, but as social formations are nationalized, the populations included within them, divided up among them or dominated by them are ethnicized—that is, represented in the past or in the future *as if* they formed a natural community, possessing of itself an identity of origins, culture, and interests, which transcends individual and social conditions. (Balibar 1994, 224)

According to Balibar, fictive ethnicity is constructed via two primary tools, language and race, both of which will be central throughout my study as I explore their roles in creating as well as queering and destabilizing the exclusionary fictive European ethnicity.[6]

The history of racialization in Europe emphasizes race as a social rather than biological construct (Mosse 1978; Gilroy 2000) and in its current configuration it is closely related to what Rey Chow in the U.S. context called "the ethnicization of labor" (Chow 2002), that is, "a flexible social mechanism for producing an internal boundary between what is considered proper and valuable, on the one hand, and foreign and inferior, on the other" (Adelson 2005, 8). Chow goes on to claim that "the experience of migration . . . simply highlights and amplifies the connection between commodified labor and ethnicization that takes place in a society even when there are no migrants, even when migrants have become citizens" (Chow 2002, 34). Thus, the "ethnic," rather than replacing the loaded and ambiguous term "race" with a neutral, precise, and nonbinary terminology of largely objectifiable regional difference as is often professed in neoliberal discourse (Hong 2008), is the outcome of hierarchized labor structures that not merely use, but produce "ethnic" difference. It is precisely the process of ethnicization that permanently defines ethnicized citizens as "migrants," creating a catch-22 inevitably reinforcing

> [t]he positivistic view that ethnics are, indeed, aliens from elsewhere, in fact end[ing] up lending support to the concept of ethnicity as an a priori, essentialist condition of foreignness . . . the ethnic as such stands in modernity as the site of a foreignness that is produced from within privileged societies and is at once defined by and constitutive of that society's hierarchical divisions of labor. (Chow 2002, 34)

As Leslie Adelson has shown for the German context (Adelson 2005), Chow's definition can be extremely helpful in analyzing how post–World War II labor migration produced an ethnicized population that despite often having acquired citizenship is continued to be perceived as migrant, as "alien[s] from elsewhere." In what follows, I propose that this argument can be extended to processes of ethnicization in postwar Europe that closely interact and overlap with longer-term, in part precapitalist processes of racialization (Balibar 2004; Goldberg 2006, discussed in more detail below).

The geographical focus of this study, continental Europe, is commonly taken to include the nations west of the Ural. All parts of Europe are arguably invested in "whiteness" as the norm against which ethnicization is read as a tool of differentiation between insiders and outsiders, in fact, that this is so is one of the key claims of this book. What this notion of whiteness constitutes in the European context cannot be presupposed however and as emerging European whiteness studies have shown, the continent's racial paradigms differ from the U.S. context, in which whiteness studies originate, in a number of ways that still need to be fully explored.[7] It is obvious nonetheless that both Eastern and Southern Europe's claim to this whiteness is more ambiguous than that of the Northwest of the continent. Since the end of state socialism, migration patterns are increasingly structured by the disparity between rich West and poor East, and Central and Eastern Europeans are by now the largest migrant group in Western Europe (European Commission 2008). Eastern Europeans, in particular from nations not yet part of the European Union, certainly constitute ethnicized labor. Southern Europeans who migrated north in large numbers in the course of postwar guest worker programs, while having increasingly gained insider status as "Christian" through the current foregrounding of a cultural-religious framing of exclusions, are still often suffering the effects of racialization (see, e.g., Klimt, in Eder 2003). Thus, when I speak of "racialized minorities" in Western Europe, groups of Eastern and Southern European descent usually will be included, in order to point out that the Othering of these groups, while closely related to the ethnicization of labor, is part of a larger system of knowledge that goes beyond the context of capitalist labor production (see Guitiérez Rodríguez, and Steyerl 2002; Ha, Lauré al-Samarai, and Mysorekar 2007).[8]

But popular discourses on migration, especially when framed in negative terms, largely target "visible minorities," represented by people of non-European descent and Muslims (including those of Eastern European descent), whose situation in some ways is thus significantly different from that of "peripheral" European migrants and minorities. The term "Europeans of color" thus is meant to reference populations defined as inherently "non-European" because of a racialized cultural difference linked to a non-European origin (an origin that, as in the case of Roma and Sinti, might lie centuries in the past).[9] As will be discussed in more detail in the next section, the means by which minority populations often originating in migrations from Africa, Asia, and the Middle East continue to be differentiated from "real" Europeans reference supposedly innate, visible, unchangeable differences from what the popular imagination considers to be European. This is a perception in other words that uses an essentialist understanding of culture that largely follows earlier ascriptions of similar qualities to the same groups under the heading of "race."

To reference race as native to contemporary European thought, however, violates the powerful narrative of Europe as a colorblind continent, largely untouched by the devastating ideology it exported all over the world. This narrative, framing the continent as a space free of "race" (and by implication, racism), is not only central to the way Europeans perceive themselves, but has also gained near-global acceptance. Despite the geographical and intellectual origin of the very concept of race in Europe, not to mention the explicitly race-based policies that characterized both its fascist regimes and its colonial empires, the continent often is marginal at best in discourses on race or racism, in particular with regard to contemporary configurations that are often closely identified with the United States as a center of both explicit race discourse and of resistance to it.

This position has been forcefully expressed for example in Pierre Bourdieu's and Loïc Wacquant's influential, and controversial, 1999 essay "On the Cunning of Imperialist Reason," which claims that the current U.S. dominance on every level of international relations, including academic discourse, globally imposed concepts and issues particular to this nation's context, causing a "globalization of American problems" (Bourdieu and Wacquant 1999, 46). One of the authors' central examples is the harmful introduction of "race" as an analytical framework into contexts that it is alien to, such as the European or Latin American one. In stark contrast to Chow's theory of the ethnicization of labor, Bourdieu and Wacquant present "race" and "class" as alternatives, ending their piece by affirming class as a universally relevant category of social analysis while relegating race to the lesser status of (U.S.) particularism (Bourdieu and Wacquant 1999, 51).[10]

While the polemical nature of the essay sets it apart from more differentiated assessments of the usefulness of categories of race for continental European scholarship in particular on migration (discussed in more detail in chapter 2), it nonetheless expresses a number of assumptions, attitudes, and strategies common primarily in political discourse, but also in continental European scholarship. Among them are the suspicion that race does little more than cloud the view of the more relevant category class; the idea that U.S. cultural imperialism destroys organic, authentic, and formally unmitigated analytical concepts inherent to the affected regions by superimposing inorganic categories like race; the discrediting of proponents of the usefulness of race as an analytical category outside of the United States as collaborators with imperialism, granting them a power by proxy they do not possess if one does not assume the full force of the world's only superpower to be behind them; and an understanding of U.S. theorizations of race that is often superficial in its grasp of in particular scholarship by authors of color (ignoring for example well-established concepts such as intersectionality [Crenshaw 1991] in favor of a simplified race and class binary. See, e.g., Griffin and Braidotti 2002).

Bourdieu's and Wacquant's overall defensive tone—"From being an analytical tool, the concept of racism becomes a mere instrument of accusation: under the guise of science it is the logic of the trial which asserts itself" (Bourdieu and Wacquant 1999, 44)—furthermore produces a sense of besiegement, of an immensely uneven battle, in which intellectual honesty and science need to be defended against the onslaught of an American-based "political correctness" often expressed within a terminology of race that ends up silencing in particular any feminist and queer critique of migrant communities (ibid., 43). This tone and this image of Europe as threatened by, on the one hand, cultural and intellectual "Americanization" and political correctness, and on the other by anti-Enlightenment migrant fundamentalism, places the continent in the position of victim, occupied with defending its values rather than imposing them on others. The imagery of a European culture faced with possible extinction or at least dilution invites a binary rather than an interactive view of cultural exchange and has become a familiar feature in European discourse in particular on the continent's Muslim population, as will be discussed in more detail in the book's chapters.

David Roediger and others have pointed out that a more constructive response to too narrowly U.S.-focused theories of racialization than their wholesale rejection would be a contextualized understanding of these processes (Roediger 2006; Patterson and Kelley 2000). In arguing for a concept of interrelated but specific "racial regionalizations," replacing paradigmatic models of racism, David Theo Goldberg uses the European case as a prime example for the necessity of this shift in paradigms. Pointing to the absence of a discourse on race not as a sign of the absence of racism, but as a severe impediment to the possibility of effectively addressing the latter, he claims that:

> Europe begins to exemplify what happens when no category is available to name a set of experiences that are linked in their production or at least inflection, historically and symbolically, experientially and politically, to racial arrangements and engagements. The European experience is a case study in the frustrations, deliminations, and injustices of political racelessness. (Goldberg 2006, 335)

The continental European case represents a form of racialization that receives relatively little academic attention both because it diverges from models traditionally dominating the discourse around race and because its strategy of denial is particularly hard to challenge: rather than explicit mechanisms by which race is implemented or referenced in political, social, and economic interactions within and between communities, the ideology of "racelessness" is the process by which racial thinking and its effects are made invisible. Race, at times, seems to exist anywhere but in Europe, where racialized minorities have traditionally been placed outside of the national and by extension continental community. Europe can thus be situated within the larger context of ideologies of colorblindness that prohibit discourses around racialized oppression (see, e.g., Marchant in Lionnet and Shih 2005; Langfur 2006 on Brazil; or Torres-Saillant 2000 on the Dominican Republic). In its European version, this ideology is characterized by the convergence of race and religion as well as the externalization of racialized populations (rather than their relegation to second-class citizen status). Recent panics around the incompatibility of Islam with modern societies, the French "riots" of 2005, or the terrorist threat posed by "second-generation migrants," indicate that there still is a substantial investment in what Stuart Hall called the "internalist" narrative of European identity, that is one in which Europe appears as a largely homogeneous entity, entirely self-sufficient, its development uninfluenced by outside forces or contact with other parts of the world (Hall 1991). Accordingly, within this narrative, European racial and religious diversity is less a reality than a threat to the continent's very essence.

Building on Audre Lorde's claim that the master's tools cannot dismantle the master's house (Lorde, in Anzaldúa and Moraga 1981), throughout this book I take a stance that is directly opposed to Bourdieu and
Wacquant's argument for the purity of regionally authentic theorizations,
instead suggesting that the dominant internalist narrative of Europe cannot be deconstructed with methodologies internal to it alone, even if, like
cosmopolitanism, critical theory, or poststructuralism, they are meant to
represent a global rather than Eurocentric perspective. In their recent volume on *The Creolization of Theory,* Françoise Lionnet and Shu-mei Shi
offer an alternative approach, presenting a methodology developed in the
Caribbean context by among others Stuart Hall and Edouard Glissant and
suggesting its careful application to other positionalities:

> [A]ll life stories of theoretical concepts begin as regional concepts,
> and they are all once historically and contextually specific before they
> are widely disseminated, applied, or assumed to be universal. It is, on
> the one hand, as Palmié notes, a matter of "conceptual politics" that
> certain concepts can overcome their particularity while others are not
> able to or not given a chance to. On the other hand, what is at issue is
> also the degree of pretensions that we attribute to a given theory. (Shih
> and Lionnet 2011)

Creolization thus works to rid theory of its pretensions by exploring the
at times tense relationship between specific circumstances and universal
conditions, local applications and global connections, without aiming to
dissolve them through an all-encompassing, unified model, instead allowing for the intersectional, sometimes contradictory workings of power
structures and subject positions shaped though not determined by them.

In the following segments, I put into practice such a creolization of
theory by using a number of approaches developed largely in U.S. and
Caribbean discourses on race, nation, gender, and sexuality, in order to
grasp the workings of European racelessness. What this book attempts
to do by creolizing, reappropriating, and extending theoretical concepts
drawn from among others women of color feminism, African diaspora
studies, and queer of color critique is to capture what Avery Gordon in
Ghostly Matters, by now a key text of American studies on the after-
shocks of chattel slavery, called "haunting," that is the "way in which
abusive systems of power make themselves known and their impacts felt
in everyday life, especially when they are supposedly over and done with"
(Gordon 1997, xvi). In the European case that means the invisible, unspeakable presence of race, the myriad ways in which it makes itself felt
from day-to-day interactions to transcontinental political structures, while

simultaneously being deemed nonexistent within European thought. In tracing this haunting, I build on the pioneering work on European racism by authors such as Essed, Balibar, and Goldberg, however, my approach diverges radically from earlier studies by placing at its center racialized minorities themselves, their strategies of resistance, and their growing impact on what it means to think "European."

In the circular logic of race as inherently un-European as expressed in the Bourdieu and Wacquant polemic, the former can be considered something that is simply not there unless brought in by non-European theories and bodies and the latter's presence in turn always seems both sudden and marginal to the continent's core.[11] It was exactly these marginalized populations and their creolization of spaces, histories, and languages from which discourses of authenticity and organic identities exclude them, that introduced the new and exciting definitions of Europeanness that inspired this study. The affinity of European racialized minorities with U.S. and in particular African American discourse and black diasporic cultural forms could be classified as another success of the "cultural imperialism" that Bourdieu and Wacquant lamented. It might make more sense however, to read them as implying that mechanisms of racist exclusions in the United States and in the rest of the world are not as completely different as the two authors claim and that class is not enough to fully address these exclusions within Europe. The works of scholars like Philomena Essed, Françoise Lionnet, or Kien Nghi Ha as well as of the artists and activists discussed in this study indicate that a fusion, a hybridization of these American models, building on European migration studies' work on class, is a more promising way out of an unmitigated imposition of U.S.-centric theories on the one hand, and the complete rejection of the relevance of race for the European context on the other.

It is one of my key assumptions that the transgressive approach to concepts of identity characteristic for the new minority activism I explore here is directly related to the specifics of the European situation: their common configuration as illegitimate and alien to the nation fosters cooperations between different racialized groups, making possible a "postethnic" understanding of identity that is not built around racial identification, but nevertheless challenges the European dogma of colorblindness by deconstructing processes of racialization *and* the ways in which these processes are made invisible. "Haunting," Gordon argues, "unlike trauma, is distinctive for producing a something-to-be-done" (Gordon 1997, xvi). Haunting thus implies an interaction of past and present, the visible and the invisible, the here and there—a connection that is hidden rather than uncovered by binary, linear models of time, space, and identity. As I will suggest in the book's chapters, haunting makes visible historical memory as a constantly (re)constructed process, shaped by interventions into the present that always also contest visions of the past. In the current construction of a European identity and history, the haunting of Europe's silent racializations and ethnicizations continues to place people of color outside the limits of the new, inclusive, "postnational" community. At the same time however, it is used by those excluded as an incentive for something to be done. In a network that includes rappers, feminist collectives, queer groups, and migration activists, Afro-Dutch, Swiss Roma, or Belgian Muslims appear not as separate, distinct groups, but as contributors to a whole that has never been merely the sum of its parts. Euro hip-hop, spoken word poetry, performance art, video, and graffiti represent a fusion that resonates with the attempt to "queer" ethnicity, since its most significant characteristic is the use of the performative nature of popular culture to emphasize the performative, constructed nature of tacit social, racial, and cultural assignments.[12] This strategy results in a situational, potentially inclusive identity, creating bonds between various ethnicized and marginalized groups.

Such bonds seem all the more important since there are few signs that the nonwhite European presence is becoming normalized in the majority's perception. Instead, racialized populations, while numbers are substantial and rising fast, are still frequently presented as incompatible with the very nature of Europeanness. My focus on continental Europe rather than particular national configurations poses methodological challenges, but nonetheless seems crucial for a number of important reasons. The national often is the means by which exclusion takes place; minorities are positioned beyond the horizon of national politics, culture, and history, frozen in the state of migration through the permanent designation of another, foreign national identity that allows their definition as not Danish, Spanish, Hungarian, etc. A look at various European countries indicates however that this in itself is a continentwide pattern, based on beliefs and strategies that cannot fully be explained within the national context. While differences exist, the perception of minorities in European public discourse shows important commonalities. Works on among others the French, Dutch, German, Swedish, and Romanian national contexts show that across the continent, there is still little awareness of the actual ethnic diversity representing not only contemporary, but also historical Europe—more sophisticated approaches notwithstanding when push comes to shove "white and Christian" seems to be the smallest common denominator to which debates on European identity are reduced, and anyone not fitting this description remains an eternal newcomer not entitled to the rights of those who truly belong.[13]

As a result, both public and policy debates lack a concept of minority identity and by implication of European racial diversity. While the migrant problem so routinely invoked in recent debates on Europe's future is usually addressed at native Europeans, that is the second and third generation and their supposedly failed integration, these visible minorities remain invisible in the unambiguous discursive divide of Europeans and migrants. This omission can also be detected in current debates on postnational identities spurred by the growing importance of the European Union. Consequently, the various minority populations of Europe are increasingly subjected to the same conditions and confront an ever more homogeneous image of a continent that fails to include its residents of color. The Europeanization of exclusion also means, however, that patterns of identification among minorities do not necessarily follow national or ethnic borders.

Interactions between different racialized communities in continental Europe are shaped by the common experience of migration and often also that of European colonization, shared by populations originating in Africa, Asia, the Middle East (and even Eastern Europe if one includes the continental empires of Austria, Russia, and Turkey);[14] and Islam for many creates an additional link to a transnational community that is ethnically diverse, but largely nonwhite. Consequently, responses to continental patterns of exclusion often work outside the logic of ethnicity and nation that still define much of European migration studies, where migrants' identities are defined along lines of ethnic classifications, and various generations of a particular ethnicity are grouped together, while similarities between populations of different backgrounds are neglected.[15] In addition, the almost exclusive focus of European migration studies on the first generation of migrants has resulted in a lack of comprehensive studies of second- and third-generation migrants either on a national or a continental level (Crul and Vermeulen 2003). Their nonrepresentation is supported by studies of ethnicity in Europe that focus on processes of migration rather than on the emergence of native minorities, implying an invincible divide between (white) Europeans and migrants (of color).[16] As a growing body of critical literature points out, this is an omission that both reflects and reinforces the belief that there are only migrants, no minorities in Europe (Guitíérez and Steyerl 2003; Crul 2003; Terkessidis 2000; Hargreaves and McKinney 1997).[17]

Racialized populations are thus externalized from contemporary Europe, and as a result, their long-standing presence within the continent is absent from most historical accounts.[18] The contemporary native population of non-European descent, in its majority the product of increased labor and (post)colonial migrations since the 1950s, seems completely detached from developments preceding its arrival, excluded from Europe's past and thus from any legitimate claim of belonging in its present. This is especially visible in the treatment of colonialism, discussed in chapter 1, expressed in an official narrative of colonial rule as largely benevolent, marginal to Europe, and most importantly without negative repercussions for the present. This lack of contextualization and historicization leads to an inability to understand or even acknowledge existing power relations shaping interactions between majority Europeans and racialized minorities. Instead, terms like "third-generation migrant," "integration," and "xenophobia" suggest that these populations permanently remain "aliens from elsewhere," replacing the vocabulary and conceptual framework needed to adequately analyze processes of internal racialization—and the ways in which this racialization is an integral part of global economic policies inseparable from the after-effects of European colonialism. This perception is intensified by late twentieth century economic developments: the invisibility of minority communities in official narrations of a uniting Europe reflects their uselessness to a postindustrial economy increasingly outsourcing the cheap labor that brought the first generation of postwar migrants to the continent. The lack of a vocabulary adequately addressing a growing minority population, however, is far from reflecting the implied indifference of Europeans to racialized difference; instead it references and reinforces a common racial archive while simultaneously rendering inexpressible its workings.

In order to support my argument with specific claims, I will present a number of border-crossing case studies focusing primarily on Western Europe. This uneven representation of the various regions of Europe, partly due to my areas of expertise and linguistic limitations, obviously is not ideal. What follows is thus less an exhaustive study of the European condition than a step in claiming that such a condition exists: In tracing an emerging postethnic and translocal discourse, I hope to highlight developments that I believe are European rather than national in nature, in important ways exceeding the limits of the nation-state and as importantly that of ethnic identifications. Building on works addressing specific national contexts, I suggest that the complex interactions of race, religion, migration, and colonialism haunting the presence of minorities of color in Europe might best be explored through a shift away from a vertical look at one ethnic group, covering various generations and their move from home to host country, toward a horizontal perspective crossing various ethnic and national divides. Together, these perspectives can be used to map a rhizomatic network that exceeds the limits of the static grid still often used by mainstream migration studies. Such an exploration I believe will uncover identifications that are translocal rather than binational, producing forms of resistance countering the image of the second generation as largely passive and isolated, stuck in the middle between origin and destiny (Soysal 2000). What gets lost in such a perception are processes that lie outside of traditional frameworks of identification, but are adequate to the circumstances of this growing population that actively establishes networks that are not primarily shaped by national allegiances and borders. The invisibility of minorities within the nation in Europe, while bringing with it a host of obvious problems, paradoxically also offers a certain freedom from prescriptive identity models that allows eclectic and subversive appropriations of disparate traditions. The resulting fusion presents multilayered challenges to established norms and concepts and provides new means of resistance to dominant, seemingly natural forms of identity, minoritarian ones included. This resistance is exactly what defines the emerging postethnic, translocal European identity I am tracing in this book and I argue that the challenges these activists pose to the system of racelessness are significant beyond the European context, offering insights into new postethnic configurations of identity that react to globally changing socioeconomic conditions.

Race and Europe

I was born and raised in Germany, speak the language natively, and am German by nationality. This reality has always been hard for the Germans to accept and growing up Chinese in Hamburg offered my own version of the "not-German-looking" episode. The incident happened in the 1970s when my brother and I took the subway home one day. We were chatting away in German and hardly noticed an older German male, sitting in a row behind us. He had obviously been eavesdropping for a while when he suddenly got up from his seat, walked over and interrupted our lively, if self-absorbed conversation. "Excuse me," he asked, and his tone revealed a mix of curiosity and annoyance, "how do you speak German so fluently?" I was totally unprepared for this interruption, but while I was still thinking of an appropriate reply, I heard my brother saying: "Well, that's because we've learned it." To which the man responded in a more hostile tone: "But how long have you been living here?" Before I could think of a reply, I heard my brother saying with a smile: "Oh, we've only been here about a year. You know, German is such an easy language!" Of all possible responses, this was certainly the last the man had expected, especially as Germans believe their language to be particularly difficult.

The man's face paled instantly and, without so much as another word,
he turned around and retreated to the other end of the subway car.
(Yue 2000, 175)

The above scene, taken from Ming-Bao Yue's deliberations on the visual
and the nation in her article "On Not Looking German,"[19] likely needs no
further explanation for either the European or the American reader. What
prompted this interrogation of two German children by a German adult
seems quite obvious: it was the children's "wrong" looks, their racial
designation as nonwhite, which to the white German passenger on a Hamburg subway train necessarily translated into their being "non-German."
There appeared to be in other words an inconsistency if not an invincible
contradiction between an aural truth, the sound of native German, and
a visual truth, the sight of Chinese. While the case seems clear, it might
still warrant further inquiry: Why was the perfect German of the children
not enough to make them readable as (minoritarian) Germans? Why did
their answer, which seemingly confirmed the man's assumption (that they
could not be German), anger him? Why did the supposed visual reality
take precedence over the aural one? And why did the children assume that
simply affirming their Germanness would not satisfy the man's curiosity
and end the conversation? This book aims at answering the above questions by putting them in the larger context of what I consider to be a particular European form of "invisible" racialization. With this I mean the
peculiar coexistence of, on the one hand, a regime of continentwide recognized visual markers that construct nonwhiteness as non-Europeanness
with on the other a discourse of colorblindness that claims not to "see"
racialized difference.[20]

The ideology of colorblindness is not a passive attitude but an active
process of suppression, that is, the kind of interaction that according to
Avery Gordon produces a "haunting." Encounters with the repressed presence of nonwhite Europeans—be it through a chance meeting on the subway or TV images of burning cars in neighborhoods the average European
has never visited—are not necessarily forgotten but rather decontextual-
ized, denied any relevance for and interaction with one another by being
defined as strictly singular. This active process of "forgetting" by rendering events meaningless, without reference and thus without place in a
collective memory means that every acknowledgment of a nonwhite presence always seems to happen for the very first time, giving each incident
a spectacular character, signifying a threatening state of exception, but
at the same time voiding it of any lasting consequences—uprisings in the
French *banlieus* ignite debates on the end of Europe (Baudrillard 2006),

but no policy changes (instead the next incident is again met with utter incomprehension); a nonwhite native speaker of Danish, Polish, or Greek again and again appears as a curious contradiction, never quite becoming unspectacular and commonplace. Europeans possessing the (visual) markers of Otherness thus are eternal newcomers, forever suspended in time, forever "just arriving," defined by a static foreignness overriding both individual experience and historical facts.[21]

The continued inability or rather unwillingness to confront, let alone overcome, the glaring whiteness underlying Europe's self-image has rather drastic consequences for migrants and minority communities routinely ignored, marginalized, and defined as a threat to the very Europe they are part of, their presence usually only acknowledged as a sign of crisis and forgotten again in the ongoing construction of a new European identity. This dialectic of memory and amnesia, in the shape of an easily activated archive of racial images whose presence is steadfastly denied, is fundamentally European I argue, in part constituting dominant notions of what "Europe" means: though rarely mentioned, race is present whenever Europe is thought, recalling a dynamic that Susan Suleiman identifies in the continent's historical (non)memory of the Holocaust:

> To forget is human, but amnesia is an illness—or worse still, an alibi. The question can then be formulated as follows: If forgetting is salutary as well as inevitable, both individually and collectively, under what conditions does it become a reprehensible amnesia? (Suleiman 2006, 217)

One could add a set of more specific questions: if this amnesia is an active rather than passive process, how is it implemented, what purposes does it serve, and what are the intended and unintended implications for present-day Europe? The following chapters will attempt to answer these questions, making the issue of historic memory, its construction and suppression, one of the book's constant themes.

It seems clear that contrary to common European wisdom, the repression of race discourse does not prevent it from being mobilized in various contexts, in unspectacular everyday interactions turned into identity policing ("How do you speak German so fluently?"), in the normalization of evocative terms such as "honor killings," (see chapter 3 for more details) or in the immediate readability of a Swiss People's Party (SVP) poster successfully used during the 2007 Swiss elections (the poster showed a group of white sheep kicking a black sheep off the Swiss flag—the caption: "Creating Security").[22]

Swiss People's Party, "Creating Security," 2007.

In each case, race is not mentioned yet referenced implicitly as a marker of not belonging, a strategy that relies on a shared iconography that remains unspoken.

Postcolonial populations in Europe challenge the European narrative of racelessness by continuously bringing the forgotten history to the fore. To include their perspective, give them a voice in the debate about Europe's identity and future would mean to contest the internalist position and to admit to the subjectivity of the dominant European position simply by providing a larger context for current inner-European developments.[23] In order to understand the European investment in the internalist narrative, one has to consider the importance of constructions of the past for perceptions of the present. The refusal to acknowledge the continent's "impure" racial history indicates another aspect of "the rise of fundamentalism" so often referenced in relation to Europe's minority populations, as Stuart Hall noted two decades ago: "If what we mean by 'fundamentalism' is a defensive and exclusive retreat into a rigid and unchanging version of the past inhabited as Truth, then there is plenty of it about, not least in the so-called 'modern West'" (Hall 1991, 19). It seems that Europe neither simply remains ignorant of, nor merely forgets, its longtime residents of color. Instead, the structures along which continental identity is formed work to constantly externalize and defamiliarize racialized populations. There are numerous illustrations of this dynamic, some of which will be analyzed in detail in the following chapters. Among the most striking and symptomatic certainly is the situation of the continent's Roma and Sinti populations, which, having been part of Europe for half a millennium, are the European minority par excellence. Nonetheless, they remain nearly invisible in discourses on Europeanness.[24] As the mass expulsions in France in 2010 and the pogroms in Italy in the summer of 2008 have drastically shown, neither long-term residency nor citizenship have anything to do with who is classified as a "foreigner" whose right to remain in Europe depends entirely on the majority's goodwill.[25] If Europe can afford to define itself as white and untouched by race matters despite the existence of this racialized native population numbering roughly ten million people, present in every single European nation's reality and imagination (see, e.g., Breger 1998); if a history of racial subjugation that includes slavery and genocide remains severely understudied while the racist exclusion itself continues nearly unmitigated; if Roma and Sinti living in Europe since the Middle Ages remain despised and marginalized "foreigners" in all of their native nations—and recent UN and EU reports indicate that this is the case— there seems to be little hope for Europe's ability to come to an inclusive, nonracialized model of belonging without a drastic discursive shift (European Commission Directorate-General for Employment and Social Affairs 2004, Ivanov 2006, European Roma Rights Center 2007).

The current racialization and externalization of Muslim populations provides another incident of the potentially explosive European relationship between racial memory and amnesia: while this discourse follows familiar patterns, it is rarely framed in relation to the long history of racialization of religion in Europe. To do so would locate the source of current "clash of civilization" scenarios within an internal tradition rather than some inherent, fundamental Otherness of the continent's Muslim communities. Instead, this supposed Otherness, expressed in religious intolerance, sexism, and homophobia, prevents Muslims from ever becoming part of the tolerant, secular European "we." Migration studies scholars such as Leo Lucassen increasingly challenge the contemporary discourse on "new," that is non-European immigrants as culturally opposed to the European tradition of religious tolerance and gender equality by pointing out how Europeans conveniently seem to forget the continent's long history of anti-Semitism (Lucassen 2005).[26] And one could add that there is also a long history of racism and Islamophobia

traditionally directed against exactly those groups that are at the center of contemporary migration discourses (while the numeric majority
of contemporary migrants to the EU is provided by "white," Christian,
Southern, and Eastern European nations). In addition, Europe's history
of anti-Semitism (and of gender inequality) might not be merely conveniently forgotten. Instead, the image of the fundamentalist Muslim immigrant is instrumentalized in order to work through or rather rewrite and
transfer this history; that is, the supposed contemporary Judeo-Christian
affinity and alliance against the lethal threat of radical Islam is naturalized and implied to be traditionally present, despite all historical evidence
to the contrary (and despite the fact that in contemporary Europe anti-
Semitism is by no means a prerogative of Muslim minorities, but on the
contrary often coexists with Islamophobic and racist positions).[27] The
Muslim presence in Europe thus is acknowledged in order to define a
new, unified Europe characterized by a tolerant secularism—a tolerance,
paradoxically, that is manifest not in the inclusion but the exclusion of
the continent's largest religious minority.[28]

    Thus, "political racelessness" does not equate experiential or social
racelessness, that is, the absence of racial thinking, rather, it creates a
form of racialization that can be defined as specifically European both in
its enforced silence and in its explicit categorization as not European of
all those who violate Europe's implicit, but normative whiteness, allowing to forever consider the "race question" as externally (and by implication temporarily) imposed. The result is an image of a self-contained
and homogeneous Europe in which racialized minorities remain outsiders permanently. Their presence is continuously delegitimized through the
workings of political racelessness, which in part manifests itself through
what Suleiman called a "reprehensible amnesia": this amnesia is reprehensible exactly because it depends on strategies of repression aimed at minimizing the incidents in which "the cracks and rigging are exposed, when
the people who are meant to be invisible show up without any sign of
leaving" (Gordon 1997, xvi). These incidents and their structural embed-
dedness in Europe's past and present are exactly what interests me here,
particularly in so far as they result in what Lisa Yoneyama calls "counter-
amnes(t)ic" practices, that is "a critical remembering in which past memories are recalled to become urgently relevant to present efforts that seek
social and cultural transformations" (Yoneyama 2003, 61).

    In order to grasp this particular configuration, I follow Hall, Balibar,
Goldberg, and others in arguing that paradigmatic models of race are inadequate in analyzing the European case, on the contrary help to support
its colorblind status by showing how Europe is different from "normative"

racialized nations such as the United States, while leaving unexplored the specific mobilizations of race in European processes of exclusion and hierarchization (Hall 1991; Balibar 2004; Goldberg 2006). The key problem in addressing and potentially deconstructing Europe's ideology of racelessness might indeed be that while the implicit though not at all subtle racialization of Europeannness as white and Christian and thus of racialized minorities as non-European seems indisputable, public—and too often academic—discourse nonetheless rejects this observation as meaningless within an intellectual framework shaped by an Enlightenment universalism that for centuries has managed to claim race as irrelevant while simultaneously treating it as all important (see Goldberg 1993).

How then can this system be effectively challenged? To name it, verbalizing the unspoken mechanisms of exclusion, seems like an obvious first step, but in itself is not necessarily sufficient. Too easily are these attempts at dismantling the system integrated into it, by defining the identification of racist structures as an act of racism itself (you are racist if you "see" race and therefore cannot be racist if you are "colorblind"), through the claim that discourses on race are fundamentally tied to the U.S. experience and thus without meaningful context in Europe, or by exclusively associating debates around race with a right-wing fringe unconnected to the European mainstream.[29] Thus, I am interested here in contextualizing "political racelessness" and in making the case for an intensified analytical interest in this configuration by presenting the challenges it poses to our understanding of racialization as well as the challenges posed to it by those representing the unrepresentable in the European model.

Queering Ethnicity

Until the 1980s, discourses on labor migration were shaped by the belief that the vast majority of migrants would simply "return home." This same rhetoric rings increasingly hollow however, when referencing a population whose only home *is* Europe. The fact that the second and third generations were born into their countries of residence, their experiences if not passports defining them as European, makes their continued categorization as external to the continent increasingly questionable and it seems less than arbitrary that in recent years, their difference is frequently framed as one of fundamental cultural opposition to everything Europe stands for—implicit in this assumption is of course the idea that there *are* distinct and immutable cultures separating Europeans and the eternal newcomers as which racialized migrant populations are perceived. As discussed in detail in chapter 3, Islam increasingly becomes the shorthand for this implied permanent difference of minorities: while migrants have been in a precarious position in continental Europe since massive immigration began in the late 1950s, over the last decade "Muslim" has replaced "Southerner" as the generic term allowing to police and permanently contain Europe's internal Others—and at the same time providing an outside threat helping to create the coveted European identity. Islam at times appears as a signifier almost as empty as race, ascribing a combination of naturalized cultural attributes to "Muslims" that has little to do with religious beliefs or even with being a believer. Instead, the trope of the Muslim as Other offers an apparently easy and unambiguous means to divide Europeans and migrants. However, this discursive centrality of the (second-generation) Muslim as cultural Other can be read as being caused by and at the same time covering a paradigm-shifting change, namely the continentwide demographic move to a migrant population that is predominantly minoritarian, consisting of so-called immigrants who were born and raised in their countries of residence.

Due to the silencing effect of racelessness, the grounding of these minority populations in Europe is neither part of dominant narratives nor is it confirmed in coherent counter discourses. A memory of their century-long history is thus not something that comes organically with being a European of color (see Campt 2005). It would be wrong nonetheless to consider this group as a people without history, but the creation of narratives of identity, both for communities and individuals, is not a linear, affirmative process of authentication, but rather rhizomatic and preliminary instead. The fractured nature of European minority communities results in complex, at times circular processes in which knowledge is produced and oppressed, recovered and appropriated, its creation a continuing work in progress conducted by a growing number of artists, activists, and academics, connected by border-crossing structures visible in the Swiss Urban Skillz Hip-Hop Festival as much as the Black Women's Summer School or the Frassanito network of European migration activists. Circumventing the structures that exclude them, these preliminary collectives use new media and popular culture in order to radically rewrite European history through a queer practice, a revised definition of political agency as well as national identification, and a reassessment of the relationship between community, space, and identity in a postethnic and translocal context.

This process of alternative community building might best be defined as the queering of ethnicity, that is, as a movement in which "[i]dentity, too, becomes a noun of process" (Gilroy 2000, 252). The constant mixing of genres and styles in this process reflects a resistance to notions of purity and uncomplicated belonging based on the positionality of racialized

Europeans, but resonating with larger questions facing minority communities and activists worldwide. At the same time, these notions of belonging are the source of the dominant perception of the second generation as "lost between cultures," eternally homeless and without claim to the kind of stable identity, both national and ethnic, naturalized by dominant society as well as the first generation of migrants. This static, unambiguous identity that frequently is uncritically posited as normative and desirable in discourses on integration in turn is not merely a reflection of reality but a narrative in whose production considerable energy is invested and on whose internalization by those it targets the system of political racelessness fundamentally depends: it remains stable as long as the structure as a whole is left unquestioned and the "failure" is instead located within those who exceed the boundaries of normative identifications.

The framing of the inability to belong as an individual and cultural failure rather than as the outcome of structural exclusions works to disempower and alienate groups who threaten the binary identifications on which Europeanness continues to be built. From this perspective, spectacular incidents like the French riots of 2005, which seemed to confirm the self-fulfilling prophecy of migrant youths' threatening and invincible difference, can also be read as part of a complicated and tense process of negotiating degrees of belonging: the supposedly lacking integration of the second generation of migrants of color might be traced to a situation that can neither be approached effectively through conventional methods of outreach nor through the traditional methodology of migration studies, namely to the coexistence of restrictive, essentialist models of Europeanness and of multiethnic minority communities defying the limits of these models. The teenagers interviewed in Trica Keaton's insightful study of Muslim girls in contemporary France, while not necessarily able to directly challenge this projection, seem well aware of the process. As one of them states:

> To say that we are French means a lot of different things; it's almost like saying that we are Christian, almost, because most of the time, French people are Christian. Maybe on the outside we're French and on the inside we're Arab. But really, our problem is that our parents are immigrants, and when we go to Algeria, we're still immigrants. So, we're somewhere in the middle. (Keaton 2006, 32)

In this book, I argue that the seeming consensus on the "failure of multiculturalism," targeting the so-called second and third generation and equating being "somewhere in the middle" with not properly belonging, with being outside of society, coincided with a rise in the native "migrant"

populations whose very presence defies the existing categories, producing a queering of ethnicity that is increasingly transformed into an active
process of cultural resistance primarily located in the continent's urban
centers.

While the delegitimizing difference of visible minorities is still most
obvious in rural areas, their presence is most contested in urban spaces,
which they are frequently accused of polluting or taking over (Buruma
2005; Bruckner 2007). Discourses of racelessness construct the homogeneous whiteness of Europe on the national and the continental level,
leaving the city as a repository of that which cannot be named: the visible
presence of racialized populations whose concentrated presence necessarily implies a threatening violation of the "normal." This perception is used
to justify a variety of control mechanisms while negating economic and
social policies forcing migrant populations into segregated neighborhoods
in metropolitan areas. One could include these urban populations among
the groups that Étienne Balibar defines as

> qualitatively "deterritorialized . . . in an intensive rather than extensive
> sense; they "live" on the edge of the city, under permanent threat
> of elimination; but also, conversely, they live and are perceived as
> "nomads," even when they are fixed in their homelands, that is, their
> mere existence, their quantity, their movements, their virtual claims
> of rights and citizenship are perceived as a threat for "civilization."
> (Balibar 2004, 129)

The undeniable presence of minoritarian Europeans is thus reframed as a
threat to the continent's foundations that needs to be contained through
new forms of spatial governance. While borders within Europe are becoming increasingly diffuse with the progressing unification, the divide
between "Europeans" and "non-Europeans" is reinforced along lines of
race and religion: the current focus on a common continental identity emphasizes a cultural difference of marginalized communities that is both
threatening to Europe's identity and inherent to these communities across
generations—a difference in other words that is racialized in the most unambiguous terms, while never quite being defined as such. In this context,
the postnational theme of the united Europe works as a way to circumvent
the consequences of the increasing native national presence of Europeans
of color.

The process of reconfiguration of external as well as internal differentiations plays out in familiar ways and while the continental union means
greater mobility for some, for others the border now is everywhere. In effect, those perceived as non-European constantly have to prove that their

presence is legitimate, for there is no space within the limits of Europe that they can claim as their own, in which their status of belonging is undisputed.[30] From the perspective of the descendants of the labor and postcolonial migrants arriving since the 1950s, the unifying Europe thus seems less open and pluralist than shaped by ethnonationalist structures excluding racial and religious minorities by assigning them a permanently transitory migrant status. With the shift to the numeric dominance of the second and third generation of migrants, events like the London bombings and signifiers such as the headscarf confirm this continued dangerous difference from the European mainstream and symbolize a migration crisis that in truth might instead be a crisis caused by the ideology of political racelessness, incapable of addressing racialized inequality.

In order to develop methodological approaches that can successfully address these complicated processes, I believe one needs to reexamine and creatively combine existing frameworks of theories of migration, race, and nation. In its fusionist approach, my analysis could be placed within the fledgling field of queer of color critique, pioneered by among others, José Esteban Muñoz (see also Eng 2001; Ferguson 2004) and defined by Roderick Ferguson as such:

> Queer of color analysis . . . interrogates social formations as the intersections of race, gender, sexuality, and class, with particular interest in how those formations correspond with and diverge from nationalist ideals and practices. Queer of color analysis is a heterogeneous enterprise made up of women of color feminism, materialist analysis, poststructuralist theory, and queer critique.
> (Ferguson 2004, 149n)

The return to black feminist intersectional analytics, a focus on class as a central category in the production of queer subjects, and an understanding of queerness that is not restricted to sexual identities, makes queer of color critique immensely applicable in the context of European racializations and cultures of resistance. The process of disidentification in particular, as described by Muñoz in his study of "queers of color and the performance of politics" seems easily applicable to this minoritarian strategy of queering ethnicity as "[d]isidentification is meant to be descriptive of the survival strategies the minority subject practices in order to negotiate a phobic majoritarian public sphere that continuously elides or punishes the existence of subjects who do not conform to the phantasm of normative citizenship" (Muñoz 1999, 4). Building on Judith Butler's notion of disidentification not as counteridentification or rejection of a dominant narrative, but instead as a destabilizing "slippage," a "failure of identification" that potentially opens a moment of disruption and reorientation, Muñoz frames disidentification as a political strategy aimed at creating a discursive network of marginalized positionalities.[31] By returning to key authors of women of color feminism such as Audre Lorde and Cherríe Moraga, he claims queer theory as part of this network not (only) because minority subjects can learn from it, but also because it has learned from minority theorizing: no queer theory without Barthes and Foucault but also not without Lorde or Anzaldúa. This interconnectedness—also expressed in works like Paul Gilroy's *Black Atlantic,* reminding us that there would be no Western modernity without the contributions of people of color—is what is missing from Europe's internalist narrative.

Disidentification thus allows for the construction of a narrative that is less rigid and exclusive than both the dominant one and than those constructed in direct opposition to it. It does not imply a clear break with the majority culture, but acknowledges the necessity of a continuous engagement with and negotiation of an often-hostile larger culture at the same time that it allows to explore tensions and differences within minority communities that also provide the means to survive the hostility of the dominant society.[32] While it so far largely focuses on the U.S. situation, though from a transnational perspective, I suggest that queer of color critique can offer important insights into the European situation, especially when one includes the closely related field of queer diaspora studies (Shah 2001; Manalansan 2003; Luibhéid and Cantú 2005; Gopinath 2006). The latter has not yet been applied to the continental European situation, nor has queer of color critique focused much on intercommunity activism (Hong 2005). Nonetheless, using the important work done in these fields allows me to combine elements of performance studies with queer theory's challenges to identity politics, diaspora studies' attention to shifting configurations of communities of color, and transnational feminism's awareness of intersecting forms of oppression.

It is important to include "diaspora" here, I believe, despite its potential overuse in recent academic discourse, since contrary to the concept of migration, diaspora transcends the binary of citizen and foreigner, the linear model of movements from origin to destination. The strategy of claiming a space within the nation by moving beyond it as practiced in the queering of ethnicity can be called fundamentally diasporic in drawing on identifications and models of identity that exist, according to Paul Gilroy, "outside of and sometimes in opposition to the political forms and codes of modern citizenship" (Gilroy 2000, 252). Since their exclusion is framed in exactly these forms and codes of modern citizenship, circumventing them appears as a necessity for European minorities. While "migration" does not grasp the experience of a population that is born into one nation, but never becomes fully part of it and "minority" does not quite encompass the transnational ties of that same population, "diaspora" can bring both aspects together, functioning like disidentification as a "third mode of dealing with dominant ideology, one that neither opts to assimilate within such a structure nor strictly opposes it . . . a strategy that works on and against dominant ideology." (Muñoz, 11).

In this study, I extend the notion of diaspora to describe a population that does not share a common origin—however imaginary it might be—but a contemporary condition. Within this broadened understanding of diaspora, the concept is transformed from a term of temporal and spatial displacement focused on the past toward one of permanent productive dislocation directed at the future—mirroring the potential of queering ethnicity as a nonessentialist, and often nonlinear, political strategy:

> Suturing "queer" to "diaspora" . . . recuperates those desires, practices, and subjectivities that are rendered impossible and unimaginable within conventional diasporic and nationalist imaginaries. A consideration of queerness, in other words, becomes a way to challenge nationalist ideologies by restoring the impure, inauthentic, nonreproductive potential of the notion of diaspora. (Gopinath 2006, 11)

Gayatri Gopinath's use of queerness in her study of the Indian diaspora would not necessarily include the minority identity I am concerned with here, since its queer elements can, but do not necessarily include sexuality, but her connection of queer and diaspora is relevant in this context nonetheless. One of the most intriguing aspects of queer of color critique after all is its resurrection of "queer" as a term that is not merely synonymous with "homosexual" but references processes of constructing normative and nonnormative behaviors and populations. The interaction of race, class, and gender in constructions of deviant sexualities creates more complicated groupings and hierarchies than the simple homosexual versus heterosexual dichotomy suggests, queer thus might also stand in opposition to *homonormative* formations (see chapter 4). From this perspective it seems not only possible, but also useful to argue that Europeans of color are produced as "queer," "impossible" subjects in heteronormative discourses of nation as well as migration. In response, without necessarily reflecting it theoretically, minority subjects use queer performance strategies in continuously rearranging the components of the supposedly stable but incompatible identities assigned to them by exploring their "impure, inauthentic, nonreproductive potential," creating cracks in the circular logic of normative European identities.

I use "queer" here as a verb rather than an adjective, describing a practice of identity (de)construction that results in a new type of diasporic consciousness neither grounded in ethnic identifications nor referencing a however mythical homeland, instead using the tension of living supposedly exclusive identities and transforming it into a creative potential, building a community based on the shared experience of multiple, contradictory positionalities. The new European minority activism demonstrates a queer practice by insisting that identity is unstable, strategic, shifting, and always performative. Its practice is grounded less in theory than in the everyday experiences of the nominal second and third generation of migrants who fall between the neat European division of insiders and foreigners. Their survival strategies—largely invisible in dominant discourses—are forms of resistance that destabilize the ascribed essentialist identities not only by rejecting them, but also through a strategic and creative (mis)use, rearranging a variety of concepts and their interrelations, among them time, space, memory, as well as race, class, nation, gender, and sexuality. And while it is important to note that this subversive approach does not necessarily always translate into progressive politics, it does represent a concerted attack on the myth of colorblindness that is long overdue in a Europe moving between unification, globalization, and ethnicization and in which competing discourses around national and continental identities are more often than not centered on the trope of the threatening migrant.

The crisis caused by the clash of the internalist European narrative of racelessness with a growing population of color could be said to produce Muñoz's "identities-in-difference [that] emerge from a failed interpellation within the dominant public sphere. Their emergence is predicated on their ability to disidentify with the mass public and instead, through this disidentification, contribute to the function of a counterpublic sphere" (Muñoz 1999, 7). These identities reflect a move toward reacting to the process of Othering directed at European migrant and minority communities by speaking from the position of ethnicized and racialized subjects, emphasizing exactly this Othering rather than accepting it as reflecting an essential truth. Practiced as an individual as well as communal strategy, this resulted in the emergence of a loose Europe-wide postethnic activist network, creating such a counterpublic sphere.

The appearance of minority youths as agents in the European public space, resisting their silencing with often innovate tactics (which however do not necessarily undermine or even question all forms of oppression, at times instead reinforcing them), is among the most important changes in the European landscape since the fall of the Soviet Empire. This is a new development that requires new modes of analysis, working on the intersections of concepts and disciplines. Such a creolization of theory has the potential of expressing exactly the positionalities deemed impossible in dominant discourses, namely that of Europeans of color, while foregrounding economic analyses often downplayed in the culturalist discourse around Europe's "migration problem." In my analysis, I thus draw on a variety of theories not necessarily usually thought together. Their adaptation to the configurations I summarize as the queering of ethnicity requires the introduction of a vocabulary adequately expressing identities long silenced. In order to capture the complex interplay of art and activism at play in European minorities' queering of ethnicity rather than to domesticate it by privileging particular topics, suppressing the simultaneity of issues and forms that is one of its defining characteristics, it is not only necessary to combine various theoretical approaches and methodologies, but also to use a structure approximating that of the topic itself.

My discussion is built around a couple of central concepts, the first of which is the idea of a postethnic minoritarian identity. In a time of renewed essentialism and clash of civilizations scenarios, it seems important to point to a tradition of radical, postnational, and postethnic cultural activism around issues of sexual, ethnic, gender, and national identity that originated in exactly those groups that in current European discourses around cultural identities appear as naturally balkanized, unable to transcend a limited and backward ethnic perspective. Contrary to this narrative, minority youths—misfits within the strict identity ascriptions characterizing contemporary Europe, not meeting the criteria of "authentic Europeanness" nor being authentic migrants since they never in fact migrated—circumvent the complicated question of national belonging by producing a localized, multicentered, horizontal community, in which a strong identification with cities or neighborhoods, perceived as spaces both created by and transcending national and ethnic limits, combines with a larger diasporic perspective.

The term that I use in my discussion of the interaction of the urban and diasporic space is "translocality." Saskia Sassen, Étienne Balibar, Achille Mbembe, and others have pointed to the important role of urban spaces both in providing border-crossing transnational network points for global economies and in containing populations denied movement even on the national level, creating increasingly localized border zones (Sassen 2001, 2006; Mbembe 2003; Balibar 2004). And while the claim that current neoliberal globalization processes weaken if not doom the nation state has been rightfully questioned (e.g., McNevin 2006), it seems undeniable that modes of citizenship, sovereignty, movement, and belonging cannot be grasped through a primary focus on the nation any-more (to the extent that they ever could). At the same time, rapidly grow-ing urban populations create megacities on every continent, and with them new forms of spatial control. The "urban splintering" character-izing late modernity (Mbembe 2003) takes different forms for different groups, groups that less and less can be classified through national and ethnic markers alone.

For the population I am concerned with, the city is the primary source of spatial identification, marking the origin as well as the limit of sov-ereignty.[33] Movement—of people, information, cultural symbols—takes place between a network of cities that is accessible because of translocal structures that circumvent modes of control ever present for European minorities largely perceived in the context of illegitimate presence and movement. Translocal mobility thus happens in a context that is rather different both from the legal privileges associated with cosmopolitanism (Benhabib 2006) and the formal networks of transnational movements as described by Sidney Tarrow (2005).

In addition to these two key terms, the book uses a number of concepts that intersect in all four chapters, each of which foregrounds different aspects of the relationship of (public) space and (national and diasporic) time, memory and identity, community and agency, and relates them to various forms of popular culture, namely music, literature, performance, and video art. Attention to cultural productions of minorities in the European context so far has largely focused on mainstream art forms; there is a sizable body of studies on "migrant literature," recently rivaled by a growing interest in film (see, e.g., Adelson 2005; Göktürk 2001; Hargreaves and McKinney 1997). A lot of the most exciting and innova-tive work by minority artists, however, takes place in the less well-defined, less respected fields of vernacular culture or public art in a variety of forms from safer sex performances in gay clubs to illegal billboards or event fly-ers. These minoritarian interventions create a new type of cultural archive, (re)inscribing the presence of racialized communities onto the European landscape. The artists and activists' use of vernacular, often ephemeral forms is what allows them to escape the institutionalized mechanisms of racelessness designed to silence positionalities beyond the white, Christian European versus migrant dichotomy, but its very ability to subvert bi-nary models of identity also poses challenges for the theorization of this situational queering of ethnicity. In order to trace the alternative archives currently created across Europe, I provide close readings of a variety of nontraditional cultural texts ranging from spoken word poetry to drag performances to the hijab worn by some European Muslimas.

Using an understanding of culture that consciously or unconsciously relates back to 1970s U.S. women of color feminism's multidirectional resistance against the exclusion of female and queer subjects from liberal, nationalist as well as antiimperialist movements (Ferguson 2003), the hip-hop artists, feminist organizers, queer performers, and migration activists that are at the center of this study represent the first concerted efforts of racialized minorities to enter and define as Europeans the debate on what it means to be European. One central aim of these groups was and is to uncover a different history of race in Europe, one in which people of color appear as insiders and agents. This book sees itself as part of this attempt by mapping the conditions under which this activism emerged and by theorizing its varied but connected agendas. Together they represent an approach to central questions of our postnational age that offers different answers to pressing questions around identity, locality, agency, and memory, if nothing else shaking the certainty of clear-cut identities, offering some hope that alternative worldviews are possible and livable.

Chapter Overview

Chapter 1, "'Stranger in My Own Country': European Identities, Migration, and Diasporic Soundscapes," explores the notion of a European public sphere and its dependence on the successful creation of a common continental history. In order to deconstruct the particular forms of racialization shaping contemporary Europe, in their continental commonalities and national differences, it is necessary to be aware of the historical formations leading up to the present point; a point at which, after the major steps of economic and political unification have been implemented, the need to define what makes a European, to create common symbols and a shared sense of history in order to gain broad support for the new continental order, has increasingly moved to the center of policy debates. Thus, I start this chapter with the current quest for a postnational European identity, reflecting the complex economic, political, cultural, and social processes that have moved Europe beyond the nation-state over the last two decades, exploring its relation to the overarching discourse of race-lessness and its role in shaping narratives of the continent's future and past as well as in conceptualizing transnational spaces.

My exploration begins with two recent incidents that could be considered exemplary for the emergence of a transnational European public: the widespread protests against the Iraq War in the spring of 2003 and the riots in the French *banlieus* in late 2005. These events and their reception allow me to map the parameters of European discourses on self and Other as they pertain to the position of racialized minorities. I approach them in the first segments of chapter 1 through the lens of two of Europe's most important public intellectuals, Jürgen Habermas and Jean Baudrillard. In their responses to the protests, both authors explicitly reject and criticize Eurocentrism in favor of a more universalist, cosmopolitan perspective, but nonetheless remain within Eurocentric parameters, limited in their ability to go beyond them, I argue, by the invisible continental "grammar of race" (Hall, in Dines and Humez 1994): different as their positions are, in their assessment of Europe's internal as well as external relationships, both philosophers seem caught in a perspective that continues to place racialized migrant and minority populations outside the limits of Europe.

The second part of chapter 1 is devoted to conceptualizations of Europeanness to be found within excluded populations. I look closer at the material consequences of this exclusion and in particular its effect on spatial relations. In addressing the severe limits posed on minority youths' mobility, and the role that local spaces play in processes of identification for these groups, I provide a different context for the urban uprisings that neither began nor ended with the riots of 2005. Continuing the earlier sections' exploration of cosmopolitanism's (in)ability to address issues of race and migration, I apply its focus on stateless migrants as the paradigmatic population in need of Kantian hospitality and Arendt's "right to have rights" (Arendt 1951) to minority youths living in European cities as largely rightless civil war refugees. In doing so, I turn around dominant discourses on legal and cultural belonging, placing the most marginalized and externalized group at the center of my inquiry into Europeanness by taking up legal theorist Bonnie Honig's question: "What if refugees, rather than (or in addition to) being the exceptions of the juridical state (or continental) system, are metaphorically its norm, the exemplary objects of the sort of power that the state system and its sovereign legalism represent but hide—Bio-power and its rule over all as bare life?" (Honig, in: Benhabib 2006, 115)

The chapter ends with what arguably is Europe's most important transborder counterpublic site hip-hop culture. When it arrived in Europe, in the mid-1980s, the metropolitan experience of a disintegration of (spatial) ethnic unity combined with an increasing ethnicization by the majority had already fostered cross-ethnic identifications among urban youths, and hip-hop immediately appealed to European minority and migrant teenagers in search of a language in which to represent themselves as distinct subjects: "We went to Switzerland and met the same people we knew here . . . those were Afro-Swiss, Swiss Turks, Portuguese Swiss, or Vietnamese—exactly the same scene as here. We got together and communicated in the common language of a shared culture" (*Advanced Chemistry's* Linguist, in Loh and Güngor 2002, 132). This discovery of a "common language" across communities and borders often amounted to an epiphany for young artists who began to use hip-hop as a tool to analyze and name their positionality as minoritarian Europeans within a continental system that continued to define them as foreigners. It was the appropriation of this U.S. born afro-diasporic art form that first allowed Europeans of color to create a language in which to define themselves as belonging to Europe.

My interest in early Euro-hip-hop culture thus lies primarily in the way in which this "shared culture" helped to articulate and create a new type of postethnic, translocal identity able to counter the continental discourse of exclusion targeting racialized populations, in particular young men of color such as those at the center of the French unrest of 2005 (for which press and politicians were fast to blame "rappers").

While I do not intend to overemphasize hip-hop's subversive, liberating, or antiessentialist potential, it is significant and worth exploring that it was this culture, inseparable from the African diaspora in the Americas, that for the first time created a forum of exchange for a multiethnic, economically marginalized native population that had been effectively silenced by being inscribed with the signs of essential ethnic and cultural Otherness.[34] In concluding chapter 1, I illustrate how hip-hop's role in creating a translocal counterpublic inclusive of minority populations relates to the deconstruction of internalist notions of European time and space—in particular the question whether colonialism should be included in a European memory discourse—by turning to an ongoing legal battle between the French government and an underground rapper of Algerian descent around the question of (post)colonial state violence against urban minority communities.

Chapter 2, "Dimensions of Diaspora: Women of Color Feminism, Black Europe, and Queer Memory Discourses," addresses the scarcity of theorizations of race in European migration studies and the potential of a reassessment of "diaspora" as used in transnational black discourses for an analysis of the continent's minority communities as well as the impact of women of color feminism on black diasporic identities, in particular those in Europe.[35] Inseparable from such an exploration is the question why black Europe has long been marginal within the African diaspora and what its fuller inclusion might contribute to an internationalization and complication of "blackness."[36] Continental Europe's negligence is largely due to its supposedly secondary role for the central source of the African diaspora in the West, the transatlantic slave trade. The focus on the latter lets diasporic populations who have entered the West through different trajectories necessarily appear as less representative of the black condition. Accordingly, African diaspora studies have so far overwhelmingly focused on the black experience in the Americas and the methodological framework developed to grasp the particulars of that situation cannot necessarily be applied to other parts of the world. It can offer, however, an important foundation for further explorations of black communities, including those in continental Europe who so far play little role in transnational diaspora studies precisely because of their divergence from the U.S. norm.

In chapter 2, I explore how the nonnormative elements of the black European experience can be used to complicate and challenge existing binaries and blind spots by decentering the U.S. diaspora experience exactly through applying its theorizations to the European context. Building on the critical examination of black diaspora identity pushed by women of color feminism and queer of color critique, I address the potentially productive complications that the European case with its particular configurations of racial, ethnic, and religious ascriptions presents. Among them are the intersections of Muslim and African diasporas, raising the question how race is negotiated in a transnational community that is largely nonwhite and non-Western, the relationship between "Africanness" and blackness, for example in regard to Europe's population of North African descent and to the (self)definition of Eastern European Roma as black— all reminding us that the latter is not a term filled with absolute and essential meaning but the result of a complicated and continuous process of, often asymmetrical, interactions and negotiations.

A new stage in these negotiations was reached in the 1980s as a direct result of transnational feminist networks, introducing U.S. discourses on race to the European feminist movement: U.S. women of color feminism offered a theorization of interrelated oppressions, creating links to "Third World women" across the globe and thus laying the foundation for postethnic coalitions among women of color in Europe within both feminist and migrant organizations. Audre Lorde in particular, who spent much time in Europe, had a tremendous impact on the continent's black feminists and by extension on the Afro-European movements that gained momentum in the 1980s, especially in Germany and the Netherlands, giving these fledgling communities rather unique gender dynamics.

The invisibility if not impossibility of black European communities, their lack of spatial and temporal anchoring in national or diasporic narratives, facilitated a further questioning of heteronormative, linear narratives of black identity that had been initiated by feminist discourses, replacing them with a fractured, dialogic subjectivity that found its primary artistic expression in (spoken word) poetry—just as hip-hop provided a form adequate for expressing a postindustrial urban experience representing what is the unnamable in the linear narrative of a constantly progressing modernity. Using two landmark feminist anthologies, *Farbe bekennen* (Showing Our Colors), published in Berlin in 1986, and *Talking Home,* Amsterdam 1999, I argue that the combination of poetry, both spoken and written, and autobiography within the early black feminist movements in Germany and the Netherlands allowed for a larger critique of (patri)linear (nation)time that resulted in an alternative genealogy of both diasporic and national belonging. This genealogy allowed for the negotiation of shifting positions in the complex field framed by race, gender, class, sexuality, and nation and was fundamentally shaped by Europe's encounter with women of color feminism. The resulting model of black European identity was one that reacted to the process of racialization itself rather than aiming at producing a legitimate racial or national identity, challenging the very idea of normative, exclusive identity formations and thus opening up a space for postethnic identifications among communities of color in Europe (and beyond).

Chapter 3, "Secular Submissions: Muslim Europeans, Female Bodies, and Performative Politics," like the preceding chapters, explores concepts of time and space in their relation to European minority communities and their queering of ethnicity. Here, the aim is to deconstruct the dichotomy through which European Muslims are produced as queer, as a contradiction in terms, both spatially and temporally displaced within a heteronormative discourse of nation and religion; a discourse that interacts and intersects with supranational liberal cosmopolitanisms in assigning Muslims a position both outside of Europe and outside of modernity—in particular through a focus on the European Muslima and her un/covered body. The third chapter links discourses around (non)normative sexualities and gender performances to the role of the female body within the (post) nation by focusing on the intersections of two tropes that have been established as necessarily and symptomatically incompatible in Western secular discourses: a European Muslim identity and progressive activism around gender and sexuality. This allows me to further explore what has no doubt become *the* context in which issues of migration and assimilation are debated across Europe: Islam, or more specifically the increasingly rhetorical question whether being Muslim is compatible with being European.

I will thus revisit from a different angle the quest for a European identity and its grounding in a problematic universalist tradition addressed in chapter 1. I begin with a discussion of the historical links between Europe, cosmopolitanism, secularism, and Christianity, effectively constructing

European and Muslim as oxymoronic. I then turn to the continent's explicitly secular North West, where I argue the discursive identification of minorities with migrants, migrants with Muslims, and Muslims with violent, fundamentalist young men and disenfranchised, oppressed women and girls has been firmly established in the wake of the Danish cartoon crisis and the assassination of Theo van Gogh in the Netherlands.

The discourses on Europeanness explored in chapter 1 constructed the male Muslim "second-generation migrant" as embodying essentialist positions on gender, sexuality, national and ethnic identity, as presenting a threat both to minority women and to enlightened European masculinity. This configuration is still present in recent debates on headscarf bans and honor killings, but the focus shifts to Muslim girls and women as passive and silent victims of their culture, the only possible affirmation of independence available to them the escape into dominant society.[37] While Spivak's trope of white men saving brown women from brown men is certainly recognizable here (Spivak 1988, 296), in its European liberal, secular version it appears in two slightly different variations, emphasizing the role of white feminists as mediators and saviors and, more importantly, granting (some) Muslimas the ability to escape on their own (though only after an intellectual awaking initiated by the encounter with Western secularism).

In chapter 3, I trace this discourse from its affirmation in both liberal feminism, exemplified by Dutch playwright Adelheid Roosen's work, and in the escape narratives of ex-Muslims such as Ayaan Hirsi Ali, to its deconstruction by Muslim feminist activists like Danish Asmaa Abdol-Hamid. My focus throughout is on the uses of performative strategies in constructing as well as destabilizing binary notions of movement and immobility, progress and stagnation in relation to West and Global South, Orient and Occident, Islam and (secular) Christianity, Muslim men and women. That is, I am following Diana Taylor in using performance as a "methodological lens that enables [me] to analyze events *as* performances" (Taylor 2003, 3). Common to these very different types of performative politics is the centrality of the image of the (veiled) Muslim woman, signifying much larger assumptions around cultural (im)mobilities and (im)possibilities. My notion of performance in this context begins with Frantz Fanon's assessment of nationalism as a scopic politics often symbolized by the clothing of female bodies. I move from traditional forms of performance illustrating this view, such as Roosen's plays, to the performative interventions of political activists like Hirsi Ali, both of which retain a hierarchy in which the authors "speak for" Muslimas, literally inscribing their perspective on generic, deindividualized female bodies. I end with feminist socialist Abdol-Hamid, who takes a radically different approach by using her own body to insist on the compatibility of supposedly exclusive positionalities, such as wearing the hijab and being a radical feminist, and most importantly on the right and ability of European Muslimas to speak for themselves.

The first part of chapter 4, "'Because It Is Our Stepfatherland': Queering European Public Spaces," continues to explore discourses around (non)normative sexualities in relation to performance and body, in particular the performance of black and Muslim queerness. Chapter 3's exploration of the implicit link between universalist humanism and Christianity in the construction of a postnational Europe is based on the assumption that while in its current version, this discourse necessarily and explicitly externalized Muslim Europeans, it is part of a larger heteronormative system that excludes all racialized minorities from the sphere of proper Europeanness. Adding sexuality to the previous chapter's analysis of the role of gender in Othering Muslims brings into focus how the positioning of both hetero- and homosexual Muslims as "queer" in relation to a heteronormative model of Europeanness is complimented by a homonormative neoliberal model of sexual identity. This model, expressed in spatialized hierarchies of the postindustrial "creative city," is explicitly racialized, again employing the culture trope in order to mainstream and depoliticize a white, middle-class gay and lesbian positionality while at the same time silencing communities of color and their alternative models of (queer) identity.

Returning the focus to urban spaces and their neoliberal reordering, chapter 4 addresses exactly these alternative models. I begin with an analysis of the impact of the Dutch queer of color collective Strange Fruit, founded in Amsterdam in 1989, whose activism combined feminist and queer politics with a grounding in Muslim and African diasporic cultures. Rejecting the normativity of a white western model of homosexual identity, Strange Fruit constantly juggled questions of race, class, gender, and sexuality, refusing to prioritize one over the other. Active for more than a decade, the group created a network that stretched across Europe and into Africa, Asia, and North America. One of these connections could be traced to Salon Oriental, a Turkish-German performance and activist collective that through its radical drag shows engaged in a queering of ethnicity, gender, sexuality, and nation that challenged, like Strange Fruit's activism, the move among white lesbian, gay, bisexual, and transgender (LGBT) organizations toward a homonormative assimilation into a neoliberal mainstream marginalizing queers of color on multiple levels. Located in the center of Berlin's largely minoritarian Kreuzberg neighborhood, the group, like the hip-hop artists working with it, was directly affected by the restructuring of deindustrialized urban neighborhoods, justified through "creative city" discourses celebrating the marginalization and objectification of communities of color as a sign of integration. Salon Oriental's use of cultural forms of resistance ignored in radical Marxist critiques of postindustrial urban spaces became part of a national discourse through Kanak Attak, an explicitly antiessentialist, translocally structured migration activism group. Since its inception following the 1997 Urban Skillz Hip-Hop Festival, Kanak Attak, consisting for the largest part of members of the second generation, spread its message of "the end of the culture of dialogue," drawing on sources as diverse as the Black Panther Party, operaismo, Giorgio Agamben, hip-hop, and queer theory.

The latter parts of chapter 4, focusing on the role of visuality in the queering of ethnicity and in particular in creating alternative public archives, uses the activism of Kanak Attak, as expressed in its performances and video work, to tie together tropes addressed in earlier chapters: local and translocal public spaces, migration and memory, performance and body politics all were central to the group's assault on dominant perceptions of the second generation and its place in European society. While Kanak Attak's antiessentialist strategy ultimately reached its limits in failing to account for the tensions emerging from the different positionalities of minorities and migrants on which it was built in the first place, it was useful, in fact necessary, in creating a minoritarian voice crossing ethnic, cultural, and religious markers used by liberal multiculturalism as well as identity politics to prevent exactly such cross-identifications. Kanak Attak can be considered the first group that explicitly built its activism around the label of "inauthenticity" that Europeans of color are invariably faced with in continental discourses of identity; that is, while aggressively claiming a space in public discourses, the activists did not aim at creating a legitimate positionality from which to speak, but instead continuously attacked and undermined the notion of authentic belonging itself.

The conclusion's three sections reflect the three levels of analysis present throughout the book and frame the preceding chapters by juxtaposing dominant notions of European identity built around an internalist, exclusive notion of Europeanness based on the ideology of racelessness, as exemplified in the EU-sponsored Museum of Europe in Brussels, with the "inauthentic," inclusive identity generated by the queering of ethnicity, ending with presenting a tentative theorization of European minority identity from a queer of color perspective.

CHAPTER ONE

"Stranger in My Own Country"

European Identities, Migration, and Diasporic Soundscapes

The fact is that the so-called European civilization—"Western" civilization—as it has been shaped by two centuries of bourgeois rule, is incapable of solving the two major problems to which its existence has given rise: the problem of the proletariat and the colonial problem.

—AIMÉ CÉSAIRE, *Discourse on Colonialism*

The hard reality is the exact opposite of the rhetoric. And it is tough. The reality is that living in our neighborhoods means that you are more likely to live with economic destitution, psychological devastation, job discrimination, precarious housing, regular police harassment, botched education, incarceration experiences, lack of perspectives, of individual opportunities, temptations to break the law . . . it means moving towards prison or death a little faster than everyone else . . .

—MC HAMÉ, *Insécurité sous la plume d'un barbare*, 2002

Race, Religion, and the Construction of a Collective Continental Past

Europe appears to be in a unique position in this post-cold war, post-9/11 world, both with regard to its internal reconstruction and to its potential role in current world politics. Seeming to have overcome the postwar state of crisis famously analyzed by Césaire in his *Discourse on Colonialism*, at a time when the "postnational," the "end of the nation-state," have become favorite buzzwords within academic and nonacademic discourses of globalization, it seems Europe, and Europe alone, has created a material manifestation of this new world order: the European Union appears as the first supranational system fit for the twenty-first century, meant to

magnify the virtues and minimize the vices of the nation-states that built
it. As concerns grow over the unilateral policies of the one remaining superpower, the inefficiency of the United Nations, and the apparent rise
of antidemocratic movements and regimes worldwide, the perception of
the European Union as a vanguard form of (post)statehood rapidly gains
ground (Beck and Giddens 2005; Judt 2005), often positioning the continent in the familiar role as bearer of global progress and keeper of humanitarian values, as Jeremy Rifkin put it enthusiastically: "The European
Dream is a beacon of light in a troubled world. It beckons us to a new
age of inclusivity, diversity, quality of life, deep play, sustainability, universal human rights, the rights of nature, and peace on Earth" (Rifkin
2004, 385). This "European vanguard" model has temporal as well as
spatial dimensions, defining the continent's position both geographically
and in relation to its own history. Debates about the state of Europe emphasize that essential to the success of the continental union beyond mere
economic and bureaucratic centralization is a sense of a transnational
European identity, based on common values, rooted in a common past,
distinguishing the continent from the rest of the world and connecting nations with vastly different cultures.[1]

Currently, the attempt to invest this European identity with meaning heavily relies on the trope of the Other, the non-European, in order
to foster internal bonds. But the turn to a Europe-wide culturalist discourse of exclusion should not have been inevitable—if the discursive ho-
mogenization of modern Europe has been managed primarily in terms of
the nation-state; that is, if racial minorities were framed as non- rather
than second-class citizens, then the European unification could have represented a turning point. The unifying continent is widely perceived as
leading the way toward a postnational type of society and the shift from
a national to a European polity and identity potentially offers a unique
opportunity to not only reconsider migrant and minority populations'
position in the emerging continent-wide community, but also their contributions to the national histories, which the European narrative is meant
to both incorporate and transcend. Potentially, the trans-European community structures of Roma and Sinti populations, for example, could have
worked to their advantage, presenting them as a model of "postnationality" within the European context. As recent events show, this is certainly
not what happened.[2] In fact, a look at the continent's postnational turn
from a minoritarian perspective warrants a rather pessimistic interpretation. It seems that instead of reconceptualizing Europe in order to include
them, the unification process creates a narrative that not only continues to
exclude racialized minorities but also defines them as the very essence of

non-Europeanness in terms that increasingly link migration to supposedly invincible differences of race, culture, and religion.

While changes in national laws and the introduction of the Euro passed relatively smoothly, the rejection of the European constitution in a number of national plebiscites led to renewed debates about the continent's essence, to an intensified search for an existing "European spirit" connecting the roughly 500 million EU citizens (Judt 2005; Anderson 2007). All too often, however, these debates devolve into an assessment of what, or rather who, is *not* European. Migration gains a central position here by functioning both as a threat uniting the beleaguered European nations and as a trope shifting the focus away from the continent's unresolved identity crisis. Current debates seem to indicate that the twentieth-century division between insiders and outsiders based on the model of the nation-state is not necessarily diminishing with the European unification, but often merely appears to be shifting to reconfigure migration as a problem that threatens continental as well as national identities.[3] Rather than entering new territory, debates around identity and political rights are frequently sidetracked by discussions around the Europe fitness of particular racialized groups, as if minorities could be returned to their place of origin if they fail to pass the compatibility test (as of course, within this setup, they inevitably will).

Worldwide movements of migration have already emerged as one of the central issues of the new millennium. Apart from the material reality of dwindling resources, economic globalization, and international financial breakdowns, immigration has gained increasing importance as a symbol of the various social, economic, and political fears plaguing contemporary Western societies. Both in its material and its discursive incarnation, migration is of additional relevance within the European context, where the process of economic and political unification includes a massive redefinition and reconstruction of borders. Europe is a densely populated continent with ostensibly clearly separated national and cultural, and often by implication ethnic, spaces. The tension between those imagined pure spheres of national identity and actual cultural and ethnic pluralities is far from a new phenomenon, and could instead be considered characteristic for modern European history (Anderson 1983; Balibar and Wallerstein 1991; Brubaker 1992; Aly 2003). It has been intensified, however, in the context of recent developments, both within and beyond the continent's borders, which have created a renewed need to define the meaning of "Europe."[4]

Race and religion function as central but largely invisible factors in this setup, the former in particular seldom explicitly referred to in public debates, but rarely absent either. The contemporary exclusionary discourse, one could argue, indeed manifests a specific European consciousness in its mobilization of images that have been central to constructing a European identity since the early Middle Ages: the racial threat of Africa and the religious and cultural threat of Islam reappear as key themes in contemporary Europe, constituting a commonality that indeed seems to transcend all national differences (it does not appear coincidental that tightened immigration policies were among the first elements of the future European legal system that the member states could agree on).[5] There is little to no public acknowledgment of the actual ethnic and religious diversity representing not only contemporary, but also historical Europe—rather, the supposed ethnic homogeneity of the latter is seen as an explanation for the persistent resistance to a multiethnic and multireligious conceptualization of the former.[6] The desire to create unambiguous European spaces, both through fortified external borders and, increasingly, internal segregations that create clearly separable zones of access, is fundamentally tied to a reconstruction of national memories within the emerging European narrative.

National identity revolves around the production and institutionalization of a common past. Whether minorities find a place in the larger community thus also depends on their relation to its narrative of national origin.[7] In Europe, migrants and their descendants are routinely denied access to this common history.[8] At the same time, they live with the national past as much as the native population, while frequently simultaneously functioning as its Other. This multidimensional position is erased by the exclusionary approach of national historiography, which, from its most populist to the most sophisticated versions, tends to firmly place racialized migrants outside of Europe's past and present. Historiography ascribes "the migrant" (including succeeding generations to the nth level) a flat, one-dimensional existence in which she or he always has just arrived, thus existing only in the present, but like a time traveler simultaneously hailing from a culture that is centuries (or in the case of Africa, millennia) behind, thus making him or her the representative of a past without connection to or influence on the host society's history (Fabian 1983; Crul 2003; Terkessidis 2004).

The "European memory" currently constructed and debated as a basis for a transnational continental identity could offer a perfect opportunity to overcome this process and the structural (self)exclusion of migrants and minorities from the nation that is so often lamented in mainstream discourses, to rewrite what "has been the dominant narrative of modernity for some time—an 'internalist' story, with capitalism growing from the womb of feudalism and Europe's self-generating capacity to produce, like a silk-worm, the circumstances of her own evolution from within her own body" (Hall 1991, 18). Despite the professed desire to integrate reluctant and hostile "foreigners" however, it seems as if the internalist focus of national histories will instead be reinscribed in twenty-first century postnational discourses, leaving unexplored the myriad ways in which minorities and migrants are part of this history. The French Revolution, the Second World War, the totalitarian systems of fascism and Stalinism with their implications that obviously reach beyond the nation-state are used as foundations for a continental European identity, incorporating as well as transcending national experiences. Their postnational Europeanization can also be read however as a continuation of exclusions already shaping "world history" in the age of the nation-state. Based on what Haitian anthropologist Michel-Rolph Trouillot calls "archival power," that is "the power to define what is and what is not a serious object of research and, therefore, of mention" (Trouillot 1995, 99), the involvement in, and effect of, the two world wars on non-Western and nonwhite populations is deemed irrelevant, events of global importance are shown to take place in the West alone, and Western ignorance about the rest of the world is permanently excused. Consequently, this model produces the claim that migrant cultures and European cultures did not touch until the postwar period and thus do not share a common, interdependent history.

While a thorough exploration of the process sketched above would exceed the scope of my study, the trope of an emerging "European identity," in relation to the national as well as the global, offers a convenient focal point for an analysis foregrounding the aspects particularly relevant to the issues addressed in *European Others*. The need to overcome century-long national rivalries and to convince the West European citizenry of the advantages of an economic and social system whose introduction coincides with the rapid dismantling of the postwar welfare state creates considerable pressure on the continental political system. This more so as added to it is the necessity to downplay regional rivalries and national myths constructed in order to create distinct peoples and to combine or replace them with a European identity that does not yet carry the same ideological and emotional power.

In the following segments, I will trace some of the complicated interactions resulting from the simultaneous construction of a European space, both materially and discursively, in the contemporary global landscape and of a normative European historical memory. My starting point are two recent incidents of what could be defined as the emergence of a transnational European public space, both directly related to the ways in which the Second World War and colonialism are (not) evoked in this process: the continentwide antiwar demonstrations in the spring of 2003 and the riots in the French *banlieus* in the winter of 2005. These incidents place the European public also within the discursive space of two dominant tropes of current global politics with deep historical roots: the war on terror and the clash of civilizations. I will approach these two events partly by way of their assessment by two of Europe's foremost public intellectuals, Jürgen Habermas and Jean Baudrillard. Habermas's reflection on the meaning of the West European resistance to the Iraq War and Baudrillard's view of the uprising on the margins of French society can be seen as emblematic of two versions of postwar Europe—one in which the European Union stands for the successful construction of a civil society out of the ruins left behind by World War II, the other documenting the failure of this attempt. Ultimately however, I argue, both interpretations are insufficient as they remain caught in a Eurocentric perspective, failing to place Europe's post- and prewar history in a truly transnational global context.

In pieces like Habermas's—centering on the Enlightenment and the French Revolution, but reaching back to the ancient Greek and Roman empires and forward to include the less celebratory realities of the Second World War, fascism, and Stalinism—a linear narrative is constructed and used as foundation for a European identity transcending national divisions but firmly remaining within internalist limits, most obvious in the exclusion of colonialism from Europe's history. "Race" thus is both at the center of postwar European identity and doubly invisible: on the one hand, it is associated exclusively with Europe's outside and nonwhite populations, consequently it, and with it the history of colonialism, is externalized and deemed marginal to European identity. On the other hand, the Holocaust and related politics of purity applied to various European populations during the Second World War are central to the continent's self-definition, but are completely "deracialized" (and ultimately as detached from postwar Europe as colonialism). This is how racelessness produces haunting: the ideology represents an active, and never fully successful, attempt to repress race rather than a mere reflection of the latter's absence, thus inevitably depending on violence to assure its success.

Nothing has made this process and its dangers more visible than the 2005 French riots. The effect of colonialism on continental European societies remains undertheorized in both migration and postcolonial studies, as are the ways in which relations between different communities of color in continental Europe are in part shaped by the common experience of colonization. As a result, politics, public discourse, and frequently scholarship explore minority populations' "difference" rather than the process by which they are produced as different again and again. The experience of those who violate the image of European ethnic uniformity has a place neither in the various national narratives nor in the European one gradually replacing them—not only allowing the preservation of illusionary notions of unambiguous, pure, and inalterable national identities, but also preventing a constructive approach to the irreversible multiethnic reality of contemporary Europe. This is especially problematic since the united Europe takes on a position of moral authority based on lessons supposedly learned from past mistakes.

The creation of an international human rights regime as a consequence of the horrors of World War II and Europe's key role in this process is central to critical theorists such as Habermas or Seyla Benhabib with (and against) whose notion of cosmopolitanism my understanding of translocality is in part constructed. In the chapter's remaining sections, I relate discourses of universalism to the voices of those silenced by and within them, namely marginalized urban youth of color who prominently figure as Europe's internal Other in dominant debates. In exploring how these marginalized youths practice the queering of ethnicity by creating a space for themselves within the European landscape, I pay particular attention to the ways in which dominant notions of nonwhite masculinity shaped the perception not only of the French uprising, but also more generally provide the framework through which young men of color are categorically defined as both deviant and threatening. My notion of queer in chapter 1 thus is one that references positionalities placed in opposition to as well as opposing heteronormative models of white European masculinity.

I take a closer look at the economic roots of minority youth's growing exclusion from the nation as neoliberal ideologies take hold of the uniting Europe and analyze how the local, the city or neighborhood, becomes an alternative public space, in part replacing national allegiances and instead creating border-crossing translocal networks. One of the most interesting examples of these is the European hip-hop community, which I see as a central source of a postethnic European of color identity, used by urban youths of the second and third generation to create a common language that allowed them to challenge their structural silencing in mainstream debates. The creolization of a culture originating in the multiethnic metropolitan neighborhoods of the postindustrial U.S. generated exchanges between minority communities across Europe, establishing translocal connections that offered an alternative sense of belonging by constructing a group identity in progress, based on common interests and experiences rather than shared ethnic or national origin and for the first time creating a sense of European minority identity.

Hip-hop not only offered a space for minoritarian voices, but also, as I show in the concluding section, a means with which to connect the fractured elements of Europe's postwar identity, doing the work of haunting "when the over-and-done-with comes alive, when what's been in your blind spot comes into view" (Gordon 1997, xvi). I use the example of Hamé, a member of the multiracial French hip-hop crew La Rumeur, who in 2001 linked the police violence he experienced growing up in a Parisian *banlieu* to the 1961 Paris massacre, in which French police killed several hundred unarmed Algerians. In doing so, Hamé made obvious the connection between Europe's history of racism, colonialism, labor migration, and contemporary exclusions that is routinely denied by the ideology of racelessness—and the state's reaction, personified by then Minister of the Interior Nicolas Sarkozy, resulting in an ongoing legal battle, brings to the open the continuous disciplinary violence necessary to keep on silencing instances of haunting that cannot be permanently repressed.

Postwar Unification, Humanism, and the Colonial Legacy

Discourses on European migration are usually placed in the chronological context of post-1945 Europe, with World War II serving as a break separating homogeneous pre- and multicultural postwar societies. This division is obviously problematic on various levels, not the least in its fundamentally flawed representation of early to mid-twentieth century Europe. What it does accurately represent however is the still central role of World War II in the perception of contemporary Europe. After the collapse of the Soviet Union and the disappearance of the communist Other within Europe's limits, the extent to which ideological cold war debates were in fact often a reworking of the experience of World War II becomes increasingly obvious (Evans 2006; Judt 2005). Support for the European unification process is frequently framed within an older model of postwar Western Europe that sees the Second World War in general and the Holocaust in particular as the "end of innocence" of modernity, the (temporary) collapse of Western civilization.[9] The challenge and moral obligation that the postwar West thus faced was to recover and modify the Enlightenment project in a way that would reestablish it as the basis of an international regime of universal human rights.

Within this view, Europe appears as the driving force behind the creation of a network of international relations and treaties effectively preventing a return to the state of "absolute war" that marked the birth of (post)modern Europe. This distinctive, paradigmatic European experience is what in the eyes of many contributors to current discussions predestines the European Union for a key role in world politics (Žižek 2001; Judt 2005; Anderson 2007). Aimed at justifying a leading role for a united Europe in twenty-first century global politics, this argument also represents an interpretation of the Second World War that responds to assessments of contemporary European humanism, and its criticism of U.S. unilateralism, not as a superior ethical position but as the result of a loss of political influence that left the United States to safeguard the global implementation of exactly these humanist values (Kagan 2002), and instead reclaims World War II as the source of European particularity and ultimately superiority: it was after all exactly the descent into (anti-Enlightenment and thus ultimately un-European) barbarism that motivated the unique success story of the European Union: during the second half of the twentieth century (Western) Europe has repented, has proven that it learned from its mistakes and reemerges exceptionally qualified for renewed world leadership.

While this position becomes increasingly common, it might have been expressed most forcefully in a piece that Jürgen Habermas and Jacques Derrida published in 2003, as part of a concerted action of European intellectuals in response to the Iraq War and the popular Western European opposition to it.[10] The two philosophers frame this opposition as a watershed moment separating good and bad Europeans that proves without doubt that (good) Europe has learned its lesson from World War II and thus marks the final paying off of the moral war debt by the peoples of Europe, allowing them to start anew and make another attempt at world leadership:

> Two dates we should not forget: the day when the newspapers
> presented to their baffled readers the oath of loyalty to Bush by the
> coalition of the willing, orchestrated by Spain behind the back of the
> other EU nations; but neither February 15, 2003, when the protesting
> masses in London and Rome, Madrid and Barcelona, Berlin and
> Paris reacted to this surprise coup. The contemporeinity of these
> overwhelming demonstrations—the largest since the end of World
> War Two—could in hindsight enter history books as the signal for the
> birth of a European public. (Habermas and Derrida 2003, 33)

The European public constructed in the antiwar demonstrations was one that explicitly referenced World War II (rather than Vietnam) in its rhetoric, claiming a voice of authority based on an experience with "total war" that Europeans (but not Americans) share. This position implies a superior moral authority that in fact becomes quite explicit in the Habermas and Derrida piece; and the argument for a European (intellectual) intervention

certainly gained weight after being expressed by two of the most influential European philosophers, representing different schools of thought,
known for their disagreement on almost everything of philosophical importance, but now united by the urgency of the occasion: Europe having
to save the world. Again. Derrida characterized the essay, copublished but
written by Habermas, as "the designation of new European political responsibilities beyond any Eurocentrism, the call for a renewed affirmation
and effective alteration of international law and its institutions, particularly the United Nations, a new concept and a new practice of the separation of powers, etc., in a spirit based on the Kantian tradition" (Habermas
and Derrida 2003, 33, my translation).

In addition to thus assigning the European Union a central role in newly
popular cosmopolitan discourses, the text touches on many of the key arguments brought forward in favor of the European Union as model for
a future world order. In a seemingly generous gesture, Europe's achievements are shared with the world, which thereby is effectively divided
along familiar lines—hardly the same as a departure from Eurocentrism:

> Because Christianity and capitalism, science and technology, Roman
> law and code Napoleon, a civil-urban lifestyle, democracy and human
> rights, the secularization of state and society have spread over other
> continents, they are not Europe's property anymore. The Western
> spirit, rooted in Judeo-Christian traditions, certainly has characteristic
> properties. But the European nations share this way of thinking,
> defined by individualism, rationalism, and activism, with the United
> States, Canada, and Australia. (Habermas and Derrida 2003, 33)

Apart from peculiarly linking "the Western spirit" to European descent,
this characterization of Europe as always creating, never receiving, repeats a favorite trope of Eurocentrism: that of the continent continuously
re-creating itself, shaping other cultures, but never being fundamentally
touched by them; a trope tying all universal concepts to the West, rejecting notions of "other" modernities, downplaying the influence of Islam on
the European renaissance, in short erasing any sense of a world in which
Europe was not the center of progress. Habermas's characterization of the
continental mentality can be seen as exemplary of this narrative, implicitly
establishing the European as the normative type of human:

> Here, citizens are distrustful of transgressions between politics and
> religion. Europeans have rather a lot of faith in the organizational and
> governing capacities of the state while being skeptical of the market.
> They have a distinct understanding of "the dialectic of enlightenment,"
> are not overtly optimistic toward the possibilities of technological

progress. They favor the securities of the welfare state and of joint guarantees. Their level of tolerance toward violence against persons is comparatively low. The desire for a multilateral, regulated international order joins in with the hope for an effective world domestic policy [*Weltinnenpolitik*]—through a reformed United Nations. (Habermas and Derrida 2003, 33)

This rather idealized representation of the European public consciousness is traced back directly to the French Revolution: "The emission of the French revolutionary ideal throughout Europe explains why here politics in both senses, as the medium that secures freedom and as structural power, have a positive value" (ibid.). The French Revolution thus functions both as the source of modern European difference (it is here that the idea of universal human rights was born) and of Eurocentric universalism (the idea of universal human rights was born here).

This narrative can be, and has been, criticized from a variety of angles. One could argue for example that the promise of the French Revolution has been taken nowhere more seriously or put into practice more radically than on the French slave island St. Domingue, which transformed itself into the independent black republic of Haiti—against the violent resistance of Europe's most powerful nations and without any support from either the French revolutionaries or those Enlightenment thinkers whose passionate commitment to the human right to freedom inspired both the French and the American Revolution, but was bizarrely detached from contemporary racial slavery (Trouillot 1995; Buck-Morss 2000; Johnson 2009). The obvious double standard applied to the black liberation struggle led Michel-Rolph Trouillot to the scathing conclusion that "[t]he Haitian revolution was the ultimate test to the universalist pretensions of both the French and the American revolutions. And they both failed" (Trouillot, 1995, 88).

The immediate application and expansion of the revolutionary ideals by Europe's colonized, enslaved subjects could have been interpreted as a sign that the "Western spirit" referenced by Habermas is no European property indeed and as an indication of the complex interconnectedness of world cultures before the current globalization. The contemporary reactions to the uprising on the other hand can draw attention to severe limitations of the European conception of universal rights, challenging the notion of a sudden fall from grace in the twentieth century. The Haitian revolution, despite its far-reaching consequences, however, is conspicuously absent from standard accounts of the age of revolutions, the Napoleonic Wars (after all, more than a decade before Waterloo,

Napoleon experienced a devastating defeat in Haiti, prompting him to give up all colonial ambitions in the Americas), or Western history in general. The investment in keeping invisible narratives that challenge fundamental tenets of the Enlightenment discourse continues to limit the West's ability to envision a non-Eurocentric humanism, and discussions on the meaning of Europe's legacy such as Habermas's, while meant to propose new political formations beyond nationalism, reinforce rather than challenge the existing ones that insist that "individualism, rationalism, and activism" are white, Western properties.

Just as Haiti is omitted from the age of revolutions—and from the list of universally significant events that seem to overwhelmingly happen to take place in the West, a West that appears as a racial as much as a geographical designation—so are people of color excluded from other markers of European historical consciousness. This is evident for example in the ways the two world wars become a completely Western affair through a denial of the link between the war and colonialism, which provided Europe with non-Western resources, battle sites, and cannon fodder. But of course colonialism itself is the giant blind spot of European history, externalized despite its indisputable qualification as a common and identity-shaping experience—and as providing the fuel for much of Europe's "internal" progress. Again Habermas's essay summarizes a dominant position that acknowledges and at the same time erases Europe's colonial past:

> Each of the big European nations went through a prime of imperial
> power, and, more important in our context, through the experience
> of loosing an empire. In many cases, this descent went along with the
> loss of colonial possessions. With the growing distance from imperial
> power and colonial history, the European nations received the chance
> to critically reflect on themselves. Thus they could learn, from the
> perspective of the defeated, to see themselves in the dubious position
> of winners who are held responsible for the violence of an enforced
> and rootless modernity. This might have advanced the rejection
> of Eurocentrism and fed the Kantian hope for a *Weltinnenpolitik*.
> (Habermas and Derrida 2003, 33)

The above characterization does imply some guilt or rather regret over colonialism. Not for the exploitation, enslavement, and willful underdevelopment of large parts of the world, however, but for an "enforced modernity" that, while overall positive, in retrospect might have been introduced more gently. This image not only denies or at least minimizes the disastrous effects of colonialism on the colonized, but also the continued post- and neocolonial exploitation from which Europe profits as much as the United States (Young 2003; Ziegler 2005). This deeply ambivalent attitude, attempting to "save" colonialism while admitting that it was somewhat wrong, emerges as dominant in European discourses, reflected among others in the European Union declaration on colonialism in the wake of the 2001 Durban conference against racism or the short-lived 2005 French law ordering high school teachers to instruct students on the positive effects of French colonialism, particularly in North Africa.[11]

This whitewashing of the colonial past has obvious implications for Europe's perceived role in contemporary global politics in which it appears as a benevolent, neutral mediator, wizened by past mistakes and without a stake in current power struggles. But the effects of this distorted perception of the colonial past are just as stark for intra-European developments: the internalist European narrative could not survive an honest scrutiny of the impact of knowledge, resources, and manpower from the global South on European "progress." Furthermore, by excluding colonialism from the list of the key events shaping the continent's identity, the complex aftereffects of colonial rule on contemporary Europe can be ignored or externalized as can its (post)colonial populations.

It is certainly entirely justified and potentially useful to ask about the particular role a united Europe might play in contemporary global politics that go beyond the simplified notions of "power and weakness," that Robert Kagan and other neoconservatives on both sides of the Atlantic propagate (Kagan 2002; Lévi 2008), about the possibilities created by a political and economic association that intends to respond to the more than obvious crisis of the nation-state. The dominant answers as expressed in the Habermas and Derrida essay pose a number of problems however, both in their characterization of Europe's past and in their suggestions for a future world order. Of course, the Habermas and Derrida argument did not go unchallenged, but the criticism focused primarily on the exclusion of Eastern Europe and the authors' wholesale dismissal of the U.S. strategy (See, e.g., Krastev 2003; James 2003).[12] Less critical attention was devoted to the matter of course way in which Europe appears as entirely self-contained, the eternal engine of historical development, and the world as divided between those who already are or aspire to become "the West" and those who reject its values.

Europe continues to imagine itself as an autonomous entity, simultaneously part and whole of the dialectic of progress, untouched by race matters, occasionally wizened but fundamentally unchanged by its contact with various Others who remain forever outside; a colorblind continent in which difference is marked along lines of nationality and ethnicized Others are routinely ascribed a position outside the nation, allowing the permanent externalization and thus silencing of a debate on the legacy of racism and colonialism. That those who are most emphatically presented as "Others-from-Without," to borrow Michelle Wright's terminology (Wright 2004), Jews, blacks, Muslims, Roma, and Sinti, always are really (also) "Others-from-Within," that the ethnic cleansing, aimed at achieving an already proclaimed national homogeneity, has been a key feature of twentieth century European population politics long before the Yugoslavian war introduced the term into the common European vocabulary, does not change this binary perception of cultural and national belonging any more than the naturalized claim that Europeans have long laid on other parts of the world.

Instead, in public narratives colonialism is remembered as having taken place outside of Europe (if it is remembered at all), the Second World War appears as a European event (while there is a dim awareness of the Pacific theater, this is certainly not true of the war's implications for colonized nations and Latin America),[13] the cold war is seen as shaping Europe's postwar history, but decolonization is not assigned a similar role and in turn seems unrelated to labor migration, which appears as a recent, reversible phenomenon. While the detrimental effects of this compulsively compartmentalized perception of postwar European history are obvious on many levels, they are most urgently felt in the legal, social, and discursive treatment of migration.

The French Riots and the Failure of Multiculturalism

In the Paris suburb Clichy-sous-Bois on October 27, 2005, after the death of two teenage boys—Zyed Benna and Bouna Traore, one of North African and the other of West African descent—who were running from the police, longstanding tensions and frustration erupted in three weeks of unrest that quickly spread from Paris all over the nation (and into neighboring countries such as Germany and Belgium). Violence was concentrated in the larger cities' *banlieus*—officially known as *zones urbaines sensibles*, structurally neglected, isolated neighborhoods with a high concentration of populations originating in France's former African colonies—and resulted in about ten thousand torched cars and almost half as many arrests.[14] The conservative government under President Chirac reactivated a state of emergency law first introduced in 1955 in response to the colonial war in Algeria and then minister of the interior, and current president, Nicolas Sarkozy took a strongman approach in defense of the nation (and Europe), among other things threatening the deportation of the ringleaders as if the vast majority of protesters had not been French (Morice 2006).

The riots garnered Europe-wide media attention, resonating with fears around migrant populations especially in Western European nations. "Could it happen here?" was a constant refrain in a debate that drew on continent-wide recognized images of violent, criminal minority youths. The destructive rampage of young men of color in the suburbs seemed to validate this perception, offering an almost perfect inversion of the public space created by the largely white- and middle-class protesters against the Iraq War: here the "civil" and "civilized," nonviolent antiwar demonstrations of a liberal European citizenry, there the violent, inarticulate, self-destructing, antidemocratic, and anti-European riots of a black and Muslim underclass. While the European media initially had difficulties classifying the rioters—Arab, African, migrant—most reports, especially those published outside of France, quickly focused on "Muslim" as a central characteristic, as if the young men's religion was an incentive for their violence (this was, after all, only a couple of months after the London bombings). The search for the roots of the riots was visibly shaped by this perception: radical Islam, hip-hop, gangs were all identified as possible culprits (Poggioli 2006). And while the marginalization of black and Muslim French youth was admitted, their own explanations for the riots, such as that of fifteen-year-old Mehmet Altun, were dismissed as sufficient justification of their violent response:[15] "The police come and hassle us all the time. They ask us for our papers ten times a day. They treat us like delinquents—especially Sarkozy. That's not the answer. It would be good to have youth clubs and other places to go—then there would be less trouble. It's not good to burn cars, but that's one way of getting attention, so people can come and solve our problems."[16]

The coverage of the riots was symptomatic in its homogenizing of a heterogeneous group, externalizing representatives of a postindustrial European urbanity as a foreign, hostile Other. The *banlieus*, though invisible in Habermas's vision of a new Europe, are a public space in many ways symbolizing the European postindustrial condition of spatial segregation and of new borders running through urban centers.[17] Containing superfluous populations, they became foreign territory, enclaves of the non-West, threateningly, finally invading Europe itself.[18] Only few, like the Mouvement de l'Immigration et des Banlieues, an activist organization founded in 1995 and situated in the projects themselves, put this sensationalized representation into context:

> Today we are told about these "young people from the suburbs"
> (by which we are to understand "these Blacks and Arabs") who burn
> things down as if they were foreigners who came to pillage France.

And yet from Minguettes (1981) to Vaulx-en-Velin (1990), from Mantes-la-Jolie (1991) to Sartrouville (1991), from Dammarie-les-Lys (1997) to Toulouse (1998), from Lille (2000) to Clichy, the message is plain and clear:

Enough with unpunished police crimes, enough with police profiling, enough with crappy schools, enough with planned unemployment, enough with rundown housing, enough with prisons, enough with humiliation! And enough with the two-tier justice system, which protects corrupt politicians and consistently convicts the weak.[19]

For the most part though, even sympathetic analyses of this decades-long history of failed communication and conscious structural neglect, creating and containing a native underclass, tended to retreat to well-established "lost between cultures" and "nation within nation" tropes. Accusing the French state (and often European societies in general) of failing the "second generation," the latter is nonetheless naturalized as foreign, denied the right to become European by the only agent able to grant this right: the majority of "real Europeans." The criticism of European integration policies thus falls short by assuming the existence of a distinct, separate, non-European "culture of poverty" dominating minority communities, who are granted little agency in claiming a space within the nation and the continent. Failing to note, as MIB does, the long history of resistance against racialized oppression in France (and Europe), the inability to contextualize within Europe's history minority communities in general and the riots in particular is reflected in the frequent reference to 1960s uprisings in the United States instead. Supported neither through a closer look at U.S. structural racism nor through a detailing of the supposed parallels, it seems instead that the similarity of "black riots" speaks for itself, leaving the United States as the paradigmatic site of racial conflict, with Europe drifting dangerously in its direction.[20]

The most prominent self-critical opinion in this Europe-wide public debate that for the largest part granted a voice only to members of the majority culture used the riots to condemn an unjustified European arrogance, reading them as the final proof of the failure of liberal democracy. Seemingly taking its inspiration from Aimé Césaire's scathing condemnation of post–World War II bourgeois Europe, but not sharing his concern with the fate of the global South, this negative Eurocentrism perceives the riots as a mere backdrop for the grander narrative of the West's decline. Jean Baudrillard, in his "The Pyres of Autumn," published in the *New Left Review* in early 2006, exemplifies this attitude that condemns Europe for its oppressive and exclusionary policies, but is not able to see those excluded as anything but a fundamentally different

Other, ultimately existing only in relation to and for the benefit of greater self-realization of the majority: "This society faces a far harder test than any external threat: that of its own absence, its loss of reality. Soon it will be defined solely by the foreign bodies that haunt its periphery: those it has expelled, but who are now ejecting it from itself. It is their violent interpellation that reveals what has been coming apart, and so offers the possibility for awareness" (Baudrillard 2006, 6).

From this perspective, the material and discursive exclusion of minorities becomes equal, and ultimately secondary, to the existential alienation of a European citizenry to whom the nation cannot offer sufficient meaning anymore and whose only remaining power lies in the rejection of Europe—the rejection of the European constitution that is, not that of actual membership (see Anderson 2007):

> [T]heir No was the voice of those jettisoned by the system of
> representation: exiles too, like the immigrants themselves, from
> the process of socialization. There was the same recklessness, the
> same irresponsibility in the act of scuppering the EU as in the young
> immigrants' burning of their own neighbourhoods, their own schools;
> like the blacks in Watts and Detroit in the 1960s. Many now live,
> culturally and politically, as immigrants in a country which can no longer
> offer them a definition of national belonging. (Baudrillard 2006, 6)

The blending of drastically different kinds of disenfranchisement and homelessness that is at play here is problematic on a number of levels, not the least of them the epistemological (mis)use of "the migrant" as a mere foil for deliberations on the European condition. Very different from, say, Zafer Şenoçak's reflections on how the Turkish minority presence in Germany and its negotiation of a place in the nation's past and present could productively reconfigure the national memory (Şenoçak 1998), here the minority remains outside and unaffected, its "recklessness" proving a point from the margins while leaving the white center intact through its daring, and convenient, refusal to be integrated: "Perhaps they consider the French way of life with the same condescension or indifference with which it views theirs. Perhaps they prefer to see cars burning than to dream of one day driving them. Perhaps their reaction to an over-calculated solicitude would instinctively be the same as to exclusion and repression" (Baudrillard 2006, 6). The subaltern stubbornly refusing to be domesticated, bogeyman of conservative migration discourses, becomes a romantic hero of this left Eurocentrism. But while he—this is definitely a male figure—might exist, the focus on the modern urban outlaw conveniently allows keeping intact a clear separation between "French" and "foreign" and ignores the larger context of the riots, born out of the frustration of a population for whom integration is not an option. Samia Amara, a twenty-three-year-old youth worker interviewed by the BBC during the riots, states: "The problem with French-style Republicanism is that you are accepted as long as you fit a certain mould. As soon as you have something that comes from outside, you are no longer viewed as entirely French. You are suspicious." [21]

If the French riots showed the failure of European integration policies, the vast majority of mainstream responses manifests the failure to envision the postnational, inclusive Europe postulated by Habermas and Derrida. After the events in France 2005, public attention briefly turned to the obvious consequences of the economic segregation underlying discourses of cultural Otherness and religious difference. But even while the need for more infrastructure, employment programs, etc., was conceded, funding for existing measures was cut. [22] Like the momentary attention granted after the *march de beurs* in 1983 or the riots in Les Minguettes in 1996, the (re)discovery of the *banlieus* by the majority had no lasting consequences. The forcible forgetting of race within the European Union is a process not only kept alive by governmental policies, but also by the willful blind spots in mainstream media analyses as well as in discourses of the Left. There still is no European frame of analysis; instead the dialectic of amnesia and memory characteristic for European racializations seems in full effect. Punctual analyses warning of a "European apartheid" lead to no lasting change in public attitudes or policies toward marginalized minorities; instead the only longtime effects are repressive measures, inevitably met with new violent responses. [23]

In order to grasp this complex interaction of commonalities and exclusions, analyses will have to move both beyond the national paradigm and beyond the postwar moment. If it is to include a break with its internalist tradition, the process of "postnational Europeanization" can offer a chance to include formerly excluded populations and narratives. So far it appears, however, as if marginalizations are continued that already shaped the nation-state, and the interventions of Habermas, Derrida, and Baudrillard, while they should not be given undue importance, do show the complicity of European public intellectuals with exclusionary state and social practices, preventing the emergence of a "new European identity" by excluding exactly the groups that are central to the continent's changed, transnational culture and from whom, against all apparent odds, one might most reasonably expect a constructive intervention. Only a European public that incorporates these voices as well as its own repressed history might indeed become truly postnational and inclusive.

Despite this continued resistance, minority voices increasingly find ways to be heard outside of mainstream discourses. Hip-hop in particular has become a key site of unauthorized but effective interventions into discourses of migration and belonging, successfully integrating experiences usually framed as unintelligible and alien. This is exemplified in Lille rapper Axiom First's "Monsieur Le President," in which he reacts to the 2005 riots and the French government's response to it by placing the events in the context of the histories of colonialization and labor migration, structural exclusion, economic inequality, and everyday racism in contemporary France, while emphatically claiming his status as part of French society. He does this not only by invoking the service of French colonial subjects in defending and rebuilding the nation, but also by stylistically referencing writers such as Victor Hugo and Boris Vian, placing himself within a long tradition of French intellectuals' resistance against abuses of state power:[24]

> "Je suis français, ai grandi dans les quartiers populaires/Mes grands-parents ont défendu ce pays pendant la guerre/Mes parents eux aussi l'ont reconstruite cette république/Rappelez vous ces ouvriers qu'on a fait venir d'Afrique/Et leurs enfants ignorés par le droit du sol/ Citoyens de seconde zone, de la naissance à l'école."[25]

Axiom First is representative of a new generation of European minority activists who appropriated hip-hop as a tool of intervention that allows racialized communities across the continent to formulate an identity negated in dominant discourses; an identity that transcends mononational assignments through its multiethnic and translocal frame of reference, but that nonetheless, or arguably because of it, effectively challenges minorities' expulsion from national discourses. An incorporation of silenced voices into a European public discourse requires, however, not only a reassessment of who might claim a positionality as European, but also of where such a positionality may be grounded, namely in (trans)local rather than (trans)national identifications. In the following two sections, I will first trace the role of the city in minoritarian identifications and then explore how hip-hop culture created translocal networks that in turn allowed minorities to claim a space within the nation.

Racialized Youths, Urban Containment, and the Right to Have Rights

The current externalization of racialized minorities as threats to Europe's identity makes use of longstanding tropes of exclusion that tend to mask underlying economic interests. Through this culturalist framing of economic exclusions in postindustrial Europe, class is not only racialized but also (de)nationalized, placing an ethnicized underclass literally outside of the nation, through a mechanism in which borders within states become as important as those between them. While claims of belonging to Europe are nominally fought over on the level of the nation, the actual sites of contest are the continent's metropolises. These "global cities," to employ Saskia Sassen's somewhat overused term, Berlin, Paris, Warsaw, or Rome, are intersections of global economic activity and centers of transnational mobility, symbols of a world "without borders." At the same time, not co-incidently but necessarily, they are also increasingly fortified border zones, divided into sections, housing populations with radically different positions and prospects in the national hierarchies, whose paths are rarely crossing. This localized segregation could be framed within what Balibar calls "the recolonization of social relations":

> Such a recolonization can be read both at the level of daily realities and at that of great effects of representation on the scale of humanity as a whole, the link between the two being more and more assured by the system of communications that reflects for each human group a stereotyped image of its hierarchical "place" in the order of the world by "virtually" projecting it onto the place it lives. It is occasionally transformed into naked violence, particularly in the urban or suburban ghettos where the public services tend to function as if on conquered territory, under siege from the hostility of the new barbarians (when they do not simply withdraw). (Balibar 2004, 41)

The recolonization of European metropolises can be related to the global context of an ever-faster urbanization, with more than half of the world's population for the first time in history living in cities, often under precarious conditions. Excluded from formal economies, these populations are increasingly managed through carceral and militarized systems (Mbembe 2003). While this development is most pronounced in the global South and in the former Soviet Empire, the movement toward delocalized capital and precarious labor, described by Donna Haraway and others as the "feminization" of the economy (Haraway 1991, 168), that is a generalization of working conditions formerly characteristic of female employment, certainly extends to the West as well.[26]

The massive deindustrialization of European urban centers since the 1980s in particular affected migrant and minority communities. While postwar industrial metropolises had been in need of unskilled migrant labor, contemporary postindustrial centers have moved to the service sector, which draws from an entirely different pool of potential employees. As a result, a working migrant population, frequently concentrated in poor neighborhoods directly adjacent to factories, has been replaced by a permanently unemployed multiethnic underclass, consisting for a large part of members of the second and third generation, as well as recent, often undocumented migrants, stuck in these increasingly deteriorating spaces. The 2005 uprisings in France were based on the economic exclusion of a heterogeneous, racialized, and largely native underclass, of mostly North and West African descent, their desperation caused exactly by the fact that they are French, not the migrants as whom they are so persistently perceived. This group represents a perfect example of "disposable populations," considered superfluous from the moment they are born with no realistic prospect of being integrated into the system and without full access to citizenship rights (Mbembe 2003; Balibar 2004).

These populations are concentrated in urban spaces, constituting the racial residue excluded from the terrain of cultural homogeneity constructed through the internalist narrative of national and supranational Europeanness, in which "cities remain the main battleground on which societies articulate their sense of time past and time present" (Huyssen 2003, 101). The experiences of nineteen-year-old Mamadou Nyang from Clichy-sous-Bois seem rather representative for those who paradoxically are only granted a voice in public discourse (however briefly) when they give up any attempt at communication and turn to violence instead: "I left school two years ago but have never had a job. As soon as I say my name and where I live, they tell me the vacancy has gone. I am happy to do any job, except be a policeman. I hate the police. As soon as they see blacks or Arabs, they just try and cause trouble."[27] Despite regional differences, in Europe marginalized populations are never fully allowed to integrate into the nation, instead they are concentrated in what increasingly appears as "extraterritorial spaces"—while simultaneously being accused of creating separatist nations within nations. Exclusion happens both discursively through the persistent definition of minority youths as migrants and legally through the denial of citizenship to descendants of immigrants, with all the implications this has for access to the labor market, social services, etc. (Crul 2003; Card and Schmidt 2003).

Post–World War II labor migration was conceived as a temporary presence, the idea being that migrants would return when their labor was not needed anymore. After the West European "guest worker" programs were stopped in the early 1970s, it soon became clear that there would be no massive movement of return, but this realization did not produce a change in policies, instead it led to the creation of a hierarchical system of rights directly tied to (remote) national origin, whose disparities become more rather than less pronounced with the progress of European unification:

> A two-tiered status of foreignness is thus evolving: on the one hand there are third-country national foreign residents of European countries, some of whom have been born and raised in these countries and who know of no other homeland; on the other hand are those who may be near-total strangers to the language, customs, and history of their host country but who enjoy special status and privilege by virtue of being nationals of states that are EU members. (Benhabib 2002, 158)[28]

This racialized pattern shows drastically that postindustrial minority communities in Europe's metropolises can lay little claim on the universal human rights that a more optimistic sociology of migration attributed to them in the 1990s. Authors like Yasemin Soysal (1994), Miriam Feldblum (1997), and Benhabib (2004, 2006) see an increasing splitting of citizenship rights into different levels, some of which are accessible to noncitizens. Benhabib, for example, characterizes citizenship as constitutive of collective identity, political membership, and social rights (2006, 45). She continues: "Entitlement to rights is no longer dependent on the status of citizenship; legal resident aliens have been incorporated into civil and social rights regimes, as well as being protected by supra- and subnational legislations" (2006, 46). While this is to a certain extent true, it glosses over the fact that the possession of citizenship does not guarantee the access to full citizenship rights. In addition, the legal, social, and political characterization of a native population as "migrant" can mask their exclusion from full participation behind the seemingly generous granting of partial rights.

It is certainly true that migrant and minority communities created structures both below and above the level of the nation in order to circumvent and counter their marginalization, but it is the lack of recognition within the nation that makes any effective claim to supranational rights difficult if not impossible. Despite all postnational rhetoric, it is still largely the state's prerogative to grant or withhold these rights and the precarious position of communities of color lies precisely in their uncertain position within the European nation. Their racialized difference permanently bars them from full membership, paradoxically ascribing to them a nomadic status while simultaneously drastically reducing their mobility.

As a consequence of their precarious position within the nation, urban youth of color are defined through an excess of movement while simultaneously experiencing an extreme lack of it. They are perceived as being in transit, coming from elsewhere, momentarily here, but without any roots in their host nation, living instead in a parallel society, refusing to either fully integrate or finally return.[29] At the same time, the everyday life of this group is often shaped by severe limitations to its mobility, some of them economic, some legal, or more frequently a mixture of both. The unified Europe manifests itself increasingly through ethnicized economic bonds, belonging to the EU primarily means having access to economic privileges not available to non-Europeans. In order to prevent or control the access of those non- (or in the case of the East not quite yet) Europeans, the continent's external borders are increasingly fortified.

"Fortress Europe" in turn means that non-Europeans may break the law—and accordingly might be treated as criminals—simply by being present.[30] This requires an increased policing of Europe's internal as well as external spaces, in order to detect and remove illegitimate presences. The latter is a category that by default includes populations of color who are expected to carry the burden of proof of belonging. This proof is complicated by the fact that many descendants of labor migrants lack European Union citizenship, putting their experiential reality of being European in sharp contrast to juridical systems that insists on their foreignness.[31] In everyday life, that means among other things that they need to constantly reapply for a residence permit in their country of birth, an application that in theory can be rejected any time, and are in need of a visa whenever they want to cross the border into a neighboring country. These groups of "foreigners," and any individual that through looks or residence is assumed to belong to them, are thus subjected to a particular kind of policing: their access to the European public space is shaped by numerous qualifications, they must be constantly ready to prove, through a variety of papers and permits, that their presence in a particular nation, city, neighborhood, street, is legitimate—a situation that makes it certainly difficult to feel at home or accepted. Italian-Egyptian rapper Amir Issa, who owns an Italian passport and lives in Torpignattara, a low-income suburb of Rome: "I feel like a foreigner in my nation. That's the title of one of my songs. A foreigner in my nation. Because if the police stopped me on the street with an Italian friend, they would definitely keep me a half hour longer and make hundreds of checks. Then after 9/11, they associate an Arab name with Islamic terrorism and other such things" (Interview Gupta, AKI 2008).

European hierarchies of racialized belonging play out in a myriad of everyday interactions and experiences in public spaces, causing an enormous amount of pressure on particular parts of the population, namely those without unquestionable ties to "Europeanness," and this more so since they are frequently presented (and asked to identify) as not the victims but the perpetrators in this process. This in turn leads to various forms of "preventive" violence, which are, however, experienced by the majority population as self-defense rather than discrimination. Trica Keaton observes this in connection with the French debate around violent minority youth:

> The discourse of urban violence intensifies these tensions when a supposedly unsuspecting public is told that, ultimately, they will be victims of outer-city youths, if they are not controlled and confined . . . [while] the degraded conditions typical of outer-city public housing and schools in the "other France" are not understood as a form of violence. (Keaton 2003, 194)

Structural violence against minorities takes various forms; some of them, such as racial profiling by the police, are at times subjects of public debates, while others remain completely invisible (and therefore are arguably even more effective). Often these forms of violence take place in the context of the regulation of mobility in the "national interest" as the criminalization of unregulated migration makes incarceration appear more and more as simply a type of legitimate population management. From the discourse around the threat posed by illegal immigrants follows a practice that unselfconsciously ties the access to full human rights to being Western and white.[32] Confinement, be it in the form of internment camps for undocumented migrants (including recognized refugees), of an increasingly privatized European prison system in which minorities are dangerously overrepresented, or simply in minorities' increasing containment in certain designated, isolated neighborhoods such as the French *cités*, appears as the deeply racialized, silenced counterpart to the much celebrated mobility and ease of movement in the new Europe.[33]

This disparity becomes especially obvious for a group to which a small but significant part of Europe's minority population belongs: aliens with an exceptional leave to remain in Europe. Often civil war refugees from Lebanon, Afghanistan, Iraq, Bosnia, Somalia, or Kosovo, who lost their citizenship when their nations fell apart or were reconfigured along new lines, they were given limited and temporary residence rights in many, especially Western European nations—rights that were to be revoked as soon as it would be possible to send them back to their homelands. Their integration into their temporary residences was thus not only not wanted, but actively prevented.[34] They are being allowed into Europe explicitly under a post–World War II notion of cosmopolitan "hospitality" that aims at isolating basic human rights—in this case the right to leave a deadly zone of war—which are allowed to temporarily supersede national and EU laws in granting a single right, the right to be there, to a group of people who

otherwise would not qualify to enter, and whose temporary presence explicitly cannot lead to the acquisition of anything beyond the bare right
to be present. Of course it is entirely up to the receiving nations to decide
what constitutes a civil war deadly enough and when the situation is such
that people can be sent (or often more accurately, deported) back. Despite
the fact that the vast majority of (civil) war refugees is received by nations
outside the West, Europe is proud of this system as one of the most obvious indications that the international community under Western leadership is committed to the "right to have rights."

While it would be ridiculous to claim that the granting of an "exceptional leave to stay" to contingent populations under the threat of im-
minent death is without importance, it is useful to look at the context of
Arendt's famous formulation. In her *Origins of Totalitarianism*, she wrote
about the "rightless":

> The prolongation of their lives is due to charity and not to right,
> for no law exists which could force the nations to feed them; their
> freedom of movement, if they have it at all, gives no right to residence
> which even the jailed criminal enjoys as a matter of course; and their
> freedom of opinion is a fool's freedom, for nothing they think matters
> anyhow . . . The fundamental deprivation of human rights is manifested
> first and above all in the deprivation of a place in the world which
> makes opinions significant and actions effective. (Arendt 1951, 296)

While one can argue that civil war refugees granted the temporary right
to stay in Europe leave the space of absolute rightlessness, this is not to
say that they enter the space of possessing rights. In fact, the conditions
of their temporary presence seem designed exactly to guarantee that they
remain without "a place in the world which makes opinions significant
and actions effective," by ensuring that they remain completely isolated
from the national community (the "right to belong to some kind of organized community" incidentally is the second aspect Arendt identified
as constituting the right to have rights).[35] In this sense, while they are a
relatively small group, their situation might not be as exceptional as their
official title implies. Rather, their situation in many ways symbolizes the
European attempt to place migrants literally outside of (normative) time
and space. Even when they are located within the nation, the internalist
impulse dislocates them as being without. In Germany, which accepts the
largest contingents, recognized civil war refugees are neither allowed to
work or study, welfare payments being their only possible legal source of
income (Martens 2006). This is a policy that creates a difficult situation
on the short term but becomes unbearable for those who spend decades

with the legal status of a *Duldung* (exceptional leave to remain) or, as descendants of civil war refugees, are born into this status, being in effect stateless.

While chapter 3 explores the tensions between the human rights discourse and Europe's repressed history of (neo)colonialism as it affects the positionality of the continent's Muslim minority, here I want to look at the concrete effect of being suspended between rights and rightlessness on minority youths who have grown up (or were born) in the "state of exception(al leave)." The only amendment to the nonparticipation rule is made for minors for whom the international human rights regime provides at least minimal protection and who are allowed to attend school—which for them however is not the road to a better future, but instead in the best case a step on the way to becoming welfare recipients or a temporary stop before the final deportation in the worst: "Show your passport, they said at school. I had to show them the *Duldung* instead, a letter-sized paper with a picture attached to it. The teachers and secretaries didn't know what to do with it. I had to explain to them that I was supposed to be deported" (Osman Teken, in Martens 2006). Youths like eighteen-year-old Osman Teken, of Turkish-Lebanese descent, live in suspended time, from month to month, until their *Duldung* needs to be renewed again, unable to plan for the future, go to college, learn a trade, find a job, do any of the things considered part of becoming an adult, while at the same time being burdened with grown-up responsibilities far exceeding an average teenager's capabilities, since often their access to public schools means that they are the only family members able to master the national language well enough to deal with the authorities: "My friends played soccer outside and I was just busy with my papers trying to prevent the deportation" (ibid.).

The youths' situation deeply affects their relationship to time, disrupting the normative notion of linear movement through progressive stages of adolescence toward adulthood. This necessarily makes them aberrations from the model citizen all "foreigners" are measured against, outsiders in all national contexts, which per definition depend on normative timelines for the nation's subjects. More than that, it is impossible for them to plan for their future in any, even the most basic way: "On the *Duldung* it says: not allowed to study, not allowed to work. No driver's license either. You can't open a bank account. You can't do anything. You can go to school, that's all" (Hassan Akkouch, in Martens 2006). There is also a fundamental effect on spatial relations. The European states' attempt to prevent the unavoidable, that is, people claiming the space they live in as "home," becoming what they are not allowed to become—Europeans—paradoxically means that they are tied to a restricted, designated space in a very literal sense: during their stay, however long it might be, refugees are not permitted to leave the limits of the community they have been originally assigned to: "I have never been allowed to leave Berlin because I only have had a *Duldung*—for all of my life" (Akkouch, in Germany since he was two years old).

Of course, the assigned place is not necessarily located in a major city and the isolation of refugees in small towns can be devastating (and sometimes create unexpected solidarities), but cities have become the source of new coalitions between a critical mass of populations who are disposable rather than displaced.

It is the local space, most often the city, that allows minority youths to create a sense of belonging, providing an alternative to the "lost between cultures" trope by using a "disidentificatory" approach to identity, in the sense José Esteban Muñoz uses the term, that is not as a simple counteridentification, but as a working with intersections and displacements, as "the third mode of dealing with dominant ideology, one that neither opts to assimilate within such a structure nor strictly opposes it; rather, disidentification is a strategy that works on and against dominant ideology" (Muñoz 1999, 11). The youths' positionality, outside of any recognized category of belonging gives a new twist, one could argue, to Judith Halberstam's conceptualization of "queerness as an outcome of strange temporalities" (Halberstam 2005, 1). Hassan Akkouch's identification with his hometown of Berlin provides an example of this strategy in which a head-on attempt at claiming a German identity that is the only accessible but at the same time completely inaccessible national identification is abandoned in favor of claiming local spaces less overdetermined than the nation, instead open to contestations, appropriated by an array of marginalized "misfits" whose coalition is not a natural one, but a strategy that makes the state's claim to the urban space less authoritative than its national hegemony, making Akkouch's identification far from unusual: "When I ask *Türkiyelis* in Berlin how they identify themselves, they do not answer with '*Türküm*' (I'm Turkish) or '*Almanim*' (I'm German) but often with '*Berlinliyim*' (I'm a Berliner)" (Petzen 2004, 22).[36] Akkouch, in permanent and acute danger of being deported to Lebanon, a country completely foreign to him—a "strange temporality" if there ever was one—gained local, and eventually national, fame as an accomplished hip-hop artist, a talented break dancer who used his art as a means to form an alternative community, a community that in turn offered a framework through which he, like Axiom First, could insert himself into a national landscape in which youths like him are still completely invisible.[37]

Without intending to minimize the specific difficulties of youths growing up under the *Duldung* status, I suggest that the young refugees' situation is more extreme, but not necessarily qualitatively different from that of minority youths in general. The poorest neighborhoods, be they located in the suburbs or the inner city, increasingly become the domain of those incapable of leaving—in the words of a youth worker in Kirchdorf-Süd, one of Hamburg's poorest and most multiethnic boroughs: "whoever is able to moves away, what's left is 'the underclass of all nationalities'" (Kahlcke 2006, 24), made up of recent migrants as well as of racialized minorities. Within European discourses, urban centers are portrayed as sights of ethnic conflict and social decay. Used to localize common fears around economic decline and cultural change, these neighborhoods appear as foreign matter, growing uncontrollably, a volcano permanently close to eruption. From the perspective of their young inhabitants however, these spaces seem to represent the opposite: time slowed down, stagnation, boredom, the lack of opportunities and conceivable futures—as one Hamburg youth states: "Ghettos are places where nothing ever happens" (Hieronymous 2001, 306). Against this background, the French uprisings seem far less surprising than the fact that they remain the exception rather than the rule. Routinely accused of being out of control, violent, and dangerous, most urban minority youths in fact either internalize the tensions they face or express them in far more complex ways than the discourse around them is willing to admit.

While employment opportunities are slim, traditional forms of organizing do not respond to their situation, and their ancestors' country of origin, often considered their home-country too, by parents as well as "host societies," is largely foreign to them, the city, the neighborhood, is less a target of destructive youth violence than a means to counter alienation and exclusion from society, creating a sense of community that encompasses both less and more than the nation. While the nations they have been born into continue to define them as foreigners on their way out, their hometown, their neighborhood, becomes not only an alternative, but also the only possible source of identification. Importantly though, this local identification is the stepping stone to a sense of belonging that is indeed supranational, providing the first forum for expressing a European minority identity. Public spaces, virtual or real, within local communities provide grounding at the same time that they connect their inhabitants to a larger diasporic culture that found its most important recent expression in hip-hop culture, connecting seemingly isolated minority youths across Europe.

Hip-Hop as Diasporic Lingua Franca

Created by African American, Caribbean, and Latino youths in 1970s New York, hip-hop soon became a worldwide movement, first picked up in Europe by minority and migrant teenagers who easily identified with U.S. old school raps revolving around racism, exclusion, and the search for a place of one's own:

> When we were teenagers, to see black American artists erupt in our world, like NWA, Run DMC, with their attitudes, with a certain pride, defying white racist America, reclaiming their history, their pride. It was earth shattering to us. For the first time, people who looked like us, speaking freely . . . it was like being branded with a red-hot iron. We still haven't gotten over it. (Hamé, La Rumeur, in Werman 2006)

As shown, (post)colonial migration patterns, economic globalization, and the continental unification had combined to create a native European population of color effectively silenced by the inscription of the signs of essential ethnic and cultural otherness. Hip-hop in particular and African diaspora discourse in general was indispensable to the creation of a postethnic European diaspora identity among them. The failure to take part in established political and (counter)cultural practices further marginalized this seemingly nonintegrated and apolitical "lost generation." In the 1980s, it became apparent, however, that strategies relevant to the situation of these multiethnic urban communities were to be found less in European political traditions or postcolonial theories focusing on formerly colonized territories than in the survival strategies of African diaspora communities in the Americas. For minorities incorporating the racial otherness inadmissible within internalist narrations of Europe, invisible within a continental progressive movement whose brand of Marxism had failed to theorize race, and excluded from structural participation in a political system that defined them as outsiders, vernacular culture, dismissed as irrelevant within all these discourses, became the site on which to create and negotiate new forms of Europeanness.

Hip-hop, more than anything else, was the catalyst that introduced these strategies to European minorities. The emergence of a continental hip-hop culture facilitated the move from a local to a translocal sense of community by pointing to commonalities that were not based on ethnic or national identifications or ascriptions, but rather on the common effects of racialized economic exclusion, on similar strategies of resistance in Europe's urban ghettos. The identifications behind the appropriation

of hip-hop by European youths were complex and multilayered, ranging from those of European with American minorities to those between
minority communities in different European nations and different ethnic groups living in the same neighborhoods. Already representing the
fusion of several cultural traditions, hip-hop lent itself to adaptation
and further creolization by groups who immediately related to its message. Like the French La Rumeur, Meli, MC of the Afro-German Skillz
en Masse recalls the dramatic effect of her first encounter with U.S.
hip-hop:

> In Germany it starts when you enter the first institution, be it
> kindergarten or school—you are confronted with rejection, being
> different, being black. And then I heard Public Enemy, got the
> T-shirts—that was liberation for me, an outlet, to rap the lyrics, feel
> the energy; that just touched me. These were people, 9,000 miles away
> from me and they said things that were relevant for my life here in
> Germany. (Loh and Güngör 2002, 103)

The tide of racist violence that swept Europe in the early 1990s politicized many young people of color who could not relate to the politics
of traditional migrant and antiracist groups. Hip-hop culture created a
framework in which European ethnic "(un)subjects" for the first time
were able to create a language through which they could express their
specific experiences, define themselves as autonomous, and position
themselves in relation to the struggles of American communities of color
that had produced the role models of European rappers, DJs, b-boys and
b-girls, and writers. While ethnic migrant organizations had emphasized
differences between ethnic communities and created homogeneous group
interests often not shared by the second and third generation, these artists proclaimed an identity that was completely ignored by mainstream
society, yet fit a growing part of the population under twenty-five (and
was reflected in the multiethnic composition of many early crews): that of
"nontraditional" Europeans, Muslims, Roma, Asian, or Afro-Europeans,
confronted with a uniting Europe that did not welcome them into its new
community of citizens. Young European artists initially closely imitated
the American model in style, dress, and language, but gradually they created a creolized, independent Euro hip-hop culture. This independence
from the U.S. original manifested itself in the inclusion of new musical
traditions, creating new subgenres such as Oriental hip-hop, but also
in the exploration of topics directly addressing the situation of European minorities. Here, shared interests and experiences rather than eth-

nic identity provided the material from which to build cross-national discourses.

Central to the sense of a European hip-hop community was the move in the late 1980s from rapping in English to using the artists' native languages. Paradoxical as it might seem, the diversification of languages was key to hip-hop becoming a continental political force, amounting to a declaration of independence from the overbearing U.S. paradigm and allowing European rappers to find their own voices. The daily practice of hip-hop forged bonds within local neighborhoods, and regional and international meetings such as the Swiss Urban Skillz brought the realization that multiethnic communities in European cities resemble each other, creating an emerging consciousness of a continent-wide community that constitutes a legitimate presence in Europe. What was important here, and what hip-hop made possible, was a dialogue that took place among and between minorities rather than one directed at the majority. After and because this had happened, minorities, again using hip-hop as their tool for communication, could intervene in national discourses, challenging their exclusion from it, importantly doing so, like Axiom First, by speaking from the position of insiders who have the right to be heard. Basel-based rapper Black Tiger, the first to make the move to Swiss German rap in 1991, recalls the border-crossing dynamic, linguistic as well as geographical, that resulted in an almost complete switch to native language rap by the early 1990s:

> France was very important to us. I was in Paris in 1987–88, there I saw
> a rap group in a club rapping in French. And the audience rapped with
> them. That was a trip. They know the lyrics—wow! That's what rap is
> supposed to be about. That's why we're rapping, so that the audience
> gets it—and reacts—with a counter-rap if they disagree. (Khazaleh 2000)

The appearance of minority MCs rapping in French, Italian, or Greek also provided a poignant comment on Europe-wide discourses on the supposed inability or unwillingness of the second generation to speak the dominant culture's language. Their appropriation of the "master's language" irrevocably transformed it, its "hybridization," "bastardization," noticed by the majority with profound ambivalence (as if language was not always in flux, transforming, incorporating new and dropping old expressions), coming full circle in current discussions like the Dutch one about *straattaal*.

Hip-hop worked as a lingua franca that enabled minorities to explore their similarities beyond ethnic differences and language barriers. At the same time, the move away from English allowed a focus on the European situation, fundamentally different from that of the United States in some ways, but showing previously unnoticed similarities between the continent's nations. That hip-hop represents a language beyond the verbal is reflected in numerous instances of continental cooperation between crews who do not always speak each others' languages, but who deal with the same issues. Turkish-German Fresh Familee's Tachi, author of "Ahmed Gündüz," the first German-language rap ever released, recalls how hip-hop always spoke to Europeans of color even if they did not understand the lyrics:[38]

> I think, as a migrant from a poor neighborhood, you automatically identified with hip-hop. Just from hearing rap's rhythm and realizing: someone's getting something off his chest here. You heard that immediately, for example, with "The Message," even if you couldn't understand a word. (Loh and Güngör 2002, 92)

The collective creative process finally resulted in a Euro hip-hop that combined musical influences from the United States and the Caribbean with those of the Middle East, South Asia, and North Africa, yet was created in Berlin, Belgrade, or Barcelona, and introduced a thematic focus on national belonging that seems peculiar to Europe.

While mainstream audiences long associated European hip-hop only with its "whitewashed," commercially successful version, a vibrant subculture continued to exist outside the media hype, its centers often close to U.S. army bases where the newest imports could be heard. An example of this is Heidelberg-based trio Advanced Chemistry—whose members were of Haitian, Italian, and Ghanaian German descent—founded in the mid-1980s as one of the first German crews, and probably the first to rap in German (Loh and Güngör 2002). Their "Fremd im eigenen Land" (Stranger in My Own Country), published in 1992, is a milestone in the articulation of a European minority identity, placing them among the most important proponents of a version of hip-hop that went beyond the apolitical fun message of commercial European rap. The song, reflecting the everyday experiences of Germans of African and migrant descent in a post-Unification Germany, remains one of the sharpest, to the point reflections on the situation of Germans of color to date:

> All das Gerede von europäischem Zusammenschluss / fahr' ich
> zur Grenze mit dem Zug oder einem Bus / frag' ich mich warum ich
> der Einzige bin, der sich ausweisen muss, / Identität beweisen muss! . . .
> Das Problem sind die Ideen im System: / ein echter Deutscher muss
> auch richtig deutsch aussehen.[39] (Advanced Chemistry, "Fremd im
> eigenen Land")

First listening to "Fremd im eigenen Land" again and again appears in the narratives of young German rappers of color as a moment of awakening, of inspiration for their own careers (Loh and Güngör 2002; Krekow and Steiner 2000). For many of them, Advanced Chemistry showed that rap could be a form of political activism, and one that perfectly fit their situation: hip-hop for the first time created a broad forum of expression and exchange, fostering interactions between minorities becoming aware of their similar situation. Advanced Chemistry's Linguist in 1993:

> In Germany you have minorities. There are minorities with a German passport. That's me for example, a black German. There are minorities in this country without a German passport. Those are Turkish Germans for example—I consciously say Turkish Germans—those are Yugoslavian Germans, Moroccan Germans, whoever. But we all belong together. We are all confronted with racism, not xenophobia. I am confronted with racism, but I am lucky, because I cannot be thrown out of the country. On the other hand there are no laws protecting my rights as a member of a minority (in Linguist 1993, 16).

This statement, simple as it might seem, was both new to German discussions and highly controversial. The claim that there was a post-1945 German racism, that Germany had minority populations at all and that these minorities shared similar conditions (and potentially a common struggle) earned Advanced Chemistry, whose sensibilities were shaped by the 1980s Afro-German movement that will be explored in the next chapter, attacks from all sides:

> The crazy thing is, that we are criticized, naturally, by people ideologically opposed to us, conservatives. Of course, they can't stand seeing a black guy holding up his green passport, stating offensively that he's German. On the other hand, and this is the crazy thing, people considering themselves progressive believe that we wanted to distance ourselves from those minorities in Germany without the green passport. That accusation came very often. (in Linguist 1993, 16)

The agreement between conservatives for whom people of nonwhite descent necessarily fell out of the German and into the migrant category and progressives whose solidarity with "migrants" did not include a reflection on their own essentialist definition of Germanness, was made possible by the ideology of racelessness, which not only left unexamined shared racialized concepts of national belonging, but which made violations of the code of silence such as the one by Advanced Chemistry unacceptable

exactly because it created the paradox of the excluded insisting to speak
from the position of insiders. At the same time, the cult status that "Fremd
im eigenen Land" gained within the hip-hop community and the number of songs addressing similar issues testifies to the growing challenge
to racelessness—and to hip-hop's success in creating a counterpublic in
which issues could be explored that were (made) unspeakable in mainstream discourse.

Neither was this in any way merely a German phenomenon as similar
discourses all across Europe show. In 2006, Italian rapper Amir published
a track that shared its title, "Straniero nella mia nazione," with Advanced
Chemistry's "Fremd im eigenen Land" published more than a decade earlier and expressed similar sentiments. For Amir, too, identification with
the nation starts with a local community representing everything that is
absent in dominant notions of belonging:[40]

> There's a mix in this neighbourhood that has really influenced and
> inspired me. I feel that in a way I represent this reality. A spokesman
> for children of immigrants, the second generation born in Italy. We
> are Italian. We feel Italian. But because of our surnames, because of
> our features, we're not treated by Italians as a hundred percent Italian.
> (Interview Gupta, AKI 2008)

And Mike Samaniego, Italian MC of Chinese-Philippine descent adds:
"Amir and I have things in common. He's the son of an immigrant and I'm
the son of two immigrants. What unites us is rap and its message. Even
though we were brought up differently, we still work together because we
have things in common" (ibid.). Across the continent, hip-hop reached a
large part of the second and third generation not mobilized by traditional
political activism, and the belated media boom around rap in the early
1990s transported this group and its views into mainstream consciousness for the first time.

The central role of African American productions in twentieth century
international popular culture facilitated the translation and appropriation of codes developed within U.S. communities. This appropriation of
the U.S. experience comes not without problems though. The danger of
what George Lipsitz calls strategic antiessentialism (Lipsitz 1994) lies in
the use of African American culture as a mere foil against which a new
European minority identity can be constructed, the former reduced to an
essential state from where it is not allowed to evolve or display internal
contradictions. In addition, the solidarities hip-hop created among racialized communities of different backgrounds are fragile at best. As Oliver
Wang observes for the U.S. situation:

That desire to identify with hip-hop's outspoken politics of identity can provide the basis for the *beginning* of a potential dialogue between different groups. It has the *potential* of bridging the gulf created by historical structures of inequality of interpersonal conflicts. Obviously, these dialogues are not guaranteed to achieve "emancipatory ends" simply on the basis of intent, but they are an attempt to bridge commonalities between communities that share long histories of disenfranchisement and marginalization." (Wang, in Raphael-Hernandez and Steen 2006, 158)[41]

Some European minority crews showed little effort to connect to the communities from which hip-hop originated. For others the repossession of a suppressed past is instrumental in constructing an open, inclusive group identity based on common interests and experiences rather than shared ethnic origin, a sense of history necessary to oppose marginalization and stereotyping by the majority. Advanced Chemistry in the cover notes to their second single, "Welcher Pfad führt zur Geschichte" (Which Path Leads to History), published 1993, explicitly connect with an urban U.S. diaspora tradition to which they add new members:

Each and every activist of contemporary hip-hop, whether in Bremerhaven or Brooklyn, acts in the tradition of the Zulu Nation, no matter if he or she admits this or not . . . In New York, this culture was initiated primarily by African Americans, Jamaicans, Haitians, Puerto Ricans . . .

It is no coincidence but due to its rebellious content that in Germany many black Germans, Turks and Kurds, Yugoslavians, Roma and Sinti feel attracted to this culture and practice hip-hop . . . The message should be clear: . . . We're going our own way![42]

Hip-hop's appropriation in Europe allowed for the creation of a remarkably fluent movement that has engaged in the process of building a community that avoids the seemingly unavoidable retreat to an essentialism differentiating between "us" and "them"—not by denying that there are fundamental differences running through European societies, but by insisting that these differences can be named and dismantled. Hip-hop became the means for marginalized youth to claim the streets of the cities they lived in, quite literally through breakdancing and graffiti, elements of hip-hop that received the least commercial recognition and in which the dominance of minorities was especially pronounced (Khazaleh 2000). This movement offered a way beyond the dichotomy of cultures and nationalities characterizing discourses around migration until this point and created a space for those who "share long histories of disenfranchisement and marginalization," silenced by the challenge to these binary structures their very existence posed. In concluding chapter 1, I will return to the dynamic between memory and amnesia, contested public spaces, and notions of a European past and identity that have been the overarching themes of this chapter. I will do so by reexamining these issues in the context of European hip-hop culture, exploring its potential in offering a perspective that links the often willfully fractured elements of postwar European history, breaking its internalist conception by situating contemporary minority identity at the crossroads of World War II, colonialism, labor migration, and cold war politics.

The 1961 Paris Massacre and Its Aftermath

What appears as an urgent task within the oft-proclaimed quest for a twenty-first century European identity is the exploration of the impact of neglected aspects of Europe's history and more so of their inextricable link to the foundational elements of Europeanness. Such an exploration would necessarily require a reassessment of national histories from exactly the transnational and interdisciplinary perspective needed to create a "postnational" positionality. While this reassessment cannot happen here, I would like to briefly illustrate its potential by pointing to various possible entry points into this history within the last half century or so, such as 1945, 1989, 2001, and perhaps less obvious, 1961. This was the year of the Eichmann trial in Jerusalem, marking the end of the "postwar" period and the beginning of a new assessment of the Holocaust; the beginning too of the hot phase of the cold war, symbolized by the building of the Berlin wall as well as the failed Bay of Pigs invasion; the same year also that the West German government signed a "guest worker" treaty with Turkey that brought to Europe what is now its largest ethnic and religious minority community, a community that is still, however, perceived as representing everything that is *not* European; a year finally in which more than a hundred protesting Algerians were murdered by French police in the streets of Paris, a largely uncommemorated event marking the repression of European colonial history (and echoing the French army's massacre of Algerian civilians on May 8, 1945). The events of 1961, all remembered in varying degrees, but never together, could be seen as symbolizing the link between colonialism, World War II, cold war politics, cosmopolitanism, and migration that is routinely ignored in discussions of either subject. I will briefly explore how such an inclusive approach to postwar history could be conceptualized by focusing on an unlikely example: An ongoing lawsuit that pits French President Nicolas Sarkozy against an underground hip-hop crew from the Paris suburbs, La Rumeur, whom he accuses of slandering the French police forces in connection with the 1961 massacre.

In 1961, the war of independence in Algeria had been raging for seven years, the French oppression against the civilian population turning increasingly brutal. Despite widespread resistance to the French colonial occupation, the government in Paris refused to consider the conflict a war, instead presenting it as an "operation of public order" against a group of terrorists. Among the effects of this strategy was the French insistence that captured "terrorists" were not protected by the Geneva convention, allowing an increasingly normalized regime of torture.[43] This regime directly affected Algerians not only in their home country, but also in France. In 1958, in reaction to an FLN attack killing three Paris policemen, police forces rounded up more than 5,000 Algerians living in France (or those assumed to be Algerian, which could include Moroccans, Tunisians, or Southern European migrants), detaining them in centers used for the same purpose in Vichy France during the Second World War. The raids and detentions continued over the coming years; eventually more than 11,000 people were imprisoned temporarily, and in October 1961, a special curfew for Algerians in Paris was introduced. The measure prompted a protest on October 17, attended by an estimated 30,000 people, most of them Algerians. Police attacked the demonstration, throwing hundreds of participants in the Seine River (often after beating them unconscious or tying their hands), rounding up others at police headquarters where they were beaten, many to death. Numbers are still contested, but at least two hundred dead civilians seems a safe estimate (Greisalmer 2002).

The police force committing the atrocities acted under orders from Maurice Papon, who had been police prefect of the Algerian province Constantine from 1949 to 1958.[44] In 1958, Papon was named police chief of Paris, where he quickly created an identification center specifically for Algerian-born French citizens, and an auxiliary police force consisting largely of anti-FLN Algerians who, under his command conducted torture and "disappearances" (one of which, of Moroccan opposition leader Mehdi Ben Barka finally led to Papon's forced resignation in 1967; see Gallisot 2005). Papon was never disciplined for his role as police prefect in Algeria or police chief in Paris. On the contrary, a protégé of Charles de Gaulle, he received the Médaille de la Résistance in 1958 and became a member of the Légion d'honneur in 1961. After his forced resignation as police chief, Papon successfully continued his career—both in politics as a provincial mayor and in the private sector, as president of the company that built the first Concorde jet—until 1981, when it was finally confirmed that the connection between colonial and metropolitan violence that Papon personified did not begin in Algeria after World War II, but rather in Vichy France during the 1940s. As secretary general of the prefecture of Gironde and supervisor of its Service for Jewish Questions, Papon was responsible for the deportation of more than 1,500 Jewish men, women, and children (Whitney 2007).

Papon's ability to evade trial until 1997, his protection by high-ranking French politicians, his release from prison after less than three years, when he had finally been convicted in 1999 (all the while insisting that he was the victim), and his burial in 2007 with full honors of the French legion drastically shows the "reprehensible amnesia" that Susan Suleiman rightly insists persists in Europe with regard to the crimes of the Holocaust, despite the latter's central role in the European "collective memory" (Huyssen 2005; Assman 2007; Novick 2007). And while Papon's case might have been extreme, it was by no means unique. Many of the police involved in the 1961 massacre had in fact served in Vichy France. In the virulently anticommunist cold war climate, it seemed safer to a postwar France cultivating the image of a national resistance to rely on collaborators of Nazi Germany rather than on resistance fighters who often had also been members of the Communist Party (de Gaulle was fully aware of Papon's past when he awarded him the Médaille de la Résistance).

Maurice Papon's career provides an exceptionally clear case against the internalist narrative of Europe: the dehumanizing violence originating in the colonial context was brought back to Europe through the Nazi state as Arendt and Césaire most prominently have argued (and the still largely taboo subject of widespread collaboration with the German occupiers in many European countries was rooted not only in an endemic anti-Semitism, but also additionally in a scientific racism made popular by colonialism). It was reintroduced to the colonial context in response to the independence movements gaining momentum after the end of the war (both through official policies and the widespread use of the French foreign legion, a mercenary army which provided a safe haven for many former Nazis and collaborators, see Baer 1999) and then brought back to the metropolis through the treatment of (post)colonial migrant populations. While these connections are still persistently suppressed in European discourses, the pressure mounts with the growth of a minority population invested in relating their marginalized status to the treatment their migrant parents and grandparents received when they arrived. In recent years, a multiethnic "counter-amnes(t)ic" (Yoneyama 2003) movement challenges the whitewashing of Europe's history. In the case of France and the 1961 events, this collective includes Jewish, Beur and

Algerian activists, historians, Communist and Socialist parliamentarians, and hip-hop activists.

In 2002, three years after the French government had finally acknowledged that the Algerian "conflict" had indeed been a war (implicitly allowing for the possibility that war crimes had been committed), decades after thousands of Algerian laborers and their families had moved to France, set up in temporary housing that became permanent ghettos, and a couple of months after socialist Paris mayor Bertrand Delanoë unveiled a plaque commemorating the 1961 massacre (members of the Conservative Party and the police force boycotted the event), hip-hop crew La Rumeur from the Paris suburb Élancourt published its first CD, L'Ombre sur la Mesure. The CD was accompanied by a zine in which one of the group members, MC Hamé (aka Mohamed Bourokba) published the article "Insécurité sous la plume d'un barbare" (Insecurity from the pen of a barbarian). The piece is a rather sophisticated analysis, linking colonial oppression, exploitation of migrant labor, police violence, and the scapegoating of impoverished urban communities of color in the name of "zero tolerance" and the "war on terror," painting a bleak picture of life in the *cités*.

It was the accusation of police violence and the reference to the 1961 murders, presenting both as expressions of a structural racism within French institutions and society in general, that motivated then Secretary of the Interior Nicolas Sarkozy to initiate a lawsuit against Hamé for "slandering the national police forces" (Brown 2008).

While Hamé is not the only French rapper of color put on trial accused of tainting the French image (Brown 2008), the issue here very clearly seems one of "archival power," of "the power to define what is and what is not a serious object of research and, therefore, of mention." Hamé's defense acted accordingly, asking historians and sociologists to testify on the events of October 17, 1961, the links between Vichy and 5th Republic police forces, and the suppression of both histories; a teacher from the *cités* spoke about the daily police harassment his students had to endure; fellow crew member Ekoué emphasized that Hamé spoke for all of La Rumeur, and a "rap expert" placed the group's political rap in a French tradition of protest music (Brown 2008). The prosecution did not do much to counter the defense's claims (beyond calling them slanderous) and Hamé was acquitted in 2003. The ministry of interior, now headed by Dominic de Villepain, decided to appeal, however, and a new trial was held in 2004. It ended with the same result and again the government decided to challenge the ruling. When the next trial was held in 2006, the 2005 riots had taken place and Nicolas Sarkozy had become president of the French republic. The prosecution reflected common sentiments in accusing La Rumeur of instigating violent behavior among their young listeners in the suburbs. This strategy did neither change the outcome of the trial nor the state's determination to go on until the bitter end. As of 2010 there is still no final ruling and while it seems unlikely that the earlier decision will be reversed, since if anything Hamé's claims have become more substantial with the evidence coming to light since the trial began, so far the proceedings have cost the rapper more than €20,000.

The events around La Rumeur's 2002 release are remarkable not only because of the government's persistence in pushing a court case against the MC of an underground hip-hop crew, nor can they be sufficiently explained with Sarkozy's apparent identification of Arab and Muslim youths with "enemies of the state." Instead, I believe, they signify a turning point in Europe's self-representation. The continental unification brought a renewed examination of the meaning of nation in the twenty-first century, debates about a common history gave momentum to a very belated and partial examination of World War II collaborations and a fledgling examination of the long-term impact of colonialism. This is no linear development though, rather a contested process, in which positions clash and racialized populations play a familiar scapegoat part. What is new in this constellation is the extent to which these populations voice and coordinate their resistance to this scapegoating. This is possible in part because of the growth of the second- and third-generation population, both in numbers and influence. Being European not by choice but by experience, they pick the only battleground they have and increasingly become a party in ongoing battles around the meaning of "Europe." Actions like Sarkozy's exemplify the last attempt to expel them and the past they represent from a clean image of (post)national identity that their very presence is perceived to taint. Hip-hop is a logical culprit because it expresses challenges from the margins to the sanitized self-image of the center more forceful than any other medium, at the same time its violent rhetoric and macho imagery feeds (and is fed off) mainstream fears of violent men of color.

European hip-hop culture no doubt is the most important contemporary translocal minority structure, dramatically changing the representation of racialized communities in the continent's landscape; providing a much needed rallying point to counter economic exclusion, moral panics around violent, terrorist male youths of color and neoliberal policies of containment of disposable populations. Discourses around colorblindness and multiculturalism notwithstanding, minority youths are disadvantaged in school, overrepresented in prisons, and disproportionally affected by unemployment (OECD 2003; Ivanov 2006; Keaton 2006). But while it lastingly troubled the rigidity of national and ethnic ascriptions, Euro hip-hop failed to do the same for notions of gender and sexual identity. This is not meant to imply that there was no female presence. Just as in the United States, women played a central role in hip-hop culture since the days of the Rock Steady Crew and Philadelphia's Lady B so did European women of color like Turkish-German Aziza A or Moroccan-Swedish Lila K.[45] The discursive construction of hip-hop identity and community, however, followed similar exclusionary patterns. Tim'm West's discussion of the constitution of the "Hip-Hop nation" in the 1990s and the implications this had for the performance and policing of gender and sexual identities (West 2005) becomes especially relevant here precisely because of the critical engagement with the nation-state central to the segment of Euro hip-hop engaging in the queering of ethnicity: while successfully deconstructing exclusionary notions of European nationhood, the hip-hop community constructed its own "fictive ethnicity," enforced through a policing of nonnormative expressions of gender and sexuality as violating norms of authenticity and "realness." But as West states:

> Paradoxically, "keepin' it real" is one's authentication of allegiance to a norm that seems to struggle against itself; realness is never proven once and for all, but must be compulsively reconfirmed. Angst around authenticity exists because, ironically, the illusion of permanence must be stabilized over and again. (West 2005, 169)

Accordingly, the discursive disciplining of queer and feminist voices through the notion of realness within Euro hip-hop activism was confirmed as well as challenged constantly, from the outside, but more importantly within collaborative processes that brought together activists of color from a variety of backgrounds. One of the key sites of this interaction was the black European movement that will be focus of the next chapter.

CHAPTER TWO

Dimensions of Diaspora

Women of Color Feminism, Black Europe, and Queer Memory Discourses

For women, poetry is not a luxury. It is a vital necessity of our existence. It forms the quality of the light within which we predicate our hopes and dreams toward survival and change, first made into language, then into idea, then into more tangible action.

—AUDRE LORDE, *Poetry Is Not a Luxury*

Relation is learning more and more to go beyond judgments into the unexpected dark of art's upsurgings. Its beauty springs from the stable and the unstable, from the deviance of many particular poetics and the clairvoyance of a relational poetics. The more things it standardizes into a state of lethargy, the more rebellious consciousness it arouses.

—EDOUARD GLISSANT, *The Poetics of Relation*

Rethinking the African Diaspora from the Margins

Chapter 1 pointed to diaspora as an alternative framework of identification for racialized Europeans by exploring dominant narrations of continental identity and minority youths' challenges to them, in particular through hip-hop, via a focus on space. Chapter 2 further builds on this notion of diaspora and its application by activists of color. The spatial situatedness of identity discourses, here around the black Atlantic, remains central, but there is an added focus on the temporal dimension of community building, more specifically on the construction of a queer diasporic memory within the black European movement. This is a memory discourse that is not built on linear notions of roots and authentic origins, but on the grounding of a community embracing its "inauthentic," fractured nature rather than resolving it through a projected, unambiguous past. With this focus, I also shift my attention rather drastically from urban minority youths to feminist activists of color, namely to 1970s women of color feminism's critique of diasporic nationalism and the spaces it opened for alternative conceptualizations of both diaspora and nation as reflected in black feminist activism in 1980s Europe.

The following discussion of the potentially fruitful relationship between African diaspora discourses and European minority communities challenges the absence of theorizations produced by the former from emerging methodologies applied to the latter. It also continues the inquiry into the limits of blackness started by queer and feminist authors in the United States and elsewhere by exploring how a consideration of "black Europe" might expand our understanding of diasporic identity. As many authors have noted, African diaspora studies have long centered on the U.S. experience (Gilroy 1993; Patterson and Kelley 2000; Edwards 2003; Wright 2004). Many also suggest that transnational black diasporas studies cannot and should not merely be additive, that the geographical expansion of our definition of the African diaspora has to go along with an expanded understanding of the very nature of this diaspora. The dominant methodological framework developed in order to grasp the particulars of the American experience cannot necessarily be applied to other parts of the world, and additionally, the growing knowledge of the black condition elsewhere in turn might change our understanding of the diaspora in the Americas. Thus, black studies scholars increasingly argue that diasporic thinking beyond the national paradigm is a necessary prerequisite for an inclusive black subjectivity, that is, one that does not create its own internal Others.

While a generalized definition of "black" is both methodologically justified and politically necessary, diaspora discourse to a certain extent produces its own subject, and this representational power needs to be examined: who is considered a proper black subject and why? A shift from a national focus to a transnational perspective requires that the specific cultural, historical, and political conditions that produced dominant notions of the black subject within Africana studies are made explicit— and challenged if necessary.[1] I argue that in some ways, this might even require thinking beyond the black paradigm as we understand it now. This does not put into question at all the validity or necessity of national black studies; it does raise the question, however, whether a growing number of these national black studies will merely coexist and occasionally interact under the umbrella of the African diaspora or whether a truly transnational and interdisciplinary diaspora studies will emerge.

The latter seems the more constructive response to a geopolitical climate in which trench mentalities thrive while old binaries are successfully revived within clash of civilization scenarios that increasingly affect academic discourse. Caught in between these exclusive binary constructions are racialized populations whose very right to self-definition is challenged in an effort to permanently limit their access to the privileges of citizenship as well as to those of "universal personhood" (Soysal 1994). This includes communities of color in a West that continues to define itself as creator and gatekeeper of the commitment to universal human rights. These groups, in insisting on the right to name themselves, question a number of dominant assumptions, among them traditional notions of blackness. An exploration of the continued importance of colonialism for diaspora identities, for example, could effectively question the marginalization of black Europe within Africana studies. This marginal position is often due to Europe's supposed irrelevance for the central theme of the African diaspora: the transatlantic slave trade (which of course is closely linked to colonialism).

The majority of theorists of the African diaspora define the Middle Passage as the central moment of the black Atlantic consciousness, and there is, of course, good reason for such an assessment: the transatlantic slave trade, Paul Gilroy (among others) argues, shaped not only the history and identity of black people in the West (whether they descend from slaves or not), but also the history and identity of the modern West itself. While the momentous impact of racial slavery can hardly be denied, its dominance in theorizations of diasporic identity has nevertheless been questioned within Africana studies. Some criticism addresses the problematic effects of essentially and eternally defining the African diaspora through slavery; others question the usefulness of attempting to identify a single, central event around which identities are built (see, e.g., Blyfield 2000).

If, however, neither the Middle Passage nor any other historic event is able to anchor an African diasporic identity, how, then, can this identity be defined beyond the far more questionable imaginary of biological race? One of the most interesting responses comes from Michelle Wright, who argues that the answer lies in a particular form of discourse rather than a shared historical or cultural trope (Wright 2004). Starting from the assumption that a black diasporic consciousness indeed exists, while at the same time acknowledging that diaspora communities have different traditions and face varying conditions, Wright claims that "[a] truly accurate definition of an African diasporic identity . . . must somehow simultaneously incorporate the diversity of black identities in the diaspora yet also link all those identities to show that they indeed constitute a diaspora rather than an unconnected aggregate of different peoples linked only in name" (Wright

2004, 2). She continues to identify an intellectual tradition that includes various positions that nevertheless share an understanding of black subjectivity as "that which must be negotiated between the abstract and the real or, in theoretical terms, between the ideal and the material" (ibid., 3).

This dialectic discourse, however, remains tied to the norm of the nation and thus reproduces its modes of exclusion: in order to come into existence as a citizen, the black male subject had to reproduce the dialectic formation that produced him as Other by creating its own Other. Within the nationalist framework of dialectic discourse, subjectivity is coded male, and the black woman necessarily remains an "(un)subject."[2] To overcome this exclusionary principle, according to Wright, theorists have to move beyond the nation and address gender and sexuality as inseparable from notions of race in order to arrive at a Bakhtinian dialogic model that allows for a "diasporic intersubjectivity," which, rather than any particular event or experience, conceptualizes the African diaspora "as a dialogic formation in which many subjectivities exist that cannot be organized into thetical and antithetical categories" (ibid., 3). Wright concludes that the first movement in this direction has taken place in the context of 1960s liberation movements, exemplified by black feminist poets such as Gwendolyn Rodgers and Audre Lorde who established a female black subjectivity that was dialogic rather than dialectic, thus overcoming the need to produce internal Others. The connection Wright draws between a dialogic understanding of diaspora and black feminism's use of poetry leads directly to women of color feminism's challenges to essentialist models of identity and to its appropriation by black European feminists.

It is both a historical coincidence and a testament to the enormous changes generated by the liberation movements of the 1960s and '70s that roughly at the same time *Wild Style*, *Beat Street*, and *The Message* arrived in Europe, providing a foundation for the translocal Euro hip-hop movement whose emergence I described in the last chapter, another U.S.-based movement became immensely influential among racialized Europeans. Women of color feminism and the community it envisioned, like hip-hop, are rooted in African American discourses while being profoundly shaped by interminority activism. In many other ways, it could hardly have been further from the identities and ideologies dominating the hip-hop scene, but the fact that both movements did merge in the queer of color activism that will be the subject of chapter 4 indicates that there might be more commonalities between transnational feminism and hip-hop culture than meets the eye.

One of these commonalities, I suggest in this chapter, is the use of nonessentialist, intersubjective models of diaspora identity in creating a transnational community that draws on disparate cultural traditions, traditions that in dominant discourses are not only often perceived as being without relation to each other, but also as without political relevance. Popular music certainly falls in this category, and so does poetry as a tool of community building. Accessible and related to oral traditions, poetry—written or spoken—was probably *the* art form of women of color feminism. Outside of the context of high art, in its vernacular form, still largely associated with "low culture" in European literary studies, poetry, where it is practiced to challenge exclusion, provides an openness of form that can extend into content, allowing the combining of the vernacular and the political and the expression of the experience of groups whose oppression is considered irrelevant in the dominant narratives of political resistance.

Few have analyzed and practiced this form as a means of resistance more effectively than queer black feminist poet and activist Audre Lorde—daughter of Caribbean immigrants to the United States—who defined poetry as an everyday tool of survival for groups silenced through their supposedly lacking ability to master the tools of proper political analysis. The solution, Lorde argued, does not lie with using "the master's tools," but with appropriating poetry, offering an alternative vocabulary of liberation: "Where that language does not yet exist, it is our poetry which helps to fashion it. Poetry is not only dream and vision; it is the skeleton architecture of our lives. It lays the foundations for a future of change, a bridge across our fears of what has never been before" (Lorde 1984, 37).

Lorde claimed poetry as a radical, feminist form of expression exactly because of its association with qualities disvalued within the Western intellectual tradition—emotion, intuition, collectivity, nonlinearity, the oral—qualities that had also been attributed to women and people of color. In the context of 1970s liberation movements dominated by the dialectic model of revolutionary nationalism described by Wright, poetry became a subversive tool for feminists of color, creating a discursive space that allowed for the coexistence of different identities, sites, voices, and ideas, opening up possibilities often suppressed in calls for black, brown, or feminist unity, namely those of intersectional positionalities. The reassessment of difference within and between communities as a source of strength rather than of disunity, as something to be explored rather than avoided and denied, was at the center of women of color feminism's approach to identity and community, opening up new avenues of dialogue by using poetry to "give name to the nameless so it can be thought" (Lorde 1984, 37).

In pushing beyond binary, essentialist notions of identity, women of color feminism initiated a shift in paradigms, lastingly shaping the search for methodological tools that allow for "fuzzy edges" and intersections rather than depending on the creation of boundaries, making possible the exploration of commonalities while paying close attention to specific circumstances. For the first time systematically theorizing intersectional identities and power structures (Crenshaw 1991), women of color feminism:

> represented a crucial break in gender studies discourse in which any naïve positioning of gender as the primary and singular node of difference within feminist theory and politics was irrevocably challenged . . . [I]t has enabled the discourse of gender studies to move beyond politics of identification and counteridentification, helping us arrive at a politics of disidentification." (Muñoz 1999, 22) [3]

Women of color feminism was a key influence not only on Muñoz and other practitioners of queer of color critique, insisting on constant attention to the interrelations of class, gender, race, and sexuality, but also—for the same reasons—on black European movements, most obviously in the case of 1980s Afro-German and black Dutch activism.

Within the European context, there certainly seems to be a dearth of theoretical approaches that provide the tools to address minorities of color as anything but Other and their art and activism as anything but trivial. These tools must also be able to reflect the challenges to the Manichean dichotomies shaping nearly all of political discourse in Europe (and beyond) represented by this art and activism, able to capture the ephemeral hauntings that binary and inflexible models of identity keep at the periphery of Europe's vision of itself. Poetry, with its ability to "give a name to the nameless," became a tool of liberation for European minorities in the context of hip-hop as well as black feminist activism. While hip-hop provided a common language for youths of color of various ethnic backgrounds sharing the experience of being silenced through exclusion from the community of citizens, so did women of color feminism provide a position of agency for migrant and minority women whose marginalization within the mainstream feminist movement was often coupled with the wholesale rejection of their cultural knowledge. When placed in a diasporic context, however, this consciousness of dislocation proved to offer important tools for criticizing the exclusions inherent in the workings of the modern nation-state as well as in movements opposing its exclusions, namely, second-wave feminism and diasporic nationalism. After all, as Grace Hong reminds us:

> While 1960s and 1970s black feminism's intersectional analytic was, as it is often narrativized, a critique of the sexism within black nationalist movements or of racism within white feminism, we must also understand the larger implications of intersectionality: it was a *complete*

critique of the epistemological formation of the white supremacist moment of global capital organized around colonial capitalism. (Hong 2008, 101)

Women of color feminism's attention to globally intersecting power structures, linking the struggles of minorities in the West and anticolonial struggles in the global South, opened a venue for the inclusion of diverse experiences that could offer new perspectives on these issues, pointing to the potential contributions of "marginal" black communities to the emerging understanding of a transnational black community defined by its diasporic intersubjectivity rather than by a single formative event. Obvious differences in ideology make it easy to forget that the subversive use of poetry by feminists of color and hip-hop originate in the same social contexts and cultural traditions, sharing a translatability that is reflected in their appropriation across continents and languages.

Afro-German spoken-word poet Olumide Popoola, coeditor of the queer of color anthology *Talking Home* (discussed in more detail later in this chapter) describes her coming of age as a poet and activist in a way that closely resonates with those of the hip-hop artists addressed in chapter 1:

To be honest, I always wanted to be a writer, from age six, when I learned to write. I used to write little stories then, in my early adolescence, it became poetry. I had my first poem published when I was thirteen, in an Afro-German magazine called *Afro-Look*. The poem was about the effect that neo-Nazis had on my life; we had a big problem in the city I grew up in, so in a way at that time poetry became a space I could feel empowered in, it was my voice in a racist environment. (Chauke 2009)

In this chapter, I focus on two feminist, queer texts that use poetry to simultaneously expand definitions of Europeanness and of blackness, both collections of autobiographical writings of various genres—memoirs in the widest sense—negotiating the authors' shifting positions in the complex field framed by race, class, nation, sexuality, and gender, and both fundamentally shaped by Europe's encounter with women of color feminism. I argue that it was this combination of form and genre—poetry and autobiography—that allowed the texts to create a counter-memory discourse grounded in a transnational diasporic community while directly challenging the amnesia erasing their presence in the nation.

The first text, *Showing Our Colors: Afro-German Women Speak Out* (1986, English 1991), widely considered the foundational text of the black German movement, is concerned with appropriating a transnational diasporic discourse and placing black Europeans within it. The second, *Talking Home. Heimat aus unserer eigenen Feder. Frauen of Color in Deutschland* (Home in our own writing. Women of color in Germany, 1999), published thirteen years later and in many ways a response to the earlier text, is a queer women of color anthology reflecting both the changes brought about by the earlier anthology and the remaining similarities. Though exceeding the national in many ways—one collection was published in Berlin, the other in Amsterdam—both anthologies focus on Germany. This nation, located in Europe's center, at once represents the problems and successes of creating a European identity out of the continent's fractured history. It also provides a particularly interesting example of the transnational grounding of contemporary communities-in-the-making with the emergence in the mid-1980s of an Afro-German movement that both claimed an identity as black *and* German (a perfect example of an oxymoron to white Germans) and as part of a larger African diaspora. Afro-Germans are representative of a black European population that for the most part did not originate in a violent mass removal and the specific group experiences it occasioned but came to Europe via direct or indirect routes as a consequence of colonialism.

It was black Europe's heterogeneous composition, its ambiguous relation to constitutive narratives of the African diaspora as well as its complicated relation to and overlap with other communities of color that left black Europeans at the margin of diaspora discourses. I argue however that it is exactly this "messiness" of black European identities and allegiances that is its potential. Europe appears as a promising terrain to explore and advance the possibilities of new conceptualizations of minority identity, inclusive of but not necessarily limited to black Europeans. Taken in its totality and national differences admitted, black European communities show important commonalities, rooted in a perception of Europe as a white continent living on in current debates on postnational identities. Consequently, the various black populations of Europe are increasingly subjected to the same conditions and confront an ever more homogeneous image of a continent that up to now has excluded its residents of color. A comparative approach to these groups thus seems of crucial importance. In order to adequately discuss the idea of a black Europe, however, I will first need to systematically explore the conditions under which not only concepts of race but also racialized minorities were created.

Racialized Europeans, Migration Studies, and African Diaspora Theory

European minority communities' affinity with African diasporic cultural productions has been widely noted (Hargreaves and McKinney 1997; Diedrichsen 1998); it is therefore surprising that there nonetheless is little overlap between ideas originating in black diaspora discourse and debates about the potential usefulness of the diaspora model in the European context. Before exploring the interactions of African diasporic discourses, transnational feminism, and black European activism, it is thus necessary to address European theorists' reluctance to engage with these intellectual traditions, especially because in recent years, diaspora has become an almost omnipresent concept across disciplines.[4] Diaspora studies is emerging as a field that by now includes among its objects of scrutiny more or less all populations that originate in migration, only loosely basing itself methodologically on the original use referencing the Jewish experience (Clifford 1994). In fact, the term *diaspora* has entered migration studies to such an extent that it can be considered one of the primary tropes used to describe contemporary migrant groups (Soysal 2000). Exactly because of this almost inflationary use of the diaspora, attitudes toward the nation-state expressed within diaspora theories can differ widely from the attempt to completely leave behind the nation model to the desire to "return home" to an ethnic nation-state.

I believe that it is the former approach that could be extremely useful in understanding European minority communities; however, it is the latter definition of diaspora that currently dominates debates within European migration studies: the model of diaspora most often represented revolves around the trope of the "lost home," in which the migrant's existence is seen as focusing entirely on his or her native land, the return to which is identified as *the* dominant life goal, and all activities in the temporary domicile of the host society appear focused on this central aim. This focus, furthermore, is assumed to shape not only the life of the migrants themselves, but also that of their (grand)children whose identification with a home they often barely know is not seen as a reaction to their living conditions in the here-and-now, but as a shared nostalgia for the then-and-there (Şenoçak 2000). It is, in other words, an understanding of diaspora that perfectly matches the internalist narrative at the heart of European racelessness in placing diasporic populations permanently outside of the national community they are part of.

The prevailing notion of diaspora in migration studies over the last decade has come under criticism for overestimating the role that the homeland plays for migrant populations of the first and later generations and for underestimating the investment of those populations in their host societies. Those critical of the use of diaspora within migration studies, however, often unintentionally reproduce the narrow perspective they rightly challenge by completely ignoring the African diaspora and its theorizations.[5] Transnational movements of people, ideas, and technologies are central to black Atlantic culture, but theoretical and methodological developments in black studies are all too often automatically assumed to be of little relevance to disciplines not primarily occupied with race or when dealing with areas such as Europe assumed to be unaffected by it. Consequently, the vast body of theory borne out of the experience of black minorities in the West is largely considered irrelevant for the understanding of continental European migrant and minority populations. This might be due to a general reluctance to conceptualize second- or third-generation migrant communities as native minorities (who thus might be compared to other minorities in the West) and to the belief that the black experience revolves around race while the concept is secondary to all other groups (and especially those who consider themselves or are considered white).[6]

Sociologist Yasemin Soysal, one of the most prolific critics of the diaspora model within migration studies, sketches a picture that indeed bears little resemblance to the African diasporic experience:

> The dominant conceptualization of diaspora presumptively accepts the formation of tightly bounded communities and solidarities (on the basis of common cultural and ethnic references) between places of origin and arrival . . . Diasporas form when populations disperse from their homeland to foreign lands, engage in movements between the country of origin and destination, and carry out bi-directional transactions— economic, political and cultural. In this formulation, the primary orientation and attachment of diasporic populations is to their homelands and cultures; and their claims and citizenship practices arise from this home-bound, ethnic-based orientation. (Soysal 2000, 2)

Understood like this, diaspora does little more than provide a new name for the old idea that migrants experience the period of migration as a suspension of their real life, which will be continued after the final return home. According to this theory, even if in reality the moment of return is endlessly postponed, it remains at the center of the migrants' identity, preventing them from ever fully engaging with the host society, though in the end they might spend the larger part of their life there (Hage 2003). Soysal and others contrast this model with the multiple forms of engagement migrants display in the receiving nations, an engagement that transcends the binational focus and is obscured by what is perceived as the diaspora's obsession with the past. Andreas Huyssen, for example, claims that "[t]oday's hyphenated and migratory cultures develop different structures of experience which may make the traditional understanding of diaspora as linked to roots, soil, and kinship indeed highly questionable"

(Huyssen 2003, 151). This traditional understanding locks the migrant out of the nation and into the past and accordingly is a concept hardly useful in capturing how migrants negotiate national belonging(s) in an increasingly postnational world. Instead, according to Soysal, "[a] more challenging and productive perspective is achieved by focusing our analytical providence on the proliferating sites of making and enacting citizenship. In a world of incessant migrations, it is in these novel geographies of citizenship that we recognize the dynamics and distribution of rights and identities, and patterns of inclusion and exclusion" (Soysal 2000, 3).

The critical inquiry into a scholarship of migration that characterizes its objects of study as forever looking backward—unable or unwilling to overcome the exclusive identification with the culture of origin—also asks for a different assessment of the policies of the receiving nations. These nations, Soysal, Seyla Benhabib, and others argue, do not, in a move mirroring the migrant's supposed refusal to integrate, exclude noncitizens from all forms of participation associated with citizenship, but are instead engaged in constant negotiations of belonging that reflect the constructed, contract-based nature of the nation-state, resulting in a citizenship model based on an individual's universal personhood rather than her passport (Soysal 1994). While the analytical focus on conceptualizations of citizenship importantly shifts the center of migrant lives to their present surroundings, the last chapter has pointed to some of the hurdles that diasporic populations face in these negotiations of national belongings, especially if they take place in a context such as the European Union's, in which citizenship is a multilayered concept to which not all migrants have the same access. Instead, they are confronted with an implicit but strict hierarchy of belonging that leaves many of them with very little negotiating power and consequently little universal personhood.

The limits of approaches such as Soysal's—which do not provide the means to deconstruct the mechanisms of colorblindness that feed inequalities in access to citizenship rights—become even more obvious when one turns to populations who nominally have possessed citizenship for generations but are nonetheless excluded from many rights implicitly assumed to be part of citizen status, something that applies to various European populations, including the Roma, Jewish, and African diasporas. Their histories point to the impossibility of assessing present negotiations of belonging without taking into consideration the way representations of the past inevitably figure into contemporary understandings of citizenship. It is precisely their persistent exclusion from Europe's past that makes it impossible for European minorities to access full citizenship rights in the current moment. This notwithstanding, however,

Soysal's criticism of migration studies' use of the diaspora concept foregrounds a central problematic of the discipline, namely: how can one theorize migrant and minority populations as integral parts of national histories and contemporary politics while at the same time recognizing their transnational components?

The answer, I suggest, lies—Soysal's and others justified skepticism notwithstanding—in the diaspora concept itself, albeit in a somewhat unorthodox approach to it. What the conservative diaspora model employed in migration studies and its critics often have in common is the desire to resolve the tension migrant and minority populations cause within the nation-state by either placing them firmly without or firmly within the nation. Both positions thus suppress what is central to these communities: their transnational affiliations that make them something different from either insiders or outsiders and thus a constant reminder of the limits of the nation model. Diaspora is a concept that ideally, though far from automatically, can express this tension without the implicit need to resolve it. In this sense and contrary to migration, diaspora transcends the binary of citizen and foreigner, the linear model of movement from origin to destination. What diaspora signifies is the fact of change, of losing a purity that one never had, thus providing the basis for a situational community of racialized European subjects engaged in the process of queering ethnicity using similarly nonlinear and nonbinary forms of artistic expression.

While migration does not grasp the experience of a population that is born into one nation, but never is fully part of it, and minority does not quite encompass the transnational ties of that same population, diaspora can bring both aspects together, and it does so most explicitly in African diasporic discourses. The unique position of blacks in modernity has produced not only particular cultural formations that are obviously adaptable to other contexts but also intellectual discourses of race, class, culture, sexuality, and gender that are in many ways more relevant to contemporary European societies than critical or postcolonial theory. The latter, while addressing questions that critical theory often ignores, nonetheless seems strangely disconnected from Western minorities, as a number of authors have noted.[7] An example of this negligence is provided by Arjun Appadurai's paradigm shifting *Modernity at Large*, laying out a possible path to a postnational global system through its analysis of the effects of the coincidence of modern mass media and mass migration that produced diasporic public spheres, creating new transnational communities and new means for social action: "[T]he imagination has broken out of the special expressive space of art, myth, and ritual and has now become a part of the quotidian mental work of ordinary people in many societies. . . . Ordinary people have begun to deploy their imaginations in the practice of their everyday lives" (Appadurai 1996, 5).

Appadurai's work, impressive and useful as it is, illustrates the problem: while his book was published a few years after Gilroy's *Black Atlantic* and addressed a number of similar issues (namely, the interrelations of popular culture and movement), his study, granting the new postcolonial diasporas a key role in an emerging postnational world order, largely ignores the African diaspora, both in its practical and theoretical manifestations.[8] This is all the more regrettable as one could argue that the new phenomena Appadurai identifies have first been present in exactly this African diaspora:

[T]hese diasporas bring the force of the imagination, as both memory and desire, into the lives of many ordinary people, into mythographies different from the disciplines of myth and ritual of the classic sort. The key difference here is that these new mythographies are charters for new social projects, and not just a counterpoint to the certainties of daily life. (Appadurai 1996, 4)

It is exactly those new social projects and their reimagining of both memory and desire for which African diaspora studies can offer useful analytical tools. In fact, Appadurai's statement could be read as a description of the process of cultural exchange and identity production at the heart of the African diasporic community since the beginning of modernity. In addition, a number of authors have convincingly proposed a close relationship between this population and the new mass technologies characteristic of postmodern public spheres (Rose 1994; Eshun 1998; Moten 2003, Weheliye 2005). That these technologies—so obviously employed and advanced, for example, in hip-hop—are nevertheless hardly ever linked to black cultural productions might be due to the visual bias of modern cultural criticism, which rarely situates technological revolutions within the sonic. This, despite the fact that, as Alexander Weheliye argues,

popular music offers one of the most fertile grounds for the dissemination and enculturation of digital and analog technologies and has done so at least since the invention of the phonograph at the close of the nineteenth century. Pop music also represents the arena in which black subjects have culturally engaged with these technoinformational flows, so that any consideration of digital space might do well to include the sonic in order to comprehend different modalities of digitalness, but also to not endlessly circulate and therefore solidify the presumed "digital divide" with all its attendant baggage. (Weheliye 2005, 3)

The lack of attention to the sonic as opposed to the visual in analyses of twentieth and twenty-first century mass technologies partially explains the persistent exclusion of African diaspora populations from histories of technological progress, but it also points to a perception of blacks as always marginal to innovation, producing a culture that is ultimately always both derivative—a fusion of elements "already there"—and raw—providing the clay to others' art and culture.[9] A similar argument could be made regarding the nonperception of black intellectual traditions in representations of (post)modernity. If we return to the idea that black people in the West constituted the first modern population (Morrison, in Gilroy 1993, 2; 175–82), confronted with conditions of displacement and questions of identity that became relevant on a much larger scale in the late twentieth and early twenty-first centuries, a different picture emerges: it makes sense to assume that black discourse explored a number of questions that other groups summarized under the heading *diaspora* are confronted with now.

This is not meant to imply that experiences are identical, that there is a hierarchy of knowledge, or that African diaspora studies could offer ready-made solutions for the situation of European minorities, but it does seem obvious that their inclusion would be useful in particular because, as seen, the notion of diaspora is already in frequent use when talking about European minority communities. An interaction of both could thus be very fruitful, I believe, and more so because African diaspora discourse itself so far has not paid much attention to continental Europe.[10] An intensified dialogue thus could be mutually beneficial. This will, however, require a reassessment of the notion of European racial configurations as well as diasporic definitions of black identity in order to include communities falling outside of both definitions. Such a cross-ethnic exploration of processes of racialization in Europe would also necessitate a rethinking of the notion of blackness dominating African diaspora studies, with regard to the diaspora itself, but also in its assessment of African racial configurations.

Africa all too often remains the authentic-but-static point of reference for diasporic identifications, offering a clarity and certainty of identity that life in the diaspora cannot provide, a stable if not never-changing entity in (and against) which diasporic identity is grounded. But cultures are fragmented and contested everywhere, and notions of identity—national, racial, or ethnic—are not necessarily less complicated and negotiable in the past or the motherland. North Africa, direct neighbor to both Asia and Europe, could be an ideal starting point in attempting to approach some of the complexities of diaspora formations. However, the region has largely been excluded from Africana studies based on a consensus that follows a framework established by Hegel's definition of Africa as divided into three distinct parts of which the North is supposedly the European, that is, not really African one (Hegel 1945). Almost two hundred years later, scholarship still largely works along the lines of this arbitrary division, even when, as in Africana studies, its inherent hierarchy is explicitly challenged. The (lacking) role of the Northern part of the continent is one facet of the somewhat essentialist perception of Africa within the diaspora. Despite its investment in challenging the racist construction of ancient Egypt, diasporic discourse tends to marginalize the Maghreb, doing little to question its categorization as white.[11]

The Sahara Desert continues to be represented as a natural border, effectively separating the North from black Africa, rather than as a negative continent similar to Gilroy's *Black Atlantic*, that is, a vibrant space of cultural and other crossings. While the latter view is much more adequate to the experience of those inhabiting the Sahara and its borders, the former reflects the European perception and thus remains dominant in Western discourse.[12] Its adherence to limits produced by a racist discourse reminds us that African diaspora studies are of the West in productive and less productive ways: The model of sub-Saharan Africa as the real, black Africa worked to a large extent for an Africana studies focused on the Americas, but it is nothing more than that—a working model, not a reflection of realities. Working models tend to limit reality's complexity and contradictions according to the demands of a particular focus. They thus cannot be generalized, rather the question whether they can and should be applied to other contexts has to be answered for each individual occasion. If this does not happen, African diaspora scholarship unwittingly affirms supposedly clear racial boundaries that in truth are ideological constructs. Within this ideology, the fact that populations in the Northern part of Africa are racially heterogeneous (as opposed to the ethnic diversity of sub-Saharan Africa) then becomes proof that black North Africans are not really black or not really African, rather than proof of an actual diversity that has been discursively erased by race theory and replaced with artificial racial distinctions that are still often taken as completely natural (Bernal 1987; Lefkovitz and Rogers 1996).

Instead, the ways in which "Africanness" and "blackness" interact need to be reexamined based on local dynamics rather than preconceived universalist notions. The regional, religious, continental, and racial identifications of North Africans create internal as well as external group relations that cannot necessarily be approached with a methodology based on a Western/U.S.-centric perception.[13] This becomes clear when one returns to Europe, which has very direct links to (North) Africa. A significant number of black Europeans are of supra-Saharan descent and their relationship both to other black Europeans and to Afro-Europeans of North African descent who are not black (but sometimes part of the same family) contribute to a different perspective on black subjectivity. As seen in the last chapter, the November 2005 riots in the French *banlieus* brought into focus a group that, though largely of African descent, is neither ethnically nor racially homogeneous. Rather, the French system produced a homogenized, racialized economic underclass based on certain markers of foreignness, including but not restricted to blackness as Islam becomes inextricably linked to notions of both Africanness and foreignness (a discourse characteristic for the whole of Europe as seen in chapter 3).

The focus on African populations in the Americas, on the transatlantic slave trade that brought them there, and on the ways in which they shaped and were shaped by Western modernity necessarily kept attention away from other aspects of the diasporic experience, less relevant to this focus, among them the link to the non-Western world of Islam, leaving unaddressed a number of important questions: Where are the similarities with and differences to racialization processes in the Christian/Western world? How is race negotiated in a transnational community that is largely non-white and non-Western? How are discourses transported, adapted, and countered between West and East, and how does Africa function as a space of contact in between? It would certainly be wrong to assume that there are no substantial connections between the African diaspora in the Occident and the Orient; rather, internalist origin narratives of Western culture, rejuvenated by current clash of civilization discourses, make invisible a history of exchange and overlap between Christian West and Muslim East that centrally involved black populations and took place on all continents, defying neat separations of pure cultural spheres (Bayoumi 2003; Prashad 2008). Its role as Europe's Other notwithstanding, Islam has become the continent's largest minority religion and, while in U.S. public discourses Muslims outside the Nation of Islam usually are racialized as Middle Eastern or South Asian, that is, "foreign," African Americans make up one-quarter to one-third of the Islamic population in the United States, estimated at around 5 million (meaning that at least 5 percent of the African American population identifies as Muslim).[14] Islam thus has long become a factor in interminority relations in the West, both within the nation and beyond it.[15] In the European context, a separation between black sub-Saharan Africa and Muslim North Africa, while prevalent in dominant discourses, fails to reflect the reality of Europeans of African descent.

Hip-hop was used by this group as a medium in which to express a more accurate model of identity. It was the interaction of music and technology more than anything else that contributed to a rizomorphic spreading of black discourses, irrevocably complicating notions of cultural or racial authenticity claimed by black nationalism and including more populations than one might initially assume: another group massively present within the early European hip-hop scene, in particular as break-dancers, were Sinti and Roma. The perception (and self-definition) of Eastern European Roma as black adds another dimension to the question of black subjectivity.[16] Discourses around black Roma neither replace nor are similar to the racialization of people of African descent within the same societies. Nevertheless, the discourses overlap: on the one hand the Roma as Eastern Europe's native black population were ascribed characteristics directly imported from the racist discourse around the black race (while still being applied to the latter). On the other hand, this inscription, in combination with a number of perceived similarities—the Roma are a diasporic people with neither prospect nor intention of returning home, most Roma in Eastern Europe were agricultural slaves until their emancipation in the nineteenth century, and economic, social, and political discrimination is still the rule—led to an identification of twentieth century Roma activists and organizations with African American activism, in particular the Black Power movement (Hancock 1987; Gheorghe and Acton 1999).[17] The focus on the Middle Passage as unifying moment, useful as it can be, tends to cover up such relationships, which crisscross the black Atlantic but are not confined to it. It also erases and hierarchizes differences within the black Atlantic community itself, marginalizing experiences not fitting the dominant paradigm.

Wright's suggestion that the African diaspora above all is a discursive formation opens fascinating perspectives and closely resonates with this chapter's larger theme of the limits of blackness—and so does her claim that while the novel is the form of the nation, poetry might be that of the diaspora, as the latter two approach nonlinearity, difference, fragmentation, and subjectivity in similar ways. Her exclusive focus on written discourses threatens however to exclude important sites of diasporic dialogues. A more inclusive model might be reached by using Wright's sense of diaspora as a particular kind of black subjectivity while reintroducing an element absent in her argument, that is, vernacular culture. In doing so I believe we can come to an understanding of a common language of black subjectivity based on a more open definition of discourse, not opposed to but including embodied forms such as popular music, dance, and performance. This would be an understanding, awareness, and acceptance of internal differences and tensions, a relational model, in which in the words of Caribbean theorist and poet Edouard Glissant, "relationship (at the same time link and linked, act and speech) is emphasized over what in appearance could be conceived as a governing principle, the so-called universal 'controlling force'" (Glissant 1989, 14). Traditional diaspora discourse does not account for these complications. But while it is certainly not in the least immune to national(ist) limitations, in this chapter, I argue that the transnational, transethnic potential of diaspora has been explored to its fullest within black minority discourse, producing a global, interdisciplinary scholarship, in which diaspora is not merely a nostalgic longing for a lost, idealized home or past. African diaspora theory, in some of its incarnations, can offer a context in which translocal practices can be explored rather than being petrified into a hierarchical dichotomy of a pure—or essentialist—home and hybrid diaspora. The move away from particular historical moments or cultural practices as markers of authentic African diasporic identities brings into focus marginal experiences of being black that might irritatingly mess with established concepts, but I believe that in the end they do so in productive ways. There certainly are and likely always will be more questions than answers, but if it is the process of creative inquiry that constitutes African diasporic identity, asking these questions can only be beneficial, rather than threatening the unity of the black community. Ideally, the continued exploration of the limits of blackness adds to diaspora's disidentificatory potential made explicit most persistently through its critical reworkings in popular music, Third World feminism, and queer of color theorizing, moving toward a fusion of theory and poetry described by Glissant as a "Poetics of Relation, in which each and every identity is extended through a relationship with the Other" (Glissant 1997, 11).

Afro-Germans, Third World Feminism, and (Trans)national Genealogies

Afro-Germans certainly are among the groups complicating Soysal's use of changing notions of citizenship in order to question the usefulness of diaspora theories for the European context. A number of authors have focused on the particular situation of black Germans as citizens who are in every but the legal sense treated as foreigners (Oguntoye et al. 1986; El-Tayeb 2001; Muniz de Faria 2002; Campt 2004; Fehrenbach 2005). They are thus a main target of the paradox of colorblindness in dominant European discourse, which presumes the importance of some factors in defining integration and belonging, such as adherence to Western values, while denying the relevance of others, namely racialized difference.[18] Black Germans, often growing up in largely white neighborhoods, are likely the most highly assimilated German minority according to official standards, that is, in regard to culture, language, education, and last but not least citizenship.[19] Nonetheless, they are the minority generally perceived as being most "un-German": through the decades and across the East-West divide the stubborn conviction persists that black Germans must "really" come from either Africa or the Americas (see Oguntoye, Opitz, and Schultz 1986; Gelbin, Konuk, and Piesche 1999; Popoola and Sezen 1999; Kantara 2000). The externalization of Afro-Germans shows the absurdity of the cultural difference argument employed to explain the marginalization of minority communities. And while the implicit racialization of Germanness as "white" and thus of blacks as necessarily nonnationals would be an obvious answer to this apparent paradox, the internalist narrative rejects this explanation as meaningless within a discursive framework that insists on the myth of colorblindness.

In what follows, I focus on the ways in which the implicit tensions of (diaspora) nationalism are made explicit in the case of Afro-Germans, whose presence appears as oxymoronic within the nation and as equally dissonant within the diaspora narrative. The desire to create a "real," authentic, tangible history and identity in accordance with dominant definitions is certainly a present reaction to this double displacement; also obvious, however, is a departure from essentialist concepts of home toward an embracing of these disidentifications. This does not preclude a desire for roots, for a sense of history on which to base positionalities in the present. This history is constructed, however, via a queer memory that directly relates to the central role of transnational black feminist positions within the Afro-German community. The black consciousness movement in Germany represented the attempt to create a past and a collective memory within the nation but simultaneously beyond it, claiming that to do one without the other is impossible. This process can be read as the response to the existence of a peculiar absence. In her important study of black Germans in the Third Reich, Tina Campt identifies memory as "an undertheorized element of diasporic relation" and continues to point to the particular importance of this element for the Afro-German community:

> The status of memory suggests a different process of cultural formation and highlights some important tensions of diasporic relation that must be engaged in any analysis of the Black German community's relation to the African diaspora.
>
> In the German context, the absence of the forms of memory so central to many models of Black diasporic identity and community raises the question of what happens when a community lacks access to such

memories, as has historically been the case for Afro-Germans . . . with the exception of the current generation, most Black German children did not grow up with their Black parents, thus hindering almost any transmission and preservation of memory in a fundamental way. (Campt 2004, 179)

Campt identifies here what must indeed be considered one if not *the* key particularity of the Afro-German (and to a lesser extent black European) experience, leading to the central question of how a community "without history" can (re)create itself.[20]

The feminist collection *Showing Our Colors: Afro-German Women Speak Out*, appearing in 1986, was the first publication to attempt an answer by expressing a collective Afro-German identity. The authors did so in part by following a traditional model of community building, pointing to the long history of a black presence within the nation:

> In the course of our research we met Afro-German women who had lived in Germany under the reign of Kaiser Wilhelm II, in the Weimar Republic, and through National Socialism. Some were immediately willing to meet with us younger ones and recount their lives. Today— several years later—it is difficult to describe how moved and excited we were at these meetings. We suddenly discovered that our history had not begun in 1945. We were brought face to face with our past, and saw it was closely linked with Germany's colonial and National Socialist history. Our unknown background and our invisibility as Afro-Germans are consequences of the suppression of German history. (Oguntoye et al., xxii)

In other ways, *Showing Our Colors* represents a highly unusual break with normative practices. The particular shape of the 1980s black movements in Germany and to a lesser extent the Netherlands had been made possible by the interventions of U.S. Third World feminism into the revolutionary nationalist discourses of the 1960s and 70s. *This Bridge Called My Back* (1981), coedited by Gloria Anzaldúa and Cherríe Moraga; Gloria Hull, Patricia Bell Scott, and Barbara Smith's *All the Women Are White, All the Blacks Are Men, But Some of Us Are Brave* (1982); *Home Girls* (1983) edited by Barbara Smith; and Audre Lorde's *Sister Outsider* (1984) are cornerstones of a concerted challenge that effectively deconstructed the pure, authentic, masculine identity of the diasporic subject, which Michelle Wright describes as the key feature of traditional African diaspora discourse. This was a challenge furthermore, that extended way beyond the U.S. borders, inspiring feminist organizing in other parts of the diaspora, including continental Europe, where racialized women could easily relate to the modes of exclusion and strategies of resistance expressed in the U.S.

context. Women of color feminism's insistence on the interrelation of race, class, gender, and sexuality provided a framework within which racialized European women could affirm experiences deemed irrelevant or impossible by mainstream opinion (including feminism).

Echoing La Rumeur's Hamé and Skillz en Masse's Meli's reaction to first listening to Public Enemy quoted in the last chapter, Gloria Wekker, Dutch Surinamese activist and scholar who became one of the key figures of women of color feminism in Europe, recalls how she and a number of other black lesbians got together in Amsterdam in the early 1980s to discuss literature by African American women: "We read everything we could get our hands on. We had a bibliography of black lesbian texts that we passed around and that had gotten all hackneyed. Barbara Smith and Gloria Hull we devoured" (in Hermans 2002, 16). Audre Lorde's work in particular proved to be a decisive influence for this first black lesbian activist group in the Netherlands that went on to provide one of the centers of transnational feminist exchange among women of color in Europe. In 1984, the group formally constituted itself as *Sister Outsider,* named after Lorde's collection of essays published that same year.[21]

Audre Lorde herself was actively searching for this emerging community, in part becoming visible in response to her own work:

> In the spring of 1984, I spent three months at the Free University in
> Berlin teaching a course on Black American women poets and a poetry
> workshop in English, for German students. One of my goals on this
> trip was to meet Black German women, for I had been told there were
> quite a few in Berlin. (Lorde, in Oguntoye et al. 1986)

Lorde was relatively well known when she arrived in Germany, since the year before a small but influential Berlin-based feminist publisher, Orlanda, had edited a volume containing texts by her and Adrienne Rich—the first German language publication on the U.S. debate on racism within the feminist movement, a debate however, that was not yet considered relevant for Europe (Schultz 1983). It is indicative of the continental silence around race and racism, and of the identification of the race problem with the United States, that it took the presence of an African American activist to create a platform for a public discussion of race in Germany. Lorde's 1984 classes at the Free University had attracted a number of students who subsequently began to address their specific situation as black German women. Many were still struggling to develop a black identity vis-à-vis a society that not only considered the terms "black" and "German" mutually exclusive, but also doubted black Germans' just claim to either identity. Anne Adams, in her 2005 article "The Souls of

Black Volk," traces Lorde's part in shaping the fledgling Afro-German movement, recalling a string of meetings with groups of black German women (as well as the Dutch Sister Outsider) who voiced their frustration at their marginalization in German society:

> At one such meeting in 1987 in Frankfurt where I served as interpreter, Lorde replied to the Afro-German women by saying, you don't have to live your lives as marginalized, outcast Germans. There is a whole other half of you, your Black self, that can be embraced by the Black diaspora. So, rather than viewing yourself merely as outcast, half-caste Germans, you can view yourself as Afro-Germans. (Adams, in Mazon and Steingroever 2005, 212)

While the transformative power of the scene described by Adams is evident and it is obvious that Audre Lorde's impact on the early Afro-German movement can hardly be overestimated, representations by Adams and others of Lorde as the mother of Afro-Germans, creating the community through the symbolic and literal act of naming, are problematic nevertheless.[22] Too easily are differences erased again as Afro-Germans are integrated into dominant narratives of diaspora in which they appear as merely imitative of the paradigmatic U.S. experience. When Adams states that "[i]n effect, Lorde was 'inviting' these black Germans spiritually to assume their birthright membership and identity in the black diaspora as a compliment to their birthright German nationality," (Adams 2005, 213) the invoked mother-child relationship between the diaspora in the Americas and Europe simultaneously reflects and obscures existing hierarchies within the presupposed unity: from a U.S.-centric position, the Afro-German community comes into existence only when it is recognized and created by a diaspora whose consciousness is firmly situated in African American experiences.[23] The dialectical model of diaspora characterized by Wright as the reflection of a patriarchal discourse in which women are made invisible and genealogies are exclusively masculine is not effectively challenged by the introduction of a female hierarchy following similar patterns.

From a different perspective, Lorde's recognition of Afro-German women as part of a worldwide black diaspora made a significant difference, not because the women had not been aware of this transnational community, but because their identification with it had been largely one-sided, an imaginary community used to counter the Otherness imposed on them by a white society:

> As Afro-German women almost all of us between the ages of twenty and thirty were accustomed to dealing with our background and our identity in isolation. Few of us had any significant contact with

other Afro-Germans and if we attempted to discuss our thoughts and problems with friends, it was always possible that we would alienate someone or be accused of being 'too sensitive.' Meeting each other as Afro-Germans and becoming involved with each other has been a totally new experience. (Oguntoye and Opitz 1986, xxi)

A sense of being part of a larger black community thus had often been achieved not through direct contact with other black Germans, but through indirect participation in diaspora discourses transported by popular and alternative media. The interactive relations between black communities worldwide are reflected in the profound influence the African struggle for decolonization and the U.S. black liberation movement had on the development of an Afro-German sense of identity. The fascination of the West European Left with the Black Panthers in the 1970s, the broad coverage of Muhammad Ali's heavyweight fights, West German TV's broadcasting of *Roots* or Diahann Caroll's *Julia*, as well as East Germany's "Free Angela Davis" campaign, and of course music, all provided material for a sense of a larger diaspora prior to the 1980s.[24] As this short list shows, a sense of diaspora was indeed very much shaped by an African American presence. Much like hip-hop, this dominant experience was not taken as normative, but used as inspiration, transformed and adapted to the particular circumstances of the rather different (yet, perhaps, close enough) German situation, in both East and West also shaped by African migration and decolonization. Radia Lubinetzki, a contributor to *Showing Our Colors* born in socialist East Germany, recalls such a movement of transformation, from the United States to Germany and from the novel to poetry:[25]

I've always read Afro-American literature. Which I discovered in libraries. Richard Wright's *Native Son*, for example, and James Baldwin— that was the beginning of the "black is beautiful" movement. Around that time I once wrote something about my feelings and thoughts, and it came out in the form of a poem. (Lubinetzki, in Oguntoye and Opitz 1992, 218)

Being black and German represented an unthinkable identity within the paradigms of racelessness and even, largely, within African diaspora discourse, and it seems less than coincidental that poetry again and again appears as key in making this identity first thinkable and then speakable, exactly because it offered a form of expression in which feelings and thoughts did not need to be separated in order to become legible, instead combining both in a poetics of relation that linked Afro-Germans to each other as well as to larger national and diasporic communities.

While black Germans struggling against the racism and isolation that they faced were often aware of larger struggles in Africa and even more so those in the United States, using this knowledge as a survival strategy, black populations elsewhere rarely questioned Germany's (self)representation as a white nation. Audre Lorde's intervention does not mark the birth of a black German consciousness, but it certainly symbolizes the transnational turn of the African diaspora. Lorde's reaching out to a black community that most African Americans still assumed to be nonexistent furthermore underscores the important role of diasporic feminist networks in the first decade of Afro-German activism. Their recognition and explicit inclusion within an international African diaspora community validated their experiences in a way previously unknown to black Germans and facilitated the nascent process of collectively exploring similarities rather than being defined through their difference from the German norm. This was a norm that continued to assume that blackness had no national context: it took Lorde's intervention to convince the Orlanda publishing house to rather than do a German translation of her own texts take on a project that became *the* Afro-German key text.

After two years of research and interviews, *Showing Our Colors* was published in 1986, edited by Afro-German activists Katharina Oguntoye and May Opitz. The book thus was the result of the interaction of a number of factors: a black liberation movement whose aims and messages had been internationally circulated, a transnational feminist network that brought Audre Lorde to Berlin and created a venue of expression through the fledgling female-owned Orlanda press, and the dedication of a group of young Afro-German feminists who located women across the country and convinced them to share their often painful stories of growing up black in Germany. *Showing Our Colors: Afro-German Women Speak Out* presented the life stories of fourteen Afro-German women between the ages of seventeen and seventy (some of them members of the same families), providing glimpses of black life in Imperial Germany, in the Weimar Republic, under National Socialism, and in the GDR and the Federal Republic. The volume provided factual and personal information on a part of German history deemed nonexistent by society, politics, and academia alike, without considering one level of narration more authoritative than the other. The anthology connected the nation's history to black life stories covering almost a century, contextualizing experiences that had hitherto been perceived as aberrant and individual, pointing to them as collective traits in the life of a part of the population that up to that point was neither perceived nor had defined itself as a community: black Germans.[26]

The lack of a formative collective memory and distinct community structures and the resulting inability to claim an accepted or acceptable identity emerges as a common theme in the volume—though interestingly much less so for Afro-Germans born in Imperial or Weimar Germany who grew up as part of a larger diasporic community structured around African migrant networks. It was exactly this lack, however, that allowed the younger generation of Afro-German activists an eclectic, creative appropriation of diaspora discourse rather than a mere imitation of a dominant model. This is most clearly reflected in the movement's gender dynamics: because of the central role of *Showing Our Colors*, the life stories of women stood for the emerging community of Afro-Germans as a whole, thus radically changing the usual pattern in which the male experience is presented as normative, a normativity that is constructed by invoking relationships and similarities to other normative male narratives, at times implicitly including the female experience, at others explicitly excluding it. In stark contrast to this, women from the beginning were a strong presence within the Afro-German movement. The focus on a female perspective in *Showing Our Colors* as well as its explicitly feminist context made sure that here, black identity was not presented as male; instead it was women's voices that first articulated experiences that laid the groundwork in constituting a larger sense of community. This differentiated black Germans from almost any other ethnic, diasporic, or nationalist movement in which typically women, as well as queers, while taking part in the struggle additionally have to fight for their inclusion in a communal We.

This was not a mere reversal of the usual either. Rather than presenting a different normative experience, the early Afro-German movement rejected the idea of the normative in general, replacing it with a fractured, dialogic, queer subjectivity, presenting a new whole, the Afro-German community, while allowing its parts to stand next to and sometimes against each other, rather than forcing them into a coherent pattern. The women telling their stories in *Showing Our Colors* grew up under a variety of conditions, in nuclear and extended families, with single mothers, grandparents, foster families, or in children's homes. Telling their stories meant the creation of a genealogy that moves as far away from essentialist notions of "roots, soil, and kinship" as possible: while blood relations, histories that are created through the parents' family lines, are of varying importance to individual black Germans, a sense of an Afro-German community and history was created primarily through a shared experience *in* the host nation. A sense of a continuing African diaspora presence in Germany, the existence of forefathers and foremothers, is built around a group of people who rarely shared family ties or even cultures a priori, but are if not a community of choice then one of chosen identification.

Michelle Wright's analysis of Gwendolyn Brooks's and Audre Lorde's poetic use of the trope of motherhood in order to reintroduce a female, dialogic notion of subjectivity resonates with Campt's identification of (collective) memory transmitted from parents to children as constitutive of diasporic consciousness, but importantly moves toward a less organic, a potentially conflicted and shattered process of transmission between generations (still largely conceptualized in terms of biological families however), allowing for the inclusion of black diasporic populations not fitting the dialectic model. The models of family and community presented in *Showing Our Colors,* in the form of interviews, poems, stream-of-consciousness narratives, and analytical essays, go beyond even the dialogic model described by Wright in analyzing Rodgers's and Lorde's work, confronting difference, resisting dialectic (dis)solution in synthesis. Not one normative form of a normal and natural family emerged from the narratives, and this was not presented as a lack that needed to be corrected in order to heal the community, as the dialectic model of diaspora would have required. Instead, a variety of possibilities appeared as equally normal, undermining supposedly authentic, organic models of both individual families and African diaspora genealogy.

The early formation of the black German movement thus illustrates how the queering of ethnicity employs disidentification as "a third term that resists the binary of identification and counteridentification" (Muñoz 1999, 97), opening up an unauthorized in-between space that resists the false dissolution of conflict through the suppression of pluralities. The taken-for-granted open presence of lesbians such as coeditor Katarina Oguntoye among the contributors further confirmed that the diaspora consciousness expressed here was not one longing for a lost home, a return to a state of innocence, purity, or sameness, but rather one that resonated with women of color feminism's perception of difference as an opportunity, bridging the dialogic and dialectic. For a group of people denied even the status of community, who had been defined through a racialized difference that was conceived of in exclusively negative terms, in itself enough to justify their exclusion from the collective of Germans, the radically subversive understanding of difference as something that "must be not merely tolerated, but seen as a fund of necessary polarities between which our creativity can spark like a dialectic" creating the ability to "act where there are no charters" expressed by Lorde in the groundbreaking women of color anthology *This Bridge Called My Back* made immediate sense (Lorde, in Moraga and Anzaldúa 1981, 98).

May Opitz (who after the book's publication changed her name to May Ayim) went on to become the best known Afro-German poet to date, publishing a number of essays and a collection of poems before she took her own life in 1996. Ayim's work as an activist, theorist, and poet was devoted not only to uncovering the hidden history of blacks in Germany, but also to their inscription into a larger diasporic counternarrative:

> borderless and brazen: i will be African/even if you want me to
> be german/and i will be german/even if my blackness does not suit
> you/i will go/yet another step further/to the furthest edge/where
> my sisters—where my brothers stand/where/our/FREEDOM/begins/i
> will go/yet another step further and another step and/will return/
> when i want/if i want/and remain/borderless and brazen (Ayim
> 2008, 48)[27]

Ayim had devoted her master's thesis in sociology to the history of black Germans, completely absent from official narrations; parts of the thesis were included in *Showing* and provided background information that ranged from twelfth century paintings of Africans in Germany to the eighteenth century philosopher Anton Amo to black youths subjected to forced sterilization by the National Socialists, insisting that their lives, erased from German history, had lasting meaning within an alternative memory discourse, in which they were recognized as ancestors to a community reinserting itself into dominant histories.

Countering the lack of a memory traded from generation to generation described by Tina Campt, *Showing Our Colors* creates a collective history encompassing a diverse community with roots in Africa as well as all parts of the diaspora, tying into it personal memories that are as diverse and full of stories of survival, violence, resilience, and death. The successful attempt to turn these silenced narratives into a source of common identity without erasing either its contradictions or the implications of failure and shame tied to it from the perspective of dialectic diasporic discourse, resonated not only with disidentification's refusal to "willfully evacuate the politically dubious or shameful components within an identificatory locus" (Muñoz 1999, 2), but also with Grace Hong's invocation of Baldwin's term "bringing out the dead" in response to the deaths of African American feminist activist-scholars like Audre Lorde, June Jordan, Barbara Christian, and VéVé Clark:

> To bring out your dead is to say that these deaths are not unimportant
> or forgotten, or, worse, coincidental. It is to say that these deaths are
> systemic, structural. To bring out your dead is not a memorial, but a
> challenge, not an act of grief but of defiance, not a register of mortality

and decline, but of the possibility of struggle and survival. It is shocking to say and impossible to prove that these women suffered early
deaths because the battles around race, gender, and sexuality were being waged so directly through and on their bodies. Yet the names bear
witness to this unknowable truth. (Hong 2008, 97)[28]

The work of black German feminists such as Ayim and Oguntoye bears
witness to the fact that these battlegrounds are everywhere, even and
especially in spaces that insist on this truth remaining unknowable. The
invocation thus can also be read as an appreciation of Ayim's life and
death, remembered too in the only Afro-German literary award established in 2004 by the black community in Ayim's honor, its first recipient
a young, queer, spoken word poet living in London, Olumide Popoola,
coeditor of the women of color anthology *Talking Home*.[29]

The Poetics of Relation: From Black Feminism
to Queer of Color Activism

The nonnormative concept of black identity at the root of *Showing Our
Colors* had an impact way beyond the Berlin group of women who initiated the project. It heavily influenced the first national meeting of black
Germans in 1985, which resulted in the founding of the Initiative Schwarze
Deutsche/ISD (Initiative Black Germans). The group, still active today as
an umbrella organization for Afro-Germans, later changed its name to
Initiative Blacks in Germany, reflecting the move from the urgent need to
confirm one's existence as insiders of the nation to a position critical of
the limits of national identifications.[30] The ISD, consisting of semiautono-
mous local chapters, early on took an explicitly feminist as well as transnational stance, and one that emphasized the constructedness of national
memory and the importance of rewriting it:

> We would like to contribute to a change in the general apprecia-
> tion of German history—all aspects of it. This includes dealing with
> Afro-German (Afro-European) history, which to a great extent must
> be compiled and recorded for the first time. This means that we
> should concern ourselves with our own biographies as a basis for a
> special, black-identified identity. We demand that white society put
> an end to prejudice, discrimination, racism and sexism, perpetrated
> against us Black Germans/Afro-Germans and against all other social
> groupings with a similar plight . . . We demand that racist stereotypes
> and discriminatory expressions, terms, illustrations and race-slanted
> reports disappear from the media . . . An important aspect of our

work is to cooperate with groups from Black world movements, with people doing anti-racism work and other solidarity groups. (*ISD*, 1989) [31]

In 1986, the black German women's association ADEFRA (Afro-deutsche Frauen) was founded in Bremen. Similar to the ISD, with which it works closely, ADEFRA consists of affiliated but independent local groups. For several years, the organization published its own magazine, *Afrekete*, in addition to providing a number of women-focused activities and participating in organizations such as the International Cross-Cultural Black Women's Studies Institute, which met in Germany in 1991.[32] ADEFRA brought an explicitly feminist agenda and strong lesbian presence into Afro-German activism. Many within the ISD, male and female, felt uncomfortable with this development; debates on the priority of racism over sexism or the "lavender menace" of lesbianism that ADEFRA supposedly introduced to the movement led to tensions not yet resolved (Hopkins 1999, 18–19).

Women nevertheless continued to strongly influence if not dominate Afro-German activism over the next decade. This was partly caused by the fact that the larger feminist network in which German racism was increasingly debated provided a platform that had no male pendent, and accordingly, publications exploring the black experience in Germany often appeared in a feminist context. Reflecting their grounding in women of color feminism and its commitment to confronting rather than fearing and suppressing difference as well as the particular situation of racialized communities in Europe, a significant number of publications (co)edited by Afro-German women addressed, often for the first time, relationships between women of color of different backgrounds trying to build coalitions, such as another Orlanda publication, *Entfernte Verbindungen* (Distant Relations), coedited by May Ayim in 1993, an exploration of anti-Semitism, racism, and class oppression, or *Aufbrüche* (Departures), published six years later, documenting cultural productions of black, Jewish, and migrant women. Afro-German contributor Ekpenyong Ani, managing editor of Orlanda Press, explains the rationale behind these projects:

> First I want to know who the other marginalized women are, want to know what connects me with the Turkish women and what might set us apart; at long last want to explore the often strenuous relationship between Black women and white Jewish women. In my vision this long overdue getting to know each other can only strengthen us. And then, yes then we would have the strength to engage with women from

the dominant culture—if we haven't found allies among them already.
(Ani, in: Gelbin, Konuk, and Piesche 1999, 84)

While dominant narrations of black feminism and hip-hop in Germany do not tend to emphasize this fact, both movements originate in the same communities and faced similar challenges. The ISD and especially its annual *Bundestreffen* (national meeting) were important in creating a sense of community for young Afro-German hip-hop artists and in many ways laid the foundation for the latter's explicitly political, diasporic Brothers Keepers project, as its initiator Adé recalls:[33]

> There [at the *Bundestreffen*] you came together for three days, watched movies together, held workshops and discussions. At these meetings, I first met people like Torch or Ebony. Many of those people I might have seen at a jam before. But in the context of the ISD meetings, you were free of the role of "rapper" and could really talk about yourself. You talked differently with each other in this Afro-German context.
> (Loh 2003)

In some ways, hip-hop marked the return to a dialectic, heroic model of diaspora, creating a patrilineal genealogy threatening to erase the contributions of women. Due to their well-known central role, lesbian and feminist activists cannot easily be marginalized as irrelevant or dangerous to a black German movement that was decisively shaped by them. At the same time, the authority of that which is supposedly authentic and normal is not easily defeated and nonnormative structures, exactly because they cannot or refuse to derive authority from dominant constructs, are in constant need of explanation and justification.[34] A closer look uncovers a more complicated situation however, defying the too easy opposition between female "dialogic" inclusiveness and male exclusionary nationalism. Old school Afro-German hip-hop was clearly shaped by the black German community in all its diversity, and contemporary artists like Brothers Keepers represent much more than a simple regression to a nationalist, homophobic, sexist essentialism, instead negotiating different traditions in an at times confusing mixture of radically new approaches and reactionary models of identity. This is an eclectic mix, though, that is far from atypical for European communities of color. Rather, a look at the constitution of a sense of black Europe in the wake of national, but diaspora-oriented, black movements such as the German one sketched here lets this fusionist approach appear as the norm rather than the aberration.

This is the context in which the anthology *Talking Home* was produced, continuing the tradition of cross-ethnic collaborations between German women of color, but for the first time making explicit the translocal component that had been implicitly present since *Showing Our Color*'s diasporic genesis. Afro-German attempts at interacting with black communities outside of Germany often focused on the United States and (West) Africa as well as Britain rather than continental Europe, but within women of color networks, the Netherlands represented an exception and a number of Dutch–German exchanges, among others with Sister Outsider, took place during the 1980s and 90s. The interaction was facilitated on the German side by the image the Netherlands generally have in the eyes of its bigger Eastern neighbor, namely that of a nation populated by easy-going, tolerant people with a liberal attitude toward racial difference. This liberalism brings with it its own set of severe problems as will be seen in the next chapter, but on a surface level the mere presence of black bus drivers, train conductors, sales clerks, even police, represented a different, more inclusive world for Afro-Germans who were still not allowed to feel at home in their nation.[35] This provided a sharp contrast in particular to Amsterdam's obvious racial diversity; the seemingly peaceful intermingling of white, black, and brown as well as the city's reputation as Europe's gay capital made it a favorite destination for queers of color from all over the world, among them many Germans.

The anthology *Talking Home* was conceived by two of them, Afro-German spoken-word poet Olumide Popoola and Turkish-German animation artist Beldan Sezen. Published thirteen years after *Showing Our Colors*, both publications nonetheless had similar motivations:

> In the summer of 1995 we had the idea to publish an anthology by women/queers of color in Germany . . . we were tired of having no voice. How was it possible that we didn't exist? We were right here after all . . . Like so many others, we ourselves had to write the words we so desperately needed to read. Words that allowed us to come to terms with our experiences in Germany and that made us visible, made us be . . . Reading the texts it became obvious that "home" was a dominant theme . . . We all seem to be familiar with this: not belonging. This never being able to "be whole," always searching, metaphorically "homeless." (Popoola and Sezen 1999, 1)

This almost verbatim repeats the statements made by the editors of the earlier volume, indicating both the accurateness of that text's observations beyond the group of black German women it represented and the lack of change in the situation of Germans of color after more than a decade. The publication of *Showing Our Colors* had a tremendous impact on the fledgling Afro-German movement, providing it with a focal point, a foundational text that became the central source of reference for black

German activists, feminist or not. The ISD's annual *Bundestreffen* as well as the Black History Month events taking place in Berlin from the mid-80s to the mid-90s brought together hundreds of activists each year and provided forums of exchange that made sure that the movement's different strands, from Afrocentrists to lesbian feminists, never completely drifted apart. The perceived need to keep ranks closed was partly informed however, by the more than hesitant reception of the black movement by mainstream society.

While the emerging black consciousness movement had dramatic effects on the ways in which Afro-Germans were able to articulate their individual and collective identities, these drastic changes clashed with a dominant perception that did not only remain largely unchanged, but also actively denied black Germans' right to name themselves. ISD activists in the 1980s and '90s achieved limited results regarding the group's goal to influence media representations of black Germans. The founding of the ISD and the publication of *Showing Our Colors* generated some interest, newspaper articles, and a number of TV documentaries reported on the fate of the grown-up "colored occupation babies."[36] In this short moment of public awareness, the central role of language, of the power of naming as a means to claim a public identity became obvious again: none of the media responses used the terms "black" or "Afro-German," so clearly favored by the subjects of their reports. Not all went as far as reviving the "occupation baby," but clearly, white journalists felt that it was up to them, not black Germans, to determine how the latter would be called (most settled, and still do, on "colored," see El-Tayeb 2003). In her autobiography, activist Ika Hügel-Marshall relates an episode that well captures white Germans' attitude toward black German self-definition:

> I receive a teaching post in Berlin. The topic of the seminar I will teach is identity. At the first class, I ask all the students in turn to say something about their identities and how they define themselves. I introduce myself as a black woman, but a white student interrupts me.
>
> "You're not black, if you ask me. It would probably be a lot easier for you if you were. But your fate is to be neither black nor white, and thus every attempt at being one or the other leads to a crisis of identity." (Hügel-Marshall 2001, 122)

Of course, it is exactly this strategy of simultaneously claiming that Afro-Germans cannot be German because they are black and denying that they are really black as soon as they confront this racism that aims at creating a crisis of identity. Within binary models, the hybrid, in terms of race, gender, sexuality, or nation, represents a threat that is contained by assigning her a state of unnatural and inferior inbetweenness that precludes a legitimate positionality from which to challenge the system or even name oneself. Repeated in one form or the other multiple times every day across Europe, this scene exemplifies one of the ways in which the ideology of European racelessness aims at suppressing the possibility of a European of color identity, resonating with Judith Butler's analysis of the effects of "injurious names" (Butler 1997, 2): "The terms by which we are hailed are rarely the ones we choose (and even when we try to impose protocols on how we are to be named, they usually fail)." The queering of ethnicity uses this failure, working with and against injurious names: "these terms we never really choose are the occasion for something we might still call agency, the repetition of an originary subordination for another purpose, one whose future is partially open" (Butler 1997, 38).

While the ongoing challenge to injurious names represented by the black German movement no doubt has had an enormous impact, the ISD has not become the envisioned pressure group able to expose racism in media and politics.[37] Clearly, many majoritarian Germans, not the least those concerned with the plight of oppressed minorities, much rather would have hundreds of thousands isolated "tragic mulattos" in need of white support than a vocal, self-reliant black community. Frustrations about failing to engage the majoritarian society at the same time emphasized the need to form alliances with black communities beyond Germany and with other activists of color within the nation. Not only through its transnational and transethnic location does *Talking Home* represent the changes that took place in black and women of color organizing since *Showing Our Colors* was published more than a decade earlier. While the latter expressed the desire to name and confirm commonalities, to create a coherent black German identity (both toward the nation and the diaspora community), without giving in to the pressure of essentialist understandings of community, the former approaches questions of identity in a more tentative, open-ended manner. This is also reflected in the different styles of the two volumes: *Showing* presented itself in an innovative form, mixing personal testimonies, poetry, and historical background, that however resulted in a linear narrative of a suppressed black presence. *Talking Home* is far more fractured, using a variety of literary as well as visual forms that do not necessarily combine into a seamless whole.

These differences could be seen as representative of a number of larger developments, such as the shift from feminism to queer politics, from the need to find a grounding in Germany both spatially and in historically to the embracing of a decentered, translocal, mobile community, including women of diverse ethnic backgrounds. In their introduction, Popoola and

Sezen make clear that the openness of form and content is indeed not co-incidental, offering what could be considered a perfect summary of the strategy of queering ethnicity:

> Queer to us meant the attempt not to give in to the pressures of pre-determined role-models. Be it within heterosexual or homosexual contexts. What exactly the term meant to each contributor was left open as we wanted to avoid prior limitations. (Popoola and Sezen 1999, 1)

This understanding of queer gives a different spin to topics already present in *Showing Our Colors,* allowing for the coexistence of continuity and breaks requiring neither solution nor rejection, while issues of home, belonging, family, and community remain central. The link to the earlier volume is never explicitly made, but nonetheless quite obviously acknowledged, among other things through the choice of the first contributor, who also provided the foreword, Eleonore Wiedenroth, one of the women who told their stories in *Showing Our Colors.* Wiedenroth complements her 1986 focus on growing up in an often extremely hostile German postwar environment as the daughter of an absent black father and an overstrained white mother with 1999 reflections on her own daughter's role in helping her maintain a sense of home and community, however fragile, in an often no less alienating contemporary Germany.

Part of Wiedenroth's quest for belonging told in *Showing* had been the frustrated attempt to move to Africa in search of an unquestioned sense of home. This theme, present for many black Germans, is taken up in a poem by Popoola, describing her accompanying a friend to Nigeria to meet her father for the first time. The poem "lagos 1996—a long way home" is both the story of a homecoming and the realization that "home" is not a point in either time or space that signifies belonging as the end of ambiguity:

> His-story / daddy took over / oh yes / there we were / two independent women / daddy-ionized / and patience got scarce // 4 weeks of / home / questionmark // the city / full of people / we kind of shy / the family / loving and demanding / we a little irritated / used to be dis-connected / not belonging (Popoola and Sezen 1999, 57–58)

Popoola's description of her friend's journey "home" can be read as a re-interpretation of dialectic models of diaspora in its refusal to assign either Africa or the patriarchal family the part of resolution to the quest of overcoming the dissonances of the diasporic subject's positionality within the West. Without denying the desire to belong, she shows both sides as fractured and engaged in the attempt to create oneness, seeing this process, rather than its inevitable failure as constitutive of a sense of community encompassing and at the same time separating African and diasporic, male and female, queer and straight subjects. What appears as the most marked difference between the two volumes are the conclusions drawn from (largely) similar situations. Rather than proclaiming a common identity, *Talking Home*'s editors claim a unity in difference: "We realized that in truth our stories are so different that this search for wholeness really is *the* commonality that connects us, lets us feel close" (Popoola and Sezen 1999, 2). This open-ended approach allows for the representation of all authors, black, Latina, Turkish, and Iranian German women, activists, artists, and educators; for a community beyond ethnic identification, based not on origin but positionality. At the same time, such an open, queer understanding of community and identity brings with it its own set of problems, central among them the need to constantly revisit the commonalities that make possible collective action, while neither allowing them to remain unquestioned nor fetishizing rather than exploring existing differences.

The understanding of "home, "past," and "belonging" as necessarily contentious processes rather than points of resolution is central to the queering of ethnicity beyond the context of *Talking Home*. This becomes obvious when we return to the potential meanings of the term diaspora for hip-hop culture as well as women of color feminism. Both movements resist the resolution of their dislocation within the nation, hip-hop negates the spatial logic of the state through a translocal counterdiscourse, and women of color feminism does something similar through its rejection of the nation's heteronormative control of time. The latter is of particular importance because the disputed question whether diaspora is a useful term in describing contemporary European migrant and minority communities has a temporal dimension that tends to be neglected. Diasporic memory relates in complex ways to discourses of origin. While it is at times "as tempted to create a unified memory of a lost homeland as the nation is to create national memory," (Huyssen 2003, 150), there are nevertheless fundamental differences between diaspora and nation: "National memory presents itself as natural, authentic, coherent, and homogeneous. Diasporic memory in its traditional sense is by definition cut off, hybrid, displaced, split" (Huyssen 2003, 152). This traditional concept of diaspora includes a sense of spatial and temporal displacement that can create a critical awareness of the processes of memory and identity formation that the national narrative necessarily suppresses. Due to the nature of diaspora, this suppression can never fully work even for its most essentialist configuration, which thus always includes the seeds of its dissolution, of an irrepressible haunting.

The notion of memory and its role in not only shaping a community's history, but also, at least as important, its present and future, is central to diasporic identity. Black Europeans seem to be doubly disadvantaged in this regard: they often are perceived as marginal with regard to the key memory trope of the black diaspora in the West, that is, the Middle Passage, while at the same time having in common with other Europeans of color the expulsion from the continent's remembered past.[38] Accordingly, counter-memory discourses and the (re)discovery of narratives of past agency are central concerns for European minority activists. The quest, on the other hand, to erase or marginalize the presence of national Others within lies at the heart not only of national histories, but also of the European (non) memory of colonialism. The experience of being written out of or misrepresented in majority histories therefore is often more relevant to minority communities in Europe than the supposed desire to re-create an ideal home. This is something that is actively confronted by "renegade," transnational understandings of the term diaspora, which seek to explore rather than resolve the discord between diaspora and the national. Huyssen in addressing the relationship between diaspora and memory, argues for an exploration of these underlying tensions: "It is particularly the relationship between diasporic memory and the memory formations of the national culture within which a given diaspora may be embedded that remains seriously understudied" (Huyssen 2003, 151). For Huyssen (who does not include the African diaspora in his discussion), part of the problem lies with diasporic populations themselves being too preoccupied with their difference to take an interest in a history shared with the host nation, their fixation on a lost past pushing into the background the question of how they might relate to that of the host country (Huyssen 2003, 154).

In order to assess the validity of this claim it might be useful to look at the opposite case, that is, a diasporic community's attempt to gain access to the past of the host country as exemplified by the African American case. While black European identity in some ways importantly diverges from the U.S. model—and it seems paramount to acknowledge this difference as enriching rather than disqualifying it as inauthentic—the African diaspora in the Americas was a necessity to the creation of an independent European model exactly because it offers a different perspective on the situatedness of diaspora within the nation, one in which the lost home is a symbolic if not metaphorical term and not necessarily the one that is most central in creating a communal "we." Instead, the diasporic community is closely intertwined with the larger society's past and present, but is confronted not only with the systematic destruction of collective memories predating the diaspora, but also with a minority memory that is explicitly at odds with official commemorations of the past, leading to radically different perspectives on national history. Accordingly, black Americans had to find alternative ways to create, maintain, and pass on a collective memory outside of the official national discourses silencing them. Diaspora theories are in part aimed at creating coherent memories for fractured communities whose experiences and subjectivity have been systematically denied, buried, and appropriated. Since countermemory is of obvious importance to marginalized communities, challenges to a systematic, coherent story of diasporic identity are at times seen as threatening to a group's collective memory and identity. Nonetheless, the most effective of these challenges come out of the same diasporic discourse. Representing creolized theory with a small "T," they replace, to use Glissant's terms, "root identity," centered on (lost) origins, with "relation identity," leaving behind the idea of "sacred territories" and moving toward the possibility of accepting the messiness of "situational communities" (Glissant 1989).[39] In this chapter, I have argued that it was a movement shaped by the African diaspora experience and 1970s women of color feminism that offered the tools with which black European women in the 1980s rewrote personal and collective memories that contributed to new nonessentialist, nonlinear, nonhomebound understandings of diaspora at the same time that they carved out a space for communities of color in the European discourse. An analysis of black Europe from this perspective could also alter African diaspora discourse's focus on the West within the black Atlantic framework by providing a means to reassess the interaction of space and time in relation to diaspora and homeland. Diaspora theory has the potential to reconceptualize this interaction away from the usual linear relationship between center and periphery, past, and future, including not only Europe, the Pacific, and other neglected areas, but also Africa itself in this process. Placed within such a larger, reframed context, the often supposed peculiarity of the Afro-German experience appears as less unique as well.

This leads me back to Tina Campt's identification of the absence of a diasporic memory as the Afro-German key experience. In doing so, she might be overemphasizing the opposition of an "organic" memory traded from generation to generation on the one hand and its complete lack on the other, positioning the former as the (African American) norm, the latter as the (Afro-German) aberration. The lack of an Afro-German "community memory" spanning the five hundred or so years of a black presence in Germany is in part due to the very different relation of black Germans to a diasporic homeland, be it in Africa or other parts of the diaspora: the connection is frequently nonexistent and simultaneously immediate, represented through an (absent) father and an extended family.[40]

Afro-Germans thus inhabit a space between the traditional diaspora and the second generation of migrants. While this sets them apart from the diasporic experience in the Americas, it does create a link to the growing second generation of Germans of color, the children and grandchildren of the first generation of the labor migrants who remained a mute(d) presence in German society. This silence was often reproduced within families, leaving children with little knowledge of their parents' experiences in a hostile host society. Even though here, traditional family structures remained intact, a break in memory discourse occurred.

Since the 1980s, a growing part of the second and third generation chooses to neither fill this gap with an idealized identification with a culture of origin providing the sense of belonging so explicitly denied to them in German society, nor with the assimilationist rejection of their parents' difference. Their search for alternatives produced a common ground with an Afro-German community facing many of the same issues. While *Showing Our Colors* marks the insertion of an explicit, politicized black German identity into nation and diaspora, *Talking Home* reflects the community's interconnectedness with the second and third generation. A dialogue between the groups became possible in those spaces that crossed ethnic lines. As seen in the last chapter, the early European hip-hop community provided such a space, as did the feminist movement for women of color. A third important venue was provided by gay and lesbian culture or rather by the search for a queer community beyond normative whiteness. This search lead many queers of color to the Netherlands, a country that more than any other represents the continent's image as enlightened, tolerant, and secular, and that for exactly this reason has become one of the main sites of an increasingly alarmist "culture war" pitching Europe against its Muslim minorities. This discourse and the precarious role of feminist and queer Muslims within it will be explored in the next chapter.

CHAPTER THREE

Secular Submissions

Muslim Europeans, Female Bodies, and Performative Politics

> The way people clothe themselves, together with the traditions of dress and finery that custom implies, constitutes the most distinctive form of a society's uniqueness, that is to say the one that is the most immediately perceptible.
>
> —FRANTZ FANON, *Algeria Unveiled*

> The body, I believe, has to be theorized in ways that not only describe the ways in which it is brought into being but also what it does once it is constituted and the relationship between it and the other bodies around it. In other words, I desire a rejoinder to performativity that allows a space for subjectivity, for agency (however momentary and discursively fraught), and, ultimately, for change.
>
> —PATRICK E. JOHNSON, *Black Queer Studies*

The Racing of Religion in Secular Northwest Europe

The European ideology of racelessness creates a double bind for racialized populations: an internalist perspective claims European exceptionality by defining the continent's identity as both entirely self-generated and self-contained, while a universalist narrative simultaneously presents the European condition as paradigmatically human and other, non-Western parts of the world as inevitably deviating from this norm. One of the most striking examples of this dynamic is the discourse around European Muslim difference, in which, seemingly paradoxically, gender and sexuality take center positions, while religion remains comparatively marginal. That is, the claim to the "incompatibility" of Islam and Europe is not framed as a conflict between a Christian majority and a Muslim minority, both of whom are European, but between European humanism, committed to the protection of rights, namely those of gender equality and sexual freedom, and a hostile, intolerant, foreign culture. Within this unequal dichotomy, Europe invariably stands for the universal, while Muslims represent the particular and thus inferior. As a result, while the European Muslim community as a whole is judged to present the "wrong," (i.e., misogynist and homophobic) type of heterosexuality, feminist and queer Muslims too appear as limited by their culture, deviating from the dominant norm of liberal and progressive cosmopolitanism. Chapter 3 will explore both the particulars of Western universalist discourse and its deconstruction by European queer and feminist Muslim activists.

Despite, or rather because of, this chapter's focus on the politicized use of the "racing of religion" (Bayoumi 2006), its geographical center will be Europe's notoriously secular North West. I argue that the ways in which this region's attitude toward Muslim minorities is shaped by its own submerged but influential Christian identity constitutes another incident of Avery Gordon's haunting, explaining in part the rapid deterioration of relationships between majority and Muslim minority in these nations. Years before tensions erupted internationally after the Danish daily *Jyllands Posten* commissioned a number of cartoons depicting among other things the prophet Mohammed as a terrorist, Denmark had been the first nation in Europe's reputedly progressive North that shifted toward a populist, draconian anti-immigrant stance, pushed by a coalition between an explicitly Christian political right and an equally explicit liberal secularism (Klausen 2006).

Soon after, a similar coalition emerged in the Netherlands, the European nation that more than any other defines itself and is defined through Enlightenment ideals and a laid-back, live-and-let-live mentality. I use the developments in these two nations to deconstruct the European notion of tolerance and secularism, suggesting that the tensions becoming visible in their wake are in fact already built into the (Western) European model of liberal tolerance, including its feminist and queer variations. Following an Enlightenment tradition of internal purging through projection on others (if they have it, we don't), comparative analyses of patriarchal systems and misogynist structures are discouraged by this model; instead the Muslim presence is acknowledged only in order to define against it a new, unified Europe characterized by a tolerant secularism rooted in Christian principles. The French uprisings in the winter of 2005 highlighted both the material consequences of European exclusionary policies and their discursive reconstruction as a fundamental culture clash, framing the growing presence of a marginalized minoritarian population as a permanent moment of crisis. In this chapter, I propose that Muslim youths—the violent male and the veiled young woman—become the central Other of the unifying Europe, exemplifying everything it is not and cannot be, exactly at a point when the existence of a native European Muslim population has become an undeniable reality.

In order to understand how second- and third-generation Muslim Europeans can be perceived as more foreign and threatening than their parents or grandparents who came to Europe from the Middle East, West Africa, or South Asia, one needs to turn to the role of culture in discourses about identity and assimilation. Contemporary tropes around the Muslim presence in Europe are framed not in the language of race, religion, or nation, but in that of culture and gender. The *hijab* in particular serves as the key symbol of Muslim difference, representing silenced, oppressed women living in parallel societies that are shaped by ancient and primitive rather than modern Western structures. Its presence underlines the perception that Muslims and Europeans are like oil and water, unable to mix and merge; instead archaic Muslim enclaves, separate *qua* space as well as time, are supposedly surviving unchanged within the larger European societies. The ways in which these larger societies constantly work to regulate and reframe "peoples' access to the resources of the nation-state" (McClintock 1995, 353) through the production of national, and increasingly continental, identities, is thus made invisible by the construction of static and exclusive cultures, in which women play a central but completely heteronomous role.

The rise of "Culture" with a capital C applies to a variety of areas, but it may be most notable in the extent to which it has replaced race in discourses directed at migrants and minorities—gender and sexuality on the other hand appear as constants, exemplifying both racial and cultural difference. In the following sections, I trace this process by turning to the scopic politics through which the *hijab* worn by some European Muslimas has become a highly charged symbol of racial, cultural, and gender, as much as religious difference. I am particularly interested in the ways in which feminist positions are invoked in this discourse and in their interaction with tropes of the body and mobility in relation to both time and space, resulting in immobilizing the veiled woman, making her readable while simultaneously silencing her. The implicit perception of the *hijab* as signifying a particular type of cultural(ist) performance becomes explicit in the plays of Dutch feminist writer Adelheid Roosen and in the public persona of Dutch Somali activist and author Ayaan Hirsi Ali. While both figuratively write their performances on the muted Muslim woman's body, ostensibly in order to liberate her, but only further disempowering her, Danish Muslim socialist feminist Asmaa Abdol-Hamid uses her own body to disrupt normative narratives and suggest alternatives modes of European Muslim identities.

Abdol-Hamid's positionality—practicing Muslim, feminist, socialist—is representative for a substantial number of European Muslimas, in particular those active in the migrant women's movement established since the late 1970s; however, that same positionality stands as an oxymoron in dominant European discourse. Not, as I argue, due to any particular traits of Islam or Muslims, but due to the intersection of cosmopolitanism's Othering of the Global South and nationalism's disciplining of female (and queer) bodies. While using Abdol-Hamid as my focal point, I show her grounding in larger movements working to overcome this dichotomy, namely Euro-Islam and migrant feminist activism.

Combining queer of color critique with new developments in performance studies, I argue that interventions like Abdol-Hamid's (recognizing the body as a site of liberation as well as repression) contribute to an embodied kind of theorizing with the potential of breaking down from within the binary model still structuring dominant European perceptions of (Muslim) minorities. They do so in part by pointing out that these dominant perceptions are so powerful exactly because they do not reflect qualities possessed by the diverse group of Muslim Europeans, who are created as a coherent community only by the discourse about them, but are rooted in larger and older models of universal humanism and its non-European Others, among which Islam held a central position from the beginning. In order to understand the discursive construction of the Muslim Other in contemporary Europe, it is therefore necessary to contextualize it within the larger ideological tension caused by renewed binary notions of West and East constantly undermined by an unprecedented real and virtual mobility.

Cosmopolitan Humanism, Postsecularity, and Western Bias

In May 2008, the conservative U.S.-based journal *Foreign Policy*, an influential bimonthly with a circulation topping 100,000 copies, cofounded by Samuel Huntington, financed by the Carnegie Endowment for International Peace, and read by academics as well as diplomats, published its second annual list of the world's "100 Top Public Intellectuals" (*Foreign Policy*, July/August 2008 issue). Including "introspective philosophers and rabble-rousing clerics," the list presented "the thinkers who are shaping the tenor of our time" and asked its readers to pick their top five among the journal's suggestions. The latter at first glance offer few surprises: there are only ten women included, more than two-thirds of the candidates live in the United States, Canada, and Europe, and the list includes many of the usual suspects, Jürgen Habermas, Slavoj Žižek, Noam Chomsky, Salman Rushdie, and Al Gore among them. But the choices also reflect a desire to be globally inclusive and representative of a cosmopolitan intellectual landscape—this is *Foreign Policy*, after all. Thus, the journal listed thinkers whose influence is felt equally or even mainly outside of the West, such as Chinese economist Fan Gang, Egyptian TV preacher Amr Khaled, or Indian environmentalist Sunita Narain.

The response to *Foreign Policy*'s online poll, conducted for the first time, was enormous—more than half a million votes were cast on the journal's Web site within a couple of days—and produced quite unexpected results: of the top ten intellectuals picked by the readers, only four live in the West and among them only one was born there (Swiss Tariq Ramadan, whom I will come back to later), the other three are exiled religious philosophers Abdolkarim Soroush from Iran and Fethullah Gülen from Turkey, and Ugandan-born cultural anthropologist Mahmood Mamdani, all living in the United States. Even more interesting: all of the world's top ten intellectuals according to *Foreign Policy*'s readers are Muslim, though representing a wide selection geographically as well as in religious practices and beliefs: Fethullah Gülen; Bangladeshi microloan pioneer Muhammad Yunus; star of Al Jazeera's popular advice show "Sharia & Life," Egyptian Yusuf Al-Qaradawi; Turkish novelist Orhan Pamuk; former president of the Pakistani supreme court Aitzaz Ahsan; Amr Khaled; Abdolkarim Soroush; Tariq Ramadan; Mahmood Mamdani; and Iranian lawyer and human rights activist Shirin Ebadi (in order of their ranking).[1]

Most interesting, however, is the narrative that the journal provides its readers with in order to frame the results within exactly the context challenged by the vote's outcome. The editorial accompanying the list starts by stating authoritatively: "Rankings are an inherently dangerous business," a claim that is then expanded by pointing out that being an influential intellectual necessitates being good at communicating with one's audience, thus some candidates, such as Chomsky, linked to the poll on their Web sites, mentioned it in interviews, and used other strategies to boost their ranking. After insinuating that popularity contests are always open to manipulation, the editors end by stating:

> No one spread the word as effectively as the man who tops the list. In early May, the Top 100 list was mentioned on the front page of *Zaman*, a Turkish daily newspaper closely aligned with Islamic scholar

Fethullah Gülen. Within hours, votes in his favor began to pour in. His supporters—typically educated, upwardly mobile Muslims—were eager to cast ballots not only for their champion, but for other Muslims in the Top 100. Thanks to this groundswell, the top 10 public intellectuals in this year's reader poll are all Muslim. The ideas for which they are known, particularly concerning Islam, differ significantly. It's clear that, in this case, identity politics carried the day. (*Foreign Policy* Sept./Oct. 2008, 1)

The argument put forward in the editorial thus starts out with an assumption, namely, some intellectuals on the Top 100 list have such command over their followers that the latter will do exactly as they are told. While there is no actual evidence provided for this claim, it is nonetheless not implausible.[2] In the last of the three paragraphs, however, this assumption has become fact: Fethullah Gülen won because his supporters hijacked the vote. The editors also seem to know that those who voted for Gülen did so because they are Muslims who in turn voted for the other Muslims on the list because they are Muslims, whether Shiite or Sunni, conservative or liberal, secular or Islamist. The unavoidable conclusion: A list of the world's most influential intellectuals that is topped by ten Muslims is a triumph of "identity politics," a term that has been thoroughly discredited in both liberal and conservative discourse over the last decade, increasingly identified as the main culprit in the failure of Western multiculturalism.

This is a failure in turn that is *the* central theme in current European debates around Muslim minorities' invincible Otherness, often reflecting the belief that Muslims are both more homogeneous and more fanatical in their religious convictions than other groups (even when they are "educated [and] upwardly mobile"). While I do not claim superior knowledge as to why *Foreign Policy*'s readers voted the way they did, "Muslim identity politics" does seem a catchphrase that achieves very little besides providing a negative foil for a Western "universal cosmopolitanism" (even if religion was the prime motivator, there still was a choice between various Muslim candidates, some of which did not make the top ten). And uncertainty about motives aside, the fact remains that nowhere in their reaction do the *Foreign Policy* editors allow for a simple possibility: maybe the ten most influential contemporary intellectuals indeed *are* all Muslims and all non-Westerners (or minority Westerners, in the case of Ramadan, the one exception); maybe there is a transnational, cosmopolitan discourse going on in which the white West is marginal.[3]

Cosmopolitanism, rooted in a European humanist tradition that arguably also justified colonialism, slavery, and the Holocaust, has been challenged fundamentally in the post–World War II era, resulting in a variety of more or less self-critical attempts at retaining a universally valid set of values allowing for global communication, while acknowledging that cosmopolitan thought has not only produced the concept of universal human rights, but also justified its systematic violation (Kristeva 1993; Gilroy 2000; Honig 2001; Habermas 2003; Benhabib 2006). For many, the strongest argument for cosmopolitanism remains human rights, the need for common basic values and international institutions that enforce them in order to create even a semblance of liberty and equality for all human beings irrespective of their origin or current position. Universalism might be full of problems, the reasoning goes, but it is still better than its opposite, relativism, which lets go of any common moral ground against which state actions need to be justified. As became evident in chapter 1, however, it remains a problem that humanist universalism seems necessarily centered in the West, dividing the world into those who share Western values and those who do not.[4]

Across the political spectrum, the relationship between the West and human rights is more often than not presented as a necessary, natural one. Some months after the *Foreign Policy* poll, the liberal British *Guardian* newspaper published an article decrying the waning Western influence within the United Nations:

> The West's efforts to use the United Nations to promote its values
> and shape the global agenda are failing, according to a detailed study
> published yesterday. A sea change in the balance of power in favor of
> China, India, Russia and other emerging states is wrecking European
> and U.S. efforts to entrench human rights, liberties and multilateralism.
> (Traynor 2008)

The link between the decline in support for human rights and the rising influence of non-Western nations in the UN remains central throughout—the article goes on to describe among other things how the UN Human Rights Council is increasingly used by Muslim states to sanction "blasphemy" rather than promote human rights—but there is no inquiry whatsoever into why those non-Western nations do not support human rights; instead it is implied that they simply have different values. Similarly, the Western commitment to these rights is presented as a given; there are no questions asked, not even obvious ones such as: How much is the international human rights system undermined by centuries of exploitation in the name of a humanist "civilizing mission" and how much is this memory kept alive by the open creation of "extralegal" zones through extraordinary rendition, secret prisons, "harsh interrogation techniques," and antiterrorism laws in the West? How important are successes in institutionalizing international human rights regulations when the very concept of "rights" is becoming increasingly irrelevant within a neoliberal globalization that privatizes everything from wars to health care to prisons—and from which Western nations profit more than anyone else? Finally, there seems to be neither a sense of non-Western concepts of "cosmopolitics," nor of the effect of slavery and colonialism on the emergence of a modern, wealthy, secular Europe and of continued interventionist policies, from "regime change" to protectionist tariffs, on its survival.[5]

While there can be little doubt that the current non-Western coalition within the United Nations is far from the ideals of Bandung and that governments in the Muslim world have little interest in sincerely pushing for universal human rights (though nothing in the Islamic tradition would prevent them from promoting such an agenda), there is also a strange lack of self-criticism or at least self-awareness among Westerners toward their own supposed value system, a lack evident in the conservative *Foreign Policy* and the liberal *Guardian* as much as in the 2003 Habermas and Derrida piece discussed in chapter 1. Habermas expands his earlier argument in a more recent article, "Die Dialektik der Säkularisierung" (Dialectics of secularism), in which he directly addresses the need for a postsecular European identity that allows for the integration of Muslim minorities. He goes on to define "postsecular" as follows:

> In order to speak of a "postsecular" society, it needs to have been in a prior state of "secularism." The contested term thus can only be applied to the prosperous European societies or nations like Australia, Canada, and New Zealand, where citizen's religious ties have been continuously, since the end of World War II even drastically, loosened. (Habermas 2008, 3, emphasis in original)

The key question here might not be whether the West alone has gone through a stage of secularism (leaving unaddressed nations like India, China, or postcolonial socialist societies), but whether "secularism" as used by Habermas and others is a concept that is necessarily linked to a Christian heritage and would better be described as "secularized Christianity." If so, the (chrono)logical timeline suggested in the above quote, in which the West already is (post)secular while others still have to follow, would not hold, as in order to become secular and then postsecular one really would have to have been Christian first (this in turn allows for the assumption that there are a variety of secularisms interdependent with the religious systems they define themselves against). If this possibility is considered, the assumption that non-Western and in particular Muslim societies are simply in a presecular state loses credibility—one could even turn the timeline around and claim that the failure of Muslim secularism in nations like Turkey or Algeria, closely tied to questions of internal equality, is something that Christian secularism is beginning to go through now; and the end of state socialism in Eastern Europe might be considered a case in point then as the revival of Christianity there, Catholicism in Poland, evangelical Protestantism in many other nations, could be linked to the revival of Islam in postsocialist nations like Syria or Egypt.

I am not necessarily advocating this alternative timeline, though its plausibility is certainly worth debating; more important, however, are the ways in which it illustrates how hierarchical constructs linking time and space contribute to the Western bias of universalist thought. In his path-breaking *Time and the Other*, anthropologist Johannes Fabian showed the importance of "political Space [and] political Time" as "ideologically construed instruments of power" (Fabian 1983, 144). That is, politicized spatial and temporal models place the Other not only in a distinctly separate space, but that space is also located in a different time relative to the West (and within a linear model of progressive time this necessarily means the Other lives not only in the past, she or he lives in the West's past). Since the end of World War II, decolonization, and the beginning of large-scale labor migration, "the necessity arose to provide an objective, transcultural temporal medium for theories of *change* that were to dominate Western social science in the decades that followed" (Fabian 1983, 144). The increasing interaction, outside of the strict boundaries of colonialism, of societies placed in different developmental stages was thus framed around the idea of "public time," a kind of Twilight Zone in which different time-space constellations interact, allowing non-Western societies to see their future—and move toward it with the help of organizations regulating international public time and space, such as the United Nations or the World Bank—while simultaneously allowing the West an educational glimpse at its own past.

Interventions into this past, that is, into the internal affairs of nations of the Global South, are increasingly framed as "humanitarian," taking place in the context of a model of universal human rights that depends on the existence of a public space and time in which these rights are negotiated, but often fails to admit to its deeply politicized nature, instead, like French philosopher Pascal Bruckner, assuming the presence of infallible self-regulating mechanisms allowing for constant progress:

> Modernity has been self-critical and suspicious of its own ideals for a long time now, denouncing the sacralisation of an insane reason that was blind to its own zeal. In a word, it acquired a certain wisdom and an understanding of its limits. The Enlightenment, in turn, showed itself capable of reviewing its mistakes. (Bruckner 2007)

Consequently, the exclusion of large parts of humanity from humanist discourses through most of the last three hundred years appears as a regrettable oversight rather than a systemic problem. An oversight in addition that the West is ready to fix as long as there is a reciprocal willingness among the former Others to be included, instead of a stubborn commitment to a premodern, antihumanist belief system.

Over the last decade, Islam became identified with such a system. As sociologist José Casanova argues: "As liberal democratic systems, all European societies respect the private exercise of religion, including Islam, as an individual human right. It is the public and collective free exercise of Islam as an immigrant religion that most European societies find difficult to tolerate precisely on the grounds that Islam is perceived as an 'un–European' religion." (Casanova 2004, 7)

The Othering and marginalization of Muslim minorities is increasingly justified with the supposed threat that intolerant, misogynist, and homophobic Muslims pose to the secular, liberal Europe they want to be part of:

> [T]he West's wealth is in a certain sense a by-product of something
> else, for it is based on an underlying ideology expressed chiefly in
> terms of absence: Here there is no censorship, there are no prisons
> full of dissidents, no powerful network of official corruption, no
> judicial power operating in the service of a political dictator or party
> programme, no fear of the authorities, and certainly no fear of a
> religion of any kind. (de Moor 2007)

Such a skewered comparative perspective hides the Christian bias of the secularism argument evoked in relation to, and increasingly against, the continent's Muslims, reflected for example in the very different reactions to an effective re-Christianization of Europe through the expanded European Union and to the potential inclusion of a majority Muslim nation among its member states, as Casanova observed:

> The widespread public debate in Europe over Turkey's admission
> showed that Europe was actually the torn country, deeply divided over
> its cultural identity, unable to answer the question whether European
> unity, and therefore its external and internal boundaries, should be
> defined by the common heritage of Christianity and Western civiliza-
> tion or by its modern secular values of liberalism, universal human
> rights, political democracy, and tolerant and inclusive multiculturalism.
> (Casanova 2004, 5)

The notion of Europe as torn between Christian and secular identifications points to an important but usually unspoken source of current tensions around the supposed "desecularization" of Europe by Muslims, namely the role of Islam in negotiating unresolved internal tensions around religion and its meaning for the continent's identity.

It also brings another, often overlooked fact into focus: the single largest national source of Muslim migration to Europe has for the last century been the most unambiguously, even aggressively, secular among all "culturally Muslim" nations. In other words, the majority of Muslims in Europe, if they were not born there, emigrated from a secular nation. Turks, no matter how religious they are, have as much experience living in a secular society as do Germans, Finns, or Italians.[6] That their presence is seen as a threat to Europe's identity, that Turkey, one of the first nations to apply for EEC membership, has not yet been provided with a definite timeline for its inclusion into the European Union, thus seems to have less to do with secularism and the implied commitment to human rights than with Christianity (and, since race is never far in Europe when religion is the issue, with whiteness). Thus, rather than committing to a linear model of human development, in which Europe not only appears as having passed through a stage that others still have to enter, but in which the rise of secularism in Europe also appears as independent from rather than interdependent with developments in the rest of world, it seems necessary to address the question how much "secular" European societies depend on largely monoreligious and monoracial populations. Put differently: does European universal humanism rely on keeping both internal minorities and the rest of the world in the position of prehumanist Other? And if so, how is this achieved?[7]

Dutch Liberal Feminism and the Mute Muslima

In chapter 2, I argued that European migration studies could profit greatly from the application of African diasporic theories to the study of European minorities (and from acknowledging the ways in which European activists of color already incorporate them). A theorist central to any such application would be Frantz Fanon, to whom all contemporary scholars of race, nation, and sexuality are indebted. While some of his positions, in particular with regard to female agency and homosexuality, are problematic to say the least (Fuss 1994; McClintock 1995; Muñoz 1999; Wright 2004), he was the first to systematically analyze the centrality of sexuality and gender to racialized power structures within and beyond the nation. This is a perspective that needs to be urgently brought to a discussion that is increasingly used to define the position of Europe's largest religious minority, namely that on the status of the Muslim woman. Incidentally, many of

Fanon's most keen observations on the uses of gender in nationalist and colonial discourses were formulated while he lived in a region that is not only predominantly Muslim, but also provided a major source of postcolonial and labor migration to Europe, that is, North Africa. Fanon's work as a psychiatrist and later FLN activist in Algeria offers one of many examples of interactions of African and Muslim (diasporic) communities—illuminating the potential as well as the pitfalls of these intersections and alliances. [8]

Of particular interest here is his essay "Algeria Unveiled," written in 1958 and published a year later (English translation 1965), which uses the trope of the veiled woman to dissect the inner workings of colonial dominations, their effect on those who dominate as well as those dominated, and the specific gender dynamics of this process. The veil in Fanon's analysis becomes a symbol for Algerian culture to both colonizers and colonized; its bearer, the Algerian woman, thus moves to the center of a symbolic politics that denies her agency exactly because she is positioned as the bearer of an intrinsic culture. Within this constellation, Muslim women faced pressure from both sides without being granted an autonomous voice in the conflict and Fanon implies that this reflects the positioning of women within all nationalisms. As Anne McClintock observes in her revisitation of "Algeria Unveiled": "Fanon perceives . . . that nationalism, as a politics of visibility, implicates women and men in different ways. Because, for male nationalists, women serve as the visible markers of national homogeneity, they become subjected to especially vigilant and violent discipline. Hence the intense emotive politics of dress" (McClintock 1995, 365). The latter are thus a means to contain women's mobility within the nation and to frame both this internal ordering of citizenship rights and discourses between competing nationalisms in the terminology of culture.

Many of the key discursive strategies mobilizing support for humanitarian and educational interventions post–World War II are gendered, often representing a variation of Spivak's "white men are saving brown women from brown men" trope. The use of this trope by the French colonizers in Algeria was dissected by Fanon fifty years ago:

> The dominant administration solemnly undertook to defend this
> woman, pictured as humiliated, sequestered, cloistered . . . It described
> the immense possibilities of woman, unfortunately transformed by the
> Algerian man into an inert, demonetized, indeed dehumanized object.
> The behavior of the Algerian was very firmly denounced and described
> as medieval and barbaric. With infinite science, a blanket indictment

against the "sadistic and vampirish" Algerian attitude toward women
was prepared and drawn up. Around the family life of the Algerian,
the occupier piled up a whole mass of judgments, appraisals, reasons,
accumulated anecdotes and edifying examples, thus attempting to
confine the Algerian within a circle of guilt. (Fanon 1965, 38)

The deployment of similar arguments in recent Western interventions in
the Middle East is obvious; what interests me here, however, are its uses
in the *internal* restructuring and fragmentation of European societies specifically through the emotive politics of dress. Fanon's analysis seems an
uncannily accurate description of contemporary attitudes toward Muslim
minorities as the most serious threat to Europe's modern identity. These
attitudes are produced via several steps: first, "Muslim culture" is constructed as not only fundamentally different from "European culture,"
but as its exact inversion, leaving little to no common ground (and erasing centuries of shared history). Where Europeans are tolerant, Muslims
are intolerant; where the West negotiates, the East attacks; where "we"
progress, "they" are stagnant; where Europe abhors violence, it is the
Middle Eastern way of life. In a second step, this outwardly coherent, homogeneous community is discovered to be fundamentally divided along
gender lines: Muslim identity is shaped exclusively by men, according to
their own interests, which are directly opposed to the interests of Muslim
women who are disenfranchised in every possible way, violated, immo-
bilized and in need of being saved from the outside, that is, Europe. In a
third step, alliances are built between former enemies who rally around
commonly shared values against the new external threat. These alliances
explain in part the compliance of European queer and feminist movements with mainstream racism in the name of defending universal values
of liberty and equality.

  This of course is not a new phenomenon and continues to occur in part
because of a fundamental ignorance toward non-Western and minority
cultures and the intellectual discourses they have produced. There often
seems to be an unspoken agreement that while people of color might create
revolutionary political movements, they are socially conservative (Johnson
2005). This allows liberal discourse to keep intact an imaginary divide
between the progressive West and the rest of the world, demanding of migrants and minorities a fundamental "Westernization" that at the same
time is permanently denied to them by an implicitly racialized notion of
ethnicity and religion. Progressive European discourse in its various incarnations thus minimizes the role of non-Westerners and minorities of color
in envisioning radically new forms of agency and identity, instead keeping

alive a world view in which the white Left remains central to change: feminist and queer responses to current European debates around Muslim men as aggressors and Muslim women as victims rarely use the tools provided by Fanon and others and as a result, they often seem engaged in dialogue not with minoritarian positions, but their own prejudices.

Islam's blanket definition as misogynist and homophobic not only erases female agency and homogenizes and stereotypes Muslim cultures, increasingly normalizing the notion that Islam is incompatible with modern societies, but also creates a false unity among European nations, suppressing necessary debates on internal homophobia and sexism. Rather than addressing the competing and often contradictory concepts claiming to be representative of the continent's value system, the model of Europeanness that is evoked in contrast to Muslim intolerance is usually closest to the Dutch one, thought to perfectly embody the Enlightenment tradition of tolerance and progress. This perception was first challenged by the meteoric rise of the charismatic, openly gay and openly Islamophobic right-wing politician Pim Fortuyn, assassinated by a white environmental activist in 2002. Two years later, controversial filmmaker Theo van Gogh (fond among other things of calling Muslims "goat fuckers," see Buruma 2006, 9) was murdered in Amsterdam. His assassin, a Dutch Muslim of Moroccan descent, directly linked his act to van Gogh's cooperation with Somali Dutch politician Ayaan Hirsi Ali on the film *Submission*, which attacked Islamic misogyny through drastic images. In the debates that followed the assassinations of Fortuyn and van Gogh, the Dutch "polder model," a society built on the cooperation of largely independent sociocultural subsectors, seemed to unravel at light speed, leaving Dutch and Muslims in opposing, incompatible camps. As a number of authors have argued (Hoving 2005; Ghorashi 2007), the polder model itself represents a commitment to tolerance as a structure rather than a value, resulting in a lack of actual engagement with difference and a perception of change as potentially threatening:

> Traditionally the Dutch seem to have only two main strategies at their disposal to deal with a variety of social, economic, political, and other differences: the passive forms of tolerance and intolerance . . . or evasion . . . Both strategies, tolerance and evasion, are considered to be based on the radical differentiation between self and other, and they both testify to a strong sense of superiority, from which stems the authority to tolerate or evade others. (Hoving 2005, 5)

This is what Halleh Ghorashi calls "liberal Enlightenment fundamentalism," (2007), which, based on the notion of clear cultural differences, sees assimilation of the Other as the only possible positive outcome of cultural interactions.

Accordingly, recently exploding internal criticisms of the famous Dutch tolerance, whether coming from progressives or conservatives, focuses on a perceived inability to ask more aggressively for this assimilation: "in the harsher debates in the wake of 2002, one is struck by a curious consensus in the right-wing and left-wing critiques of the concept.

Right-wing speakers, the so-called 'new-realists,' analyse Dutch tolerance as a national silence about the severe problems of migration and as the cowardly, politically correct *evasion* of difference, instead of an *openness* to difference" (Hoving 2005, 5). The new Dutch openness to difference thus follows familiar patterns in avoiding any introspection: the cultural preference for passive relations with the Other creates a desire for mediation, a way to indirectly interact that avoids concrete challenges to one's own way of life. This in turn allows us to see Dutch, or European, culture not as something that is subject to change, to "democratic iterations" of its population, but as an absolute, universalist and at the same time internalist standard, designed to externalize and thus invalidate all potential criticism. This is a liberal model of colorblindness built on the same implicit norms of whiteness reflected in 1970s mainstream feminism—challenged by feminists of color—as well as in contemporary queer theory, assessed by queer of color critique as "invested in protecting the institutional structures that have accommodated it, including, most significantly, white patriarchal structures of knowledge" (Perez 2005, 188).

The link between colorblind liberal discourse and feminist and queer movements' investment in whiteness is relevant in the Dutch context as well. Symptomatic for the mediated engagement with Muslim difference in the new Netherlands are the works of feminist playwright Adelheid Roosen, whose *De Gesluierde Monologen* (The Veiled Monologues, 2003) and *Is.man* (2007) address the mystery of the Muslim woman and Muslim men's violence against her respectively, aiming at explaining both to a Dutch public moving within a completely different cultural framework. The connection between both topics (summarized by a U.S. review of Roosen's plays as "European Muslim women—and the men who murder them" [Sellar 2007]) is increasingly normalized through the "honor killing" trope that has become omnipresent in European discourses on "Muslim culture" in recent years, despite having no agreed-upon definition. One used in a recent study commissioned by the Dutch Social Democrat Party can be considered representative for a commonly held understanding however: "Honor-related violence is each form of mental or physical violence motivated by a collective mentality as a reaction to a (potential) violation of a man's or woman's honor and thus of his or her family's that is (potentially) known to the outside world" (Gazic et al. 2006, 6).

There are no reliable statistics on the prevalence of honor killings; in the Netherlands, only one county, Hagueland, attempts to keep track and estimated that in 2003, 11 of 119 local cases of deadly domestic violence were "honor-based" (Gazic et al. 2006, 10). Since the police fail to identify any common motivations for the 108 non-honor-based cases, one is left with the assumption that they resulted from individual circumstances rather than the collective mentality assumed to be behind a form of violence that becomes representative for Muslim or Middle Eastern culture (frequently used interchangeably). This culture then is contrasted with a Dutch model of gender and family relations to which this type of violence is incomprehensible ("individual" domestic violence notwithstanding), resulting in a failure of communication across a seemingly unbridgeable gap that in turn becomes the motivation for Roosen's artistic intervention: "Killing your child out of a perception—that is something we do not understand in Holland . . . But, if I can look at someone, starting with the idea that there is no difference between them and me, I can learn" (Roosen, in Sellar 2007).

Is.man, loosely based on interviews Roosen conducted with Muslim men in Dutch prisons serving time for so-called honor killings, follows three generations of a Turkish family living in the Netherlands in order to explain how the father ended up killing his daughter to uphold traditional Turkish honor codes. The family's story is largely told through the son who translates the father's Turkish into Dutch, functioning as a mediator between his father's and the audience's culture, physically taking up the in-between space assigned to second-generation immigrants (see Roosen in: Martin 2010). While Roosen portrays all characters as struggling to negotiate contradictory cultural expectations and pressures, her attempt to present them as individuals not fundamentally different from the Dutch audience fails—and, I would argue, not primarily because of wrong perceptions of the Other, but blindness toward her own liberal, Enlightened European culture.

The point obviously is not in any way to defend men who view a threat to their (family's) "honor" as a sufficient reason to murder a female relative, but the claim that they do so because and only because they are Muslims automatically puts every act of misogynist violence committed by a non-Muslim into a different category, one that is by implication less serious, less dangerous, and less systemic. The current honor killing discourse in Europe not only sees merely a gradual difference between those Muslims who commit honor killings and those who do not, but also enables dominant society to continue to perceive endemic violence against women as a private, personal matter as soon as it happens outside of this politicized—and thus supposedly relevant—context and structural economic gender inequality within European societies remains as unexplored as the systematic exploitation of undocumented migrant women as domestic and sex workers. In short, violence against women is transformed from a global phenomenon fed by interactive structures in which Western nations are centrally involved into a by-product of premodern Muslim culture.

This is a culture that is so different from Europe's that it needs to be literally unveiled through a scopic politics of gender in order to become comprehensible; which is what Roosen does in her earlier, hugely successful play *Veiled Monologues*, whose inspiration is easily identifiable by its title:

> "Vagina Monologues" is beautiful, but it's about Western women. Where are the veiled women? The Arabian world knows so much about eroticism and sensuality and the whole sensitive world. In the West, we are so afraid and cannot accept an image from the Arabian world that is more beautiful than something from the west. We can only see terrorists and people living in holes. (Roosen, in Rathe 2007; English in original)

Roosen's *Veiled Monologues* premiered in 2003, in a post-9/11, post-Pim Fortuyn Netherlands, shortly before the assassination of Theo van Gogh, and clearly hit a nerve. The play successfully toured nationally and internationally (including a performance in the Dutch parliament broadcast nationwide on TV) and was explicitly and frequently used to "explain" Muslims to a largely Christian audience in the context of a growing sense of a culture clash between Islam and the West.

The *Veiled Monologues* also appeared, however, toward the end of a general move away from the Western European social market economy model. While the end of state socialism in the Eastern part of the continent meant a harsh transition to a largely unregulated capitalism for many former Warsaw Pact nations, the West throughout the 1990s slowly moved away from a concept of governance that implied state responsibility in minimizing economic and social inequality. This shift meant a sharp rise in temporary employment, cuts in social programs, unemployment benefits, and health care plans, and a new emphasis on individual responsibility and on the looming destruction of the welfare state by irresponsible and undeserving groups (Balibar 2004; Willenbücher 2007). In the Netherlands as in the rest of Europe, the latter were first identified as migrants in general and then more specifically as the nation's Muslim community.

I argue that the factual dismantling of a system that very much defined Western Europe's, and in particular the Netherlands', identity—capitalist yet socially responsible; guaranteeing individual freedoms yet defined by a sense of shared responsibility for the community; competitive yet caring; noninterventionist yet committed to global human rights—created a crisis that was solved by a discursive scapegoating of the continent's Muslim population onto which a reactionary identity was projected that reaffirmed Western liberal ideals in crisis and at the same time justified their rejection by posing excessive liberalism, multiculturalism, and state support of minorities as having enabled reactionary, antidemocratic, misogynist, homophobic, nonwhite, non-Western Muslim groups threatening the liberal West much more than economic neoliberalism ever could.[9] If one assumes that the newly discovered fundamental "foreignness" not of immigrants but of the already present and established Muslim minority was used to manage this "sacrificial crisis" (Honig 2001, 34) of Dutch liberalism, the reception of the *Veiled Monologues* gains another dimension, one that brings into focus what Bonnie Honig termed "the work that foreignness does, the many ways in which it operates as a way to frame other issues of democratic theory and citizenship" (ibid., 7).

Like *Is.man*, the *Veiled Monologues* are based on interviews, this time with Muslim women asked about their views on and experiences with a variety of issues related to sexuality.[10] Their responses were then condensed into twelve monologues, which in turn are performed by three actors (using index cards to underline the texts' representational nature). The monologues cover a number of positions and perceptions, from the predictable stories of oppression and violence to tales of disappointment about Dutch lovers' shortcomings or an openly lesbian daughter bonding with her father over soccer (Roosen 2007). The exploration of sexuality as something in which Muslim women take an active part is certainly commendable, but the assumption that this can only happen through Western intervention is more than questionable, as is an almost aggressive presentism refusing to acknowledge how the play itself as well as its perception is shaped by a long Orientalist tradition of sexualizing Muslim culture in general and the veil in particular (Alloula 1986). Finally, while the play explicitly aims at representing European Muslim women, the interviewees were all born in the Middle East (or are formerly Christian white Dutch converts). This emphasizes Islam, like the colored bodies representing it, as something that is not native but external to Dutch culture, justifying the introductory claim that the play constitutes "[a] journey as a tourist in your own land" (Roosen 2007, 23), visiting an exterritorial "Islamic" space within a larger Netherlands that is completely separate from it.

Just as the French *cités* appeared as foreign, threatening islands in the
European landscape in November 2005, so do Muslim communities remain distinct, separate, and strange territories in liberal European cosmopolitanism. The introduction to the first long monologue, representing
the voice of a white Dutch convert, exemplifies this mixture of exoticism
and condescension, the desire to understand mixed with a need to clearly
distance oneself, the construction of "Dutch" and "Islamic" as mutually
exclusive:

> Woman 2: When word got around in the Netherlands that Islamic women
> were being interviewed *to give them a voice*, a number of Dutch women
> of Christian background called. They were eager to tell how they had
> become Muslim and how their sensitive and erotic lives had changed
> since they were involved with a Kurd, Iraqi, or Turkish man.
>   We then decided to do a number of joint interviews with these Dutch
> and Islamic women. It sometimes got very heated. The Islamic women
> often felt tormented: According to Islam, if you are born Muslim, you're
> not allowed to renounce your religion. You Dutch women are free to
> choose. So why become a Muslim? A Dutch woman can embrace and
> abandon any religion without fear of retaliation; that's the difference.
> (Roosen 2007, 24–25, emphasis mine. Also note how "Islamic" and
> "Dutch" not only become exclusive opposites, but also are treated as
> similar categories, as if a Muslim's (only) nationality was "Islam.")

Despite the author's stated intention to show Muslim women as active
(sexual) agents, mobility is again explicitly presented as a prerogative of
Western, Christian (or at least non-Muslim) women—more than that, it is
Muslim women who state this as a fundamental and invincible difference,
thus giving even more credibility to the claim.

  In consequence, the attempt at communication represented by *The
Veiled Monologues* (as well as *Is.man*) underlines rather than undermines
the perception that Muslims and Europeans live in completely different
worlds, allowing enlightened liberal Western feminists to take on the
role of "translator," explaining the secluded world of Muslim women to
white European audiences, mixing exotic thrills with a fuzzy feeling of
"we're all not so different after all." Ultimately however, the veiled Muslim woman is not considered capable of engaging in a direct dialogue—in
order to do so, to become "not too different," she has to shed her cultural
baggage, that is, her veil. The latter is a demand that is made most explicit in the "escape narrative" genre, whose immense popularity played
a large part in the shift from a moral panic discourse around male migrant and Muslim youths as delinquent in the 1990s to the current focus

on oppressed women. The genre perfectly illustrates both Fanon's and Fabian's models: tales of women escaping the horrors of medieval Islam, crossing into enlightened Europe and, necessarily, burning all bridges behind them. The idea that there is a clearly marked border between the two worlds, that there is neither an in-between zone, nor the possibility of moving freely between them, that one lives in either one or the other, is at the heart of these narratives, and the women who do the crossing become the crown witness for this binary opposition.

Escape Narratives from the Muslim Underground

Escape narratives establish the connection between political time and space by explicitly representing the women's journey from Orient to Occident as one that necessarily means a journey from the Middle Ages to modernity. The West is the present (and future); the East is the past. But while these narratives are built around a model that has been in use since the early days of colonialism, their aim is not merely to reinforce it; instead the point is to show how formerly clear separations collapse as the archaic East is, part and parcel, transplanted *into* the West through migrants' "ethnic enclaves." The West thus is forced to travel back in time and reface challenges that it would have already overcome, at least within its borders, had it not been infused with a population arriving not only from a different space, but also a different time. Adelheid Roosen's countrywoman, Somali Dutch politician Ayaan Hirsi Ali—number fifteen on *Foreign Policy*'s list of the world's most influential intellectuals—is the paradigmatic representative of the gendered native informer at the heart of the escape narrative and the most prominent of the Muslim converts testifying to this epic battle in which Europe is faced with various of its past ghosts simultaneously, creating an alarmist mood that is reflected in the hyperbole of many debates, supposedly making this confrontation the most dramatic ever.[11]

Hirsi Ali's life, as it unfolds in her autobiography (2007), presents itself as a linear progression from darkness to light: "I left the world of faith, of genital cutting and marriage for the world of reason and sexual emancipation. After making this voyage I know that one of these two worlds is simply better than the other. Not for its gaudy gadgetry, but for its fundamental values" (Hirsi Ali, in Bruckner 2007). Starting with her childhood in tribal, war-torn Somalia, through the escape to Kenya and teenage conversion to Wahhabism, to an arranged marriage when she was in her twenties, Hirsi Ali's life seemed on an inevitable trajectory that was stopped suddenly, dramatically, by the fact that the husband her father had picked for her lived in Canada, necessitating a stop-over in Germany on Hirsi Ali's long flight into a future not chosen by her. Seemingly as soon as her feet touched European ground, decades of fundamentalist indoctrination began to fall away and she made the first step toward freedom by running off, eventually applying for and receiving asylum in the Netherlands where she became a parliamentarian and successful campaigner against Islam's oppression of women.[12]

As this brief summary already indicates, Hirsi Ali's story is almost too good to be true; her journey can be, and repeatedly has been made to represent the ideal coming-of-age narrative for the global South "from devout believer to fearless opponent, from a loyal clan member to being renounced by her family, from Africa to Europe, and from blind faith to unbending reason" (Anthony 2007).[13] Her frequent public statements comparing the culture of her origin to that of her chosen home indeed read like complete wish fulfillment for Western societies in postmodern identity crises: Muslims live in the Middle Ages and Western civilization is superior— check; migrants exploit the welfare state and disrespect European values— check; Africans should stop complaining about racism and Europeans should stop feeling guilty for colonialism—check; Islam is misogynist and white men must save brown women from brown men—check. In return for these ego-stroking messages, European media elevate Hirsi Ali to a status similar to that of her intellectual heroes, all of whom can be found in Europe's past. Renowned Dutch novelist Margriet de Moor calls her "a female Islamic Luther, and a black one to boot . . . Or rather, since she isn't a theologian, perhaps a black Voltaire?" (de Moor 2007).[14]

Women like Hirsi Ali, German Neçla Kelek, or Fadela Amara in France, who have not only gained unprecedented media attention, but also are among the first minority women ever to be granted a public voice in European affairs, albeit only when speaking about the threat of Islam, share certain talking points: the authors describe themselves as both secular and culturally Muslim, claiming deep theological knowledge of Islam on which they base statements such as that there is no tradition of textual interpretations, which supposedly explains why all Muslims think alike; a comparison of Christianity and Islam along Weberian lines, that is, rational, Western Christianity versus atavistic, Oriental Islam; a strict binary between Europeans and Muslims, placing themselves firmly in the European camp; the claim that Muslims exploit a European feeling of guilt that leads to an excessive, dangerous tolerance; a characterization of the minority as aggressive and of the majority as too passive; of veiled women as both victimized and as actively intolerant; the use of shocking anecdotes emphasizing the dangerous difference of Islam, replacing facts and numbers; and the rejection of dialogue with (Muslim) critics by claiming a status of absolute knowledge and absolute uniqueness (Kelek 2005; Hirsi Ali 2007; Ates 2008).

The following dialogue between a TV journalist and Turkish-German lawyer Seyran Ates, legitimized by her own suffering at the hands of her family and hailed as a defender of Muslim women's right by the mainstream press, is quite symptomatic for the interaction of these talking points and the ways new tropes build on older ones, managing to evoke emotional responses without need for factual evidence:

> ATES: Many Muslim women still live in an archaic parallel world, where structures dominate that are familiar to us from the Middle Ages . . .
>
> Q: Can you quantify this? How many migrants live in this parallel society?
>
> ATES: There are no studies. But my feeling is that at least 80 percent of the people coming to Germany from Turkey live in this parallel society. They never really arrived here—and that is transmitted to the next generation. (Bentele 2007)

The use of political time and space in this construct, paired with the intuitive insight of someone who once was part of this secret, scary parallel world, creates a moral imperative for majoritarian Europeans not only to save their own cultural achievements from being destroyed by Muslims, but also to save these Muslims from the culture pinning them down in a time that has passed centuries ago (in fact, within this model, proponents of "traditional Islam" are not only refusing to move forward, they have to run backward in order not to be swept away by Europe's constant progress).

It is not my intention to minimize misogynist violence experienced by Muslim girls and women, but the question simply is whether Hirsi Ali and others' public presentations are the best way, or a way at all, to fight this violence. This question is especially vital since the authors of these narratives as well as the mainstream public persistently ignore the work done by Muslim and minority women who struggle to change structures *within* their communities rather than condemning them wholesale as not up to Western standards, in particular feminist activists pointing to the underlying sexist structures shared by majority and minority cultures. At issue is not whether there is a need to combat sexism in Muslim communities, but the instrumentalization of this aim in order to silence and segregate Muslims, including women, while emphasizing European difference and superiority. Hirsi Ali, Kelek, and others contribute to and depend on this segregation by presenting themselves as brave travelers between incompatible worlds, as necessarily separate from the mass of the women in whose name they speak—and on whose silence they depend in order to continue to fulfill this function for a white (neo)liberal audience. Muslim women as independent actors have no place in this conversation, in particular if they are critical of it. Dutch politician Fatima Elatik points out that minority women are virtually excluded from debates about them (Anthony 2007, 4). Hirsi Ali's response to this criticism is both predictably in accordance with the rules of the escape narrative and blatantly inaccurate:

> I started off in a position where none of these women were visible anyway except as proxies to be put forward to get subsidies from the government. Just keep singing we're discriminated against. No Muslim women are allowed into this debate by their own groups. So it's way too early. By the time these women are assertive enough, I won't be around. It will be one generation on. (ibid.)

The image of by default disempowered Muslim women is instrumental to her own empowerment, but of course there were many assertive Muslim women already present when Hirsi Ali appeared on the Dutch scene, engaged in long-term feminist activism.[15]

A 1993 portrait on one of these groups, ARGAN, a Moroccan youth center founded by second-generation women, published in the women of color magazine ZAMI *krant*, indicates that not much has changed in media representations of minorities over the last decade and a half: "During our conversation the phone rings. Fatima gets involved in a long discussion. When she returns to the table she is visibly agitated. The woman wanted an item on Moroccan problem youths. This happens frequently lately. They want something and are not interested in what you have to offer" (Weiss 1993, 46). Existing feminist migrant organizations are rarely approached or acknowledged in debates on Muslim women; there is suspiciously little interest in their grassroots perspective, critical of sexism and homophobia in migrant communities, emphasizing that in the "homeland" too these issues are hotly debated, but also verbal about the racism, sexism, and homophobia within the dominant society (the women's movement included). More than that, programs for migrant and minority women and youths have faced devastating cuts throughout the 1990s all across Western Europe, giving a distinct ring of hypocrisy to current laments about the passivity of migrant communities (Gazic et al. 2006, 35).

While feminist migrant organizations point to the structural failure of European governments from the local to the continental level to put their money where their mouth is, namely with the commitment to gender equality, there seems to be little interest in responding to these criticisms.

Instead, the image of a self-isolating, hostile Other, refusing to engage in dialogue, is cherished by conservatives and disillusioned progressives alike. Within the narrative construction of the clash of cultures in Europe, the veiled female can easily shift in position from victim to accomplice, voluntarily wearing the headscarf as an act of aggression against Western society, implicitly condoning all crimes committed in the name of Islam, as happens in a review of Neçla Kelek's *Die Fremde Braut* (The Foreign Bride) by the staunchly leftist German daily *Die Tageszeitung*:[16]

> It is the simultaneous aura of oppression and aggression that makes
> [us] so helpless. Because the cover does not only hide oneself, it makes
> the other naked. Naked and sinful. It is a statement, not folklore. These
> Muslimas "don't want to deal at all with the Germans, the impure.
> They despise the dishonored life of Western women, they feel strong and
> morally and intellectually superior to the impure." (Zucker 2005, 22)

Veiling thus becomes a convenient act of self-segregation and simultaneously aggression, the female version of the male youth setting the suburbs on fire; like Baudrillard's angry young men who prefer the burning of cars to owning them, these women have no interest in Western values such as individual freedom and equality. This dichotomy, repeated across the political spectrum, not only presents Islam as inherently illiberal, but also justifies European practices of intolerance through the evocation of Enlightenment traditions, which unselfconsciously affirm tropes of Western superiority, particularly evident in the discussion around headscarf bans in France, Germany, Norway, or Denmark, which assume that a conversation on equal terms is prevented by Muslims' cultural limitations (Rommelspacher 2002; Weber 2004; Benhabib 2006).

The transnationality implied in cosmopolitan humanism is inseparable from translatability, but translation still is largely a one-way street, preventing a "cosmopolitan conversation" (Appiah 2006) on equal terms. This references a larger problem: in order to take part in discourses in which rights are negotiated, less powerful groups have to represent themselves in a shape that fits the one that is already there. Dialogue with marginalized communities thus often only takes place after they have restructured themselves along existing patterns, expressing themselves in the dominant language, while diverging voices are silenced and ignored. With regard to Muslim communities in Europe, attempts at integration often reinforce rather than weaken patriarchal, undemocratic structures as communities are asked to be represented by the kind of leaders they are expected to have. [17] This contributes to a self-fulfilling prophecy in which a diverse group of Eastern and Southern European, Middle Eastern, South

Asian, North and West African background, with different religious practices and different degrees of religiosity (including a large group of "secular Muslims") is homogenized along the lines of the dominant discourse.[18]
Ali et al., of course, deny that they themselves contribute to enforcing
patriarchal structures by denying the presence of diversity and resistance
within Muslim communities, instead insisting that they "are a couple of
exceptional migrants . . . We also need the average people, workers and
cleaning women, who say: it's enough, we don't want that anymore. We
need a migrant feminist movement" (Bläser and Oestreich 2008; also see
Kelek 2006; Anthony 2007). With this claim to exceptionalism, they enter
a strange coalition with those they claim to fight, namely ultraconser-
vative Muslim authorities, both insisting in the necessary link between
Islam, patriarchy and antisecularism. Both groups are invested in keeping
invisible negotiations of identity within minority communities: internal
differences and conflicts already present in the origin societies, urban versus rural, religious versus secular, poor versus upper and middle class, are
externalized. Within the dominant perception of Muslim communities as
homogeneous, the question of what is part of the culture that supposedly
sets minorities apart from the majority becomes increasingly reduced to
exclusive binaries and what is perceived as diverging from "traditional"
structures becomes identified with Westernization, positively or nega-
tively. Ignoring the histories of Kemalism in Turkey, early twentieth century Egyptian feminism or democratizing projects in Iran, Indonesia and
elsewhere, violently aborted by Western intervention, internal conflicts
characteristic of all societies come to represent a clash of civilizations.
As a consequence, European Muslims' attempts at self-articulation are
stifled by seemingly antagonistic groups with supposedly opposing aims
who are, however, united in their claim to authenticity, be it authentic European or authentic Muslim values, allowing them to "speak for" rather
than with, not to mention listen to, European Muslims who are primarily
defined through their lack of authentic claims to either identity or culture.

   In his *Murder in Amsterdam*, reflecting on the Netherlands after the
assassination of Theo van Gogh, Dutch American writer Ian Buruma describes an encounter with a young Moroccan Dutch woman. "M. L.,"
who works in a battered women's shelter, is equally critical of the practice
of veiling and Hirsi Ali's notion of female liberation, and offers an analysis
of gender relations that echoes Fanon's:

> M. L.'s father, like most fathers who came to find work in the
> Netherlands, is religious in a customary way. That is, he tries to stick
> to the traditions of his native place without making a fetish of them,

or even giving them much thought. When M. L. is home and her father comes back from the mosque, she asks him "what nonsense the imam was talking this time." The answer usually comes in a comment about his daughter's habits. It's always about the daughter, said M. L., "the daughter, the daughter, how we dress too provocatively, blah blah blah." (Buruma 2006, 131)

M. L. and her sisters, who wear the *hijab*, negotiate a complicated space in which they are confronted with contradictory expectations and demands. In spite of the messages of dominant discourses however, these contradictions, shaping the daily lives of millions of minority women and girls across Europe, are livable. Rather than "experiencing trauma with one leg in each culture . . . tormenting their hearts" as liberal discourse would have it (Roosen, in Rathe 2007), women of the second and third generations have developed coping mechanism adequate to the complexity of their situations. As various studies have shown, the presence of the *hijab*, prime symbol of the supposed oppression and marginalization of Muslim women by their communities, does not correlate with levels of education or income, marriage age, or other measures of successful "integration" (Rommelspacher 2002; Weber 2004). Rather, it can reflect a number of strategic choices, often geared toward gaining agency in a context in which the women and girls face obstacles from various directions.[19]

I suggest that the current discursive centrality of the *hijab* if anything is an indication that these strategies work. While popular tropes equating headscarf and oppression locate the source of the conflict in isolated, unassimilated communities, the territory over which these cultural battles are actually fought is found right in the heart of society. Not coincidentally, the continent's education system was the primary site of the *affaire(s) du foulard*, the headscarf controversy in France. Key to the naturalization of the nation as inevitable and permanent are institutions reproducing the national narrative, constructing its "fictive ethnicity" (Balibar 1990).[20] Universal schooling plays a central role in this process: it is here that children are turned into subjects of the nation. This process is based on partially deconstructing and subsuming various primary identities—class, region, religion, and family—to the secondary identity of the nation. Islam in contemporary Europe, however, is considered a primary identity that cannot be incorporated into the nation (Balibar 2004). Muslim girls wearing the *hijab* are the visible incarnation of this incompatibility—and as Fanon has shown, politics of the nation are primarily scopic politics, so the way one dresses can and will be read to signify much more than personal choice. But while Muslim students wearing headscarves can relatively easily be represented as willing or unwilling victims of their culture, requiring the state to protect them (from themselves), this argument is harder to make for teachers. As the (female) protestant provost of the German Rhine province, Helga Trösken, stated in 1998:

> Would a Muslim teacher wearing the headscarf in a public school not have the opportunity to positively use this signal to facilitate an enlightened dialogue, needed especially in our nation's public institutions? Then it might also become obvious in the ideologically neutral state that next to the big Christian churches and the Jewish community the third largest religious community has arrived and become visible but is still discriminated against in the name of neutrality. (Klingst 2003)[21]

Trösken's argument reflects a strain of German public opinion that often seems to fail to register or permanently influence debates, pointing to the discursively erased heterogeneity of not only minoritarian, but also majoritarian positions. Legislative, juridical system and media tend to take a much more hostile stand, interpreting German teachers wearing the *hijab* as a fundamental threat to both the nation's secular foundations *and* its Christian identity (Rommelspacher 2002; Weber 2004). This position leaves not only unresolved the question how Christianity and secularism can coexist in a way that neither of them can with Islam, but also fails to address another key issue of the headscarf debates: while the presence of the *hijab* is taken to represent the continued existence of Muslim enclaves at the margins of European societies as well as the margins of modernity, the explosion of public interest does in fact signify the entry of Muslim women into the European middle-class.

Danish Socialism, Euro-Islam, and Muslim Feminism

The Muslimas who are under attack for wearing the *hijab* are high school students, teachers, policewomen, and parliamentarians. This indicates that the issue is less their oppressed status than the fact that visibly Muslim women cannot be accepted as representatives of European institutions—in particular, institutions producing citizens and maintaining state power. Headscarf-clad women have long been a massive presence in the hallways of Europe's schools, universities, and court houses, but while they populated these central public spaces only as members of the cleaning force, dismay about their oppression and culture clash scenarios were conspicuously absent from mainstream debates.[22] This indicates that the new centrality of these discourses does not signify marginalization and insurmountable (cultural) differences between minority and majority, but on the contrary symbolizes class mobility and the arrival of Muslims in the center of European nations. This arrival, rather than being perceived as the success of the oft-demanded "integration" of Muslim minorities, is instead framed as a threatening invasion of foreignness, inviting a reaction like the one satirized by Lille-based Axiom First and multiethnic hip-hop crew Ministère des Affaires Populaires' "Des Youyous Dans Ma Mairie" (Ululations in my Town Hall): "Dans ma mairie ya des fat'mas et des youyous / Des foulards, des babouches et des boubou / Des Voyous, des Zoubida, Des mamadou / Au secours, on est plus chez nous."[23] Scopic politics focused on the *hijab* are thus used to displace and hide the centrality not only of nation, but also of class in current discourses on Muslim women. Importantly, this works both in the sense of blaming economic disparities on cultural difference and as a means to keep the Other in the position of object and victim. Images such as this campaign poster by the conservative Christian Danish People's Party are visual representations of a process in which the fear of being ruled by foreigners is combined with the fear of being ruled by women.

Denmark, of course, has become one of the key sites of the perceived failure of multiculturalism, culminating in the infamous 2005 "cartoon affair," supposedly dividing Danes, Europeans, and Westerners committed to and able to handle free speech and Muslims (in the West and outside of it) who place religion above civil, democratic rights (Klausen 2006). This representation fits the dominant narrative: Denmark appears as a nation in which Christianity peacefully coexisted with a tolerant secular state that granted freedom of religion to all its citizens. The model worked as long as Danish society was largely homogeneous—until the mid-1980s, less than 3 percent of the population were immigrants, a number that had doubled in 2002, primarily due to migration from Turkey, Pakistan, and the former Yugoslavia (Skyt Nielsen et al. 2003, 758). This largely Muslim migrant population, the narrative goes, proved incapable of adapting to the secular-liberal lifestyle of North West Europe, leaving the nation's tolerance overstrained with a population irresponsive to values such as free speech and gender equality. The tension finally exploded through something that should not have been an issue in a democratic society, namely the exercise of the freedom of the press in the form of a depiction of a religious prophet in a way that could be perceived as blasphemous by his followers, leading to an excessively violent reaction from the latter.

There are other narratives hidden beneath this dominant one, of course, some relating to German Protestant provost Trösken's claim of a double-standard expressing itself through "discrimination in the name of neutrality,"

ALLAH ER LIGE FOR LOVEN

UNDERKASTELSE

Danish People's Party: "Allah Is Equal before the Law—Submission."

obvious for example in *Jyllands Posten*'s 2003 refusal to print cartoons depicting Jesus, so as not to offend Christian readers ("the editor explained back then, 'I don't think *Jyllands-Posten*'s readers will enjoy the drawings. As a matter of fact, I think that they will provoke an outcry. Therefore, I will not use them,'" quoted in Klausen 2006). Another rarely mentioned aspect of the cartoon affair is the fact that the spokesperson for the eleven Danish Muslim organizations filing claims against the paper based on European Union antidiscrimination regulations was a twenty-three-year-old, second-generation, feminist Danish Muslima named Asmaa Abdol-Hamid.

Before turning to Abdol-Hamid and her embodiment of a European Muslim identity that in dominant discourses is largely presented as a contradiction in terms, it might be useful to contextualize her position through a return to the *Foreign Policy* poll cited earlier, or more specifically, to the sole European represented among the journal's top ten: Tariq Ramadan, the Egyptian-Swiss religious scholar and philosopher. As the leading representative of "Euro-Islam"—which focuses on Muslims as Europeans, aiming at adapting the religion to the needs and circumstances of the continent's practitioners—he has been a central, though highly controversial, figure in many academic and policy debates around Islam in Europe (Bechler 2004a; Sid-Ahmed 2004). While Ramadan is arguably the most influential European Muslim intellectual, and one of the few who relatively regularly appear in mainstream media, his role in dominant discourse, obsessed as it is with the topic of European Islam, is rather marginal; there is an unwillingness to seriously engage him, accept him as an intellectual peer who is a genuinely European intellectual, drawing on a tradition as rich as the Christian or Jewish one, and closely related to both. Instead, there often is an antagonistic approach, driven by an immense sense of suspicion, a desire to "unmask" him, to show the thoroughly foreign radical behind the mask of the Westernized liberal.[24]

Born and raised in Switzerland, fluent in several European languages in addition to Arabic, trained in classical continental philosophy, Ramadan seems to be as "at home" in Europe as possible. But it is exactly because of this that he seems threatening—for dominant European discourse, but also for traditional Muslim hierarchies—through confidently claiming an independent voice for European Muslims. As firmly grounded in Islamic as in European history, he aims at combining both traditions in what could be called a Muslim version of universalism:

> At the level of universality, "Western" and "Islamic" values are
> converging. For me, justice and equality come from my Islamic teach-
> ing: it has reached the level where these universal values are the same

for you as they are for me . . . For example, from the Greek concept
of democracy we take at least four principles: state of law; equal
citizenship; universal suffrage and accountability—the main universal
principles in the western model of democracy. These four principles
can also be extracted from Islam, merging at that point with the
universality of this system. (Ramadan, in Bechler 2004b)

One of the central and most successful arguments of "ex-Muslims"
like Hirsi Ali is the claim that Muslims as a group have been incapable of adapting to modernity, because their beliefs are based on a literal,
outdated reading of the Qur'an, since the art of exegesis practiced by
Christians and Jews for centuries is still unfamiliar, and sacrilegious, to
them.[25] Ramadan directly tackles this claim, advocating increasingly explicitly for a reinterpretation of Islamic sources, including Qur'anic ones
(Ramadan 2009), while fulfilling the implicit request to speak the dominant language: "The main focus of my critique is not European societies, where I see no obstacle to Muslims remaining Muslim, but on the
way that Muslims' behavior is governed by scriptural sources and a legal
inheritance which has to be revisited" (ibid.).[26]

Young Muslims across the continent heed this call to revisit Islam in a
contemporary European context, creating positionalities and forming coalitions that defy essentialist notions of European liberalism and conservative Islam alike. Among them are queer Muslims and their straight allies.[27] Stories such as that of twenty-seven-year-old Moroccan Dutch Leyla
confirm the inclusive, pragmatic adaptation of religious practices among
Muslim Europeans on an everyday basis:

> My best friend is a devout Muslim and when I am with her, we pray
> the official way . . . At first I was terribly at war with Allah. I did not
> know if I could be both lesbian and Muslim and whether I could praise
> Allah as a lesbian. This same friend helped me a lot then. She helped
> me understand that as a lesbian I am not less in the eyes of Allah.
> (el Kaka and Kurşun 2002, 73)

Nonetheless, an explicitly Muslim identity, especially when accompanied
by the charged marker of the *hijab*, is still read as necessarily representing sexist and homophobic beliefs. Enter Asmaa Abdol-Hamid—a feminist, *hijab*-wearing, queer-friendly Muslima of Palestinian descent, who
as member of the Danish Socialist Party, parliamentary candidate, social
worker, and former TV show host has gained a high public profile, defying
the expectations of both the Danish majority and the Muslim minority.

Abdol-Hamid's story in some ways seems as generically representative of European Muslimas as Ayaan Hirsi Ali's is for the supposed fate of women in majority Muslim nations—one of six children, she is the daughter of Palestinian refugees who came to Denmark in 1986 when she was five years old. What makes Abdol-Hamid unusual is her successful insistence on having her own voice heard. And while she shares this attribute with Hirsi Ali, Abdol-Hamid's perspective does not fit into preexisting narratives, but tends to defy normative expectations, starting with the teenager's active participation in her small town Christian church community in spite (or rather because) of her commitment to Islam, to becoming the only student in her school wearing the *hijab*, to her fight with the authorities about educational opportunities: "At school my siblings and I could clearly see that the teachers didn't have the same high expectations of our academic abilities as they did of the ethnic Danish pupils . . . and I eventually had to threaten legal action before my lower secondary school would enter me for upper secondary school" (Abdol-Hamid 2007).[28] After her family's move to a multiethnic, working-class suburb of Odense in her last year of high school, Abdol-Hamid started a local girls' club, recognizing that female teenagers received little support from either their communities or the state (thus showing exactly the kind of initiative and independence that Hirsi Ali and others claim nonexistent among devout Muslimas):

> I thought there was a need for activities aimed at the girls living in Vollsmose; I had grown up going to recreation and sports clubs, whereas the girls' lives here were: school—home, home—school. In addition, I found it unacceptable that, in Vollsmose at the time, immigrant boys who were troublemakers were getting all the attention. A lot of money was spent on them. There was total disregard for the fact that many immigrant girls also had problems, but reacted in a different way—maybe by staying at home and isolating themselves. (Abdol-Hamid 2007)

Acting in the tradition of women of color feminism, Abdol-Hamid draws strength from her community while simultaneously pushing its limits, the avowed feminist studied to become a social worker and joined the socialist party, motivated by the increasingly hostile tone of the national immigration debate and determined to make herself be heard.

After entering the national stage as the representative of Danish Muslims during the cartoon controversy, Abdol-Hamid made headlines again in 2007 when she became a national candidate for the socialist Enhedslisten (Unity List). Given her explicitly class-focused politics, Abdol-Hamid's candidacy seems logical.[29] Nonetheless, both the party and Abdol-Hamid faced strong criticism, caused not by the latter's political positions, but by the fact that she wears a *hijab* (and displays other public signs of her religious belief, such as greeting men without shaking their hands). While the presence of the *hijab* itself was enough to feed an extensive campaign by the Danish People's Party, for many members and sympathizers of Enhedslisten, it became a stand-in for Adbol-Hamid's politics, assumed to be necessarily at odds with their own progressive positions. It is worth it to take a closer look at how the controversy played out within the socialist party, since criticism of Abdol-Hamid was based both on the party's identity as a(nti)religious and on supposedly fundamental differences between Protestantism and Islam, again underscoring the seemingly intrinsic link between secularism and Christianity in European discourse (far beyond the political right).

As Signe Kjær Jørgensen points out in her study of Danish "headscarf-wearing Muslims," the socialist Unity List is the only Danish party not aligning itself with the "protestant secularist discourse" that creates a more or less explicit link between political parties and the state's dominant church (Kjær Jørgensen 2008, 3). It is this distance to institutionalized religion that formed the basis for the first strand of internal criticism of Abdol-Hamid, however the *hijab* was immediately introduced into the argument as symbolizing what was wrong with her particular religious practice. As one disgruntled party member stated:

> It is because religious values form the basis for her political identity. Her religious beliefs, among other things, urges [sic] her to accept that women wear headscarves, i.e., to accept some degree of inhibitedness— and a hierarchical, unequal relationship between the sexes. (*Politiken* September 20, 2007, 9, quoted in ibid., 6)

The *hijab* is thus taken to have a static, clearly defined meaning, namely the one dominating European discourse post-9/11, when the NATO invasion of Afghanistan reminded Europe of its concern for the liberation of Muslim women. According to this definition, the presence of the *hijab* manifests the absence of progressive positions on gender and sexuality. The emotive politics of dress at play here reduce Muslim women's consciousness to the symbolic limits provided by the *hijab*, linking culture, ideology, and beliefs in predetermined ways that leave them without agency, therefore offering enough grounds to demand the exclusion of Abdol-Hamid from the socialist party:

> The party ought to be culturally inclusive, according to some of your members, and there ought to be room for someone like Asmaa. No, society as a whole ought to be culturally inclusive, and there ought to be room for Asmaa. It is a fundamental political right to create parties

based on a well-defined and explicit ideological basis, a basis that
excludes people who have different beliefs. (ibid., 7)

In the course of the argument for the exclusion of "someone like Asmaa,"
the focus thus shifts from "different beliefs" as "religious values" to different beliefs as the inherent gender inequality propagated by Islam. This shift
facilitates the inclusion of Christianity into the secular defense of freedom
and equality against religion, allowing socialist party member Bente Hansen, feminist and practicing Christian, to deploy a similar line of attack on
her Muslim colleague: "This isn't just about religion, but about gender and
women as viewed by the different branches of orthodox Islam" (*Information*, September 26, 2007, quoted in ibid., 9). While Abdol-Hamid via the
hijab is identified with orthodox Islam, Hansen affirms the diversity of
Christianity, which allows Christians, and Christian women in particular,
an autonomy and independence of thought precluded by Islam:

Sometimes people ask how I can be a Socialist and a practising
Christian, and the only reason why this is possible is that the Danish
National Church unlike most other Christian churches allows women
to preach. If it did not allow them to do so then I would not be an
adherent and would if I so may say "do it in private." I will use the
same argument as regards Enhedslisten: If they do not support equal
opportunities I will leave. It is that simple. (ibid., 9)

Importantly, the superiority of Christianity is manifest through national
differentiation, that is, the enlightened commitment of Danish Christianity
to gender equality, which is contrasted to the Muslim cultural coding of
gender inequality, superseding national difference and expressed in primitive symbolic politics, that is, veiling. This recalls Bonnie Honig's analysis
of Julia Kristeva's assessment of the French Muslim community vis-à-
vis their "host country's" universalist tradition, namely the Manichean
binary Kristeva constructs of French abstract beliefs and Muslim concrete
symbolism of the headscarf, thus assuming a hierarchy of values that precludes dialogue, because it is already clear who is right and who is wrong:
"[T]he problem with Kristeva is her failure to engage others in her deliberations about the project, goals, and instruments of a cosmopolitanism she
values too much to risk by including it in the conversation as a question
rather than as the answer" (Honig 2001, 66). Albeit certainly less refined,
Hansen's argument mirrors Kristeva's in using the symbolism of the *hijab*
to avoid engaging in a conversation among equals (that is, a conversation
whose outcome is not predetermined) and to imply that Abdol-Hamid's
intellectual path is predetermined by. the way she covers her body: "she
has to affiliate herself with a party that promotes hierarchy between the

sexes, as her headgear shows that she does" (*Information* September 26, 2007, quoted in Kjær Jørgensen, 9).

While the invocation of secular and Christian traditions combines to justify the exclusion of Abdol-Hamid from the Unity List, she refuses to accept the conclusiveness of the circular argumentation employed by her white Danish critics and instead intervenes by claiming parity between them and her own feminist, socialist, Muslim positionality, demanding the kind of dialogue denied by Kristeva and other defenders of Christian universalism:

> I am aware that in some countries, for instance Iran, the headscarf is a univocal symbol of the subordination of women in society, and I have disassociated myself clearly from that. Right now, I am witnessing the contrary: people want to force me not to wear a *hijab* at least if I am to "be allowed" to call myself a Socialist . . . And, Bente, in fact we already have female preachers of Islam and I think we ought to have more of them. (*Dagbladet Information,* September 29, 2007, 16–17, quoted in ibid., 11)

With her statement, Abdol-Hamid constructs a conversation on equal terms, calling out the unquestioned certainty that the heirs of the Protestant secularist Danish tradition are to allow or not allow "foreigners" in and forcing them into "deliberations about the project, goals, and instruments of a cosmopolitanism" by decentering Europe as well as breaking up the supposed homogeniety of Islam, introducing a relationship between culture, nation, and religion that is as dynamic for Muslims as it is for Christians and thus deconstructing the latter's discursive hegemony:

> You perceive the headscarf as a symbol of repression and as a symbol of male domination. This is not what the headscarf means to me. Wearing a hijab is a personal choice that only shows my religious affiliation and religious symbols change throughout the ages and have different meanings ascribed to them due to changing circumstances. Wearing the Christian cross does not mean that you are affiliated with the Ku Klux Klan. (ibid.)

Unwilling to fit into predesigned categories, instead creating new ones, Abdol-Hamid works on intersections that represent the potential of a fusionist "Euro-Islam" as suggested by Tariq Ramadan (though she might be a little more than he can take). Key to her approach are coalitional politics between minority, feminist, queer groups, and a grounding in community work.[30] Contrary to Hirsi Ali, Abdol-Hamid does not pit Islam against

Enlightenment and Europe against the Middle East; instead she insists on combining her identities as Muslim, feminist, socialist, and European, affirming that all those identities are legitimately owned by her. Women like Abdol-Hamid represent an image that is unacceptable within European discourse (be it progressive or mainstream), because they show that Islam and commitment to "Western values" such as gender equality are compatible, and because they are representative of a larger group: as seen in the last chapter, feminist activism has been part of migrant and minority communities for decades, and these grassroots activists often face resistance from ethnic communities, dominant feminist organizations, and the state alike; their insistence on addressing simultaneous oppressions not only makes them important and effective, but also prevents them from gaining a prominent place in debates about their fate, exactly because of what they have to say about these intersectionalities.

The Scopic Politics of Progressive Islamophobia

Contrary to the claims made in popular escape narratives, Abdol-Hamid and others do provide progressive Muslim voices—it is the majority that is unwilling to hear what they have to say. This refutes the popular claim that there are no articulate Muslimas, that only women who have left the repressive culture of Islam are brave enough to speak up, that they need to completely break with their religion and community in order to be liberated: women like Hirsi Ali appear as homeless, outcasts, without community, until they are adopted by the enlightened West, thus leaving them forever indebted. What is problematic about them thus is not their criticism of Islam, but the unquestioned assumption that it is only Muslims who bring religion, intolerance, and inequality to the table—Europe, like whiteness, is the forever unexplored norm, Christianity remains invisible behind a secular cloak—until, that is, it is challenged by the growing presence of non-Christians. This presence in turn will always seem both threatening and illegitimate until the connections between Christianity and the secular state are addressed. The inability to tolerate not to mention engage with difference, characteristic for all heteronormative systems, is covered by a discourse of universalist humanism in which the Other increasingly appears as attacker, enabled by an excessive tolerance borne out of a guilty liberal consciousness, resulting in a naïve multiculturalism leaving Europe incapable of defending itself. Within this increasingly martial logic, the need to "close ranks" combines with the demand to choose sides, making it harder for dissenting voices to be heard and more dangerous to position oneself or to be positioned outside of or between the warring camps.

In dominant discourses on Muslim Europeans' place in the continental community, the scopic politics of (post)nationalism and the emotive politics of dress are successfully combined to justify aggressive demands for assimilation that are based on the assumption that Islam, contrary to Christianity, is incompatible with modern, secular societies. This discourse leaves Muslims with two basic options: in its liberal version, as exemplified in Adelheid Roosen's plays, they bear the responsibility of reforming Islam, making it compatible with twenty-first century realities, exactly because through migration they, as opposed to Muslims in the global South, have become citizens of the modern world. In its conservative variation, represented by Ayaan Hirsi Ali, Pascal Bruckner, and others, the discourse questions Islam's very ability to reform itself, seeing this as a somewhat doubtful, long-term solution at best, in effect demanding of Muslim Europeans to either leave behind their religion or their (European) home countries, confirming Islam as a fundamentally "un-European" religion. The *hijab* has become the dominant visual shorthand for this discourse, continuing a largely unacknowledged colonial use of a similar symbolism (Alloula 1986) and allowing the critics to fit Muslims into a narrow and homogeneous ideological framework, while sharply separating them from other minority communities, their identity supposedly primarily structured around this visual difference and all it implies.

Hirsi Ali's 2004 film *Submission Part I* (Part II was meant to focus on Islam and homosexuality), directed by a rather unenthusiastic Theo van Gogh (who thought the script lacked humor), is singularly illustrative of this strategy. The film's message unambiguously reflects Hirsi Ali's worldview, representing the violence experienced by Muslim women as a direct and necessary outcome of Islam's teachings. The juxtaposition of readings from Qur'anic surahs with women's stories of oppression and violation implies that the problem is not religion, but *this* religion, repeating the by now familiar claim that there is only one possible interpretation of Islam, which thus either has to be rejected completely or accepted in its most extreme fringe versions. Visually, the short film seems to take its clues from the *Veiled Monologues*, which had an immensely successful run in the Netherlands during the months that *Submission* was produced. The posters for the play used the image of a woman completely covered by a burka, made however, of see-through material, revealing her nude body underneath. *Submission* takes this a step further, using the exact same image of a nude woman in a see-through burka (representing the four female characters telling their stories), removing, however, all possibilities for ambiguous interpretations by revealing the women's bodies as literally marked by both Qur'anic surahs and signs of brutal male violence.

The film, first aired on Dutch public television in August 2004, was predictably condemned by conservative Muslim organizations, but it also received little support from the women for whose liberation it advocated. Many white liberal and feminist supporters of Hirsi Ali contributed this to the firm grip that a patriarchal religious indoctrination still had on these women:

> In one of the Dutch shelters for battered women, 80 percent of whose residents are Muslimas, Ayaan held a discussion with four young women following a screening of the film *Submission*. She received no applause. The women, women who had been beaten by their husbands, were deeply offended, angry, hurt by what they saw as the blasphemy of projecting Qur'an texts onto naked women's bodies, never mind whether these texts sanctioned violence against them or not. (de Moor 2007)

The largely negative reactions from Muslim women could of course also, and more convincingly I believe, be attributed to the fact that the film is as committed to denying them any agency as is the ideology it attacks. Hirsi Ali not only rejects any possible female investment in the religion that might exist independently of a strictly heteronormative and heterosexual context, but also completely discounts the possibility that their faith might empower some women to revolt against dominant patriarchal interpretations of Islam. While decrying women's complete submission under the religion's violent, misogynist rule, the film itself represents a completely message-controlled performance, in which Muslimas appear only as bodies and objects.

In stark contrast, women like Abdol-Hamid, who wear the *hijab* while practicing types of agencies supposedly incompatible with its presence, challenge the implicit visual logic of racialized and gendered hierarchies hidden beneath the discourse of colorblindness and contribute to the queering of ethnicity by working on and with contradictions and impossibilities.

Images such as this poster announcing an event with Abdol-Hamid at a Danish queer club violate the visual logic of racelessness, always imagining the Other as external and separate (much as Euro-hip-hop's intervention into discourses of citizenship and language violated racelessness's aural logic). They thus symbolize an alliance that not only continues the tradition of coalitions as an alternative to the mainstreaming of marginalized communities, but also strengthens the position of queer Muslims who, if they resist the binary logic of oppressive Islam versus liberated West, constitute an even more disrupting presence.

Poster for event with Abdol-Hamid at Copenhagen queer club Dunkel Bar, 2007.

The adaptation and interpretation of Islamic texts by average Muslims, denied by Hirsi Ali, Kelek et al., is an everyday practice across the world, including Europe: Islam's positions on women's rights and homosexuality are already vigorously debated in Muslim communities, often invisible to a dominant society still not ready to enter an open dialogue—and to a gay and lesbian community not ready to include Muslim queers. Instead, there is a muted reaction whenever these voices try to enter a mainstream that seems largely preoccupied with Islam's inherent homophobia. Repeating the model described in the last section with regard to Muslim women, homophobia among Muslims is defined as inevitably produced by their culture/religion, Islam itself representing the threat, which in turn, is present in every Muslim—and every Muslim is held fully responsible for the behavior of the community as a whole. While gay voices such as U.S. journalist Bruce Bawer or politician Pim Fortuyn gain additional credibility when supporting the image of Islam's inherent intolerance, Muslim queers—like women wearing the *hijab*—appear as silenced victims, their only salvation the rejection of Islam and their ethnic community and the embrace of a majoritarian gay identity.

Within this binary discursive formation, the Western LGBT community has the role of civilizer, while queer Muslims have nothing to offer, as they, like all Muslims, are products of a culture that is fundamentally inferior to the secular West.[31] This dichotomy puts all nonwhite, non-Western queers in a similar predicament: communities of color appear as by default homophobic and heterosexual, the queer community as by default white, reflecting a global discourse of progress and human rights in which the white West invariably takes the lead, maybe not always progressively enough, but certainly always more so than anyone else. The trope can be reinforced quickly because it references well-known clichés perceived as truth, since they align with the overarching binary discourse affirming Europe's status as the center of progress and humanism. A successful challenge to this mechanism therefore requires a simultaneous engagement with all of these discursive tropes and their anchoring in European conceptions of public space and time used to subordinate the rest of the world and people of color. The next chapter will explore such challenges and their impact on the European narrative of racelessness, ranging from queer of color groups like the Dutch Strange Fruit to migration activists such as the German Kanak Attak.

CHAPTER FOUR

"Because It Is Our Stepfatherland"

Queering European Public Spaces

This is a landscape where the historical remainders never add up to seamless wholes and where the meaning of ethnoscape no longer relies on ethnicity as strong multiculturalism defines it. As world upon world turns, this too is part of the ongoing labor of imagination, which is not confined to diasporic public spheres alone.

—LESLIE ADELSON, *The Turkish Turn in Contemporary German Literature*

[W]e compete for a new attitude of migrants of all generations that we want to bring on stage, independently and without compromise. Whoever believes that we celebrate a Potpourri out of Ghetto-Hip-Hop and other clichés will be surprised. We sample, change and adapt different political and cultural drifts that all operate from oppositional positions. We go back to a mixture of theory, politics and cultural practice. This song is ours.

—KANAK ATTAK MANIFESTO

Gay Consumers and Queer Commodities in the Neoliberal City

Chapter 3 highlighted how a discourse on Europe's universalist, secular identity as threatened by the particularist politics of the continent's Muslim minorities not only seemingly manifests the failure of multiculturalism, but also characterizes racialized minorities as inhibiting the inevitable progress toward a postnational twenty-first century Europe. Embodying the failed essentialism of identity politics, religious fundamentalism, political correctness, and the doomed industrial class system of twentieth century capitalism, they position themselves in opposition to the new values of diversity, tolerance, and mobility. In other words, through accusing marginalized communities of clinging to an outdated, binary worldview, a new system of domination allows for the continuation of old binaries while discarding the vocabulary developed to criticize it, in particular within the context of the worldwide liberation movements of the 1960s and '70s. One of the most important result of these movements' interventions was a move away from a system of white supremacy, working through both abjection and assimilation, toward a seemingly inclusive, depoliticized model of governance that has rendered ineffective forms of resistance created in response to earlier forms of domination:

> The most successful ruse of neoliberal dominance in both global and domestic affairs is the definition of economic policy as primarily a matter of neutral, technical expertise. This expertise is then presented as separate from politics and culture, and not properly subject to specifically political accountability or cultural critique. Opposition to material inequality is maligned as "class warfare," while race, gender or sexual inequalities are dismissed as merely cultural, private, or trivial. (Duggan 2005, xiv)

This shift is reflected in current European measures of regulation and oppression, which are presented as necessary to the survival of threatened values of liberty and tolerance, as in fact enhancing them. The limits of the acceptable are determined by an altruistic progress that ultimately leads to ever greater freedom and welfare, excluding only those who refuse participation in this democratic process. While such an argument proposes that in contemporary Europe, self-exclusion is the only form of marginalization, the reality of course is rather more complicated. European commitment to equality with regard to gender and sexuality, manifest in domestic partnership and same-sex marriage legislation as well as anti-Muslim rhetoric, is in fact limited to particular expressions, compatible with a larger structure of exclusion and strict binaries, in other words with a system of heteronormativity. As a result, both implicitly heterosexual Muslim minorities and queer Muslims appear as deviant, characterized by an excess that makes them uncontrollable and thus dangerous. That is, it is the kind of difference from the norm that is decisive here, not its content: in accordance with the overarching model of Fabian's Public Time described earlier, both queer and straight Muslims appear as not quite able to handle twenty-first century models of identity: while the former, still culturally stuck in the age of shame, are incapable of embracing a modern queer identity, the latter cling to a repressive model of heterosexuality, out of synch with the age of neoliberal consumer-citizens, offering participation to anyone willing and able to pay the price, including those formerly excluded, such as women and queers.

In order to effectively address this system as not only one of exclusion, but also of interpellation, it is helpful to introduce the concept of homonormativity (Duggan 2002), that is, a mainstreamed gay discourse attempting to expand rather than dismantle heteronormativity by internalizing a conceptualization of lesbian, gay, bisexual, transgender (LGBT) identity that constructs legitimacy and rights along established lines, challenging neither the exclusion of those who do not or cannot play by the rules, nor a system whose very existence depends on exclusions:

> Homonormativity is a chameleon-like ideology that purports to push for progressive causes such as rights to gay marriage and other "activisms," but at the same time it creates a depoliticizing effect on queer communities as it rhetorically remaps and recodes freedom and liberation in terms of privacy, domesticity, and consumption. In other words, homonormativity anesthetizes queer communities into passively accepting alternative forms of inequality in return for domestic privacy and the freedom to consume. (Manalansan 2005, 142)[1]

Homonormative identity appears as ideally complementing a playful yet competitive apolitical citizenship in which rights are primarily defined in terms of consumption, in which every level of society is framed in economic terms, offering individualized, market-oriented solutions to structural problems revolving around the ability to consume. The resulting depoliticization of capitalism, according to Wendy Brown, "as a political rationality . . . involves a specific and consequential organization of the social, the subject, and the state," along the lines sketched in the Manalansan quote above, one that "governs the sayable, the intelligible, and the truth criteria of these domains" (Brown 2006, 693) in a way that produces the "undemocratic citizen," manageable and controllable because she or he has internalized a notion of political activism as outmoded, an unproductive expression of intolerant political correctness.

This discursive turn is embedded in everyday practices, especially visible in urban zones through spatial politics, in which marginalized groups are not completely expelled, but excluded from rights through their failure to achieve consumer-citizen status, making their primary value that of products to be consumed. The apparent dissolution of binaries that have characterized modernity is also visible in conceptualizations of the city that move away from a functional model, in which urban spaces figure largely as containers into which different populations are sorted. Instead, the relationship between cities and their inhabitants appears as dynamic, both constantly shaping each other, creating unique forms of "spatial consciousness." These new theories react to the crisis of the industrial city that began in the 1970s, a crisis that in turn produced new forms of situated resistance such as the squatter and hip-hop movements. Arguably, theorists such as Richard Florida appropriated and tamed the subversive impulses produced within these movements into a neoliberal market model of the "creative city," postulating a creative class as the new driving force behind the resurrection of urban spaces (Florida 2002; Reckwitz 2009). While related to the service sector, within the new terminology, these "symbol analysts" belong to "professions that are not only about service or knowledge, but also about the creative use of symbolizations and the creation of something 'new'" (Reckwitz 2009, 3, my translation). This model of symbolic production relates to the neoliberal concept of citizenship in multiple ways, celebrating fluidity and cosmopolitan mobility as well as uniqueness and diversity, turning them into cultural capital and combining all to make performance—of identity, culture, and lifestyle—the privileged mode of urban experience.

As cultural sociologist Andreas Reckwitz and others have shown however, this postmodern model, while superficially celebrating a dynamic mode of living opposed to the static restrictions of the modern age, in fact contains and constrains the shifts taking place in late twentieth century city life and integrates them into a new binary, whose Other is quite familiar, namely "the non-Cultural, that is the sphere of that which does not see itself as cultural or is not (initially) accessible to culturation" (Reckwitz 2009, 18), in other words: the ethnic. Florida's (pseudo)quantitative creative city model offers ethnic diversity, patent applications per head, and the number of gay (male) residents as the three main indicators of an urban community's desirability within the new "creative" economy (Florida 2002). While this index seemingly legitimizes the presence of sexual as well as racial minorities, thus presenting a move beyond earlier models aimed at pushing nonnormative populations outside the city limits, there is a difference not only between types of culture, but also between those embodying creativity, the gay residents, and those representing ethnic diversity, with the former defined along the lines of a rather tired stereotype—the wealthy, artistic (white) gay man, favoring the aesthetic over the political, consumption over activism, and participation in the status quo over change—that gained new credibility and positive value with the discovery of the gay market in the 1990s.[2] Thus, despite the stated openness of the creative city, white middle-class men seem to end up once again in the position of the normative, and certain groups occupy similar marginal positions in hetero- and homonormative discourses, among them the Muslim community, which provides color, exotic food, and sexual objects but also stands for restrictive morality, crime, and poverty.

This is symptomatic of the unexplored inequalities that remain or are intensified despite the achievement of limited equality, in particular those of race and gender. The "'gay equality' branch of multi-issue neoliberalism" as Duggan terms it (Duggan 2005, 47), marginalizes if not outright suppresses analyses built around intersectionality (Crenshaw 1991), that is, the assumption that systems of oppression do not work separately but through complex and shifting interactions (a concept largely absent from contemporary queer theory's primary focus on sexuality):

> The market is constructed to be the filter of gay freedom and progress so much so that dominant discourses in the gay community disregard how this kind of freedom is predicated on the abjection of other groups of people who are not free to consume and do not have access to these symbolic and material forms of capital . . . on closer inspection what is seemingly a chaotic assemblage of political culprits fuses into the figure of the female and the feminized, the foreigner, the colored, the sexually deviant, and the poor. (Manalansan 2005, 142)

The multiple positions and identities present within the queer community become visible when the qualifier "gay" is taken off the list that defines the nonnormative, leaving the question how the acceptable gay subject living the heteronormative timeline of good citizenship looks like. In his analysis of post-9/11 interactions between gay men in the New York City neighborhood Jackson Heights, Martin Manalansan points to the fundamentally different positionalities of middle-class white gay men and poor gay men of color whose relationships in part exist within a queer context, in part within a larger context of spatial governance in which race and class become more important than sexuality with regard to access to public space (see Stein 1997 for an discussion of lesbians and public space). Thus, what is perceived as a gay-friendly gentrification by an affluent Manhattan-based queer community appears as part of an increasing policing and exploitation of poor people of color to the neighborhood's nonwhite queer population.[3]

The regulation of space, the question of who has legitimate claims to it and to whose needs it is meant to cater to, is as relevant in European cities like Amsterdam, Warsaw, or Berlin, where the rise in popularity of creative city models goes along with an increasing pitting of gay against migrant communities that completely erases class as an analytical category and instead replaces it with the understanding of culture that we encountered in the last chapter, namely one in which the legitimate inhabitants of the creative city, central among them gay men, produce desirable, that is, apolitical, forms of culture, while its illegitimate inhabitants, central among them communities of color, provide the raw cultural material that increases the city's value (without being considered part of the creative class themselves). This hierarchy is hidden under a claim to inclusiveness in which—as Hong writes in her analysis of "diversity management" in the contemporary U.S. university system—"'diversity' is tokenistically, but not substantively prioritized, racialized and 'gendered management' currently does not occur solely through . . . denigration . . . but also simultaneously through a form of valorization and fetishization, albeit of a limited and facile type. This is the ideological and epistemological formation of contemporary global capital" (Hong 2008, 102).

This formation also expresses itself in the new dynamic model of urban spaces, framing the latter not as constructed and controlled from above, but as both produced by and producing practices of living, as both created by and creating citizens. Public spaces thus are no neutral ground but sites of production and consumption, contested markets in which "diversity" is a coveted cultural product. In order to deconstruct and repoliticize this process and to address the simultaneous appropriation and denigration of minoritarian cultural agency and productivity, it is useful to follow Hong, Ferguson, Manalansan and others working in the field of queer of color critique in their return to women of color feminism's reassessment of culture within its intersectional critique of liberal capitalism, which:

> helped to designate the imagination as a social practice under contemporary globalization. In a moment in which national liberation movements and Western nation-states disenfranchised women of color and queer of color subjects, culture, for those groups, became the obvious scene of alternative agency. In the process, these subjects reformatted culture as a site of oppositional agency that eschewed nationalism, rather than facilitated it. Culture became the field from which to imaginatively work against the disfranchisements of nationalism and the debilities of global capital. (Ferguson 2004, 117)

This understanding of culture shows important differences to the one expressed in the neoliberal privileging of the urban "creative class" as exceptional: an understanding built on a Western definition of art that tends to pit the individual against the collective as well as a specifically European juxtaposition of "high" and "low culture," that identifies the former with progress and liberation and the latter with the masses' reactionary impulses. This distrust of vernacular forms is also expressed in an elitism from the Left that works to stifle subversive uses of culture by communities of color and tends to ignore the impact of queer of color activist groups like the Dutch Strange Fruit, founded in Amsterdam in 1989. The collective, whose name simultaneously references queer positionalities and African diasporic traditions, almost perfectly represents the subaltern of contemporary European discourses around race, religion, and migration in its implied impact on gender and sexuality: its founders were queer youths of Muslim and Afro-Caribbean background, for the most part welfare recipients and sex workers, who came together intending to challenge their marginalization within both their ethnic communities and the Dutch gay scene. Committed to a self-help approach, the group offered an insider's perspective to other queer youths of color; rather than that of aid workers delivering "expert knowledge," it used the expertise present within the community itself. But exactly its focus on cultural activism and ephemeral forms, in particular performance, classified Strange Fruit as not properly "political" within a progressive discourse shaped by a Frankfurt School view of mass culture still dominating much of Left politics in Europe (unsurprisingly, members of the collective had little connection to the traditional Left politics invariably central in progressive white queer communities). Activism such as that of Strange Fruit represents a reappropriation of a depoliticized notion of culture, its various social sources usually unrecognized as sights of diversity and creativity. The group's queering of ethnicity challenges this perception by drawing on a notion of culture and art based on women of color feminism's insights, reemployed toward a radical understanding of "oppositional agency" within queer of color critique (and first introduced to the Netherlands by black feminist activists closely working with Strange Fruit, such as the Sister Outsider and ZAMI collectives).

In chapter 4, I explore how multiethnic cultural artist and activist collectives like Strange Fruit, Salon Oriental, and Kanak Attak create a "poetics of relation," reclaiming public spaces through visual and performative strategies, creating alternative archives that record silenced narratives of Europeanness. I will thus revisit from a different angle the quest for a European postnational identity addressed in chapter 1, the interaction between cultural activism and theorizing in (diasporic) communities of color explored in chapter 2, and the performative queering of ethnicity analyzed in chapter 3. All of these strategies use public space as the site of negotiating (im)possible identities and in this last chapter, I address various forms of artist and activist interventions inscribing the negated past and presence of racialized populations into this space by returning to the city. I explore the meaning of public space in a neoliberal discourse bent on controlling the public through privatization and its role as a site of consumption and intervention that produces new visual strategies reacting to these changes, while also framing them within this book's overarching exploration of the specific workings of the ideology of racelessness. Chapter 4 explores the notion of "inauthenticity" as central to the strategy of queering ethnicity, showing it as a culmination of the destabilizing of binary notions of Europeanness traced through the preceding chapters and affirming its roots in women of color feminism's, hip-hop's and queer of color activism's challenges to heteronormative models of gender, race, class, sexuality, and nation.

Queer of Color Activism between Homonationalism and Identity Politics

Amsterdam in many ways exemplifies the neoliberal creative city, with its mixture of quaint architecture and edgy metrosexual culture, idyllic canals and multicultural markets, liberal drug and prostitution laws—and its own version of the *cités*, such as the (mostly black) Bijlmer and (mostly Muslim) Slotervaart, housing an increasingly segregated, criminalized, and policed multiethnic population of color, disproportionally poor and young (see Open Society Institute 2007a, Amsterdam-Slotervaart City Council 2007, 2008): out of sight of the millions of visitors who come to the city each year, but at the same time available when needed to mobilize fears around a foreign, fanatical, violent Other or to provide an accessible, exotic, and titillatingly dangerous site for the more daring traveler, straight or gay, local or international. It is exactly this combination that made the city one of Europe's most popular tourist destinations and the prime site of what Hiram Perez calls gay cosmopolitan tourism (Perez 2005). This is a tourism that affirms a particular gay identity as normative by tying liberation to specific types of mobility. At the same time, "the mobility that modern gay identity requires is not universally available. Here we encounter trouble in the form of noncanonical bodies (not surprisingly, also quite often brown bodies) nonetheless interpellated as gay. Gays who cannot properly be gay" (Perez 2005, 177).

Gay cosmopolitan tourism thus requires, and produces, the same kind of seemingly fluid, but in fact strictly hierarchical urban spaces provided by the neoliberal creative city, including poor communities of color in its cityscape, but containing and isolating them to ensure that movement takes place only in one direction, conceiving of them primarily as a resource—of labor, food, sex, and other commodities valued by the consumer-citizen. These racialized communities are thus both defined as lacking the individualized and commercialized mobility of the (homo- and heteronormative) Western subject, while they are at the same time forever reduced to a mobile, uprooted state, as Chow's "aliens from elsewhere," whose presence is a marketable touristic commodity exactly because it includes an element of danger, of the excessive exotic within the confines of the civilized city, a permanent potential threat to the humanist consensus of postnational Europe.

As traced in the last chapter, over the past decade, cracks in the idealized narrative of Dutch liberal tolerance have largely been defined as caused by the nation's growing Muslim population, unwilling and unable to partake in the *polder* model that for centuries managed to maintain a delicate equilibrium between diverse populations.[4] Several studies devoted to the issue of Islam and homosexuality in the Netherlands produced results that seemed to confirm the adversarial relationship between the two. In 1996 the city of Amsterdam published a survey of the local high schools identifying rampant homophobia among minority youths. This claim gained wide attention in part by feeding into an ongoing larger debate on "senseless violence" originating in migrant communities, in part by tying into growing concerns about the rise of "black schools," that is, schools with a high number of students of color, and the supposed negative effect of this trend on white Dutch students (see Arts and Nabah 2001). The study's findings were complemented by a 2003 Forum (Institute for Multicultural Development) report on "Homosexuality and Citizenship" focusing on queers from migrant and minority communities. The study's narrative presents the familiar dichotomy of stories of oppression representative for queers of color and stories of liberation reflecting "Dutch" queer identity (with "Dutch" and "minority" being conceived of as mutually exclusive); thus migrant and minority queers appear as "not there yet," as victims not of Dutch racism but of an oppressive, archaic ethnic culture:

> The many personal stories of gays of color are to a certain extent comparable. A coming-out like the one experienced by many Dutch gays is not (yet) seen as a necessary step by the majority and is not common. Many migrant/minority gays and lesbians live a double life and do not see any chance of living openly as gay, because, according to them, that would bring shame for their families within the community. They perceive an openly gay lifestyle as a sign of disrespect for family and community. The risk of expulsion from family and/or community is real. Thus, these are reasons to avoid a confrontation with cultural and/or religious traditions and to hide their sexual preference from family and community. For gays of color it is often already a big step— towards self-realization—to use the meeting places created by migrant/ minority gays. Initiatives such as Strange Fruit and Secret Garden of

the Amsterdam COC and the Melting Pot of The Hague's COC. These initiatives have diverse aims: from help and support to the organizing of informal meeting nights. (*Forum* 2003, 11)

One of the groups mentioned in *Forum*'s report, Strange Fruit, had become the main contact point for press and politicians after the 1996 study on migrant—and in particular Muslim—antigay attitudes. A growing media and policy focus on "Muslim homophobia" put the activists in an increasingly exposed position, sought after by journalists as well as policy makers. The resulting tension, caused by the group's refusal to be treated as native informers, while at the same time trying to use the influence they gained to open up spaces for other queers of color, remained a central challenge to Strange Fruit throughout its existence. The organization had been founded seven years earlier by a dozen gay, lesbian, and transsexual youths of color, many of them sex workers and most, being of Moroccan and Turkish descent, with a Muslim background. Transgendered members were a small but vocal presence from the beginning and while most of its founders were men, the group soon included an equal number of women and became increasingly ethnically diverse, with activists of North African, Caribbean, Middle Eastern, Afro-Dutch, Asian, and Asian-Dutch background (as well as some white queers).[5] Strange Fruit's declared aim was self-help, providing peer support under the precarious conditions of sex work, against the isolation within often homophobic ethnic communities and the racism of the Dutch queer scene. The collective was also the first to explicitly represent queer of color perspectives, emphasizing shared experiences and goals rather than offering "ethnic" support as a number of other groups focusing on particular migrant communities did, thus challenging the dominant Dutch (and European) gay and lesbian consensus of the mainstream white community as normative, as the model of emancipation to which migrants and minorities from less enlightened backgrounds necessarily aspire to.

Central to this dichotomy as Marlon Ross and others have argued is the closet as "ground zero in the project of articulating an 'epistemology' of sexuality" (Ross, in Johnson and Henderson 2005, 162; also see Perez 2005). Strikingly reflected in the *Forum* report, this understanding of the closet provides a key connection between mainstream gay and lesbian activism and queer theory, as both "argue with great rigor and sophistication that the binary between closeted and uncloseted sexual desire is a primary determinant of modernity and modernism" (Ross 2005, 162). By employing this binary, queer discourse buys into a system of heteronormativity fundamentally depending on legitimate and illegitimate subjects, privileging an either-or binary that rejects the negotiating of in-between spaces and precludes disidentification as a strategy that questions the idea of a clear cut "before and after" of (queer) identity construction. The link between linear mobility and progress ties the normative coming out story to the escape narratives of (ex)Muslim women analyzed in the last chapter: both present communities of color as spaces of oppression that need to be left behind in order to enter the domain of the liberated consumer-citizen: "The closet narrativizes gay and lesbian identity in a manner that violently excludes or includes the subjects it names according to their access to specific kinds of privacy, property, and mobility" (Perez 2005, 177).

By focusing on minority queers' inability to come out and live openly, the Forum report puts them firmly on the wrong side of the binary and presents the step of approaching one of the minority LGBT organizations working under the umbrella of larger Dutch queer organizations, namely the COC, as the way to cross over to the right side, out of the (cultural) closet.[6] This characterization drastically differs from Strange Fruit's assessment of why minority queers are ambiguous about white organizations like the COC:

> It is often assumed that all minorities have psycho-social problems, leading to lots of questions about "problematic" behavior, . . . criminal behavior, runaways, drugs, prostitution . . . sexuality and supposed taboos in the diverse communities, often based on the assumption of backwardness/underdevelopment.
>
> It is hardly ever discussed what problems these minority youths encounter within the Dutch society/the Dutch education system, in gay and lesbian organizations, subcultures, in contacts, friendships, relationships with Dutch peers/adults, hardly ever is there room for survival strategies, statements by the youths themselves or for the insights of black/migrant experts. (Strange Fruit 1997, 23, my translation)

The group was speaking from experience: founded without any resources, Strange Fruit had constituted itself as a workgroup within the Amsterdam COC. This proved problematic later as changes in the COC's management structure brought about more formal control of the workgroups' budgets, use of space, and the requirement for each group to name an official coordinator with extended powers. This demand clashed fundamentally with Strange Fruit's radically nonhierarchal structure. The collective functioned through largely independent subgroups, organizing themselves around particular themes that covered an immensely broad spectrum from a refugee support group to weekly Safer Sex and Culture evenings, focused on AIDS education through various media; the weekly local radio program *Global Perspectives* covering everything from Amsterdam news to queer activism in Zimbabwe; a monthly party and performance event; the weekly *Women of Color Café*, in part devoted to numerous cooperations with feminist organizations, in part spawning new groups like ALOA (Asian Lesbians Outside Asia); and the Strange Fruit Machine, responsible for the group's visual art production, from flyers to posters and slide shows. This variety of activities was driven by Strange Fruit's internal diversity, combining artists and activists, feminists and AIDS educators, refugees, and members of the second generation, believers, and atheists.

While productive and contributing to the group's unique position, this diversity also frequently led to tensions, which were primarily resolved through a radically democratic structure, granting far-reaching autonomy to subgroups while retaining overall coherence through biweekly, open round-table meetings at which all decisions were made:

> One of the strongest forces keeping Strange Fruit together is the principle of self-help. Connected to peer education and expressed in a nonhierarchical decision making process, known as the roundtable. Initiatives are not created by an acting board and then delegated to the members of Strange Fruit but are suggested by the members of the roundtable. They are expected to put their ideas into practice themselves and receive the necessary financial, technical, and practical support to do so. (Strange Fruit 1997, 40)

Due to the centrality of these principles, the group refused to reorganize according to the COC's demands, choosing its nonhierarchical structure over the financial security provided by the larger organization. This response in turn was read by the COC mainly in terms of culture (and class), as reflecting a Third World dependence on collective structures preventing the level of organization and effectiveness provided by the Western commitment to individuality—an attitude that had led to tensions earlier:

> In the eyes of Strange Fruit's target groups, the image of the COC was defined by a "Western, white" view of homosexuality. An understanding of individual identity construction that wasn't shared by the Strange Fruiters against the backdrop of their own cultures. Homosexual behavior is indeed universal, homosexual identity is not. (Strange Fruit 1997, 39)

Consequently, Strange Fruit split from the COC and in order to be able to operate independently and receive direct funding, officially constituted itself as a foundation. This too required the introduction of a certain hierarchy and while the positions of chairperson, secretary, and treasurer were treated as largely symbolic, leaving the round table as the actual source of decisions, the move toward a formal organization created a conflict with the group's mission that was never fully resolved. An additional source of tension was the constant expansion of activities over the more than ten years of the group's existence. It speaks to the success of Strange Fruit's strategy that it gradually became a main hub of queer of color activism in the Netherlands if not continental Europe, a major access point for people looking for help and information, increasingly sent there by other organizations or the state. This process despite its positive implications put increasing stress on the organization (whose core membership never exceeded twenty people), especially since it remained vigorously peer group focused, keeping the main emphasis on empowerment and self-help. As the group stated in its 1996 annual report:

> Strange Fruit's crucial reason of existence since its creation in 1989 is to increase offers for self-help and to support individual strategies of resistance and this will certainly remain true for the future. All other organizational activities need to be seen as "created and put into practice" in the service of this central task.
>
> Professionalization is thus no end in itself but a "means to": Within Strange Fruit we have tried our best over the last couple of years to respond as seriously and professionally as possible to the quests for help addressed at us. Not by taking on the methods and jargon of social service workers. But through trying to learn about the society we live in and about the norms and values we are dealing with. (Strange Fruit 1997, 7)

While this approach worked as long as Strange Fruit remained an informally organized group, structured around biweekly round-table meetings, it became increasingly difficult with the group's growing interaction with authorities and the social services sector, forcing the activists into a position they had always resisted, namely that of representatives, spokespeople, mediators, and service providers for migrant and minority queers, demanding from them a complicated balancing act between autonomy and playing by the system's rules.

A key example of this is Strange Fruit's work with and for queer refugees, symptomatically initiated by members who were refugees themselves, aware of the plethora of problems facing this group. While the Netherlands are more likely than most other European nations to grant refugee status on the grounds of sexual orientation, there are still a number of often-unrecognized hurdles to overcome. For their application to succeed, refugees need to provide proof of antigay policies in their home countries, something that is often hard to do not only because this kind of information is not easy to get, but also because the subject of homosexuality is difficult to discuss not only with, but also for lawyers, social workers, and health care professionals (as a result, lawyers too busy to gather the necessary background information tend to advise their clients not to mention their homosexuality and to apply for asylum on other grounds). Strange Fruit took a radically different approach to empowering queer refugees, turning to art in order to create an alternative archive aimed at providing legal as well as emotional support:

> The documentation we are looking for consists of personal stories, articles about people in similar situations, information on politics and the nation in general for the lawyer, poetry, prose, and other literature expressing the feelings and experiences of homosexual migrants in the West, and finally regular news in the form of newspaper clippings or newsletters . . . Many refugees do not talk about being persecuted due to their sexual orientation. They do not identify as gay or lesbian. Their behavior, not their identity is homosexual. Exactly because of that it is so important to have information from and about people in similar situations in the form of literature—prose or poetry. In there, you recognize your feelings and experiences as a refugee. (Strange Fruit 1997, 29)

Accordingly, Strange Fruit's refugee work consisted not only of finding competent lawyers, cooperating with Vluchtelingenwerk, the nation's largest refugee support organization, and protesting against Dutch cooperation with nations like Romania and Zimbabwe known for their homophobic policies, but also of poetry workshops. The refusal to separate "culture" and "politics" helped the group not to dissolve into specialized segments while at the same time allowing refugees who had sought support to take an active position as participant rather than as client or victim. An example of this strategy is the Strange Fruit Machine's poetry poster project for the 1996 feminist Dansen op de Denkvloer (Dancing on the Thinkfloor) conference, in which the group's female members and supporters created one hundred posters with poems written by lesbians of color from across the world as well as by the Strange Fruit women themselves (Strange Fruit 1997, 33).

The group's highly creative and eclectic appropriation of elements of both queer culture and the various ethnic communities represented by its members, combined with queer and feminist "body politics," is reflected in the central role of performance in their activism, starting with the earliest activities in AIDS education work. Strange Fruit's first outreach project took the form of safer sex performances targeting clubs frequented by queers of color, including the Strange Fruiters. Handing out condoms, dental dams, and safer sex promo materials produced by themselves, the activists resisted the separation of pleasure and education, body and mind, something that was continued later when the group organized its own, widely popular parties, providing a low-threshold outreach site and platform for performers from within and beyond their membership.

The Safer Sex and Culture work group, eventually spinning off into the independent Together We Live group focusing exclusively on AIDS education, targeting minority and migrant communities and organized by long-time Strange Fruit member Jay Haime, was another key site of the group's cultural activism. Drawing on the very direct ways in which the AIDS crisis brought the body back into discourses of queer identity and on the radically different material positions of the affected bodies, the weekly meetings were both local and diasporic in their approach. Meant to empower participants and to allow them to function as multipliers within their respective contexts and communities, activities drew from the various strengths and experiences present, from cooperations with female leaders within the Surinamese community through *Tai Anjisa* (a style of headscarf tying) courses, using Afro-Surinamese dress as a means of communication in AIDS education, to African American activist Reggie Williams introducing participants to the work of black queer U.S. artists and activists like Barbara Smith, Marlon Riggs, and Essex Hemphill.

The latter connected Strange Fruit to an argument rooted in women of color feminism and situated in the broader field of queer of color critique, which actively aims at the queering of ethnicity by returning critical attention to the reality of raced and gendered bodies. This is in part in reaction to a trend of disembodiment in queer theory (Halberstam 2006, 16), a detachment from the experiential knowledge central to the theorizing strategies of communities of color. This detachment in part was borne out of a justified critique of identity politics, but nevertheless replicates dominant Western forms of intellectual discourse separating mind from body and theory from practice, to such an extent in fact that queer studies threaten to become a sanctuary of white high theory. While queer of color critique shares queer theory's skepticism toward identity politics, it is grounded however in a critical sense of community as a necessary part of resisting interlocking systems of power (including those presented by queer and diaspora discourses). The body as site of repressive performativity as well as performative disidentification thus is necessarily central to queer of color theory as well as activism (as it is in hip-hop), since strategies of racialization rely heavily on a mind-body divide, relegating cultural productions, traditions, and modes of resistance of racialized populations to

the latter, something from which queer theory is not exempt: "poststructuralist theories of sexuality frequently build a case for the instability of
sexual identities by using black bodies as their stable foundation, as the
deep well of empirical experience on and beyond which their own fluid
identities can be playfully manipulated and differentiated" (Ross 2005,
176; also see Perez 2005).[7]

Strange Fruit persistently explored this tension, resisting the divide
through multiple strategies. One of the group's earliest members was
filmmaker Andre Reeder, whose 1996 documentary *Aan niets overleden*
(Cause of Death: Nothing), is a moving portrait of the Dutch Surinamese
community's response to the AIDS crisis, which—without excusing
homophobia and sexism—reflects Strange Fruit's commitment to self-
help, empowerment, and engagement with and within communities of
color. The film follows Shanti Paraga, a gay, HIV+ Indo-Surinamese
man, lovingly supported and taken care of by his siblings; Ethel Pangel, a
straight Afro-Surinamese mother of two who had been living with AIDS
since the 1980s, moving from internalized shame and marginalization
to becoming an outspoken activist for women living with the virus; and
Marlène Ceder, a social worker and Winti (an Afro-Surinamese religious
practice in which women play a key role; see Wekker 2006) practitioner
who uses her role in the Surinamese community to promote sex education
(Reeder 1996). The film reflects Strange Fruit's insistence in going against
the dominant dogma by drawing on traditions of migrant and minority cultures, persistently seeking contact with community organizations
and elders while maintaining explicitly queer positions. This resulted for
example in the incorporation of Afro-Caribbean practices such as *toris*,
storytelling events that offered an alternative to and creolization of the
Western coming-out narratives resisting dominant before and after binaries of Western queer identity discourses, instead emphasizing the complex and ongoing dynamic between queers of color and their communities which can be and often are both safe havens and sites of oppression.[8]

In some ways, Strange Fruit's eclectic, fusionist approach was similar
to Euro-hip-hop, allowing further creolizations, a mixture of African diaspora with "Oriental" traditions, resulting in specifically European forms,
both politically and artistically and creating new strategies appropriate
for a multiethnic community rejecting the normativity of a white Western
model of (homosexual) identity, resisting and creating alternatives to the
supposed dichotomies between cultures and the pressure to choose one
side, to assimilate into the Western queer discourse or into a heteronormative "culture of origin." In all of this, Strange Fruit built on the central
role of vernacular culture, music, dance, storytelling, in both the African

and Muslim diasporas. While this centrality of the vernacular in dominant discourses is read as a sign of traditionalism, a means to keep alive
outdated norms and values clashing with a dynamic majority culture sur-
rounding self-isolating minorities, Strange Fruit placed it at the center of
a poetics of relation, turning it into a disidentificatory source of European
queer of color identity.[9]

For more than a decade, the group was able to maintain an antiessentialist, dialogic practice in which identities and discourses were eclectically
appropriated, rearranged, and transformed without a single model of ethnic, gender, or sexual definitions becoming normative. This rather unusual
success I believe is due to a number of factors: the fusionist approach to
cultural influences as well as outreach strategies; the self-help principle
minimizing the hierarchy between members and target group; the gender
balance bringing different perspectives into constant dialogue; and a local,
peer group focused activism combined with a global perspective connecting the group to a large transnational feminist and queer of color network,
reaching as far as Morocco, South Africa, South Korea, and Zimbabwe,
but just as importantly, across national borders to other European queer
and feminist of color groups, facing very similar conditions and debates.

Genderqueer Terrorist Drag in Europe's Center

In November 2006, Tom Sellar, editor of the journal *Theater* and admirer
of Adelheid Roosen's plays, attended a performance of *The Veiled Monologues* in Berlin's multiethnic Kreuzberg neighborhood, later summarizing
and contextualizing the event for his U.S. readers:

> The actors had been preparing for weeks to perform the piece in
> Turkish, hoping to speak more directly to an audience from Germany's
> enormous immigrant community. It was a damp and chilly Tuesday
> night, and the crowd was small. But its response was unmistakable.
> A cluster of Turkish men sat in a middle row, some with their arms
> crossed, and did not laugh. At the back, a group of Turkish women
> looked unhappy to hear the stories, and one noisily made her way to
> the door in the middle of the performance, sobbing uncontrollably. The
> drama's troubling resonances for them were clear. (Sellar 2007, 15)

Sellar's reading of the audience (more than of the play) encapsulates
dominant notions of the clash between radical art addressing taboo subjects (here, both criticizing the dominant society for stereotyping the
Muslim community and said community for failing to address its own
shortcomings) and the atavistic ethnic cultures providing the diversity

attracting the creative class, including playwrights, to the new metropolises, but who prove incapable of appreciating, or even understanding, the art their exotic presence inspires. The silent, hostile men and silenced, unhappy women in the Kreuzberg cultural center appear as encapsulating the essence of migrant communities in Europe and it is likely not coincidental that Sellar chose this location to make his point as more than any other in Northwest Europe, Berlin's Kreuzberg neighborhood has come to symbolize this tension. Situated just west of the former wall dividing the city, Kreuzberg is the German capital's smallest borough, with one of the highest population densities and the youngest inhabitants. A traditional working-class neighborhood, post–World War II, its location and rent-controlled, low-quality housing made Kreuzberg one of West Berlin's less desirable neighborhoods. Consequently, it became home to the groups with the least bargaining power in the Federal Republic's burgeoning economy, primarily the so-called guest workers, whose often abysmal living conditions were justified with the assumption that they would return home after having worked a couple of years in the nation's automobile industry, shipping yards, or on its construction sites. But just like the substandard "temporary" housing in the French suburbs, these quarters became the permanent home of a growing migrant population brought in from Spain, Italy, Greece, Yugoslavia, and Turkey in the 1950s and 60s (Göktürk, Gramling, and Kaes 2007). Over the years, Kreuzberg's population became primarily associated with the latter nation, the oft-repeated fact that Berlin houses the largest "Turkish" population outside of Turkey gaining it the moniker "Little Istanbul."

In the 1970s, Kreuzberg with its blocks of decaying early twentieth-century buildings was a center of the squatter movement, and the fledgling punk scene further contributed to the edgy image the borough became famous for over the next decade, with its unique mixture of activists, artists, and "ethnic" communities.[10] Today, Kreuzberg has the highest number of minorities in all of Berlin—with over half of its one hundred fifty thousand inhabitants, of multiple backgrounds, a majority being of Turkish or Kurdish descent, with one-third of the population not possessing German citizenship (most often due to the *jus sanguinis* practiced until 2001, which did not grant citizenship to residents born in Germany of non-German parents). And despite a recent gentrification—resulting in signifying neighboring borough Neukölln, with a similar demographic, as the new primary "problem zone," symbolized by an excessive number of minorities—Kreuzberg remains one of Berlin's poorest neighborhoods.[11] During the height of liberal multiculturalism in the 1980s and the early days of the "creative city" hype, the presence of minorities made

Kreuzberg a colorful, exotic, and exciting site of consumption of foreign-ness; more recently, the discourse shifted to tropes of parallel societies, ethnic enclaves, and the Islamization of Europe. This makes Kreuzberg fairly typical for the urban neighborhoods in which the activism I am focusing on originates, with disproportionally high numbers of minority populations, because of postwar labor migration to the continent's indus-trial hubs, which in turn were heavily affected by the massive deindustri-alization of the 1980s.

While the increasingly harsh anti-immigrant rhetoric of recent years does not necessarily imply an actual attempt to expel all "migrants," it works to remind racialized minorities that being in Europe for several gen-erations does not translate into the acquisition of permanent rights, not to mention full legitimacy as "European." Instead, the growing economic exclusion of racialized populations as neoliberal ideologies take hold of the uniting Europe leaves minority youths in a space of precariousness and permanent insecurity as they become increasingly identified as a violent threat. This discursive shift can be traced back to the mid-1980s when media and police began to identify minority youths with the presence of gangs, ignoring the fact that many of these groups, such as Antifascist Genclik (Antifascist Youth) were organized in response to a rise in racist skinhead gang activity, escalating after the fall of the Berlin Wall in 1989 (Engelschaller and Pieper 2005). While right-wing violence remained a downplayed issue until well into the 1990s (and even then largely being perceived as an East German problem, exemplifying the former social-ist Europe's missing out on the West's postwar process of redemption), gangs and people of color easily fell into a naturalized connection within the U.S.-focused frame of reference already introduced in response to the rising popularity of hip-hop culture (and again employed in France dur-ing the 2005 uprising). While the racism to which the gangs in part re-sponded thus remained unexamined—the default term when it was ever mentioned being "xenophobia," thus allowing to keep the externaliza-tion of nonwhites intact even when condemning violence against them—"culture" as a driving force behind the existence of primarily Turkish gangs became central in media discourses. But notwithstanding that gangs usually were (self)identified as ethnic, they were primarily neighborhood- or street-based. One of them was the 36ers, originating in Kreuzberg's Naunynstrasse. Filmmaker Neco Çelik, a former member, recalls[12]:

> For the 36ers' group dynamic, the important thing was that we were
> friends and that there was no outside leading or organizing us. We
> just were a bunch of people on the same wavelength. It had nothing

to do with Turkish, German, Kurdish or other nationalities. It was
about where you lived and who you had grown up with. You just
needed to share a certain history. We were people who grew up
together on Naunynstrasse . . . In the end it was the same for us as it
was for German youths breaking out and rebelling against authoritar-
ian family structures. We lived double lives then: at home the one our
fathers wanted and the life we wanted on the street. We wanted to
be recognized, respected, and of course score with chicks. (Çelik, in
Interface 2005, 212)[13]

As discussed in chapter 1, the local, the city or neighborhood, became an
alternative public space for minority youths, in part replacing national
allegiances. Youth centers played a big part in this: the 36ers (as well as the
36 Girls) congregated in the Naunynritze, a progressive community center
that offered a variety of activities, including access to audio-visual equip-
ment, allowing budding filmmakers like Çelik—who later returned as a
youth worker—to take their first steps, and becoming the home of some of
Berlin's first hip-hop crews, such as Islamic Force, founded in 1986 by four
Kreuzberg youths from different ethnic backgrounds—Spanish, Albanian,
and Turkish German—drawn together by the common experience of being treated like "strangers in their own country" (Körberling, in Interface 2005). Through their fusionist style, they were one of the pioneers of
Oriental hip-hop—the first genuinely European appropriation of hip-hop,
created by minority artists drawing on Middle Eastern influences—and by
choosing a name that was less a reflection of religious affiliation than a
tongue-in-cheek yet confrontational reaction to common mainstream stereotypes about Kreuzberg's inhabitants, Islamic Force employed the same
strategy Strange Fruit and Kanak Attak would after them.

While the presence of different groups (squatters, punks, the antifascist
Left) shaped life in the borough, interactions between them and second-
generation youths were sporadic and fraught with miscommunication
(Engelschall and Pieper 2005). This began to change as hip-hop became
more popular in Kreuzberg in the 1980s, introduced by black U.S. soldiers
stationed in West Berlin through clubs like the SO36 (Çelik 2005, 212).
The SO36 Club, or simply "SO," located centrally on Kreuzberg's Ora-
nienstrasse, could look back on a long history: it came into existence as
a beer garden the mid-nineteenth century and became a rallying point for
the squatter, punk, and new wave scenes in the 1970s.[14] In between being
temporarily closed down several times, the SO became Berlin's most famous alternative event venue, but had little to offer to the neighborhood's
minority communities. After its reopening in 1990, the club began to cater
to a somewhat more diverse audience, staging hip-hop concerts as well as

queer nights. Both merged in the immensely popular Gayhane, a monthly event organized by the Salon Oriental collective, attracting a mixed audience of queer and straight, white and minority, by combining live music and performance, including the Oriental Dancefloor featuring openly queer Turkish-German DJ Ipek, who had gained international recognition with her mix of Middle Eastern and hip-hop styles.

While the Gayhane parties are ongoing and growing in popularity, its roots within the activism of the Turkish-German genderqueer drag collective Salon Oriental have moved to the background. Founded by Sabuha Salaam (aka Cihangir) and Fatma Souad in the late 1980s and active into the early 2000s, Salon Oriental produced multimedia trash performances addressing a range of topics affecting racial and sexual minorities in postcold war Germany from a perspective rarely, if ever, seen before. Salaam and Souad, a gay man and a transwoman (later joined by white German drag queen Edeltraut Plörrenhöfer, who describes the group's style as "trash, comedy, and dance"), had a background not too different from that of the Strange Fruit founders: having grown up in working-class, migrant families and ending up more or less permanently unemployed, they had little connection with Kreuzberg's radical white Left and were instead politicized though their precarious position within Berlin's queer and Turkish communities, requiring a constant process of negotiation and translation that provided ample material for their performances.

Salon Oriental's style, a mixture of classic drag show, physical comedy, and agitprop, is reminiscent of Los Angeles–based Vaginal Davis's performances, categorized as "queer drag" by José Esteban Muñoz, who argued that the latter unlike commercial drag "presenting sanitized and desexualized queer subjects for liberal consumption" stirs up desires beyond social rules (Muñoz 1997, 99).[15] Vaginal Davis's "terrorist drag," at odds with conventions of academic queer theory as well as those of an increasingly commercialized gay scene, according to Muñoz uses "parody and pastiche as strategy to create queer black power" (Muñoz 1997, 99), and this is an approach that can certainly be recognized in Salon Oriental's performances such as Fatma's Wedding, about two Turkish-German families meeting at the wedding of their children (who turn out be queer); What I Always Wanted to Know About Belly Dancing, addressing the trivialization and appropriation of Middle Eastern culture in(to) the German mainstream; Kidnapping of the Promised, about arranged marriages between Turkish-German men and Turkish women; and Maria 2000—The New Christmas Story, in which transwomen mess up heteronormative gender relations and bring about salvation by becoming able to bear children (Becker 1999).

Like Vaginal Davis, Salon Oriental failed to meet dominant standards of "political art." Viewed through the lens of queer of color critique, however, the group's performances at queer clubs show an intersectional approach to identity and community as exemplified in their Oriental Airlines or How Do I Get to the Black Sea Clinic? performance, inspired by the widely publicized case of "Mehmet," a fourteen-year-old repeat offender, German-born but with Turkish citizenship, who in 1998 was deported to Turkey, while his parents remained in Germany (Wild 2008). Concerned with the rising number of "repatriations" of delinquent so-called second-generation migrants, who actually were born and raised in Germany, meaning that they were largely or completely unfamiliar with the countries they were being sent to, Salon Oriental created a story in which, as Fatma Souad explains:

> A Commisssioner for Aliens, trying to make the deportation as
> pleasant as possible, organizes a training session: "In order for you as
> a *Deutschländer* not to stand out in Turkey too much, you have to go
> through a little re-integration program. You will see how useful this
> is for you. After all, according to our files you haven't been in Turkey
> for 30 years and aren't really up-to-date anymore." Unfortunately, the
> plane needs to make an emergency landing and the commissioner ends
> up in the Black Sea Clinic, where everything is possible from guy to
> girl and the other way around. That is the second topic, transgender.
> (Becker 1999)[16]

Salon Oriental's piece on the "returkification" of Turkish Germans in preparation for their repatriation to a strange homeland perfectly illustrates the erasure of minority identity within the European migrant-citizen binary. At the same time, the inclusion in the narrative of migration and integration of the seemingly unrelated challenges transgender identities pose to a different set of binary constructions in itself undermines the dominant uses of gender and sexuality in migration discourses, thus making Salon Oriental's queer drag exemplary of the strategy of queering ethnicity on various levels. In the course of the play, certainties about national, gender, and sexual identities unravel at light speed, as do notions of civilization and progress. This is achieved through stylistic means, employing a repoliticized version of camp able to reflect destabilized and destabilizing notions of identity and belonging, and following Muñoz's definition of camp as "a strategic response to the breakdown of representation that occurs when a queer, ethnically marked, or other subject encounters his or her inability to fit within the majoritarian representational regime. It is a measured response to the forced evacuation from dominant culture that the minority subject experiences" (Muñoz 1999, 128).

Location too, played an important part in the group's impact. Rather than focusing on entering the dominant culture from which it had been evacuated, Salon Oriental, like Strange Fruit before them, staged its interventions in a subcultural space that—contrary to for example the progressive theater scene, with which Kanak Attak later collaborated—allows for, even desires the presence of colored bodies, but does not necessarily grant them more definitional power, where the rules of engagement within this space are concerned. By turning the queer club scene into the site of their performances, Salon Oriental initiated an explicit engagement with these rules, involving the audience as much as the artists. As Ann Cvetkovich observed: "Queer performance creates publics by bringing together live bodies in space, and the theatrical experience is not just about what's on stage but also about who's in the audience creating community" (Cvetkovich 2003, 9).

Salon Oriental's performances created and queered a community in particular after the group moved to the SO36 in the mid-90s (as a result of Fatma Souad briefly being employed there through a workfare program, see Becker 1999), staging the now internationally famous Gayhane nights, starting with a "Tea Salon" at which the artists greeted each of the usually several hundred visitors personally, followed by performances that built on the audience's familiarity with the interactivity of drag shows in order to engage them in a politicized discourse smoothly transitioning into the Oriental Dancefloor, ending the events in the early hours of the morning. Like Strange Fruit's parties, Gayhane's mixture of political performance and clubbing succeeded in attracting a large and varied audience, in particular one that had mostly stayed away from the SO36, namely the local straight minority youth. Fatma Souad explain this with the latter discovering common ground—both of shared cultures and shared exclusions: "The breeder youth here in the hood wakes up, too, and says: 'Hey, we're here and you won't get rid of us'" (Becker 1999).

Thus, Salon Oriental's introduction of a minoritarian voice, disrespectful of dominant hierarchies of representation with regard to nationality and ethnicity as well as gender and sexuality did not only center the experience of queer minorities but allowed other segments of the audience to relate to and identify with this usually discarded perspective, letting the performances work as a kind of testimonial through interpellation, that is, using "[t]estimony as cultural and historical genre, an event that seeks a witness but may not find one, an interactive occasion in which the relation between speaker and hearer is crucial to the narrative, which becomes performative rather than constative" (Cvetkovich 2003, 28). Through Gayhane, Salon Oriental managed to create witnesses, carrying its performances as embodied archives of an unwritten history. This made it the first local, that is, German of color voice staging a successful and lasting intervention into an artist and activist space in which minorities and migrants had long been present only as objects without representational power. In doing so, the group forged coalitions with other minority artists doing the same, such as rapper Aziza A, the most prominent feminist voice within political hip-hop since her debut in the mid-90s and a frequent guest at Gayhane, or DJ Ipek Ipekçioğlu who has long been part of Turkish–German LGBT activism while negotiating the various spaces she inhabits as a Turkish–German queer woman.[17]

Like Salon Oriental, these artists were the product of a postethnic, translocal context, a positionality reflected in their performances, which eclectically mix influences, challenging the link between purity, authenticity, and legitimacy dominating European—as well as migrant—discourses of belonging by embracing the impure, inauthentic, illegitimate position assigned to Europeans of color. As in the discursive space opened up by Euro hip-hop and the queer memory constructed by black feminism, this combination worked to express positionalities negated in dominant identity formations, making them the source of a new discourse rather than attempting to enter the existing one as legitimate subjects. This inter-minority counterdiscourse began to directly engage with the German mainstream in the late 1990s through the media-savvy, anti-identitarian activism of the translocal Kanak Attak collective.

Subverting the Multicultural Gaze

Germany, Europe's most populous country, and Turkey, the continent's largest Muslim majority nation, have longstanding ties, politically and economically as well as culturally (Adelson 2005). In the current context, however, their relationship is primarily framed within the guest worker discourse, that is, the process widely perceived as ending European ethnic homogeneity by causing a massive influx of foreigners bringing with them fundamentally different cultures whose presence puts an increasing strain on contemporary continental societies. While the perception of labor migrants as outsiders to the nation remains a constant in postwar Europe, the locus of foreignness gradually shifted from a broad definition of the "South," which included Southern Europeans, primarily from Spain, Portugal, Italy, and Greece, contracted by Northwest European nations beginning in the 1950s, toward the Muslim world—and within the

German discourse, Turks have come to symbolize the category *foreigners* as a whole. About four million people, labor migrants and their families, many of them Kurds, entered Western Europe from Turkey through the guest worker programs, roughly half of them moving to German cities like Berlin, which now houses the world's largest Turkish-descended population outside of Turkey; Hamburg, home of the nation's biggest industrial harbor; and Cologne, center of car manufacturing, with Ford, Toyota, Mazda, and others employing tens of thousands of workers, many of them migrants (Göktürk, Gramling, and Kaes 2007). While postwar labor migration made Turkish Germans the nation's largest minority, they are nonetheless still primarily perceived as threatening rather than contributing to German culture, remaining forever foreign and assumed—as Leslie Adelson puts it in her groundbreaking study of Turkish–German literature—"to embody Turkish national culture, as if they had swallowed it whole" (Adelson 2005, 85).[18]

The German mainstream's inability to envision minorities as a legitimate part of the nation, to perceive Turkish Germanness as a viable concept, instead seeing the two attributes as mutually exclusive, an internalized clash of civilizations incapable of coexisting, is exemplified in the celebrations held in Cologne in October 2001, forty years after the German Federal Employment Agency and the Turkish Labor Administration had signed the first recruitment agreement, bringing an initial contingent of migrant workers to Cologne's Ford factory. The city decided to celebrate the anniversary with a festive act held at the Philharmonic Hall. Sponsored by Ford, presided over by the mayor, the event was attended by the Turkish consul and the mayor of Istanbul as well as local notables. In his opening speech, Cologne's mayor, Fritz Schramma, traced the century-long shared history of Islam and Europe, moving between cooperation and conflict, to the current coexistence of Turks and Germans within the city, framing it along similar lines:

> I am thinking here for example of the high concentration in some neighborhoods, in which Turks live completely among themselves, having cut themselves off in somewhat of a ghetto. But how much commonalities dominate is shown not the least in how elements of Turkey have entered our everyday lives, our culinary culture. Ayran and Döner Kebab, Börek and eggplants have become permanent parts of our diet (Schramma 2001).[19]

The mayor's celebration of the positive contributions of "Turks" remains well within the limits of multicultural liberalism and visions of the creative city, presenting them as ideally providing nonthreatening color, adding items to be consumed by (proper) German culture without challenging it (and as in the worst case choosing self-segregation). Nowhere in his speech does Schramma reference the possibility of a Turkish–German identity, despite the fact that the celebrated arrival of the first Turkish "guest workers" four decades earlier makes the presence of a German-born "Turkish" population inevitable. The event, however, does not only reflect the dominant perception of minorities as permanent migrants, forever exiled in the no-man's land of unclear national allegiances, but also the inevitable cracks opening up in this narrative, the unexpected appearance of the suppressed.

The media were of course a massive presence at the celebration of forty years of Turkish migration, including a crew from Kanak TV. Identifying itself as representing Turkish television (and interacting largely in English), it approached military dignitaries, former mayors, and other German attendees with questions like "Where do you come from?" and "When are you going back?" asking them to define German culture, inquiring whether wife beating (as evidenced by the case of a prominent singer and producer in the headlines during this period) or drug use (just having lead to the demise of one of the nation's most prominent soccer coaches) are part of it, citing statistics showing numbers of female university professors in Arab nations being significantly higher than in Germany, and soliciting comments on Bible passages demanding women's subordination to men.

While some of Kanak TV's subjects seemed to quickly get that they were being put on (a *Bundeswehr* officer in particular increasingly angrily called out the "reporters" on the stereotyping and manipulating nature of their questions), most interviewees answered eagerly and earnestly, obviously not sensing any foul play. This response is all the more surprising as the crew's name bears a more than a fleeting resemblance to the term "*Kanake*," the most common derogatory term for "foreigner" in the German language, no doubt familiar to everyone present (but commented upon only once, when a Kanak TV member noted the ethnic divide between guests and workers at the event, the former being mostly white, the latter largely "*Kanaken*," only to be reprimanded by her interviewee for her choice of words)—and a term that with its roots in Germany's colonial past in itself provides a striking example of how the suppressed history of colonialism haunts present day European race relations.[20]

Kanak TV, in fact, is a part of Kanak Attak, an organization founded in 1997 at the Swiss Urban Skillz Hip-Hop Festival by activists from various German cities, most of them second generation from various ethnic backgrounds.[21] The group appeared on the political scene amidst discussions of "the end of multiculturalism" and the "failed integration" in particular of Muslim migrants (similar to the discussions taking place in other parts of Western Europe, such as the Netherlands, at the same time). Kanak Attak entered the debate by proclaiming "the end of dialogue culture," replacing it with "the autonomy of migration," the refusal to justify migrants and minorities' presence in Europe, claiming the right to unrestricted movement for everyone and rejecting regulatory frameworks like refugee policies that leave the right to grant access with Western nations. The crashing of the 2001 celebration of "forty years of migration"—later turned into a ten-minute video shown on local public access TV as well as at Kanak Attak events and short film festivals—was the Cologne group's first intervention, based on the simple plan to use against them majoritarian Germans' objectification and externalization of minorities—in particular through the constant interrogation of origins scathingly summarized by Sheila Mysorekar (who was a founding member of the Initiative Black Germans):

> We invite you to our new show: Guess my Genes. Entertaining gene-guessing with Joe Clueless around the theme "Where do you come from?" Never heard of it? Two groups of candidates, here the Germans (White), there the "Others" (usually German, too, but whatever. The important thing: they don't look like it. Do I have to be more specific? Ok then: those are not the Whites). Then the guessing starts, i.e. the Whites guess the genetic composition of their counterparts. Correct continent: one point, correct country: ten points. The "Others," i.e. the other team, give true and false hints . . . There are more and more candidates for this show. Not only in the U.S. and England. Even right! Here! In! Germany! (Mysorekar, in Ha, al-Samarai, and Mysorekar 2007, 161)

This strategy turned out to be successful beyond expectations as Sun-Ju Choi and Miltiasis Oulio, two members of the group, recall: "The amazing thing in this filming situation was how well it worked to intervene into a societal event with this method and to turn the tables. We were surprised ourselves. After all, we put on the former and the sitting mayor in our interviews" (Choi and Oulis, in Interface 2005, 225). Taking advantage of the "compulsion to answer" that their subjects exhibited in front of a camera, the group pushed the limits of the acceptable—not in order to initiate a "constructive" dialogue, but to expose hidden discursive hierarchies, an approach that was not always well received by a white progressive audience: "The clip produced from the material criticizes the whole integration and multicultural debate in a pointed and self-confident manner and shows that we set rather different norms. At the same time at screenings it caused discomfort for the self-satisfied. The usual claim then was that we would just edit together the statements we needed. Our answer: exactly, that's how the media work" (Choi and Oulis, in Interface 2005, 226).

Kanak Attak's strategy not only deconstructed the workings of media representations of racialized groups, but it also, more importantly, uncovered them as part of the mechanisms of colorblindness. Taking as a starting point the debilitating experience of being forced to justify one's presence that minoritarian subjects have to go through constantly, the group turned it into an empowering tool by transforming individual resistance into communal activism. In forcing the silent codes of colorblindness into the open, Kanak Attak violated the rules of European political discourse.[22] The group criticized cultural hybrid chic and exclusionary essentialism as two sides of the same coin, rejecting identity politics as a response to globalized power structures (while recognizing its importance under particular historical circumstances). The activists defined their aims in the 1998 founding manifesto, published in German, Turkish, English, and French:

> Kanak Attak is not interested in questions about your passport or
> heritage, in fact it challenges such questions in the first place. Kanak
> Attak challenges the conservative and liberal orthodoxy that good
> 'race relations' is simply a matter of tighter immigration control. Our
> common position consists of an attack against the 'Kanakisation'
> of specific groups of people through racist ascriptions, which denies
> people their social, legal and political rights. Kanak Attak is therefore
> anti-nationalist, anti-racist and rejects every single form of identity
> politics, as supported by ethnic absolutist thinking. (Kanak Attak 1998,
> English in original)

The term "Kanak Attak" is clearly evocative of this programmatic—one founding member of the group explains its rejection of colorblind discourses: "The good thing about the name, it reflects the constructedness, it cannot be confused with supposed self-determination, because it transports the racism that cannot be undone with goodwill alone" (Mestre Vives, in Karkayali and Spenkoch 1999, 1). While they come out of a similar context (including direct intersections, such as the involvement of Aziza A and DJ Ipek), Kanak Attak activists drew much more explicitly on the political tradition of the European Left, in particular Italian *operaismo*, than hip-hop artists, black and Muslim feminists, or Strange Fruit did. This is likely due both to some members' close ties to the migrant labor movement and to the stronger presence of academics within the group (most of them students and lecturers). A nationwide association of political and cultural activists,

Poster for Kanak Attak event "Ab einer Million bist Du kein Kanake mehr!" in Hamburg 2001. Copyright Kanak Attak.

organized in informal local groups in most of Germany's urban centers, Kanak Attak combined eclectic theoretical inspirations, ranging from the Black Panther Party to queer theory, and infused them into nontraditional methods of political activism, including hip-hop performances, multimedia shows, billboards, and the Cologne-based video activism of Kanak TV.

The refusal to act "responsibly" and engage with majoritarian progressive movements on their terms, instead calling them out on their own prejudices in the worst possible way by making fun of them, is characteristic for Kanak Attak's overall attitude toward a German Left that saw itself as speaking for subaltern migrants: "The starting point for our Cologne group was to find a method that shows that we don't accept this talking above the heads of migrants. Premise of our work was the rejection of the predefinition of certain terms and discourses. Our camera method is disrespect towards racist hierarchies that usually cannot be challenged" (Choi and Oulis, in Interface 2005, 223).

In practicing this challenge, Kanak TV took advantage of the desire for "diversity" within multicultural neoliberalism that opened spaces for minority visibility in restricted areas, using it as a starting point to voice a critique of the very limits of this discourse by constantly violating its rules. Kanak Attak engaged much more aggressively with dominant culture than the self-help focused Strange Fruit, and German Left and liberal venues were initially quite willing to grant the group a platform, though their desire to give up their uncontested position as the nation's progressive voice turned out to be much less pronounced. The group's early media exposure created an instant forum, but included the risk of being domesticated into mere entertainers, potentially undermining the attempt to introduce issues such as structural racism, economic marginalization, and migration regimes into the mainstream debate. For some time however, Kanak Attak seemed able to pull off its queer strategy: popping up everywhere but avoiding to be nailed down anywhere, dancing circles around the logic of white antiracism and multiculturalism, fulfilling their mission of introducing the postethnic discourse among minorities into the mainstream, reminding the majority that their self-positioning as the norm is not natural and open to contestation.

At a moment when migrants and minorities were beginning to be recognized as a semi-permanent presence under the heading of "foreign fellow citizens" (*ausländische Mitbürger*) or "fellow citizens of migrant background" (*Mitbürger mit Migrationshintergrund*), the group's insistence on the term *Kanake* brought to the open the continuing inequalities hidden under the new terminology. Within this construct, *Kanake* appears not as an identifiable and containable identity, but as a concept that, similar to David Halperin's definition of queer, incorporates "whatever is at odds with the normal, the legitimate, the dominant . . . an identity without essence . . . [that] demarcates not a positivity but a positionality vis-à-vis the normative . . . a horizon of possibility whose precise extent and heterogenous scope cannot in principle be delimited in advance" (Halperin 1995, 62). Resonating with diasporic as well as queer understandings of identity, Kanak Attak's activism rejected the burden of representational power while simultaneously claiming the right to reject majoritarian definitions, not by offering "positive" alternatives, but by disrespectfully deconstructing hidden hierarchies. Kanak TV used this method not only in their initial video, but also in later projects such as "White Ghetto," in which the activists interview inhabitants of an exclusively white German middle-class neighborhood in Cologne, confronting them about their problematic self-segregation—a tongue-in-cheek response to statements such as that of the city's mayor cited above, claiming that minorities are kept from full integration into society only by their own unwillingness, their "self-ghettoization."[23]

Kanak TV's strategy starts within the parameters of identity-based antiracism, only to turn them upside down, illustrating their failure in responding to a steady normalization of racist exclusions through the vocabulary of "postideological" liberal multiculturalism:

> It is important not to fall back on identity positions. Those aren't the center, they are being used. Power relations are at the center and are being questioned. The question is not what is what? It is about processes. Who does what to whom? It's about finding the media language to inscribe us as actors and subjects into societal processes. The clips anticipate discursively the desired change in power relations. And they thematize those that are already happening. (Choi and Oulis, in Interface 2005, 228)

This strategy depends on remaining unpredictable and provocative in order to avoid becoming just another consumable hip pop culture phenomenon, and Kanak TV arguably suffered from this constant pressure to reinvent itself, with later projects being less effective than the group's earlier successful attempts at challenging media representations of minorities. Nonetheless, Kanak TV's interventions succeeded in making visible processes rather than postionalities, shifting the focus from the racialized subjects to those engaged in racializing them.

Recovering the Hidden Histories of Migrant Agency

Establishing a visual counterdiscourse among marginalized groups was central to Kanak Attak's strategy in remaining politically effective and avoiding absorption into mainstream pop culture. As important however was the group's grounding in traditions of migrant resistance that had often been ignored in accounts of both the labor movement and histories of migration. A key strategy in resisting commodification was the activists' ability to contextualize their politics both horizontally—in association with various other migration activists in Europe, mainly through the Frassanito network[24]—and vertically, by placing their work within a continuous history of resistance. In employing an understanding of cultural politics similar to the one developed by women of color feminism in the 1970s, the Kanak Attak activists referenced a political tradition made invisible by the dominant division between politics and culture: the everyday resistance of migrants and minorities that takes place, often spontaneously, outside established political structures. Recovering this subversive history was one of the group's main goals, as a founding member recalls: "We wanted to uncover a tradition that had worked partly hidden and was buried. The idea was: If you have your own history, you gain power, you have something to refer to, something to hand down and make your own" (Bojadzijev 2001, 14).

Kanak Attak's first large-scale attempt at doing this took place in 2001 with the multimedia KanakHistoryRevue (titled "Opel Pitbull Autoput") at Berlin's prestigious Volksbühne theater, which had played an important role in progressive art and activism throughout most of the twentieth century.[25] The revue brought together minority and migrant artists and activists from a variety of fields, staging readings, film screenings, and performances—among others by Salon Oriental and hip-hop artists such as Aziza A—as well as Kanak Attak activists offering reenactments of forty years of labor migrant presence in Germany, its fractured, nonlinear presentation radically differing from mainstream commemorations such as the one satirized by Kanak TV in Cologne. Central to this construction of an alternative history of migration was the "wild," that is, spontaneous strike of migrant workers at Cologne's Ford automobile factory in 1973. The Ford strike, unsupported by the strong German unions (who long refused to see migrant workers as part of their constituency) and organized largely by unskilled Turkish laborers, is an example of the *operaismo* that figures prominently in Kanak Attak's model of resistance. Theorized by neo-Marxist authors such as Mario Tronti and Antonio Negri and appropriated in the 1960s by factory workers in Italy frustrated with the European Left's preoccupation with "structures" as opposed to their concrete workplace struggles, the *operaist* direct action approach influenced a variety of movements from the situationists to the autonomists and the Zapatistas (Tronti 1974). The strike at the Cologne factory, where 14,500 of 35,000 workers were migrants, 12,000 of whom came from Turkey (the rest were for the largest part Italian), was caused by the mass firing of three hundred Turkish employees and lasted for three days, before the several thousand workers who had occupied the factory were finally defeated by the combined forces of management, police, the Turkish labor ministry, scabs brought in from Belgium, and not least the media, which in a radical twisting of what had actually happened titled "German workers liberate Ford" when the strike was broken and concluded: "Those people are not guests anymore" (Kraushaar 2004, 4).[26]

The strike at Ford in the summer of 1973 violated the rules of all accepted discourses around nation, migration, labor, and integration: it did not fit in narratives of the labor movement due to its "unorganized" nature, taking place against union orders and carried out by a part of the labor force these same unions considered apolitical if not prepolitical; the workers singing the Turkish national anthem before marching were off-putting to an antinationalist radical German Left; their rejection of the authority of the Turkish labor ministry's representative (who called them "deserters from the Turkish army") was an embarrassment to the Turkish government; the lack of overt political organizing (despite the German of the two spokesmen being a member of the Communist Party); their singing, dancing, and reciting poetry instead of producing pamphlets did not provide the right material for heroic tales of resistance. Kanak Attak approached the strike in a way that did not require a homogenizing of its fractured and spontaneous manner, but instead valued exactly these qualities. Meant to represent "organized and unorganized forms of resistance against racism" (Kanak Attak 2001), the KanakHistoryRevue mixed film clips, interviews, performance, and music to retell spectacular and unspectacular instances of postwar migrant history invisible in dominant accounts.

The focus on the neglected everyday experiences of the first generation inscribed traditions of resistance into a German postwar history in which migrants remain extremely marginal.[27] This strategy did affect dominant representations and opened communication between different generations of migrants whose relationship was often made tense by the lack of a vocabulary with which to address radically different but interrelated experiences of the first and second generation. The revue was less successful, however, in reaching its intended audience of fellow *Kanaken*. The cooperation with the Volksbühne theater provided an attractive venue, representing a long radical tradition, and generated an impressive public response. It drew however, as one Kanak Attak member put it, "the wrong audience," consisting largely of members of the majoritarian left and liberal art and activist scene (Cheesman 2005, 192). While the genderqueer activists of Strange Fruit and Salon Oriental explicitly chose venues and forms familiar to its target audience, risking (or even welcoming) the absence of the white Left, Kanak Attak, much closer to mainstream debates even while being critical of them, chose the opposite strategy, with somewhat predictable results, repeated a year later for the second large project that brought together activists from local Kanak Attak groups across the nation. Konkret Konkrass took place in May 2002, again at Berlin's Volksbühne and a couple of days later at the Schauspiel in Frankfurt, a comparable venue in the German city with the highest percentage of migrant and minority populations.

Following a pattern largely similar to the first event, the second revue added an exploration of dominant gender perceptions largely absent in the group's first rewriting of migrant history. All self-representations of first generation migrants only enter the public memory filtered, but there is more than one level of suppression and the stories of migrant women are generally less accessible, even through alternative archives. While almost a third of labor migrants in Germany were women, they are usually absent from migrant, labor, and feminist histories as economic and political agents (Weber 2004; Göktürk, Gramling, and Kaes 2007). In contrast, Kanak Attak's 2002 revue featured a performance based on the experiences of a cleaning woman—the single most important identity for first-generation migrant women, both economically and discursively; in the 1970s, the image of the headscarf-clad cleaning woman became *the* primary cultural symbol for the Turkish minority presence as a whole (complimented by the male garbage man, often generically dubbed "Fatima" and "Ali" respectively). In presenting these women as autonomous subjects negotiating the limited space granted to them in their position of extreme economic powerlessness exactly through transgressing the line between the political and the cultural, Kanak Attak's retracing of the female migration experience avoided both the romanticizing of female solidarity and the victim discourse shared by the dominant culture of Western feminism as well as the first generation of migrant writers and filmmakers, who often presented migrant women as mute, passive objects of repression.[28]

In both revues, Kanak Attak succeeded in making visible the repressed presence of first-generation migrants in the early decades of the Federal Republic exactly by focusing on their interventions into German society, their daily practices of covert and open resistance. The refusal to see migrants primarily in the context of their origin or journey rather than through their impact on the societies of destination worked effectively at destabilizing comfortable notions of Us and Them shared by a majoritarian Left unwilling to confront its own racist practices. Kanak Attak's strategy was less successful, however, in forging bonds with other multiethnic migrant organizations, especially those holding on to various levels of identity politics. This became most pronounced in the group's increasingly tense exchange with the refugee rights group Karawane für die Rechte von Flüchtlingen und MigrantInnen (Caravan for the Rights of Refugees and Migrants). Disagreements escalated around the Kanak Attak slogan of the "autonomy of migration," rejecting as divisive all justifications for migrants' presence in Europe.

Kanak Attak defended the necessity of this strategy in undermining hierarchizations of migrants and the separation of refugees into "good ones," persecuted in their homelands, and "bad ones," who leave for economic reasons, while the Karawane emphasized the ongoing neocolonial exploitation of the Global South as the reason for the very presence of migrants in the West. The group, consisting of political refugees from Africa, the Middle East, and Latin America as well as German activists, focuses its work among other things on the *Residenzpflicht*, the law forcing refugees to remain within the limits of the—often rural— community they have been assigned to, discussed in chapter 1 with regard to civil war refugees; on preventing deportations; and on police violence, frequently directed against African men. Their slogan, "We are here because you destroy our countries," expresses a sentiment diametrically opposed to Kanak Attak's "we are already among you, deal with it." Maik Adebayo Alabi, a Karawane member summarizes the disagreement:

> The conflict between Kanak Attak and the Karawane is based on different political backgrounds. Kanak Attak focuses on the situation of migrants without asylum background, while the Karawane puts the living conditions of refugees and the situation in their home countries in the center of its activism. The Karawane often sees Kanak Attak as a privileged group of migrants that did little or nothing in support of refugees—even though they are at the bottom of the social ladder. (Kanak Attak und Karawane, in Interface 2005, 362)

The Karawane assumes an internationalist, anti-imperialist, antiracist stance, holding European governments responsible for centuries of exploitation continued into the present, putting an emphasis on the liberation of the home countries whose conditions are posited as the root cause of migration to the West. In doing so, the group uses the European human rights discourse, showing how the continent's governments persistently violate their own declared humanitarian agenda by exploiting the

Global South, supporting corrupt dictators, and violating the basic rights of refugees in their care. Kanak Attak, referencing Agamben, Negri, and others, rejects this engagement with European humanism as irrelevant if not counterproductive in achieving real change by accepting migration as an aberration from the desired norm:

> I find it problematic if migration appears as a side effect of violent dispersal, signified by the extreme desperation of death. Migration is no desperate fate. What does "we are here" mean? Does that imply we'd like to stay where we came from if that was possible? And if we're here after all, should we be treated with humanity and respect, because we've been through so much misery? (Kanak Attak und Karawane, in Interface 2005, 364)

Ideological disagreements ran deep and were multilayered but often culminated around the question of identity. The two organizations made repeated attempts to overcome their different approaches, recognizing their shared interests, as referenced by Kanak Attak member Effi Panagiotis, offering an assessment of difference drawn from women of color feminism: "It seems of little use to me to follow a capitalist divide and conquer logic, even if inadvertently. The point after all is to produce a common language, helping us to play out the arrangement of difference, beyond harmonizing and 'respect discourses'" (Kanak Attak und Karawane, in Interface 2005, 365).

The failure to develop this common language, which would have allowed them to find common ground on which to express positionalities that did not converge, but which also might not have been mutually exclusive, is illustrated in the 2005 video project Recolonize Cologne, created by members of both groups. Like all Kanak TV productions, the video constitutes a direct intervention into German public spaces. It begins by documenting a performance that stages the fictional recolonization of contemporary Cologne by the King of Cameroon, using this a starting point for a discussion of German (neo)colonialism and its impact on refugee politics. Apart from its focus on reclaiming public spaces, the video seems to exclusively reflect the position presented by the Karawane however, that is, a pedagogical "we are here, because you were there" approach, the claim to rights based on clearly defined, antagonistic identities of victim and perpetrator, bearing little resemblance to earlier Kanak TV productions questioning such binary ascriptions. But while the Karawane's rather essentialist position certainly has numerous weaknesses rightly criticized by the Kanak Attak activists, a major factor in the failed communication seems the latter's unwillingness to claim any positionality at all, in particular that of minoritarian rather than migrant subjects. In its founding manifesto the group had stated:

> Kanak Attak wants to break the assignment of ethnic identities and
> roles; the 'we' and 'them.' And because Kanak Attak is a question of
> attitude and not of heritage, origin, roots or papers, non-migrants and
> Germans of the 2nd and even 3rd generation are part of it too. But . . .
> [n]ot all constructions are the same. So our project is caught up in the
> whirlpool of contradictions concerning the relation of representation,
> difference and the ascription of ethnic identities. (Kanak Attak 1998,
> English original)

In refusing to acknowledge that and how the positionalities of "second-generation migrants" are not only different from those of the first generation and in particular political refugees, but also that these (long unexpressed) positionalities fundamentally shaped its own understanding of politics, Kanak Attak fell short of heeding its call to remain aware of differences in identity constructions, failing to investigate how the group's composition shaped its ideology and thus ignoring women of color feminism's key lessons on the constructive uses of differences, instead replacing intersectionality with antiessentialism (Crenshaw 1991, 1,296).

While its strategy prevented Kanak Attak from being pinned down within a liberal multiculturalist framework, creating subversion when directed at majoritarian discourses, it had a different effect when used toward other migrant and minority activists. The absolutist refusal to allow for strategic essentialism affirmed rather than destabilized hierarchies among racialized groups as it did not allow for an open exploration of positionalities, including the privileged access to certain cultural resources minoritarian and second-generation status implies. Neither did it produce a meaningful analysis of the shortcomings of the Karawane's uncritical use of an identity formation defined in diametric opposition to dominant German society, failing to account for differentiations within and intersections between both constructs (as exemplified by the teenage civil war refugees discussed in chapter 1). Kanak Attak fundamentally critiqued and subverted the legitimacy of origins, most effectively and hilariously in their video productions, but in so doing ignored the ways in which origins constitute power: even if there is no "authentic" origin, the moment when a linear narrative is introduced is a real event and constitutes an act of violence that must be addressed in order to be overcome.

The Autonomy of Migration and Its Discontents

Kanak Attak's categorical rejection of identity politics, while focusing on processes of racialization, was a challenging and often successful strategy that suffered, however, from a failure to critically ground the group's own position within its alternative model of "migrant" identity. While the activists were the first to successfully introduce a minoritarian voice into German political discourse that effectively rejected their externalization, the group failed to claim a minoritarian positionality out of fear of falling prey to dominant divide and conquer politics. Kanak Attak shared with Strange Fruit a practice of queering ethnicity that insisted on combining supposedly incompatible positionalities and the refusal to "speak for" anyone. But Strange Fruit's radical insistence on the self-help principle, determined to channel resources exclusively into self-empowering projects and rejecting attempts at adjusting its activism to either dominant queer or anti-racist politics, resulted in a type of theorizing that seemed less prone to implicit hierarchizations and totalizing models of resistance than Kanak Attak's. This might be rooted in part in Strange Fruit's approach to the language of politics, drawing on a African diasporic tradition of poetics ranging from Lorde's claim that "[p]oetry is the way we help give name to the nameless so it can be thought" (Lorde 1984, 37) to Glissant's Poetics of Relation as "learning more and more to go beyond judgments into the unexpected dark of art's upsurgings" (Glissant 1989, 137). In drawing on this tradition while simultaneously creolizing it further, Strange Fruit offered an answer to some of the questions Avery Gordon raises when she introduces the concept of haunting, cited at the very beginning of this study, as a trope with which to grasp the concrete effects that structures of oppression have on people's everyday lives (Gordon 1997, 23).

While Kanak Attak's unwillingness to differentiate situationally between minority and migrant status inevitably led to a "speaking for" groups with different priorities and concerns, the activists were successful in responding to the troubling "contrast between conceptual or analytical descriptions of social systems and their far more diffused and delicate effects" (Gordon 1997, 23), namely through the creation of an innovative visual language. The community proclaimed by Kanak Attak and the other activist groups discussed throughout this study proposes a denaturalized concept of belonging that is both fluent and open, but it still requires some of the classical elements of maintaining social communities, namely a sense of shared history and a common language; a language that in this case is not primarily verbal—the diversity of languages being one factor potentially separating postethnic communities in Europe—but rather visual and sonic. The realization that an invisible minoritarian identity in Europe does not result in a positionality outside of identity constructs but in unstable, multiple identity fragments that can lead not only to disempowerment, but also to successful resistance along Glissantian lines of diversion is expressed primarily in Kanak Attak's visual productions. One of the last is the short video *Schland ist das Land*,[29] shot in Hamburg during the 2006 Soccer World Cup hosted by Germany.

Soccer, national sport number one in almost every nation across the world and a source of intense identifications from the local to the continental level, fostered by frequent national and international competitions, is a primary site of negotiations of identity, centrally revolving around questions of belonging. European soccer, whose fans are notorious for their racism, arguably offers a venue in which the implicit racist worldview that allows the system of racelessness to function smoothly is expressed explicitly.[30] In preparation for the competition, Germany did its best to contain the "hooligan" problem, but faced a moment of crisis when a highly publicized racist attack led to discussions on the potential effect of "national liberated zones"—parts of the nation, primarily but by no means only located in the East, declared no-go areas for people of color by white supremacist organizations—on World Cup tourism (see, e.g., Pilz 2007). The crisis was averted and channeled into a tolerance campaign around World Cup events, and debates on national identity soon shifted from xenophobic violence to national pride, namely to Germany's apparent problem with expressing the latter openly, due to its past as occupier of most nations on the European continent during World War II.

In contrast to the World Cup taking place in West Germany in 1974, the 2006 event saw an explosion of German flags on cars and buildings, and frequently wrapped around enthusiastic supporters of the national team. Both the fact that Germans seemed capable of displaying these symbols without the accompanying urge to invade neighboring nations and the generally positive reception of this display by other European countries led to the consensus that a state of "normalization" had been achieved that related directly to Germany's central role in a postnational Europe that had learned to identify around a common past and common values, overcoming centuries of internal continental antagonism (see, e.g., Scheuble and Wehner 2007). The World Cup's motto, "At home among friends," beyond its perfunctory gesture toward benevolent humanism that all global sports events are required to perform, was an attempt at reviving a European identity that seemed to have been largely reduced to its bureaucratic functions, while lacking a more "spiritual" dimension.

As I have argued throughout, the common European ground is still rather shaky, largely because central components of Europeanness, such as racism, colonialism, and the Holocaust, remain buried underneath it. Consequently, European minorities—Muslims, Afro-Europeans, Roma—function as the glue that holds Europe together precisely by being excluded. As I have also argued, this dynamic is both intensified and becoming increasingly unattainable with the growing presence of these minorities within European societies—as witnessed for example in the composition of the French national team, dominating continental soccer after the 1998 European championship (its victory celebrated as a success of liberal multiculturalism, while its defeat by the lily-white Italian team in the 2006 World Cup seemed to imply a similar larger failure of integrationist ideologies). While they were occasionally used as a silent backdrop to the "tolerance campaign," German media remained largely uninterested in exploring minorities' position within the display of newly discovered national pride and its implications for a Europe needing to combine national and continental allegiances. This however, was exactly the focus of the local Kanak TV crew when it set out to question migrants and minorities about integration and their soccer allegiances on the eve of the Germany-Argentina World Cup match in Hamburg.

Approaching everyone who was identifiable as a *Kanake* and displayed some kind of German national symbol, the group encountered a variety of complicated positionalities and approaches to the question of (national) belonging that went far beyond simple German versus migrant binaries, showing the pressures caused by the erasure of minoritarian Germans, exemplified by a teenager with a Ghanaian passport who had spent almost all of his life in Germany, but still felt unable to claim any "Germanness" (though he did root for the German team). Also present however, are the ways in which their erasure is creatively circumvented daily by marginalized groups that are far more than victims, reflected in exchanges such as this between the Kanak Attak interviewer and a group of teenage boys wearing national team jerseys:

> Q: Who are you rooting for tonight?
> A: Germany!
> Q: Why?
> A: Because it is our stepfatherland!
> Q: What?
> A: It's our stepfatherland. Because we are Turks and we are born in Germany.

Just as the white, Christian family of nations posited as the heart of Europe is in practice supplanted by a variety of creolized communities and just as black feminists and queer of color activists formulated alternative models of (diasporic) families, so do minoritarian youths construct their relationship to the national identities offered or denied to them in unpredictable ways that circumvent dominant options and move within contradictory frameworks in defiance of linear conceptualizations of belonging. Their fractured, dynamic positionality—as invisible in dominant European discourses as in the traditional anti-imperialist and pan-Africanist politics represented by groups such as the Karawane—is neither the hip, unproblematic "postmodern zapping between identities" referenced in the Kanak Attak Manifesto, nor the tragic "lost between cultures" of progressive and liberal multiculturalism. Instead, it represents a queering of ethnicity that draws from the voluntary or forced mobility of populations, ideas, identities, that is becoming increasingly normal in the united Europe and beyond and that refuses to be channeled toward either a point of arrival or departure, but that lives with and through contradictions, permanently reconfiguring itself in an intersectional network that escapes containment because it constantly "relinks (relays), relates."

"An Infinite and Undefinable Movement"

Relation relinks (relays), relates. Domination and resistance, osmosis and withdrawal, the consent to dominating language . . . and defense of dominated languages . . . They do not add up to anything clearcut or easily perceptible with any certainty. The relinked (relayed), the related, cannot be combined conclusively.

—EDOUARD GLISSANT, *The Poetics of Relation*

My art is action: it is not a goal but a tool. It helps me to reach completeness, where art is no longer needed. It is when I do not need art that I know I have reached completeness. What is completeness? It is accepting opposites, experiencing universality, re-evaluating values.

—JENÖ ANDRÉ RATZSCH, *Paradise Lost. The First Roma Pavilion*

"It's Your History": Old Narratives of a New Europe

In October 2007, after a ten-year planning period and in time for the fiftieth anniversary of the Treaties of Rome, which had laid the foundation for the continental unification, the Museum of Europe opened its doors in Brussels, one of the institutional centers of the European Union. The EU-funded museum was conceptualized—by a committee consisting largely of historians from various universities in Europe—as "the 'place of memory' that Europe needs . . . [T]he permanent collection and the temporary exhibitions will offer all Europeans (and their guests) a reasoned history of a Union portrayed as a diverse but unique civilization" (Museum van Europa 2007, original in English). The inaugural exhibit, "It's Your History," ran from October 2007 to May 2008 and attracted more than 100,000 visitors, about half of them school classes. Spread over several rooms and themed "containers," combining commissioned art works, video and audio installations, as well as more traditional museum pieces, the exhibit was divided into various sections, namely "1945 Europe: Hour Zero"; "The European Revolution, 1946–1951"; "Divided Europe, 1951–1989"; "1989: The Wall Comes Down"; and "After the Unification of Europe, 1989–2007." It was framed as follows:

> From the devastated Europe of 1945 to the challenges that are today facing our continent, visitors will come face to face with History with a capital H, but also with their own more personal history. As you will realize as you make your way around the exhibition, we are all protagonists in this incredible adventure, this ongoing quest to unify Europe. (Museum van Europa 2007)

The exhibit, like the museum itself, directly responded to the crisis of "European identity," the lacking emotional investment in the idea of Europe by its citizens expressed in, among other things, the much publicized "No" votes to the continental constitution in the Netherlands and France, as well as the notoriously low participation in European parliament elections (in which, additionally, nationalist parties tend to do unusually well, see Waterfield et al. 2009). Personalized through the life stories of twenty-seven "average" Europeans, one for each of the union's member states, "It's Your History" strived to reflect Europe as a lived experience, and in doing so, the exhibit unwittingly illustrated all key aspects of the internalist narrative of racelessness traced throughout this book.

Starting with the collection of individual life stories of eleven women and sixteen men, none of whom represent racial or religious minorities, the exhibit creates an image of Europe that is both (culturally) "diverse" and (racially) homogeneous. According to the catalogue: "The twenty-seven people we gathered here are not representatives, but symbols of the Union. However unique their stories are, they are European stories and this is exactly what makes them so valuable" (Museum van Europa 2007, 27). While this arguably relieves the organizers from having to be inclusive, it leaves unanswered the question why minorities' stories are not considered valuable enough to be included in the European narrative. The combination of universalist and isolationist perspectives implicit in the European model, leading to the replication of the same, dominant image in endless variations rather than allowing for an actual diversity of representations of Europe, also is visible in the central question of a continental memory, presented as a necessary prerequisite for a notion of Europe that goes beyond the purely bureaucratic. Echoing Habermas's and Derrida's 2003 argument, this shared memory is claimed to have been proven by the very existence of the Union—without common culture, values, and past, there is no "such thing as Europe."[1] The tension growing out of national memories interpreting this shared history in at times diametrically opposed ways is acknowledged, but assumed to be inevitably dissolved as the Union progresses: "The European identity is not exclusive but inclusive. It doesn't replace other identities, it is added on top of them (*bovenop*)" (Museum van Europa 2007, 3). What this process looks like, and whether all "other identities" are really considered subsumable under "Europe" is left open, in part because the exhibit leaves the pre-1945 period largely unexplored.

The use of the common trope of 1945 as Europe's "Hour Zero" means that a shared past can be referenced while its implications for the present are left unexplored, if not outright denied by the representation of 1945 as a radical turning point (at least for the Western part of the continent). The Holocaust in particular can thus both figure as *the* foundational memory of postwar Europe and as completely outside of the experiential world of "everyday" Europeans, both those represented in the exhibit and those visiting it.[2] Colonialism, or rather decolonization, is dutifully addressed within the "Divided Europe" segment, in a manner that is again reminiscent of Habermas's characterization, in turn reflecting the dominant liberal humanist cosmopolitan discourse in postwar Europe, namely one in which colonization somehow happened out of necessity (and more *to* Europe than inflicted by it), while economic interests, not to mention exploitation, never seem to be a factor: "Without decolonization no European unification. With colonization, the colonial powers have to involve themselves with problems outside of Europe. With decolonization they can concentrate on Europe" (Museum van Europa 2007, 60). The visual centerpiece of the space devoted to decolonization is an installation evoking an African airport with a DC-6 surrounded by left luggage, representing featured stories such as that of Belgian writer Lieve Joris, who as a child fled the Congo with her family.[3] While the end of Europe's colonial empire is thus embodied by the experience of the former colonizers, there is no further reference to any ongoing after-effects of this period in Europe, either through returning colonizers or postcolonial migration. The internalist narrative that is meant to show this period's importance for Europe while keeping it firmly outside its borders is instead very traditionally built around the images of "great men"—quite literally through oversized portraits—like Ghandi, Nehru, Kenyatta, Nkrumah, Sukarno, or Lumumba.[4]

This rather conservative understanding of history as created by exceptional leaders is not limited to the representation of the Global South, however: the founding period of the Union, too, is translated into the story of "the fathers of Europe." In keeping with nationalist history's omission of women as agents and creators, criticized by McClintock, Wright, and many others, an "inclusive" European identity is created with the tools of exclusive nationalism, producing predictable results. This is nowhere more obvious than in the striking, unexplained, and almost complete absence of migration from the exhibit. The scant references to migratory movements that are present show them as a very recent phenomenon, largely reduced to stories of desperate refugees—presenting migration firstly as an anomaly, caused by some kind of crisis in the region of origin and secondly as something that happens to Europe without the continent having any active part in it. While this last aspect differs drastically from the Karawane's framing of migration, which focuses on the West's active participation in creating "crises" in the Global South, the representation is otherwise in keeping with an understanding of migratory movements as tied to exceptional conditions, deviating from the norm and requiring a solution.

The "container" devoted to migration reflects this quite literally, being the copy of an actual container in which seven young Moroccans had hidden to clandestinely enter the European Union. Migrants are thus presented as breaking the law, intruders into a space they have no ties to, as well as victims of disastrous circumstances that seem to appear rather naturally in the Third World. A number of questions such as "What policies are needed to offer immigrants perspectives while preventing an upset of the demographic, economic, and cultural balance of the host nations? How should we react to the daily horrors of people risking their lives to reach the promised land called Europe?" frame migration as a new and urgent crisis, detached from the continent's "hour zero" and the resulting need for cheap labor, decolonization, or "the fall of the wall," resulting in a mass migration from East to West—instead forever suddenly appearing on the horizon of an unsuspecting Europe that feels obliged to react, within sensible limits, due to its commitment to human rights, not because it already is an active, powerful participant in the process (Museum van Europa 2007, 125).

The Museum of Europe's "It's Your History" with its attempt at representing a European Union that is relevant, organic, diverse, and open, ends up reflecting much of the weaknesses of postnational Europe in its insistence on defining the terms of inclusiveness and diversity, the claiming of authority through "authenticity," and the inability to decenter its perspective. The museum, like the European Union and the internalist narrative of racelessness, creates Europe through a streamlined memory whose binary structure demands the dialectic construction of an Other that can only do its work on the inside, while being forever discursively placed on (and as) the outside of Europe. In doing so, it uses Trouilliot's archival power, selecting and hierarchizing memories, assigning them meaning within a coherent, teleological story of Europeanness that has no space for any true diversity of experiences—in terms of not only race and religion, but also gender and sexuality[5]—rendering all those experiences that are perceived as nonnormative as (still) "unspeakable" in the new postnational Europe. As I have argued throughout, one of the main goals of the queering of ethnicity is to create the conditions of speakability for minoritarian identities and I end by indicating how a postnational, "postethnic" Europe built on these conditions might contrast, for the better, with the one celebrated in the Museum of Europe.

Unspeakable Identities and Methodologies of Diversion

> I am asked frequently: "Where do you come from?" If I answer
> "The Netherlands," the follow-up question is almost mandatory:
> "No, no, where do you really come from?" Of course, this question is
> not asked if the person asking cannot see me. After all, my behavior or
> accent do not indicate that I am "foreign." Say, I'll have children with
> a native white Dutch man with blond hair and blue eyes. The child
> will probably be a magnificent mixture, but well one with dark skin.
> According to the official definition my child will be a native citizen
> [autochton] since both its parents were born in the Netherlands. But
> despite an authentic Amsterdam accent and his or her autochthonous value system people will keep on asking "Where do you come
> from? The Netherlands? No, no, where do you really come from?"
> Through how many generations will this question persist? Unless the
> laws of genetics are turned upside down my grandchildren and great-
> grandchildren won't have lilywhite skin either . . . (Ahmed 2006)

The strategy of queering ethnicity traced in this book, practiced across the continent by multiethnic hip-hop crews, black and Muslim feminists, queer performers, urban guerilla video artists, and many others, is born out of the shared, peculiar experience of embodying an identity that is declared impossible even though lived by millions, of constantly being defined as foreign to everything one is most familiar with. The particular forms of exclusions produced by the ideology of racelessness require methods of resistance that cannot always be direct; instead they have to use detours, disidentifications, and diversons in order to produce positionalities from which to break the silence around Europe's deeply racialized sense of self.

A primary scene for the erasure of minorities from the discursive landscape of Europeanness is the "Where do you come from?" inquiry familiar to all racialized Europeans and described above by Moroccan Dutch blogger Fiza Ahmed as well as in Ming-Bao Yue's recollection of her childhood subway encounter in Hamburg quoted in the introduction. The social existence of minorities is negated through silence, but just as importantly through an active process of denial that reinforces the discursive rules of racelessness in everyday exchanges. In their most basic version, these exchanges police minority identity through the endlessly repeated questioning of origin, at times elaborate, often reduced to the plain "Where do you come from?" Importantly, this question usually is not motivated by curiosity, but a desire to affirm a preexisting knowledge, namely "You are not from here." In this context, Yue's subway experience discussed earlier gains additional significance: the white German man's inquiry can be interpreted as not only a reaction to a situation that violates the European logic of externalizing race, but also as an active attempt at reconfiguring reality along acceptable lines, while projecting the tension of Otherness, of incompatible identities, onto the minority subject.

That is, the "Why are you here/How can you speak my language/ Where do you really come from?" trope creates a discursive but very real paradox since the "true" answer, "I am from here," is precisely the one that is not acceptable as it falls outside of the logically possible, the thinkable and thus speakable—and "[t]o move outside of the domain of speakability is to risk one's status as a subject. To embody the norms that govern speakability in one's speech is to consummate one's status as a subject of speech" (Butler 1997, 133). Because of this, the questioned minoritarian subject lacks the discursive power to shape the exchange to such an extent that it could cause a radical break by introducing a new option that would in effect destroy the existing paradigm. Thus minorities remain invisible and mute between the antagonism of native norm and foreign aberration, only able to become subjects of speech if they take on a fake but acceptable identity ("Oh, we've only been here about a year"). If one's existence depends partly on being addressed by another, "the conditions of intelligibility" become fundamental to hierarchies of power, so basic that they tend to go unnoticed, leaving minorities of color only the choice between being unintelligible or misinterpellated.

To be "constituted by discourse, but at a distance from oneself" as Butler states in her 1997 *Excitable Speech* (in which she aims at situating Althusser's concept of interpellation in concrete power relations through a discussion of legal regulations around hate speech), seems to perfectly summarize a key condition shaping the situation of European minorities:

> Imagine the quite plausible scene in which one is called by a name and one turns around only to protest the name: "That is not me, you must be mistaken!" And then imagine that the name continues to force itself upon you, to delineate the space you occupy, to construct a social positionality. Indifferent to your protests, the force of interpellation continues to work. One is still constituted by discourse, but at a distance from oneself. (Butler 1997, 33)

Among the practical implications of the invisibility of racialized minorities is a Catch-22 leaving them with only two, impossible options: The first, to identify as an Insider of the national community, is a position that inevitably clashes with the assigned status as Other ("[P]eople will keep on asking: 'Where do you come from? . . . No, no, where do you *really* come from?'"). The second option is to accept the Outsider status, that is, the identification as migrant and foreigner. This move complies with the dominant discourse and offers a "legitimate" point of resistance through ethnic migrant organizing that addresses the native majority from the position of newcomer to the nation. It nevertheless creates its own set of problems: a movement built around ethnic solidarity and an identification with a "homeland" that is neither the place of residency nor of birth often clashes with the actual encounter with the imaginary home, in which the second- or third-generation migrant is again perceived as an Outsider (and it is in part because of this conundrum that black diasporic explorations of the relationship to "Africa" resonate so well with racialized Europeans). Both positions create a conflict that cannot successfully be resolved within the system of colorblindness, because this system makes it impossible to name its root.

This process of silencing minority voices might be theorized by appropriating Butler again, namely her "Imitation and Gender Insubordination," one of queer theory's key texts, and its conceptualization of lesbians as "unviable (un)subjects" of the economy of law (Butler 1993, 312). Within her analysis of sexual power regimes, Butler differentiates between those who in discourses around gender and sexuality represent the opposite of the norm, and who are thus indispensable for its definition and explicitly targeted by prohibitions, in this case male homosexuals, and those who do not even appear within the discourse, who are an invisible aberration without discursive space, not qualifying as "an object of prohibition" and instead are relegated to a "domain of unthinkability and unnameability" (Butler 1993, 312), thus remaining without a place from where to resist their normative exclusion, since as Butler states in *Excitable Speech* "by being called a name, one is also, paradoxically, given a certain possibility for social existence, initiated into a temporal life of language that exceeds the prior purposes that animate that call" (Butler 1997, 2). With necessary caution, one might transfer these analyses to the discourse around implicitly racialized normative European identities in which only the seemingly unambiguous and opposing options of white, Christian, European, and migrant are presented as valid, "speakable" identities while ambiguities and transgressions are discursively silenced—without ever being fully contained—and racialized populations are turned into unviable (un)subjects whose positionality is incomprehensible within the language of identity permissible in European discourses.

The disparity between the lived experience of minoritarian Europeans and their (non)perception by the majority creates an obvious alienation, a breakdown of communication. This, however, does not completely succeed in silencing the misinterpellated subjects who intervene in a discourse not meant to include them, creating not a legitimate positionality, discursive or otherwise, but a temporary disruption of a normative order that cannot recognize their existence: in everyday exchanges, through verbal diversions in response to the ritualized questioning of origins, or through spectacular incidents such as the French uprisings. This process necessarily transcends the limits of the national as dialogue takes place not only in reaction to and addressed at a majoritarian audience refusing the minoritarian subjects the right to define their own subjectivity, but also becomes part of a collective move toward creating alternative modes of belonging. Without necessarily reflecting this theoretically, racialized Europeans use queer performative strategies in continuously rearranging the components of the supposedly stable identities assigned to them. The realization that identity is not "natural" but highly performative is thus the result of the daily fight for recognition in a system that offers no space for minorities of color.

It is useful to employ queer theory to analyze the situation of these European ethnic minorities not only because of the methodological tools it offers, but also because political minority movements in Europe increasingly make use of queer strategies, particularly through a politicizing of popular culture. Queer theory's value as a political strategy is rightfully disputed, especially among communities of color that have different investments in questions of identity and subjectivity than the white, middle-class positionality that too often is the default dominating queer theory. Nevertheless, the potentially shared investment of sexual and ethnic minorities in denaturalizing and complicating categories of identity becomes

persistently evident, be it in coalitional politics or the intersectional theorizing of queer of color critique.

A queering or creolizing of theory, working on the intersections of
concepts and disciplines, opens the potential of making thinkable lived
identities erased in dominant European discourses, namely that of Europeans of color, foregrounding the latter's transgressive strategies of resistance often downplayed in culturalist debates around Europe's "migration
problem." Butler's work is useful in deconstructing how the seemingly
individualized, confusing, and repetitive process of interrogation that minority subjects constantly face is feeding into the larger framework of
political racelessness, but it is less helpful in addressing minoritarian responses to this alienating experience. The minority subject is not completely powerless in the exchange: while question, and expected/accepted
answers stay the same in an endless, almost compulsive process of repetition, minoritarian subjects can explore a variety of "false answers," all
of which are acceptable if compatible with the "you are not from here"
premise: within the clear limits of this discursive framework it is possible
to challenge, subvert, and parody its normative expectations ("I heard
my brother saying with a smile, 'You know, German is such an easy language!'"). However, this strategy, frequently practiced by minoritarian
subjects in one form or another, can be gratifying and create an instance
of disruption, momentarily throwing a wrench in the machinery of racelessness, but does not yet change the discursive rules.

In its uses as well as limits, it can be linked to the tactic of "diversion" that Edouard Glissant develops for Caribbean narratives of identity
(Glissant 1989, 18). Diversion then, is the reaction to an oppression that
is total, but at the same time diffuse, so that its source cannot be identified immediately and instead needs to be approached through dislocation,
through experiencing the source of oppression as being elsewhere:

> Diversion is the ultimate resort of a population whose domination by
> an Other is concealed: it then must search *elsewhere* for the principle
> of domination, which is not evident in the country itself: because
> the system of domination . . . is not directly tangible. Diversion is
> the parallactic displacement of this strategy. (Glissant 1989, 20)

In the European context, this would mean that the impossibility of minoritarian identity *within* the (post)nation is so fundamental, so ingrained
in the structure of society that it cannot be initially addressed, in fact cannot be initially conceptualized by the minority subject itself. The conceptualization (for the subject) as well as the problematization (for society)
is only possible through the detour of repetition and diversion: the "I am

(not) from here, but . . . ." Glissant cautions, however, that "diversion is not a useful ploy unless it is nurtured by reversion: not a return to the longing for origins, to some immutable state of Being, but a return to the point of entanglement, from where we were forcefully turned away; that is where we must ultimately put to work the forces of creolization, or perish" (ibid., 26).

Glissant's notion of creolization seems one of the most interesting and successful attempts at moving beyond the binary model of thinking so ingrained in the ways we are taught to perceive the world. His concept of diversion implies a kind of absolute displacement that requires a move back to an origin that is not a place of resolution or peace, but rather the point at which a linear, hierarchical narrative was introduced. This narrative in turn hides the potentially productive chaos that can better be grasped with "relation" than roots and that would necessitate letting go of the quest for a particular endpoint. Creolization thus allows for a type of diasporic thinking that invokes the past without burdening it, or the "homeland," with housing some kind of solution, instead suggesting a constantly shifting, chaotic, unstable network of relations that produces "situational communities" that can never be trusted to last but nonetheless offer the best starting point for change (though it cannot be estimated what the results will be). It offers not a return to an unconflicted origin or to the possibility of "integration" thus, but a return to the "point of entanglement" at which conflicting identity models clash, before they are resolved into "possible" and "impossible" identities.

In their *The Creolization of Theory*, Françoise Lionnet and Shu-mei Shih offer a framework for such a process, concluding: "Our hunch is that without being Theory with a capital 'T,' theory can engage with the objects of one's analysis in multiple ways and to different levels of intensity" (Shih and Lionnet 2011). Theory without a capital "T" as Shih and Lionnet envision it has to be mindful of the relation between the specific and general, the reciprocal process of translation, between the local, regional, national, and global. In this sense, it is closely related to Wright's notion of the dialogic and to Muñoz's use of disidentification, offering an alternative to the "History with a capital H" presented by the Museum of Europe. Again drawing on Glissant, such a theory would question Europe as the "sacred territory," as which it appears in dominant, internalist narratives: according to Glissant, the Caribbean became a center of relational identities and situational communities exactly because their inability to claim the "sacred roots" of these territories excluded its inhabitants from a world order in which both dominance and resistance were built on notions of sacred land (Glissant 1989).

This is a positonality shared by racialized minorities in Europe. An origin that does not imply sacredness or authenticity thus is the point from which minoritarian resistance can be articulated, a position as subject of speech achieved. In order to arrive at this stage however, a different archive needs to be accessed, one based on the experiences of marginalized, silenced communities, without presence in dominant manifestations such as the Museum of Europe. Traditional archives in Trouillot's sense are places that house "facts," knowledge that has already been accepted as such and thus is deemed worthy of being incorporated into a space designed for the purpose of conserving materials relevant to the community. Because of their position as exclusive centers of dominant wisdom, archives often play an ambiguous role for minorities. For them, they are sites of exclusion, manifestations of their irrelevance to their nation's history, rather than taken-for-granted containers of established history. Out of necessity thus, minority communities have created a variety of strategies to create alternative archives.

Throughout this book, I have highlighted attempts at introducing such archives into European public spaces, based on everyday practices of resistance like those performed by Ming-Bao Yue's brother, which create temporary cracks in the European narrative of racelessness, suggesting an alternative reality already lived by those silenced (un)subjects. What remains invisible in dominant discourses are forms of resistance destabilizing the ascribed essentialist identities not only by rejecting them, but through a strategic and creative (mis)use. By themselves, these uses do not create a lasting change in the perception of minorities within the narration of national and continental belonging, but I suggest that it is this persistent resistance to erasure, Sisyphean as it must appear to the individual whose very existence is casually and constantly negated by society, that is the first step toward a queering of ethnicity, the source of a postethnic, translocal minoritarian movement creating a counternarrative, told in various languages, that makes visible and thus ultimately ineffective the mechanisms of colorblindness.

Race, Religion, and Resistance in Postnational Europe

A few months before the Museum of Europe opened its doors, in the summer of 2007, in the Austrian Graz (and before that 2005 in Vienna), a multiethnic collective of artists and activists created a rather different type of archive of Europeanness. Organized under the heading "*Arbeiten gegen Rassismen*" (working against racisms), they staged an intervention into Austrian public spaces that can be read as a continuation of the performative self-defense practiced by racialized Europeans, from Ming-Bao Yue and her brother on a Hamburg subway in the 1970s to Kanak Attak's video activism in the 2000s. Billboards in, on, and around the cities' numerous streetcars addressed a number of "unmentionable" issues from the construction of whiteness and the invisibility of minorities in school curricula to the silence around the disappearance of the nation's Jewish population and the relationship between postwar migration from Austria's Eastern neighbors and their wartime occupation. The event, meant to "make visible the modes of operation of racisms and of resistance against them," created a situationist disruption, a gash in the seamless logic of political racelessness. At the same time, it used these moments of irritation to reconstruct an alternative European history, emphasizing suppressed connections, for example those between racism and anti-Semitism, offering a reading of contemporary Europe that contextualizes excluded populations as well as the mechanisms of exclusion itself.

In opposition to the dominant attempt at creating a common, coherent narrative, the activists work toward what Susan Suleiman calls a "crisis of memory," a conflict over "the interpretation and public understanding of an event firmly situated in the past, but whose aftereffects are still deeply felt" (Suleiman 2006, 1). These after-effects—Avery Gordon's "haunting"—originate from Glissant's "point(s) of entanglement," at which differences and discrepancies were suppressed and externalized. Most obviously so with regard to racialized and religious minorities, but as has been argued by feminists of color since the 1970s (and earlier), these constructs depend on heteronormative conceptualizations of gender and sexuality that are no less restrictive in their negation of what is not acceptable as is the discourse of colorblindness with which they are interwoven. The queering of ethnicity, diversion, situational communities and diasporic intersubjectivities employed by racialized minorities all work against the attempt to cohere them out of existence, resisting not only their erasure from the contemporary European landscape but also from its past. Queering ethnicity has the dual function of inserting European minorities into the ongoing debate around the continent's identity and of reclaiming their place in its history, the creation of alternative archives working as a bridge between the two.

Strategies of resistance challenging notions of purity and authenticity, inhabiting the impossible space of being simultaneously inside and out, disidentifying with the stepfatherland Europe, counter the quest for a common continental European space and memory by creating alternative visual, sonic, poetic languages inserted into a public space formerly free of signs of minority presence. With this, the activists impact virtual

Monument of "Arianization." The image of the Vienna Ferris Wheel (made famous by Carol Reed's *The Third Man*) is accompanied by an open letter to the company owning the wheel, which in its official account of the wheel's history does not make any mention of its former Jewish owner, murdered in Auschwitz in 1944, nor of the problems his heirs had in recovering the stolen property (they were forced to resell the wheel in 1964). Copyright Martin Krenn.

Black studies must be part of the curricula of all schools and universities. Copyright AFRA Schwarze Frauen Community.

as well as "real" spaces, in which minorities and migrants are usually only present as objects without representational power, be it hip-hop establishing a translocal European soundscape, or the Austrian *Arbeiten gegen Rassimen*'s subway billboards, reminding the nation not only of the marginalized presence of migrant and minority populations, but also of the ongoing effects of the suppression of the nation's role in the Holocaust.

I have argued in this book that the strategy of queering ethnicity is symptomatic for a larger movement and in the course of this argument, I have built an alternative understanding of radical cultural interventions into urban spaces by tracing the activism of a number of groups aiming at constructing queer networks undermining new and old binaries, creating counternarratives to the (hetero and homo)normative construction of Europeanness currently under way. I am particularly interested in the material grounding of definitional power over urban spaces and this leads me necessarily back to time and its relation to such a grounding, of the effects of twentieth century exclusions on twenty-first century models of belonging. Faced with the public image of their free-floating, nomadic, unattached continental presence, marginalized communities need a historical anchoring to "prove" their belonging: the failure to do so has very material spatial consequences, namely exclusion through gentrification, incarceration, or deportation.

Such a grounding, however, is easily equated with essentialism within progressive discourses, including queer theory, and while this is certainly at times an accurate assessment, I argue that there are also systematic theoretical shortcomings at play in the perception of minoritarian cultural activism by majoritarian left theorists and activists. Building on the methodological approaches used throughout this study—in particular women of color feminism, African diaspora theory, queer of color critique—I suggest an alternative reading of the queering of ethnicity in response to the European ideology of colorblindness. Since the dogma of racelessness is centrally built on silencing, on making certain identities, processes, and structures unspeakable, I have explored a number of alternative languages, all circumventing the mandate to silence by making specifically European taboos around race speakable. These sonic, performative, and visual languages use the haunting presence of repressed histories and connections to map an alternative spatio-temporal European landscape—built around rhizomatic relations rather than borders.

I believe that this strategy succeeded, at least partially, through its focus on interaction and networking between racialized individuals and marginalized communities, creating a situational community that is more fragile, but also more inclusive and adaptable than those built around identity politics. However, in order to lastingly challenge the dominant (non) discourse, these alternative networks must communicate with those who continue to discursively erase their voice and thus their very existence as legitimate European subjects. In his *Cosmopolitanism*, Anthony Appiah argues that if people with vastly different religious, sexual, and political attachments are to live together peacefully they must master the art of conversation (Appiah 2006). This claim could be considered a humanist version of Seyla Benhabib's "democratic iterations," the idea that concepts shaping societies' self-representations evolve through constant collective application (Benhabib 2006). Neither statement leaves much to disagree with, so what seems to be at stake here are the conditions under which these conversations and collective applications take place: who is allowed to speak and who is not, what can and cannot be said, from which position(s) are we speaking and with what authority? No honest dialogue is possible until these questions have been addressed and this study is meant as a step toward offering some answers. The most important answers, however, are provided by the artists and activists at the center of my book.

One of them is visual artist André Raatzsch, who contributed to the first Roma art exhibit at the Venice Biennale in 2007. The "Roma Pavilion" was one of the few occasions at which this quintessential European minority was recognized as such. The Roma, a term that subsumes a transnational, mulitlingual, multireligious community, are closely tied to the still marginalized history of the "second world," Europe's East— transit zone for non-European migrants, enforcing European racial difference, while itself possessing a rather ambiguous claim on whiteness. Roma populations play a central part in the uniting Europe's history, while being nearly completely absent from its memory, as evidenced in the continued silencing of the Porajmos, the murder of half a million so-called gypsies in German extermination camps. Artists like Raatzsch use their work to counter this silence: his definition of completeness cited above resonates with women of color feminism's approach to difference not as an obstacle to, but as the source of unity (Anzaldúa and Moraga 1981) and might well function as a motto for the whole movement of queering ethnicity. The activism analyzed here lastingly changed the political landscape not by offering clear-cut solutions, but by emphasizing possibilities, the irrepressible openness of an "infinite and undefinable movement," (Glissant 1989, 175) signaling a departure from essentialist notions of identity and a move beyond national histories and ethnic boundaries that in the face of a globally strengthened essentialism seems more urgent now than ever.

Introduction

1. The Dutch term *zwarte scholen*, black schools, referring to high numbers of nonwhite students, is striking in its unusually explicit racial reference—more so since the term *black* is not generally used to reference black citizens (or Dutch of color in general), for the former instead the majority still favors the term "*neger,*" similar in meaning to the English term *Negro*, but supposed to be without negative connotations in the liberal Dutch context. "Black schools" signify, in official as well as popular discourse, schools with more than 40 percent of *allochton* students. *Allochton* in turn is a Dutch administrative term that includes migrants as well as Dutch citizens with at least one parent born in a non-Western nation (not including Japan). In its popular use, *allochton* differentiates people of color, regardless of citizenship, and white, autochthonous Dutch. Schools with a large number of *allochton* students invariably are located in poor neighborhoods, but rather than focusing on class, the racialized use of "black schools" emphasizes the link between underachievement and overrepresentation of minorities (Arts and Nabha 2001; Hoving 2005).

2. Unless otherwise noted, all translations are mine.

3. This book focuses on continental Europe since the British discourse, while sharing some general European tropes, addresses race in different, more explicit ways than the debates on the continent and does so as part of an Anglophone discourse to which the rest of Europe only opened up recently. This is not meant to imply, however, that both can be sharply separated. On the British discourse see, e.g., Baker, Diawara, and Lindeborg 1996.

4. It seems important at this point to explicitly address the connotations of the term *migrant* in the continental European context, even though or rather because my analysis focuses on racialized *minorities* rather than migrants (and on the former's persistent exclusion from the community of Europeans). It is

impossible, however, to discuss one issue without the other, particularly in this context. Key to the ability to define minority populations as nonmembers of the nation is the racialized European understanding of the concept of "(im)migrant," which contrary to the U.S. use of the term implies a strictly temporary presence—expressed most clearly in the concept of "guest worker"—but at the same time indicates a permanent state across generations. That is, whoever is identified as racial or religious Other is necessarily conceptualized as a migrant, that is, as originating outside of Europe, even if this origin is two, three, or more generations removed. The term thus is less related to legal status or place of birth, but to a perceived immutable diversion from "Europeanness." Assimilation of the second and succeeding generations into the nation still largely depends on the ability to pass for a member of the national majority in a quite literal sense (notwithstanding that this ideal member of the national community against which assimilation is measured is him/herself an artificial construct, based on the national imaginary rather than its reality), creating irresolvable tensions for those possessing signs of difference considered inassimilable. Apart from the obvious racialization at play in this construct, it neglects the significant differences that exist between a first generation that physically migrates and its descendants who are in effect minority citizens, but in continental Europe remain defined through the paradigm of migration: the children (and grandchildren) of migrants of color, rather than becoming first- or second-generation citizens, are considered second- or third-generation migrants.

5. The terms *second-* and *third-generation migrant* are used for minority citizens across Europe, from Sweden to Italy, Romania to Spain. In addition, there are specific concepts such as the Dutch *allochton*, mentioned above, referencing those who are Dutch citizens by birth, but not entirely of autochthonous Dutch parentage, in practice applied to Dutch citizens of color. The recent German category *Bürger mit migrantischem Hintergrund* (citizen with migrant background) has a similar function in being applied exclusively to "racially different" Germans and not for example to "ethnic German" white immigrants (the latter, descendents of Germans who migrated to Eastern Europe and Russia in the eighteenth century, have privileged access to German citizenship due to the nation's ethnic understanding of belonging. See Brubaker 1992).

6. Language, through universal education, creates ethnicity as linguistic community, but the latter's potential openness needs to be countered in varying degrees by race as creating ethnicity as a closed, biological community (Balibar 1994).

7. While the origins of whiteness studies can be traced to early twentieth century African-American discourse and W. E. B. Du Bois's 1910 essay "The Souls of White Folk" (see Rabaka 2007), its origins are more commonly associated with 1990s publications such as Toni Morrison's *Playing in the Dark*, Ruth Frankenberg's *White Women, Race Matters*, or, in the British context, Richard Dryer's *White*. The reception of whiteness studies in continental Europe is a more recent phenomenon,

exactly because of a widespread skepticism toward the usefulness of racial categories within the continental context; see, for example, Gabriele Griffin's and Rosi Braidotti's 2002 essay "Whiteness and European Situatedness." Making the case for a European whiteness studies by proposing that "[t]he culturally constructed and biologically seemingly validated racism which has informed, at least intermittently, the politics of most, if not all, European countries over the past two hundred years is an issue which we as Europeans have not even begun to address adequately" (226), they go on, however, to point out that the "racialization of culture" (229) in the European context led to the violent exclusion of groups falling within the category "white" (exemplified in the Holocaust as well as the Balkan wars). While this is an important observation—and one that my own studies aims to incorporate through its focus on the interaction of ethnicization and racialization as well as the racialization of religion—it is unfortunately contrasted with a simplified model of a "black-white binary" seen as symptomatic for U.S. racial relations. This falsely assumes that a complicated, culture-based rather than biological notion of "race" is somehow specific to Europe as opposed to the United States, neglecting both the important contributions of, for example, Asian-American/Asian diaspora studies to a more differentiated image and the work of whiteness studies itself in breaking up the homogenizing function of the category white (see, e.g., Lowe 1996 or Eng 2000). It is this simple black-and-white model of U.S. racial relations that is often evoked in arguments against the necessity of European whiteness studies, rather than a thorough exploration of Anglophone theorizations of race—which in fact often come to the very same conclusions used by its critics to reject it (see, e.g., Kerner 2007).

8. In particular since the rise of scientific racism in the late nineteenth century, this system of racialization included the explicit division of Europeans in three "subraces," of which only the "Nordic" was assumed to be fully white, while Eastern Europeans were believed to be tainted with "Asiatic," Southern Europeans with "Semitic" and "black blood" (see El-Tayeb 2001).

9. Both "ethnicization" and "racialization" put the analytical focus on the process of Othering rather than on supposed qualities innate to the objects of ascription. While these terms reflect as closely as possible categorizations employed within European societies as a means to create seemingly clear boundaries between insiders and outsiders, they are not meant to imply that the ethnicized and racialized groups are stable or all face similar conditions. It is exactly the simultaneous claim to the obviousness and staticness of these categories and their constant rearrangement and reconstruction that defines processes of racialization and ethnicization (see, e.g., Gualtieri 2001; Koshy 2001; Bayoumi 2006).

10. For a critique of this position and its own inherent ethnoimperialism, for example, in its wholly inadequate understanding of the Brazilian situation, in particular the long history of internal, rather than U.S.-imposed, debates on race. See, for example, Merchant, in Lionnet and Shi 2005.

11. Too often, continental European academic writing on race and migration fails to recognize what Stuart Hall calls "inferential racism," that is structural patterns that allow if not enforce the repetition of racist assumptions and behaviors without necessary intent. Frequently, while explicitly racist positions are rejected and purposeful discrimination is explicitly defined as undesirable, the basic assumption that racist attitudes and policies in European societies are caused by the presence of racialized populations is left unquestioned (Hall 2003; see Weigl 2009 for an example).

12. This is not meant to deny the important differences between the concepts of performance and performativity, in particular with regard to agency—(almost) necessarily present in the former and absent in the latter. It is, however, exactly the intersectionality between the two that has led to some of the most productive explorations of multiple identity formations—see, for example, postcolonial studies arguing against a celebratory understanding of performance, mimicry, enactments of someone else's identity as empowering or liberating for marginalized groups (Fanon 1965; Fuss 1994; Babbha 1996) and queer of color critique's pushing queer studies to reflect on the link between collective performance and (individualized) performativity (Muñoz 1999; Johnson 2005).

13. In recent years, a growing number of younger authors join pioneers like Stuart Hall and Philomena Essed in challenging the notion that race has no place in the ideological framework shaping Europe, and it seems far from coincidental that this literature, often authored by members of racialized groups, draws on postcolonial and diaspora theories still largely ignored in mainstream European scholarship on migrants (Essed 1991). While this new scholarship is slowly gaining ground, the consensus that Europe's Others come from outside (where they will ideally return to) makes it especially hard for minority voices to enter public debates, including those of academia, leaving continental European migration studies a largely white field. See, for example, Ha 1999; Gelbin, Konuk, and Piesche 1999; Guitiérez and Steyerl 2002 for Germany; King 2001; Amiraux 2004; and Keaton 2006 for France; Arts and Nabha 2001; Hoving 2005; Ghorashi 2007 for the Netherlands; Gheorghe and Acton 1999; Grigore 2003; Mudure 2005 on Romania; and Rooth and Ekberg 2003; Sawyer 2000 for Sweden; or Card and Schmidt 2003, Crul and Vermeulen 2003 for a European focus.

14. I am not suggesting that these empires can be equated with colonial overseas possessions. I do believe however that they constituted a form of spatial and ideological governance much closer to the colonialism practiced by other European nations than to the inner-European contestation and shifting of borders taking place at the same time. Another important issue relating to inner-European divisions deserving further exploration is the central, but complicated role of the former "second world" of Eastern Europe, on the verge of becoming a first-class member of the West, and the stakes of whiteness involved in this process. There is a growing body of literature exploring Eastern Europe from a postcolonial

perspective; for a theorization of this development see, for example, Kania 2009; Korek 2009.

15. This is partly due to the sociological approach dominating migration studies, requiring classifications and divisions of populations into clear-cut groups that do not necessarily reflect their reality. This perception is being challenged within sociolinguistics however, which has been tracing the growth of multiethnolects, reflecting the increasingly creolized character of urban European neighborhoods (Quist 2000; Wiese 2009).

16. The point here is not to drive a wedge between migrant and minority populations; there are obvious intersections and common stakes shared by both groups. The definition, however, of people as migrants whose grandparents already were born in the nation they supposedly "migrated" to is not only methodologically questionable, but also politically dangerous.

17. The European definition of "national" minorities largely refers to populations originating in another, often neighboring, European nation; populations who have often been minoritized through the redrawing of borders.

18. For an example see the European Union funded "Museum of European History," discussed in detail in the conclusion.

19. Many thanks to Lisa Yoneyama for bringing this article to my attention. For other national variants of the "not looking European" experience, see, for example, Ahmed 2006; Keaton 2006; Khemiri 2006; Kantara 2000.

20. While this regime is moderated by significant national and regional differences, comparative studies of minorities, that is "second- and third-generation migrants," in Europe indicate similarities despite different national rhetoric and policies (Crul 2003; Rooth and Ekberg 2003). This presence of underlying common attitudes shaping the treatment of racialized groups makes it possible, in fact necessary, to talk about a European ideology.

21. While the claim that migrants of color are a recent European phenomenon is rather standard, there are of course numerous counterexamples: Jews, Muslims, and Roma have lived on the continent in sizeable numbers since the Middle Ages and the presence of Asian and black populations is not a twenty-first or even twentieth century phenomenon either. See, for example, Mosse 1978; Mudure 2005; Eder 2006.

22. The billboard campaign was accompanied by an online game on the party's Web site where visitors could personally "kick out" black sheep (Haegler 2007). The SVP also was behind the successful 2009 campaign to ban minarets in Switzerland, a campaign accompanied by similar incentive billboards, showing minarets rising like missiles from a Swiss flag (again) behind a dark-skinned woman wearing a burka (Jakobs 2009).

23. Apart from the more obvious contestations of colonialism's effects on the colonized, this history also includes episodes of inter-European policies such as the massive forced resettlement of several million people in South-East Europe after

World War I, repeated on an even larger scale after the next war (Aly 2003). These structural interventions could be seen as signs of "the persistence of administrative methods and habits acquired during contact with 'indigenous' populations, which, after having been 'projected' into colonial space during the decisive period of the formation of the republican state apparatus, were reintroduced and 'naturalized' in the metropole" (Balibar 2004, 39).

24. Instead, Roma tend to only appear in the context of the dangers of "migration" or as victims of an Eastern European "democracy deficit" due to forty years of communist rule (European Commission Directorate 2004; Ivanov 2006).

25. Italy has seen a surge of racist violence against Roma—both recent migrants, mostly from Romania, and Italian citizens—drawing heavily on century-old stereotypes. In May 2008, a Roma camp near Naples was torched for example after a Roma woman had been accused of stealing an Italian baby—the "Gypsy baby stealer" trope is as common and as exploitable for the instigation of pogroms in Europe as that of the Jews' ritualistic slaughter of Christian virgins was at least until the end of the Second World War and that of the black rapist is to this day. The popular right coalition of Prime Minister Silvio Berlusconi, rather than doing anything to curb the violence, engaged in a policy of blaming the victims by ordering the mandatory fingerprinting of Roma (including children). See Popham 2008; Povoledo 2008; Owen 2008.

26. The history of Jews in Europe is of course inseparable from the racing of religion characterizing Europe's perception of marginalized minorities. Despite the central place of the Holocaust in European rituals of remembrance (Suleiman 2006; Huyssen 2005; Judt 2008), its lasting effects on European societies remain understudied: in an astonishing act of suppression the "ethnic homogeneity" of postwar Europe upset by the beginning of large-scale labor migration often remains unrelated to the unprocessed "disappearance" of the Jewish minority population. See, for example, Amira Hass: "I found my answer years later, during the eighties, while studying in Amsterdam. Living there, I felt the true force of the void left after 1945, of how Europe, home to millions of Jews for hundreds of years, had simply spewed them out; how most people had collaborated with Nazi Germany's antipluralistic psychosis and accepted the gradual and final removal of the Jews with indifference. But more, I felt tormented by the ease with which Europe had accepted the emptiness that followed, had filled the void, and moved on" (Hass 2000, 8).

27. British novelist Martin Amis in a recent interview gave a bizarre but at the same time representative example of this revisionism when talking about the Lebanon war: "For Nasrallah [the head of Hezbollah], it's a power play; for Israel it's survival. And they always have this hanging over them. It's our fault because we put them in it. There couldn't have been a worse place on earth than where they are. They should have been in Bavaria and then they would have had a couple of leather-shorted scoutmasters from the BLO throwing Molotov cocktails at them,

from time to time . . . at least they wouldn't have been surrounded by millions of people who thirst for their death. So I think you've got to bear that in mind" (Amis 2006). A number of scholars have argued that within the U.S. context, Jews have successfully moved toward whiteness throughout the twentieth century (Brodkin 1998; Jacobson 1998; Novik 1999). To a certain extent this is true for Europe as well, in particular in relation to the increasing racialization of Muslims (as shown in the above quote, which manages to erase and reverse the fact that Bavarians, and other Germans, *in fact* have murdered millions of Jews, while Middle Easterners have not), but the European situation is shaped by significantly different historical and contemporary parameters as well.

28. According to a widely quoted 2006 poll for example, 63 percent of the Dutch believe Islam to be "incompatible" with Europe—this despite a European Muslim population numbering at least fifteen million (Angus Reid, *Global Monitor*, June 7, 2006).

29. This is by no means meant to downplay the disturbing rise in right-wing violence since the 1990s or the constant successes and mainstreaming of extreme right organizations and parties (see Thalhammer 2001). It is exactly the inability to address racialization, its consequences, and its material effects that creates the discursive vacuum that these groups are attempting to fill with an explicitly racist discourse.

30. The extended jurisdiction of border police now includes the right to check papers anywhere, independent of "suspicious circumstances," if they suspect a violation of immigration laws. Numerous complaints indicate that this translates into the profiling of people of color and Muslims—while in fact the majority of illegal immigrants in the union are white, Christian Eastern Europeans, as well as Ukrainians and Russians. See Becker 1998; Thalhammer 2001.

31. See Butler 1993, 219: "What are the possibilities of politicizing disidentification, this experience of misrecognition, this uneasy sense of standing under a sign to which one does and does not belong? . . . [I]t may be that the affirmation of that slippage, that the failure of identification, is itself the point of departure for a more democratizing affirmation of internal difference."

32. Disidentification does not necessarily reject separatism as a political strategy, but recognizes that it often requires race and class privilege.

33. This means that my analysis focuses on urban communities, where the vast majority of minority populations is concentrated (see UCEU 2004).

34. This identity and the new vocabulary it produced begin to enter the mainstream, for example in the Dutch discourse around *straattaal*, and with this mainstreaming comes increasing commercialization and appropriation. A relationship between hip-hop and "queer ethnicities" might seem a stretch in light of the routine association of hip-hop with misogyny and homophobia in U.S. as well as European media. But while certainly not without foundation, this discourse works to hide a far more complicated and sophisticated exploration of identity and community at

the roots of hip-hop culture, placing it in a long tradition of cultural antiessential-ism and posthumanism that reaches from Afrofuturism to the feminist cyborg (see, e.g., Rose 1994).

35. In light of the continued marginalization and silencing of black popula-tions by European mainstream discourses, academic as well as political and popu-lar, it is important to note that the black Other is a key trope in the European mi-gration discourse—a discourse that in truth often is much more one of an internal racial policing. This role has very real consequences, among them the dispropor-tionally high number of black victims of institutional as well as "informal" racism, something that disturbingly is still routinely denied in European public discourse. The degree of this denial became obvious for example in a 2006 incident in which a middle-aged black German man was almost beaten to death in Potsdam in the east of Germany by two white attackers whom he had never met before. His cell phone's mailbox recorded part of the attack, documenting that among other things he was called a "dirty nigger." Nonetheless Germany's Secretary of Interior, Wolf-gang Schäuble, publicly criticized the federal general attorney for treating the case as the German equivalent of a hate crime (in itself an extremely unusual charge and one that was later dropped by the GA). In his attempt to prove that the mo-tives of the attack were entirely unclear, Schäuble added insult to injury by stating that, "blond and blue-eyed people get attacked as well, sometimes by foreigners." In addition to providing an example of the persistent equation of people of color with "foreigners," the reaction illustrates a structural European insistence on re-jecting racism as an explanation for violence against minorities. See "'Blonde Op-fer' Empörung über Schäuble," *SpiegelOnline*, April 20, 2006, http://www.spiegel.de/politik/deutschland /0,1518,412195,00.html (last accessed July 30, 2008).

36. There is, however, a growing body of work on the black experience in Eu-rope, see, for example, Essed 1991; El-Tayeb 2001; Lemke Muniz de Faria 2002; Campt 2003; Edwards 2003.

37. Western European guest worker programs from the 1950s onward were in part a result of internal struggles around gender roles, resulting in the favoring of im-migrant labor over a massive entry of Western European women into the labor force. This issue and others around female migration, including their complicated effects on gender perceptions in and of minority communities, growing female migration from Eastern Europe, sex work, "mail-order brides," and domestic work, are usually invisible in these debates (see, e.g., Brussa, in Domenig et al. 2007, 1–13).

1. "Stranger in My Own Country"

1. See, for example, "Constitution 'Key for EU Success,'" BBC News, Jan 17, 2007, http://news. bbc.co.uk/2/hi/europe/ 6269349.stm.

2. See the grim assessment of the first "European Roma Summit," orga-nized by EU Social Affairs Commissioner Vladimír Špidla, which took place on

September 16, 2008, in Brussels, but failed to produce any concrete results (http://www.euractiv.com/en/socialeurope/eu-roma-summit-draws-crowds-controversy/article-175463 [last accessed January 24, 2009]).

3. It is certainly no coincidence that as of August 2008, not a single European nation has signed the "International Convention on the Protection of the Rights of All Migrant Workers and Members of Their Families."

4. Central among them the collapse of the Soviet Empire, leading to the (re)creation of a host of new nations in Europe's East. These nations are busy constructing a national memory and identity largely externalizing their Communist past, while emphasizing their "Europeanness" (at least in part in order to facilitate their inclusion into a European Union whose identity is still largely shaped by Western Europe).

5. See the 1985 Schengen Treaty and its implementation as European Union law through the 1997 Treaty of Amsterdam (http://eur-lex.europa.eu/en/treaties/dat11997D /htm/11997D.html [last accessed January 23, 2009]).

6. The assumption of a longstanding, "natural" ethnic balance in Europe, upset only by the massive arrival of "guest workers" since the 1950s, demands a rather strained reconstruction of European history. It not only suppresses centuries of massive Muslim influence and minimizes the lasting effects of the near destruction of the continent's Jewish population and the continued marginalization of Roma and Sinti, but also ignores the systematic "ethnic cleansing" taking place on the continent since the end of World War I, leading to the forced migration of more than forty million Europeans (Aly 2003, 28–34). This attempt to reorder Europe according to ethnic criteria necessitated the use of an essentialist notion of identity, assigning singular ethnic-religious signifiers to heterogeneous populations in order to allow for example the "repatriation" of 50,000 Muslim Greeks and Albanians to Turkey and of 350,000 Christian Turks to Greece after the Convention of Lausanne 1923 (Aly 2003, 28–34).

7. This narrative has lost none of its importance in these postnational times: in part it reappears in debates around a European identity, in part, as Balibar claims, the discourse on the end of the nation-states is really one on its origins (Balibar 2004, 14).

8. Zafer Şenoçak writes about the situation of Turkish Germans: "One can immigrate into a country, but not to its past. In Germany, history is read as a diary of the 'community of fate,' the nation's personal experience, to which Others have no access" (Şenoçak 1995, 53).

9. This understanding of modernity has long been criticized within diaspora studies. See, for example, Paul Gilroy: "The concept of postmodernism is often introduced to emphasize the radical or even catastrophic nature of the break between contemporary conditions and the epoch of modernism. Thus there is little attention given to the possibility that much of what is identified as postmodern may have been foreshadowed, or prefigured, in the lineaments of modernity itself.

Defenders and critics of modernity seem to be equally unconcerned that the history and expressive culture of the African diaspora, the practice of racial slavery, or the narratives of European imperial conquest may require all simple periodizations of the modern and the postmodern to be drastically rethought (Gilroy 1993, 420).

10. Jürgen Habermas and Jacques Derrida, "Unsere Erneuerung. Nach dem Krieg. Europas Wiedergeburt," *Frankfurter Allgemeine Zeitung*, May 31, 2003. Simultaneously, articles were published by Umberto Eco in *La Repubblica*, Adolf Muschg in the *Neue Zürcher Zeitung*, Fernando Savater in *El Pais*, Gianni Vattimo in *La Stampa*, and Richard Rorty in the *Süddeutsche Zeitung*.

11. European Commission, Council Conclusions 2001. The EU commission statement failed to define colonialism as a crime against humanity and instead condemned only aspects of it. The French law, passed in February 2005, was repealed a year later after massive protests (Liauzu 2005). A similar sentiment was expressed by French President Nicolas Sarkozy in a speech on Africa's future he gave in Senegal in the summer of 2007 (Johnson 2007).

12. For a more thorough critique see Young 2003. Young, among other things, points out that the starting point of Habermas's argument, the huge antiwar protests all over Western Europe on February 15, 2003, which he terms the birth of a new European public, were in fact part of a *global* movement in which Europe was involved but not central (Young 2003, 2).

13. This is exemplified by the Dutch case: the dates of both the invasion of, and the liberation from, the German occupiers are keystones of ritualized national memory formations, the internment of Dutch colonizers in Indonesia after the Japanese invasion is marginal by comparison, but nevertheless part of the mainstream narrative. Surinamese colonial soldiers fighting for the Dutch on the other hand have been written out of this narrative; only in 1996 were they for the first time officially recognized as war veterans (and could thus receive benefits), while the suffering of the Indonesians at the hands of the Dutch is rarely if ever related to the Dutch suffering at the hands of the Japanese (Ministerie van Defensie 2005).

14. The aim of this chapter is not to give a comprehensive overview of the events in December 2005. For that see, for example, Coleman 2006 and Vaterlaus 2006.

15. See, for example, Smith 2005, which is also indicative in its historical analysis, contrasting the marginalization of African Americans, based on centuries of racial oppression, with the "new" phenomenon of postwar ethnic minorities in France, completely ignoring the effects of centuries of colonial rule on the structural racism shaping the relationship between the majority and these groups.

16. Mehmet Altun from Clichy-sous-Bois, interviewed for BBC News during the riots (http://news.bbc.co.uk/2/shared/spl/hi/picture_gallery/05 /europe_paris_ riot_suburb_residents/html/6.stm).

17. In his 2006 speech "Die Erweiterung des Horizonts" (Broadening Horizons), Habermas does reference the riots in passing, assessing that Europe needs to view

integration as a two-way street in order to achieve the internal strength necessary to play a decisive role on the global stage.

18. See, for example, "Segregatie op basisschool al ver gevorderd," *Trouw*, Nov 16, 2007. Also see the recent study "Identity in Britain," pointing to the increasing spatial segregation of classes in contemporary European societies (Ward 2007).

19. I am using here the English translation published at: http://sketchythoughts. blogspot.com/2005/11/communique-from-mouvement-de.html#jumpto (last accessed August 12, 2008). For the French original of the MIB statement, published on November 9, 2005, see: http://lenumerozero.lautre.net/spip.php?article743 (last accessed August 12, 2008).

20. See, for example, Kleeberg 2005: "What France thus currently experiences is a problem of apartheid. Whoever wants to study where it came from, how it will develop, what good and bad solutions are available, has to look to the United States of the 1960s, to the situation of the colored population" (my translation). Also see Charim 2005; Smith 2005; Baudrillard 2006.

21. See: http://news. bbc.co.uk/2/hi/europe/4376500.stm (last accessed August 12, 2008). The riots took place twenty-two years after the March of Beurs, attended by more than a 100,000 people, high point of a nonviolent movement demanding equal rights for French minorities (Ireland 2005). According to a 1995 poll, 70 percent of second-generation Maghrebis said they felt closer to the French than their parents' culture, 90 percent wanted to be integrated into French society. At the same time, less than one-third of the majority population saw the *beurs* as French and almost 80 percent of acts of racist violence and more 90 percent of racist murders were committed against Maghrebis (Hargreaves 1997, 19).

22. Doug Ireland counts "60 percent cuts over the past three years in subsidies for neighborhood groups that work with youths, and budgets slashed for job training, education, the fight against illiteracy and for neighborhood police who get to know ghetto kids and work with them. (After the first riots in Toulouse, Sarkozy told the neighborhood police there, 'Your job is not to be playing soccer with these kids, your job is to arrest them!')" (Ireland 2005).

23. See Coleman 2006. Most recently, French President Sarkozy, whose "zero tolerance" stance during the 2005 riots arguably both helped to escalate the situation and helped him win the presidential elections, ordered a sweep of the Parisian suburb of Villiers-le-Bel, center of the November 2007 riots, taking place after two youths were hit by a police car. The deployment of more than one thousand police systematically searching the neighborhood and arresting several dozen people hardly qualifies as a change of policy.

24. "I am French, I grew up in a poor neighborhood / My grandparents defended this country during the war / My parents were among those who rebuilt this republic. Remember those workers brought over from Africa / And their children ignored by the law of the land / Second-class citizens, from birth to school."

25. "J'accuse trente ans de racisme et d'ignorance / La répression sans préven-
tion en France / J'accuse votre politique, vos méthodes archaïques / La centralisa-
tion, la défense unique de la loi du fric / Au lieu de rassembler car tous français /
Vous n'avez fait que diviser, laissant l' extrême droite avancer." (I charge thirty
years of racism and of ignorance / repression without prevention in France / I
charge your policies, your archaic methods / centralization, defense of the law of
money / Instead of uniting all who are French / You did nothing but divide, allowing the rise of the extreme right).

26. According to Mbembe 2003, neoliberal globalization works through the
spatial control of life and death not so much in the sense of killing or "letting" live,
but rather through creating populations of "living dead," deprived of almost all the
privileges that come with being alive. While he focuses on the (neo)colonial spaces
of Africa and Palestine (and one could certainly add Iraq now), a striking example
of this system of the living dead in the West is provided by the U.S. prison system.
An increasing number of people, currently more than one in a hundred, disproportionally African American and Latino men, spend part of their adolescence and all
or most of their adult lives in the prison system, many without ever committing
more than petty crimes. This system of incarceration, like the exploding use of "detention centers" in European migration control is not primarily about punishment,
correction, or protecting society from criminals, but about population management, in particular the populations Mbembe calls "disposable"—their crime being
primarily that they are useless to the global economy, whether they live or die does
not really matter, thus they are kept in an in-between state.

27. Mamadou Nyang, 19, Clichy-sous-Bois (http://news.bbc.co.uk/go/ pr/fr//1/
hi/world/europe /4376500.stm [last accessed August 12, 2008]).

28. The situation is complicated by a two-tiered EU membership, which grants
Eastern European states lesser influence in the Union. Perry Anderson writes: "The
role configured by the new East in the EU, in other words, promises to be something like that played by the new South in the American economy since the 1970s:
a zone of business-friendly fiscal regimes, weak or nonexistent labor movements,
low wages, and—therefore—high investment, registering faster growth than in the
older core regions of continentwide capital" (Anderson 2007).

29. While this position is defined as an entirely new phenomenon, caused by
a type of globalization that did not exist before, it in fact fits neatly into a long
European tradition of perceiving racialized minorities, Jews, Roma, and Sinti, as
"rootless nomads" incapable of becoming fully European.

30. See European Council on Refugees and Exiles; People Flow.

31. Germany, Austria, Italy, and Switzerland traditionally practice a *jus sanguinis* that makes "blood," that is descent, the only or primary factor in acquiring
citizenship, excluding residents of "foreign blood" for generations. After the collapse of the Soviet empire, a number of Eastern European nations have returned to
similar laws (Brubaker 1992).

32. European Union refugee and immigration policies are part of the increasing use of prisons and internment camps as a way of population management, incarceration is not based on an individual criminal act or even a court sentence but on belonging to the wrong group, lacking "legitimate" ties to privileged spaces. See European Council on Refugees and Exiles. In 2008, the UNCHR criticized Germany for violating international law by denying recognized refugees the right to free movement, assigning them residences that they are not allowed to leave ("UNCHR wirft Deutschland in Flüchtlingsfrage Völkerrechtsbruch vor" 2007). For a study of illegalized migrants as the postfordist *homo sacer* see Willenbücher 2007.

33. In July 2008, the European Union harmonized regulations for the detention of undocumented migrants (including minors) introducing a maximum detention time of 18 months in the continent's over 200 detention centers, housing approximately 30,000 prisoners (two of the eight EU nation that formerly had no detention limits, Denmark and Britain, opted out of the new law). While human rights organizations criticized the measure for its violation of the detainees' human rights, there was little public debate about it (Brothers 2008). In Switzerland, which is not part of the European Union, asylum laws have recently been tightened: applicants now need a valid passport, certificates of birth or driver's licenses are no longer accepted. This already presents an impossible demand for many, in addition, if applicants are "uncooperative" they can be jailed for up to two years before being deported, and while applying for asylum, refugees neither receive government support nor are they allowed to work. Citizens in all twenty-six Swiss Cantons gave the measure the necessary support, the lowest (51 percent) in Geneva, which has both the highest migrant and the highest unemployment rate in Switzerland (Zumach 2006, 10).

34. That is, contrary to political refugees, civil war refugees are given residence rights as a group, independent of their individual story, which means that they do not have to prove persecution, but also can never gain a permanent residence permit, see Herrmann 2008.

35. Arendt continues: "They are deprived, not of the right to freedom, but of the right to action; not of the right to think whatever they please, but of the right to opinion. Privileges in some cases, injustices in most, blessings and doom are meted out to them according to accident and without any relation whatsoever to what they do, did, or may do. We become aware of the existence of a right to have rights (and that means to live in a framework where one is judged by one's actions and opinions) and a right to belong to some kind of organized community, only when millions of people emerge who had lost and could not regain these rights because of the new global political situation" (296).

36. A 2009 study of Muslims in eleven European cities shows them identifying significantly more with their hometowns than their home countries. See Open Society Institute 2009.

37. Akkouch and his siblings are the subject of a documentary, "Neukölln Unlimited," coproduced by German and French TV, which premiered at the 2010 Berlinale and won the Generation 14 Plus (youth program) award for Best Feature (http://www.rbb-online.de/themen/dossiers/berlinale/news /news_teaser_2010/_neukoelln_unlimited.html).

38. Fresh Familee's "Ahmed Gündüz" was published in 1990. The song is a reflection on the experiences of first generation migrants, written by a member of the second generation, introducing a decidedly minoritarian German point of view. During most of the 1980s, German hip-hop crews had rapped exclusively in English. It is probably the Afro-Italian-German crew Advanced Chemistry who can be credited with first introducing German language rap in 1989. But it was Fresh Familee, whose "Ahmed Gündüz" was the first published and thus widely available rap song in German. See Loh and Güngör 2002.

39. "All this talk about European Unification / If I cross the border with a train or bus / I wonder why I'm the only one who has to show papers, prove his identity! . . . The problem is the ideas in the system: / A real German needs to look real German."

40. Many thanks to Alessandra di Maio for bringing this to my attention.

41. For a European example of this dynamic see, for example, the controversy around the German Brothers Keepers, a collective of successful hip-hop artists that was explicitly created as a black German pressure group, using its music to draw attention to racist violence in Germany and supporting antiracist networks. The group's unambiguous identification with a black German position was not only challenged by white critics, but also by nonblack hip-hop artists of color, reflecting tensions between different minority communities in Germany's hip-hop scene and society at large (El-Tayeb 2004).

42. The Zulu Nation was founded in 1973 by hip-hop activist Afrika Bambaataa as a youth self-help organization in New York's South Bronx. Its message spreading with the international rise of hip-hop, the Zulu Nation now has chapters worldwide, trying to create an awareness among contemporary hip-hop fans of the culture's history and political message. The Nation provided a means for black European hip-hop activists to relate to a transnational black diaspora and to their African heritage, but it also seemed to make it easier for Muslims to bring their faith into hip-hop culture: Cozkun (aka Tuf Kid), break dancer from Basel-based City Attack, expresses a not uncommon sentiment: "The Zulu Nation is also influenced by Islam and challenges this focus on business. Afrika Bambaataa used hip-hop to get people off the streets. Instead of fighting, they competed in Djing, rapping, breaking, and graffiti. You were supposed to think positive, not eat pork, lie, drink alcohol, or use drugs. There are many similarities with Islam" (Khazaleh 2000).

43. The strategy of denying colonial conflicts the status of proper wars and the codex of behavior going with the latter was by no means limited to the French (or to the colonial period for that matter).

44. With the exception of 1954–56 when Papon served as general secretary of the protectorate in Morocco.

45. Swedish-born Leila El Khalifi became Europe's first crossover rap star in 1989 when her (completely apolitical) "Got to Get" reached the top ten charts in several nations. Aziza A (Alev Azize Yıldırım) is of a rather different caliber, her raps—primarily in German in the 1990s , mostly in Turkish since then—addressing issues of nation, gender, and sexuality, have importantly contributed to the Oriental genre. In addition, she was quite involved in German minority activism, more about her in chapter 4.

2. Dimensions of Diaspora

1. This is not to imply that such an exploration does not take place already; to a certain extent this in fact could be said to be precisely what the African diaspora discourse is all about. The limits of black identity as they are constructed within this discourse have long been challenged by feminist and queer authors. See, for example, Hull, Scott, and Smith 1982; Johnson and Henderson 2005.

2. See chapter 3 for a discussion of the relationship between patriarchy and the nation. The black female "nonsubjectivity" sketched by Wright is a different one in so far as she is made invisible through the denial of any agency rather than through the ascription of another, "acceptable" identity as is the case with Europeans of color (or lesbians in Butler's original use of the term).

3. Muñoz however also points to the largely symbolic engagement with women of color feminism within mainstream queer and feminist theory: "The powerful queer feminist theorist and activists that are most often cited—Lorde, Barbara Smith, Anzaldúa, and Moraga, among others—are barely ever critically engaged and instead are, like the disco divas that Riggs mentions, merely adored from a distance"(Muñoz 1999, 11).

4. See Baumann 2001: "Phil Cohen points out that Black and Jewish history or culture are overwhelmingly dominant as the point of reference for diaspora studies." Nevertheless there is often little interest in the methodological content of African diaspora studies.

5. See Soysal's summary of the use of the term: "Diaspora is not a new concept. In its classical usage, it provides a normative model for Jewish history and experience, lived in a state of 'worldlessness.' Lately, however, it has found much usage as an analytical category in the vast immigration literature on the global dispersion of migrant population. It captures much of our analytical and popular imagination, and claims explanatory fortitude in narrating the presence and condition of immigrant populations," (2000, 2) or Huyssen's overview from "the classical case of the Jewish diaspora to the whole spectrum of expats, exiles, and expellees, immigrants or political refugees" (Huyssen 2003, 159). The consistent exclusion of Africana studies from the modern genesis of the uses

of diaspora, despite its affirmed key role, seems indicative of the degree to which black contributions to modern discourses are still ignored within academia (and outside of it).

6. The only systematic analysis of racializations in Europe has been conducted in the context of Holocaust studies, which however tend to sharply differentiate between anti-Semitism and racism, meaning that key texts of race studies are rarely considered in theories of anti-Semitism (Mosse 1979).

7. See, for example, Wright: "While prominent postcolonial scholars such as Gayatri Spivak and Homi Bhabha have offered numerous possibilities for a postcolonial subject, their derivations ignore all but those of South Asian descent, often "reinventing the wheel" by bypassing those African diasporic works of theoretical significance in favor of dialoguing with their colleagues in poststructuralism. Like its postcolonial sister, poststructuralist theory is explicitly committed to questioning, subverting, and ultimately replacing oppressive epistemologies of Western European colonial thought. Yet it unwittingly acts on the very racist assumptions it seeks to overturn by failing to consider that the direct targets of these epistemologies and practices—peoples of African descent in the West—might in fact possess their own body of sophisticated counterdiscourses that is valuable far beyond the ethnographic information it offers" (2004, 26).

It is important to note, however, that there is a younger generation of scholars who successfully try to bridge the gap between postcolonial and diaspora studies. See, for example, Gopinath 2005; Guitiérez and Steyerl 2003; Nghi 2001.

8. The omission of the African diaspora becomes especially grating in chapter 8, "Patriotism and Its Futures," built around an analysis of race relations in Appadurai's chosen home, the United States, which makes no reference whatsoever to the vast body of literature on the topic produced by scholars of the African American experience.

9. This position achieved scientific credibility with the theories of Artur de Gobineau (1816–82) who granted the African an innate artistic talent, but not the intellectual capacities to exploit it. See, for example, El-Tayeb 2001; Wright 2004.

10. This is slowly changing however, in part in response to the black European activism described in the latter part of this chapter. See, for example, the Black European Studies Project or Hine, Keaton, and Small 2009.

11. For the far-reaching effects of this perception see, for example, the case of Egyptian immigrant Mostafa Hefny who unsuccessfully sued the U.S. government over his automatic classification as "white" after his naturalization (Morsy 1994).

12. See Taiwo 1998. Egypt has a different role especially in Afrocentric discourse than the Maghreb, which is almost completely ignored, but nevertheless the identification of "black Africa" with the sub-Saharan regions leaves out the North as a whole. The strict division between North Africa and sub-Saharan Africa implies clear racial and cultural differences between "Arabs" and "Berbers" on the

one hand and (sub-Saharan) "blacks" on the other. However, the Sahara has not only been regularly crossed by traders since ancient times, it has inhabitants who physically bridge the supposedly "natural divide." A different perspective could perceive the Sahara as a space of contact and exchange bringing into focus links that have been obscured by nationalist and Eurocentric narratives, links that are reflected in the fusionist character of Ali Hassan Kuban's music, but also Algerian Raï's or Ibn Chaldun's eclectic philosophy.

13. In fact, "blackness" and "Africanness" are taken as synonyms only outside of the continent itself, where ideologies of regional differences, including ethnicity and race, appear compatible with Panafricanist politics.

14. Numbers are based on estimates by the American Muslim Council's 2000 poll and the 2001 American Religious Identity Survey (see: http://theislamproject.org/education/United_States.html and the 2001 FACT survey of regular mosque attendees (http://www.cair-net.org/asp/populationstats.asp).

15. The legendary internationalist transformation of Malcolm X after experiencing the multiethnic community worshipping in Mecca, for example, constitutes an important point of reference for European Muslim communities and especially for young second-generation men who can identify both with Malcolm X's personal trajectory and his nonconciliatory politics. See, for example, the "Belgian Malcolm X," Dyab Abu Jahjah, founder of the Arab-European League.

16. Another example is the effect of Bob Marley's 1979 tour through Australia and New Zealand on the fledgling transnational black consciousness movement among Aborigines and Maori (Lipsitz 1994, 142). These colonized populations, whose identification with blackness is neither based on African ancestry nor on the common experience of the Middle Passage and who live as racialized minorities in their native countries, certainly strain even inclusive definitions of African diaspora. But their experiences as "black" communities in white-dominated Western nations created enough common ground to allow an identification with and modification of Marley's Panafricanism. And their position as both "Other-from-Without" (as antagonistic *and* irrelevant to modern Australian and New Zealandian societies) and "Other-from-Within" (as native, but "unintegrated" minorities) resists the resolution of grating contradictions, a resistance one could argue that lies at the very heart of a dialogic understanding of diaspora: it continuously asks what it means to be black but does not rely on definite answers as it is the process of asking itself through which the community is formed.

17. Michaela Mudure traces the similarities between "black" Roma and African Americans further back to tropes of their literary productions in the nineteenth century (Mudure 2006). This claim allows for the potential inclusion of Roma populations in a diasporic intersubjectivity, and while it certainly requires more research, it might be strengthened by a return to the vernacular. After all, music is central to Roma culture and Europe's most brilliant jazz musician was a French Roma, Django Reinhardt. His music has rarely been connected to diasporic

discourses though, in part certainly because the binary of intellect and emotion, art and criticism, individual and collective that black music itself defies is still very present in European critics' responses to popular (black) music. This perception of artists as expressing collective feelings (rather than thoughts), in need of critics translating their art into theory remains ignorant of the role of musicians as "vernacular intellectuals" (Farred 2003) in the formation of a transnational black counterdiscourse, leaving unanswered the call for a reassessment of their relevance for diasporic identities. Thus, Reinhardt's talent is often naturalized through the stereotypical equation of gypsies and soulful music in European discourse, while his contributions to jazz history are presented in purely aesthetic terms, detaching them from any sense of community (or communication) and the diasporic and transnational history of Roma culture often expressing itself in musical fusions (Michael Dregni's 2004 biography, which also recounts the anecdote of Reinhardt's repeatedly exclaiming, "My brother, my brother!" when first listening to an early Louis Armstrong recording, does consider such a diasporic element while also heavily drawing on the cliché of the gypsy as an instinctive musician. Contemporary Roma music reflects questions of authenticity and identity, fusion, and assimilation as much as it did in Reinhardt's days). Placed in this tradition, in leaving behind notions of cultural purity, Reinhardt, like Oriental hip-hop did decades later, created new venues of dialogue between diasporic communities.

18. For an example see the German discussions around the "naturalization test" aimed specifically at Muslims applying for citizenship, who are suspected not to share Western values such as tolerance toward homosexuality and commitment to the equality of women—acceptance of these values is supposedly tested in the process. While this discourse has many of the characteristics of a farce—clearly many if not most Germans, certainly including the Pope, would not pass the test—the public discussions around it have quite serious consequences for Germany's largest religious minority by further stigmatizing it as antidemocratic and premodern (for English-language sources see Islamic Human Rights Commission 2006; Tzortzis 2006).

19. Until 2001, Germany practiced a strict version of *jus sanguinis*, permanently denying citizenship to the descendants of millions of labor migrants, most of them from Turkey and Yugoslavia (Brubaker 1994). The changed law grants citizenship through birth (with some qualifications), but allows dual citizenship only toward European Union member states, again excluding residents of Turkish descent. Afro-Germans in contrast often have one white German and one black, non-German parent, meaning that a much higher number of them have German citizenship (at least since 1976 when German women were allowed to pass on their citizenship to their children when married to noncitizens). See El-Tayeb 2001.

20. As we will see later in this chapter, the process of collective memory preservation and construction might be more complicated however than this understanding suggests.

21. Amsterdam's self-organized center for "zmv" women (*zwart, migrantisch, vluchteling*—black, migrant, refugee) is called Zami, another sign of the enormous impact of Lorde's work on European feminists of color (see www.zami.nl)

22. Adams's in many ways informative and thoughtful article is most certainly undervalued here by using it merely as an example of a larger trend in U.S. feminist scholarship fascinated by the idea that by inventing the term "Afro-German," Lorde also "invented" Afro-Germans (see, e.g., Blackshire-Belay 1996).

23. This hierarchal approach is quite opposed to Lorde's own vision of a diasporic dialog between Afro-German and African American women as laid out in her foreword to *Showing Our Colors* and practiced in her interactions with black Germans during her frequent visits to the country.

24. Autobiographical texts by Afro-Germans, such as those collected in *Showing our Colors*, almost unanimously speak of an identification with African Americans as the only visible blacks in German media, children's books, films, etc. Also see Hügel-Marshall 2001; Huber 2005.

25. Africa might have played an even bigger role in the Afro-German imaginary, where it appears a loaded concept on many levels: as the home of an often absent father and unknown siblings and routinely assigned as the "real" place of origin in encounters with white Germans—at the same time, North and West Africa are geographically relatively close, so to go there from Germany is far from impossible. Accordingly, the first trip to Africa often appears as a deeply ambiguous cornerstone of Afro-German narrations of identity. Especially in narratives of women it does not represent the desired place of belonging, of finally being able to "blend in," but a site of another experience of difference—resulting not necessarily in alienation or the rejection of one's African heritage, but in rejecting an essentialized, imaginary Africanness, potentially opening the way toward a nonessentialist version of black diasporic identity: "For a long time I wanted to emigrate. I wanted to go to an African country, to a place that promised me an identity, a little piece of an ideal world . . . I took several trips, moving around in northern and western Africa. Particular in Liberia I had a decisive experience that forced me back to the realization that I am not African, that I couldn't become a Liberian just like that, or slip into another skin and wipe away my past" (Wiedenroth, in Oguntoye and Opitz 1986, 170).

The experience of travelling to Africa appears as more of a "return home" in the memories of male Afro-Germans, and while I have no empirical proof, it seems to me that this is likely related to gender-specific experiences and expectations that make it harder for women, especially if they visit family, to overlook the fact that African societies have their own sets of normative rules that are not only unfamiliar to them, but produce new demands and restrictions.

26. Black Germans have been discursively constituted as threat to the nation's (racial) identity in the wake of the colonial war of 1904 as well as of World Wars I and II (El-Tayeb 2001). Not knowing about the history of Afro-Germans is thus

not based on a lack of information but on its periodic suppression, leading to a strange dialectic between the master narrative of the inexistence (and impossibility) of a black German identity and the underlying narrative of a black threat, readily mobilized in times of crisis.

27. Translated into English by May Ayim in 1990.

28. Ayim herself continued to take part in this ongoing collective process of bringing out the dead after the publication of *Showing*; see, for example, her poem *soul sister*, written in 1992 in response to Audre Lorde's passing. Black British dub poet Linton Kwesi Johnson in turn paid tribute to Ayim after her death in his *Reggae fi May Ayim*.

29. See http://mayayimaward.wordpress.com.

30. While "Afro-German" and "black German" were used largely interchangeably by activists, it is important to note that in practice the definition of "black" was more inclusive as evidenced in the important role of South Asian German activists such as Sheila Mysorekar.

31. "Get to knows us. I.S.D. The Black German Initiative," 1989, original in English. In the years following the first meeting in 1985, a network of ISD chapters emerged throughout Germany. Activities were wide-ranging, including an annual national community meeting (which has been attended by hundreds in recent years); the Black History Month in Berlin; the publication of a magazine (*Afro Look*, preceded by the short-lived *Onkel Toms Faust*); and cooperative projects with other minorities (see www.isdonline.de and www. cybernomads.net).

32. See http://www.globalinstitut.org/Origins&Objectives.html.

33. While black German artists were disproportionately present in the German underground hip-hop scene, they were long ignored by mainstream producers and consumers. This changed in 2000 when forty of them used their increasing popularity to form the all-male project Brothers Keepers (Sisters Keepers followed some months later). Their song "Adriano—Letzte Warnung" (Final Call), announcing resistance against the rising tide of racism in Germany, as exemplified in the brutal killing of Alberto Adriano to whom the song was dedicated, reached the top ten as did their self-titled CD. Building on this momentum, Brothers Keepers have initiated a variety of antiracist projects aimed at empowering black youths, supporting refugees (who independent of their ethnic origin live under deplorable conditions in Germany) and fighting police brutality against African migrants (see El-Tayeb 2003).

34. Challenges to this nonnormativity on the other hand can be established by referencing larger traditions in which the Afro-German experience is then naturally integrated. A recent controversy over homophobic positions expressed at an international Panafrican meeting in Hamburg shows however that Afro-German lesbians in particular are still able to effectively counter attempts to normalize larger heteronormative diaspora discourses by evoking the particular Afro-German tradition of feminist activism (Peggy Piesche, personal conversation).

35. Hip-hop, aggressively addressing this exclusion brought the conflict into the open. Advanced Chemistry's experiences after publishing "Fremd im eigenen Land" in 1991, described in the last chapter, were mirrored in the criticism facing the Brothers Keepers project a decade later, again caused by the rappers' insistence that they were German as well as black: failing to reflect on the privileges of uncontested national belonging that come with being white, a large part of the German left rejects any such statements as reactionary. Thus, black Germans' attempt to make their country their home by creating a space for themselves on its imaginary map—a step, which if successful, would mean a dramatic reconfiguration of Germanness—is held against them by exactly those white Germans who most decry the nation's anachronistic and exclusionary concept of identity.

36. For a discussion of the position of black children in postwar Germany, see Lemke Muniz de Faria 2006.

37. The relative success of Afro-German actress, activist, and musician Noah Sow's 2008 Deutschland Schwarz Weiss (Germany Black and White), which popularizes analyses of German racism originating in the black community rather than white academic discourses, represents one of the inroads into mainstream society twenty-five years of black German activism have made. Günther Wallraff's 2009 feature film *Schwarz auf Weiss* (Black on White), on the other hand, in which Germany's most famous investigative journalist goes undercover in blackface as an "African" to unmask German racism, and the controversy following the movie's theatrical release, show the strict discursive limits to which mainstream debates around racism in Germany are still confined (see Sow 2008; Büscher and Wahba 2009).

38. Black Europeans challenge both exclusions simultaneously by insisting on the inclusion of the history of slavery in commemorations of Europe's past. Progress in this regard is painfully slow but present: while slavery is still largely absent from European textbooks when the topic is Europe itself rather than Africa or the United States, a number of nations, including the Netherlands and France, have recently begun to recognize their nation's involvement in transatlantic slavery, see van der Made 2007 and Horton 2004.

39. Black diasporic discourse complicates more issues than the quest for a foundational, definite group experience however. Language is another factor playing into the particulars of the black Atlantic in complex ways. In contrast to the Jewish or Roma diasporas, the African diaspora does not possess a common language in the traditional sense. To Edouard Glissant, this lack represents "the difference between a people that survives elsewhere, *that maintains its original nature*, and a population that is transformed elsewhere *into another people*" (Glissant 1989, 15; italics in original). While this link between language and "original nature" might be too simple, it certainly is true that the need to create a common language transcending linguistic separations forms

the very grid in which the concept of an African diaspora can be placed, that is, the process of transformation "into another people." Hierarchies and exclusions are obvious nevertheless. And while colonialism provided new "common languages" for the African diaspora and Africa itself (and the problematics of this have of course been excessively analyzed by Glissant and Chamoiseau among others), Arabic as the language of another part of the diaspora remained beyond the horizon of interest of most of the intellectuals identified by Gilroy, Wright, Stephens, Edwards, and others as key figures in the creation of a diasporic consciousness.

40. It also seems important to note that the effect of the Nazi rule on the black German community (or communities of color in general), has not yet been fully analyzed (Campt's book is an important step in that direction). Pre-1933 Germany, in particular Berlin and Hamburg, was a center of internationalist anticolonialist activism, in 1930 the first International Conference of Negro Workers took place in Hamburg (though London had been the organizers' first choice) and African migrants in Imperial Germany developed strong informal and formal networks, from the conservative Deutscher Afrikanerbund (German Union of Africans) to the radical *Liga zur Verteidigung der Negerrasse* (League for the Defense of the Negro Race). See Reed-Anderson 1995, 38–40; Oguntoye 1997, 76–101.

3. Secular Submissions

1. *Foreign Policy* decided to also include the next ten readers' choices and here, things looked much more familiar: Noam Chomsky, Al Gore, Bernard Lewis, and Umberto Eco represent positions 11–14, somewhat balancing the Muslim domination of the first ten spots. Positions 15–20 were occupied by Ayaan Hirsi Ali, Amartya Sen, Fareed Zakaria, Gary Kasparov, Richard Dawkins, and Mario Vargas Llosa.

2. Especially if one considers the poll's top write-in candidate, comedian (and Catholic) Stephen Colbert, who has been known to successfully order the members of the Colbert Nation to vote en masse for him on various occasions.

3. For the sake of argument, the question how exactly *Foreign Policy* defines either "influential" or "intellectual" is not addressed here. It should be understood that both terms require scrutiny, but what is important in this context is primarily the discursive construction of "influential intellectuals," not necessarily their actual impact or status.

4. The notion of the "West" itself, based not on geographical realities but on implicit moral hierarchies, reflects this bias.

5. In reality, the West's support for UN human rights regulations is far from impeccable: while all EU member states, and recently also the United States, supported the UN General Assembly's demand to decriminalize homosexuality, of the

forty nations who have signed the UN Convention on the Rights and Dignity of Persons with Disabilities only five—Germany, Austria, Sweden, Spain, and San Marino—are European and as of 2009 no Western nation has signed the International Convention on the Protection of the Rights of all Migrant Workers, passed by the General Assembly in 1990. See http://www.un.org /News/ Press/ docs/2008/ ga10801.doc.htm; http://www.un.org/disabilities/default.asp?id=257; http://www.un.org/News/Press/docs/2003/LT4371.doc.htm.

6. I am not claiming that migrants from Turkey do not identify as Muslim nor am I making any claims about actual religious impartiality or freedom in Turkey, what I am suggesting is that Turkish secularism is as "successful" in the separation of state and religion as Western European secularism—it bears keeping in mind that in secular nations like Germany, more than 90 percent of the population are members of the recognized Christian churches (Rommelspacher 2002, 130).

7. This leads to a number of additional questions: Can cosmopolitanism do without a center and a periphery—and if not, is Europe able to accept a cosmopolitics in which the traditional "West" constitutes this periphery? Are identity politics the other of cosmopolitanism or an integral part of it? Can an Enlightenment-based universalist discourse address the fundamental power differences shaping all global dialogue (and is it this awareness that separates cosmopolitics from humanist cosmopolitanism)?

8. Especially fascinating is the question of translation and the power structures language reproduces: while Fanon identified with the traumatized Algerians he treated unofficially, he was able to converse directly—a process central to therapy—only with the French soldiers who were his "official" patients. The common colonizer made it possible for him, the Martinician, to interact in French with French colonizers and Algerian intellectuals; the vast majority of his native patients, however, spoke only Arabic or Berber, preventing direct exchanges (this notwithstanding the fact that in his writings, Fanon erased the role of the Algerian translators). See Fuss 1994.

9. See Honig paraphrasing Girard: "A scapegoat is a figure made to represent some taint borne by the community as a whole, in particular, the loss of distinctions that defines the sacrificial crisis from which the community is trying to recover. The attribution of that taint to a scapegoat allows the community to unanimously disavow it, and the ritual murder of the scapegoat cleanses the community and reestablishes the lines of proper order that had become so dangerously attenuate" (Honig 2001, 34).

It seems likely that in the Dutch case, this process is also fed by a perceived loss of liberal values in which Muslims originally appear as victims, namely the role of the UN *Dutchbat* contingent in the Srebenica massacre in 1995. The mass murder of at least eight thousand Bosnian men and boys and the raping of thousands of women within a couple of days in full sight of Dutch troops who did not interfere (most Bosnian Muslims in the area had fled to the UN compound in hope of protection from the Serbian troops) led to a national crisis culminating in the resignation of the Dutch government in 2002, after an official report had attributed at least partial responsibility to the Dutch UN commanders. In recent years, public assessment has shifted dramatically, however, and in 2006, *Dutchbat* III was officially honored for its conduct by the Ministry of Defense (Marlet 2006; also see: Honig 2001b; Runia 2004; Leyesdorff 2007). The fact that the first recognized case of genocide to occur in Europe after the end of World War II was directed against a native religious minority, Bosnian Muslims, in plain sight of the European (and international) community whose "humanitarian intervention" failed miserably is a central chapter in recent European history that remains conspicuously absent from discussions about European identity or the role of the continent's Muslim minority.

10. The interviews were conducted by non-Muslim Dutch women (Roosen 2007).

11. Apart from the Middle Ages, the Enlightenment, and arguably the 1960s, terms like "Islamo-fascism," coined by Bernard-Henry Lévy and widely used by now, point to a less than subtle attempt to rewrite Europe's reaction to the rise of Nazism, allowing to shift the blame onto the "new fascists," worse than the old ones, just some years after nations like France or the Netherlands finally began to address their history of collaboration and anti-Semitism. See for example, Diana Pinto, historian and Senior Fellow at the Institute for Jewish Policy Research London, for such a revisionist argumentation, which absolves the majority from responsibility, while pitting minorities against each other (in part by drawing on racist stereotypes): "The old anti-Semitism came from above, from the elites, and was used to mobilize the lower classes. The people who destroyed synagogues in 1938 did that on orders and had wives at home who ironed their brown shirts. The new anti-Semitism comes from below, from aggressive thugs with a violent potential that is directed toward Jews but not limited to them . . . Since about ten years, Jew-hatred is growing among blacks too. It is based on arguments such as: 'Enough of the Holocaust! Our ancestors suffered under slavery; which lasted longer and cost more lives than the Holocaust. That is what we want to talk about!' Black anti-Semitism is lower in numbers than the Muslim one but much more violent" (in Schmidt 2008, 14).

12. Her final move away from Islam, according to Hirsi Ali, came with the 9/11 attacks, which in an 2007 interview she directly relates to Qur'anic teachings: "She also describes how horrified she felt as an adult after Sept. 11, 2001, reaching for the Koran to find out whether some of Osama bin Laden's more blood-curdling statements—'when you meet the unbelievers, strike them in the neck'—were direct quotations. 'I hated to do it,' she wrote, 'because I knew that I would find bin Laden's quotations in there.' And there were consequences: 'The little shutter at the back of my mind, where I pushed all my dissonant thoughts, snapped open after the 9/11 attacks, and it refused to close again' (Applebaum 2007, BW05).

13. Of course, Ali's story is quite literally too good to be true: the lies she told about her past in order to be granted asylum in the Netherlands were used by her own party, the neoliberal VVP (Volkspartij voor Vrijheid en Democratie—People's Party for Freedom and Democracy, for which she had been a member of parliament from 2003 to 2006) after she fell out of favor, to revoke her Dutch citizenship (a decision that was later revised, see Anthony 2007).

14. As has been pointed out by Ian Buruma and others, the Voltaire comparison, despite its popularity, is far from accurate, since Muslim authorities in twenty-first century Europe hardly have a status anywhere near that of the continent's eighteenth century Catholic Church. If at all, the label might be more usefully applied to public intellectuals within the Muslim world like Fatima Mernissi, Shirin Ebadi, or Riffat Hassan (this in addition to the fact that a differentiation between faith and religious institutions, central to Voltaire's attack on the church, is virtually nonexistent in Hirsi Ali's world view). But the presentation of Europe's interaction with Muslim migrants as an encounter with its own past has the benefit of allowing to place contemporary battles into existing frameworks, giving rise to "new Voltaires" like Hirsi Ali—who under secular European supervision, might lead the continent's new medieval population out of the Dark Ages of homophobia, sexism, and anti-Semitism. In the words of Salman Rushdie: "Having recapitulated the Enlightenment for herself in a few short years, Hirsi Ali has surveyed every inch of the path leading out of the moral and intellectual wasteland that is traditional Islam" (Harris and Rushdie 2007).

15. To name just a few: in 1992, when Hirsi Ali arrived in the Netherlands, *Stichting El Sambra* focused on health education and access for Moroccan and Turkish women by addressing their specific situations rather than trying to make them fit into the existing system structured around the needs of Dutch women; the Medusa Foundation targeted sexual violence against black and migrant women by educating health care and education workers; Organisatie Marokkaanse Vrouwen Amsterdam housed weekly discussions on issues relevant to Moroccan women from immigration legislation to STDs; ZAMI, center for black, migrant, and refugee women, offered a wide array of daily activities from language classes to poetry workshops and queer women's groups; and ARGAN, a center for Moroccan youths with a focus on girls, was one of the first organizations of its kind created by the second generation, with a majority of women on its founding board (see *ZAMI Krant* 3, 1993).

16. Kelek's 2005 publication mixes personal experiences with an analysis of forced marriages within the Turkish community, identifying "Muslim culture" as the culprit. Placing herself in a position similar to that of Ali, whom she explicitly mentions as a model, she claims a unique position as both possessing authentic, "inside" knowledge of Islam (identified with the Turkish community) and a grounding in a Western Enlightenment tradition that necessarily eludes Muslims unable to shed their oppressive culture: "In this book, I report from the inside of

Turkish life in Germany, of forced and arranged marriages, I tell of women whose families deny them elementary rights" (Kelek 2005, 11). Kelek underscores her importance by constructing a drastic Manichean dichotomy, casting the fight between democracy and Islam as one of "life and death" and repeating Leon de Winter's claim that Islamism is the fascism of the twenty-first century (Kelek 2005, 17).

17. A symptomatic example is the much-touted "first national Islam conference" that the German government organized in 2006, aimed at addressing "problems" caused by the presence of a Muslim minority within the nation—central among them the position of women—in the spirit of dialogue rather than through accusations. Among the invitees were representatives of Muslim organizations, public intellectuals such as Turkish–German writer Feridun Zaimoğlu, and critics of Islam like Neçla Kelek—but not a single practicing Muslima. Naime Cakir, women's representative of Hesse's Muslim community aptly comments: "Muslim women, who might even signal allegiance to their religion, which supposedly is the conference topic, by wearing the headscarf, are presented as resistant to integration or even as symptoms of a failed integration . . . An invitation to the Islam conference would thus have been a highly symbolic gesture toward these women, since it would have had dual implications: it would have signaled political support for women fighting for the equality of men and women. And all those conservative Muslims who like to reduce women's role to children, kitchen, and church, in this case mosque, would have seen that the commitment to gender equality is real. The lack of competent interlocutors representing relevant groups of Muslim women cannot have been the problem" (Cakir 2006, 11).

18. This process certainly is in part self-enforced. In order to take part in this discourse the subordinate group profits from defining itself according to dominant perceptions: all problems admitted, the appropriation of the "Muslim" label in spite of its negative connotations and partial inaccuracy potentially opens a crack in the usually firmly closed definition of Europeanness, allowing for the idea of a European—rather than national or transnational—Muslim identity.

19. Interestingly, Neçla Kelek—who since the publication of *Die Fremde Braut* in 2005 plays a role comparable to Hirsi Ali's in German discourses—did make this exact claim in her dissertation, published in 2002, stating that an identification as Muslim among the second generation of Turkish Germans was primarily social, not necessarily implying strong religiosity, but rather a reinterpretation of the role of religion in a new context. But only a year later, she categorically denied the possibility of such an adaptation "because Islam as religion is godgiven. This cultural pattern shapes the actions of Muslim migrants in Germany into the smallest detail of their everyday lives—their life, attitude, the way they raise their children. And these values have little in common with the norms and values of the German majority" (see Terkessidis and Karakasoglu 2006).

20. According to Balibar, every nation is built around a "fictive ethnicity" (fictive in the sense that no nation has a "natural" constituency but must permanently

construct its citizens as such). It is constructed via two primary tools, language and race. Language, through universal education, creates ethnicity as linguistic community, but the latter's potential openness needs to be countered in varying degrees by race as creating ethnicity as a biological community (Balibar 1990).

21. For a discussion of the German headscarf debate focusing on the case of high school teacher Fereshta Ludin, see Beverley Weber's excellent 2004 article.

22. Discussions around the right of Muslim girls to cover their heads in the secular space of public schools shift the focus away from European education systems' massive failure to grant equal opportunities to minority populations: studies across the continent show that the second generation continues to lag behind the majority in terms of job market access with regard to both income and unemployment level. The studies also show unanimously that this disparity already starts in school and affects boys as well as girls. There are a number of factors that translate into disadvantages across national systems, having one or two non-European parents and living in a neighborhood with a high density of minority populations ranks high among them; while the parents' educational level (which is below average for non-European migrants) has less influence, religion, or more specifically the headscarf, is not considered as a factor (Crul 2003; Riphahn 2003; Rooth and Ekberg 2003; Skyt et al. 2003).

23. "In my town hall there are Fatmas and ululations / Headscarves, slippers, and bubus / Thugs, Zoubidas, Mamadous / Help, they are already here!"

24. While his descent from Hassan El-Banna, founder of the Egyptian Muslim Brotherhood, is no doubt one source of this suspicion, reactions to Ramadan seem to be in part fed by a trope already used against assimilated Jews in the nineteenth and early twentieth century, namely that of the Other who pretends to be like us and thus becomes all the more dangerous.

25. For a critique of this argument and an analysis of its function in post-9/11 U.S. foreign policy, see Saba Mahmood 2006. Mahmood examines the work of a number of "Muslim reformers" attempting an exegesis of the Qur'an (among them Abdolkarim Soroush). It is striking however that "feminist" critics of Islam like Kelek and Hirsi Ali completely ignore the historicizing of Qur'anic interpretations produced within Muslim feminism (see, e.g., Afzal Khan 2005).

26. Ramadan is familiar with and does not fundamentally challenge Europe's self-perception as the cradle of modernity, an enlightened continent, built on a Judeo-Christian tradition; rather, his aim is to show that Islam can be integrated into this model. His founding of the Muslim European Network, bringing together Muslim "leaders" from across the continent (prominently including women and Eastern Europeans) exemplifies his attempt at uniting and representing Muslim Europeans by theorizing the parameters of a distinct European Islam. This approach is not necessarily appreciated by conservative Muslim organizations, often defining themselves in relation to dominant non-Western practices of Islam. His insistence on raising a voice that is European at the same

time that it is shaped by Muslim culture is equally challenging to Europe's secular identity.

Particular striking, as well as controversial, are not necessary Ramadan's ideas about the role of religion in secular societies but his criticism of French liberals' support of U.S. and Israeli policies in the Middle East as less the expression of a humanist perspective than of a communitarian identity-politics. Here Ramadan presents himself as closer to the ideals of Enlightenment universalism than secular thinkers such as Pascal Bruckner, Bernard-Henri Lévy, or Pierre-André Taguieff, whom he accuses of rejecting cosmopolitan ideals in favor of particularist interests (Ramadan 2003). The suggestion that the continent's Muslims might be as (or more) European that the intellectuals most vocally advocating the need to defend Europe's secular identity against them was meant and perceived as a provocation, leading to accusations of anti-Semitism (since most of the intellectuals he attacked were both Jewish and ardent supporters of Israel's policies) and arguably affecting the U.S. State Department's decision to deny Ramadan a visa after he received an invitation to teach at the University of Notre Dame (see Preston 2006). At the same time, his insistence that a European Muslim identity is not only possible, but also necessary in order to overcome the (self)destructive binary static that puts both groups at odds garnered Ramadan a huge following among young Muslims in the West (in North America as well as Europe), putting into question claims that "secularization" is the only path to integration for minority youths and that a turn to religion necessarily reflects a rejection of "European values."

27. Some of them tell their stories in Imad el Kaka and Hatice Kurşun's anthology on gay and lesbian youths of Muslim background (though not all of them religious) in the Netherlands (el Kaka and Kurşun 2002). Unlike Roosen, who created composite stories from the interviews her researchers conducted in order to create "representative" images of Muslim women, the anthology's editors emphasize the heterogeneity and individuality of the contributors, offering less an explanation than an engagement with positions that are not always compatible. They range from the relaxed attitude of Rafi, who states: "I definitely still feel Muslim, but I drink a glass of wine occasionally and well, I don't worry about that too much. A typical case of a second- or third-generation Muslim in the Netherlands, that's what I call myself" (114) to the tormented Sidi: "I am afraid that I will become schizophrenic at some point. Maybe I am just a big coward. I am afraid to be who I am, but Allah wanted me this way. The Qur'an condemns homosexuality. People who deny this did not read the holy book" (150). Most of the religious contributors, however, while continuing to engage with Islam have come to their own interpretations, like Nazha, who left Morocco to escape an intensely homophobic climate (that however did not include her family), on their own: "Each night before I go to sleep I silently say the Muslim profession of faith, that there is no God but Allah and that Mohammed is his servant and prophet. I read the Qur'an frequently, because it calms me down and brings me closer to Allah" (60).

28. Abdol-Hamid's experience of being automatically recommended for a lower educational track, usually precluding the possibility of entering the university system later, is shared by racialized minorities across Europe (OECD 2006).

29. See Abdol-Hamid 2007: "Ethnic minorities are not a problem in themselves; when identifying reasons for the lack of integration in Denmark, I prefer to talk about social classes and look at people's class background rather than their ethnic identity."

30. While Abdol-Hamid is quite explicit in her feminist positions, she is less so with regard to homosexuality; however, she turns around Tariq Ramadan's demand toward queer Muslims to "keep their homosexuality private" by denying that religion provides the basis for policing sexual orientation: "People's sexual orientation is not important to me. I don't want to enter people's bedrooms and see whom they're sleeping with. It's not my right as a politician or as a Muslim. I can't judge people. As far as I'm concerned, the only one who can judge people is God" (in Wheeler 2008).

31. They have nothing to offer that is, besides their bodies, invested with a certain commodity value of exoticism to be consumed by the mainstream queer community like other exotic culinary contributions for which migrant communities are valued (and granted little more agency than those other goods)—more about this in the next chapter.

4. "Because It Is Our Stepfatherland"

1. In introducing the term homonormativity, Duggan clarifies: "I am riffing here on the term 'heteronormativity,' introduced by Michael Warner. I don't mean the terms to be parallel; there is no structure for gay life, no matter how conservative or normalizing, that might compare with the institutions promoting and sustaining heterosexual coupling" (Duggan 2005, 94n).

2. As Alexandra Chasin has shown, the research behind early 1990s studies claiming above average income for gay men and lesbians was deeply flawed, focusing disproportionally on white, middle-class men (Chasin 2000, 36). Thus, while the discovery of the "gay market" was clearly a symptom of the larger developments described here and an important step toward the ideology of homonormativity, which sees the interpellation of gay men, and to a much lesser extent lesbians, as consumers as a sign of integration and integration in turn as symptomatic of equality, this discursive shift is not reflective of any actual economic gains.

3. The other side of this political divide splitting the LGBT community materially and discursively is represented among others by Bruce Bawer, a neoliberal (or in his own terms "postideological") author—who after his move to Europe, where he expected to find a more secular and thus more gay-friendly environment than in the United States, has become one of the leading anti-Muslim voices within the gay movement—writing in 1996 in *The Advocate*: "More than ever, it seems reasonable

to suggest that much of gay America's hope resides not in working-class revolt, but in its exact opposite—a trickling down of gay-positive sentiments from elite corporate boardrooms into shops, farms, and factories" (quoted in Duggan 2005, 53).

4. Fittingly, the Netherlands' first ever "anti-radicalization" task force was established in Amsterdam-Slotervaart in 2008, targeting Muslim youths and thus confirming that it is this group, and this group alone, that embodies a radicalism threatening the nation (Amsterdam-Slotervaart City Council 2007, 2008)

5. Full disclosure: I was a member of Strange Fruit from 1996–2000, though I focus here on the group's activism prior to this period.

6. The COC, short for *Cultuur en Ontspanningscentrum* (Center for Culture and Leisure) was founded in 1946, making it the oldest surviving LGBT organization in Europe. Today, it functions as an umbrella group with a national board focusing on lobbying, and has about twenty local centers organizing a variety of activities.

7. Biddy Martin made a similar argument for female bodies: "But I am worried about the occasions when antifoundationalist celebrations of queerness rely on their own projections of fixity, constraint, or subjection onto a fixed ground, often onto feminism or the female body, in relation to which queer sexualities become figural, performative, playful, and fun. In the process, the female body appears to become its own trap, and the operations of misogyny disappear from view" (Martin 1994, 104).

8. The first of these *toris* was held in 1994 at the Cosmic theater in Amsterdam, the center of Dutch black theater; it had two Surinamese men, an Antillian boy and a Moroccan girl talk about their identities and understanding of queerness (Strange Fruit 1997, 10).

9. An early symbol of this discourse is the ethnic video store, Turkish in Germany, Arab in France, Indian in Britain, supposedly allowing migrants to ignore the educational integration programs put on public television in most Western European nations since the early 1980s, and to instead indulge in the nationalist, anti-Western messages hidden in non-European popular culture. While it is certainly true that stores and stands selling videos, bootlegged music tapes, and later CDs were ideal sites of agitation for among others Islamist movements that had embraced popular culture as a political battleground long before the Left did, a fusionist approach to culture was simultaneously present. Just as Latin American *telenovelas* swept Eastern Europe after 1989, Bollywood movies were widely popular among Turkish and North African migrant families long before they became a Western mainstream craze, offering an ideal field of disidentification for queer minority youths.

10. West Berlin's status as a capitalist enclave surrounded by socialist East Germany brought with it a number of special regulations, among them the exemption of the city's male citizens from the West German draft. This made Berlin attractive for youths opposing military service, many of whom settled in

Kreuzberg, keeping alive a Left movement that had been strong since the 1960s student movement galvanized by the protests against Reza Pahlavi's 1967 visit to the city (but largely uninterested in the living conditions of the nation's migrant population) and today manifests its continuous though dwindling presence in largely ritualized annual labor day riots in Kreuzberg's center.

11. In March 2006, the Rütli School in Neukölln became the center of a moral panic around violent Muslim minority youths that combined elements of the Dutch "black school" discourse and the reception of the French riots. Initiated by the media and stoked by conservative as well as liberal politicians, the school, with 83 percent migrant and minority students, more than three quarters of them at least nominally Muslim, was styled into a symbol of the decay and chaos brought about by multiculturalism, requiring law and order solutions. Largely ignored were the effect the economic downturn and drastic cuts in state funding had on an already poor borough with above average unemployment and a high proportion of civil war refugees among its population (in 2005 not a single student who had left the school with a diploma had found a job). See Pomrehn 2006.

12. Çelik's movies, such as *Alltag* (2002) and *Urban Guerillas* (2003), reflect life in postindustrial, multiethnic urban neighborhoods such as Kreuzberg. In 2006, Çelik and Feridun Zaimoğlu, the most successful Turkish-German author and enfant terrible of the progressive literary scene, collaborated on the play *Schwarze Jungfrauen* (Black Virgins), presenting the life stories of ten "neo-Muslim" women in Germany. Based on interviews Zaimoğlu conducted, the play, while a lot more confrontational in its approach, can be read as response to *The Veiled Monologues*. Written by Zaimoğlu—who gained national fame with his 1997 *Kanak Sprak*, presenting stylized "interviews" with Turkish-German men reflecting the same Scorsese-inspired gangsta mentality as contemporary rap culture—and staged by Çelik at the renowned experimental Hebbel am Ufer theater, also located in Kreuzberg, the play despite its intended edginess addresses a largely white audience, whose assumptions about Muslim women are challenged without, however, forcing viewers to fundamentally question the notions of race, gender, and sexuality on which those assumptions are based (Zaimoğlu and Senkel 2008). More successful in bridging the gap between art(ists) and community is Kreuzberg's Ballhaus Naunynstrasse, located in the same street as the Naunynritze youth center and sharing the latter's focus on providing a site of expression for the second and third generation dominating the neighborhood's population. Since its reopening in 2008, the theater has shown work by more established artists, such as Çelik and Zaimoğlu, as well as projects—spoken theater, dance, films—by a variety of upcoming minority artists. See: http://www.ballhausnaunynstrasse.de.

13. The Naunynstrasse girls had their own gang, which according to Çelik came much closer to the media image of dangerous gangs than the boys did: "The girls just like us felt somehow useless and wanted to be part of this hype. The wanted people to pay attention to them too. That's why they started the 36 Girls. They were quite

active and the teachers and social workers were freaked out, because the 36 Girls were really dangerous. They handled knifes and attacked boys" (Çelik, in Interface 2005, 215). The 36 in the gangs' names refers to the postal code of Kreuzberg's Eastern part (supplemented with an SO, for South-East and SW, for South-West), while the borough's Western, more middle-class section had the postal code 61.

14. For an overview of the club's history see http://www.so36.de.

15. Vaginal Davis in turn attended various Salon Oriental events while living in Berlin in 2001 (Davis 2002).

16. *Deutschländer* (Germanian) is the German version of the Turkish *almançi*, the term used in Turkey to refer to "Turks" born or raised in Germany. "Black Sea Clinic" is a spoof on the extremely popular German soap "Black Forest Clinic."

17. While her fusion style has made her increasingly popular, Ipekçioğlu initially faced resistance from the white feminist and queer scene for playing music from "misogynist" cultures, as well as from the straight Turkish–German community for queering Turkish culture (see Petzen 2004).

18. In her own work, Adelson counters this perception with the idea of "touching tales," which "suggests that Germans and Turks in Germany share more culture (as an ongoing imaginative project) than is often presumed when one speaks of two discrete worlds encountering each other across a civilizational divide. Touching tales thus takes conceptual leave from a model of incommensurable differences to stress a broad range of common ground, which can be thicker or thinner at some junctures" (Adelson 2005, 20).

19. Fittingly, catering for the event was provided by a Turkish restaurant.

20. The German use of *Kanake* is most frequently traced to the nation's colonial past in the South Pacific: the term, now identified with the largest ethnic group in New Caledonia, in the early twentieth century was broadly used by Europeans to describe Pacific Islanders (see Buschmann, in O'Hanlon and Welsh 2000, 58).

21. *Kanake* as a term of resistance had been popularized within hip-hop and first entered the mainstream through Feridun Zaimoğlu's crtically acclaimed and commercially successful *Kanak Sprak* (1995), a collection of "protocols," offering fictionalized first hand accounts of the lives of young minority men living on the edge of society. Adelson describes the text's stylistic roots in hip-hop: "Although only two interviewees are designated as actual rappers, most of the interview 'protocols' . . . read like rapid-fire, rap-like burst of transgressively linguistic material, much of it involving scatology, criminality, and sexuality. Defiantly rejecting the xenophilic myth of the lovable oppressed Turk, the author and his subjects dismissively reserve the word 'Turk' for those deemed 'socially acceptable'" (Adelson 2005, 96; also see Cheesman 2002). But while it is highly stylized, seemingly inspired not only by hip-hop, but also a prefascist literary German tradition represented by authors like Alfred Döblin (who like Zaimoğlu was both a physician and a novelist), the book was largely read as ethnological nonfiction by German media. For many second- and third-generation (male) youths, the book had an effect comparable to that of

Showing Our Colors, published almost a decade earlier, in inspiring a sense of community and identity beyond the German/foreigner dichotomy.

22. When I showed the "Philharmonie Köln" video while teaching in Germany, students were divided along clear lines: those with a migrant background immediately recognized what Kanak Attak was doing, expressing satisfaction with majoritarian Germans having to go through an ordeal that was a daily reality for them. White German students on the other hand tended to perceive the group's strategy as unfair and unproductive, designed not to foster communication but to humiliate. Most however, did not recognize this as an experience society imposed on their classmates on a regular basis.

23. The piece, together with *Philharmonie Köln—40 Jahre Einwanderung* and a third video, *Das Märchen von der Integration* (The Integration Fairy Tale) is part of *Kanak TV Vol. 1* (see www.kanak-attak.de).

24. The Frassanito network, an association of migrant rights groups from several European nations, was founded in 2003 in Southern Italy at a no-border camp, an activist gathering protesting a nearby refugee detention center. The network's position on migration is very close to Kanak Attak's, rejecting the view of migrants as victims, emphasizing mobility as a social movement, and focusing on Europeanizing the struggle against racism. See Frassanito 2006.

25. The Volksbühne (literally "people's stage"), located in Berlin's former East and founded in the 1920s as a private theater closely tied to the city's strong socialist movement, is one of Germany's most venerable progressive venues. In her insightful analysis of German theater's struggle for survival in a neoliberal economy, Katrin Sieg presents the Volksbühne as a positive example of traditional institutions' attempts to navigate an increasingly difficult funding situation while remaining politically relevant in a globalized cultural discourse. Much of this success according to Sieg is because the management's "concept of creating a 'people's theater' prioritizes the fostering of cultural, technological, and electronical literacy and refers back to a long socialist tradition" (Sieg 2008, 23), a strategy expressed among other things in cooperations with nontraditional media activist groups such as Kanak Attak.

26. The three hundred fired workers had returned late from their summer vacation, something that happened frequently, since the workers and their families had to drive thousands of miles to Turkey and back each summer. Usually, they were allowed to make up for the lost time with additional shifts, but in 1973, Ford changed its policy, leading to spontaneous protests by five hundred Turkish colleagues, soon joined by all eight thousand workers in the late shift. Within a couple of days, the whole factory was on strike and demands had grown from rehiring the fired workers to wage increases, longer vacations, and better working conditions. The automobile workers' union, the influential IG Metall, representing a majority of all industrial workers, was unsupportive to say the least. While it had begun to allow workers from non-EU member nations to run for shop

committees the year before, at Ford Cologne it refused to seat an elected Turkish worker, despite his winning almost a third of the vote, supposedly due to his lack of German language skills. The workers thus had little faith in the union and elected an independent committee with a Turkish worker and a German intern fluent in Turkish representing them in negotiations with the management. The latter's first reaction had been to close down the factory, leading to its occupation by workers, the majority of them Turks, who used the lockdown to strengthen communal ties (that this included making music, singing, dancing, telling stories, and reciting poetry all night lead to baffled media reactions claiming that Cologne had "turned into Istanbul"). After the second night of occupation, two thousand workers staging a demonstration on factory grounds were attacked by a group of foremen, plainclothes policemen, and scabs with clubs and brass knuckles, and several dozens of the workers were arrested, which in effect, meant the end of the strike (Kraushaar 2004).

27. The attack on traditional notions of knowledge and history in the United States, coming out of the U.S. Civil Rights movement, utilizing ignored materials within existing collections and recording ignored voices through oral history projects, inspired similar activities in Europe, not only in collecting the everyday histories of "average people," but also at making them accessible through neighborhood centers, which since the 1970s featured regular exhibits of the collected materials. In theory the "everyday people" whose stories were to be rediscovered could have included migrants and minorities, who had almost completely been written out of mainstream history. It turned out, though, that the leftist, union, gay, or feminist activists behind the "history from below" movement did not differ much from their more conservative compatriots or from professional historians in their views on the potential ethnic diversity of the German population. The only incarnation in which racialized subjects entered the "history from below" was that of guest workers who appeared within the context of workers' histories. Their representation differed from those of other groups in a fundamental way though: while the movement aimed at breaking down the barrier between the powerful, authoritative "expert" on the one hand and the powerless, passive object of research on the other (intending to return agency to "the people"), the guest worker was still assigned the role of the mute, oppressed object that needed the enlightened German to tell/translate his story. All good intentions aside, what was collected thus inevitably reflects the bias of dominant society. This situation was mirrored within migration studies, which, while challenging the exclusion of migrants from German history, nevertheless left untouched the barrier between white, majoritarian scholars and ethnicized migrant objects (see El-Tayeb 2005).

28. The by far most successful film, both commercially and critically, by a Turkish–German filmmaker (until Fatih Akin's *Gegen die Wand*, Head-on, came along in 2004) was Tevfik Başer's 1986 *40 qm Deutschland* (40 square meters Germany), telling the story of a Turkish woman brought to Germany by

her husband who had come as a guest worker and, disgusted with the immoral German culture, permanently locks her up in their small Hamburg apartment.

29. "*Schland* is the land"—Slogan used by fans during the World Cup. *Schland* is short for *Deutschland*, Germany.

30. Racism in soccer stadiums is routinely expressed in rituals such as collective monkey sounds and throwing bananas on the field in response to black players. This has become such a normal occurrence in Europe that the international soccer association FIFA, not known for its progressive politics, held an extraordinary meeting in 2001 and published a statement requiring clubs, the media, and referees to intervene (available at http://www.ifxsoccer. com/fifacongress.htm). The statement had little effect beyond a number of clubs being fined nominal sums for their fans' racist attacks on players of color, and over the coming years the situation escalated to such an extent that most national soccer associations were forced to take additional measures (while Britain's approach was drastic, and successful, continental Europe so far has largely paid lip service to antiracism). See Wolf 2007; Bandini 2009.

Conclusion

1. See the organizers' *Manifesto*: "We could have only done this, because there is such a thing as Europe. Nobody should get the idea to attempt a similar exhibit for, say, Asia: the smallest child can see that various civilizations exist on this vast continent. And [while] Europe might be very diverse, culturally speaking it forms a unit" (Museum van Europa 2007, 3, my translation).

2. The Holocaust, it can be argued, has become the central memory point of the twentieth century, constituting not only a key element of remembered modern European history, but also, as Alida Assman, Andreas Huyssen, and others have argued, of modern global history (Assman 2007; Huyssen 2005). However, insofar as these commemorations primarily constitute a means to establish a consensus meant to end rather than encourage debate, they validate Peter Novick's critical assessment of their actual meaningfulness: "[I]t seems to me that there is something illegitimately 'homogenizing' about establishing a 'shared' memory that . . . would have all Europeans think of themselves as perpetrators—and also as victims . . . Furthermore, it has always seemed to me that there is something absurdly 'minimalist' about a moral consensus based on affirming that, indeed, murdering six million men, women, and children is an atrocious crime" (Novick 2007, 31).

3. See the exhibit blog entry for December 8, 2008, focused on this part of "It's Your History," entitled "De dekolonisatie en de geheimen van de brousse" (Decolonization and the secrets of the bush), http://blog-nl.expo-europe.be/de-dekolonisatie-en-de-geheimen-van-de-brousse/.

4. While a number of these leaders were forced out of power with European help, this is referenced only in the case of Lumumba (Museum van Europa 2007, 67).

5. Neither does this Europe allow for regional difference, if one takes the complete marginalization of pre-1989 Eastern Europe into account.

Abdol-Hamid, Asmaa. 2007. "Her Choice to Wear a Headscarf." *KVInfo*. May 16. http://www.kvinfo.dk/side/674/article/61/ (accessed December 8, 2008).

Abou Jahjah, Dyab. 2005. "The Thirty-Year War on Terror." March 8. http://www.opendemocracy.net/debates/article-2–124–2362.jsp (accessed November 30, 2008).

———. 2005. "Open Letter from Dyab Abou Jahjah to AEL Members and Sympathizers." January 26. http://www.arabeuropean.org (accessed November 30, 2008).

Abraham, Ibrahim. 2007. "The Veil and the Closet: Islam and the Production of Queer Space." *Queer Space: Centres and Peripheries*. http://www.dab.uts.edu.au/ conferences/Queer space (accessed November 16, 2008).

Adelson, Leslie. 2005. *The Turkish Turn in Contemporary German Literature: Toward a New Critical Grammar of Migration*. New York: Palgrave MacMillan.

Afzal-Khan, Fawzia. 2005. *Shattering the Stereotypes: Muslim Women Speak Out*. Northampton, Mass.: Olive Branch Press.

Agathangelou, Anna, Daniel Bassichis, and Tamara Spira. 2008. "Homonormativity, Global Lockdown, and the Seductions of Empire." *Radical History Review* 1000:120–43.

AG Mov!ng On. 2005. *Mov!ng On: Handlungen an Grenzen—Strategien zum antirassistischen Handeln/Border Activism—Strategies for Anti-racist Actions*. Berlin: Neue Gesellschaft fuer Bildende Kunst.

Ahmed, Fiza. 2006. "Nu even niet." April 20. http://hoeiboei.weblog.nl/hoeiboei/fiza_ahmed/index.html (accessed November 7, 2008).

Alexander, M. Jacqui. 2005. *Pedagogies of Crossing: Meditations of Feminism, Sexual Politics, Memory, and the Sacred*. Durham, N.C.: Duke University Press.

Alloula, Malik. 1986. *The Colonial Harem*. Minneapolis: University of Minnesota Press.

Aly, Goetz. 2003. *Rasse und Klasse, Nachforschungen zum deutschen Wesen.* Frankfurt a. M.: Fischer.

Amiraux, Valerie. 2004. "Restructuring Political Islam: Transnational Belonging and Muslims in France and Germany." In *Transnational Political Islam: Religion, Ideology, and Power,* ed. Azza Karam, 28–57. London: Pluto Press.

Amsterdam-Slotervaart City Council. 2007. *Slotervaart Action Plan: Countering Radicalisation.* April. http://www.nuansa.nl/documentatie/beleidsstukken/countering-radicalisation (accessed March 10, 2010).

_____. 2008. *Progress Report Slotervaart Action Plan: Countering Radicalisation.* February. http://www.nuansa.nl/documentatie/beleidsstukken/progress-report-slotervaart-action-plan (accessed March 10, 2010).

Anderson, Perry. 2007. "Depicting Europe." *London Review of Books,* 29, no. 18:13–21.

Anthony, Andrew. 2007. "Ayaan Hirsi Ali: Taking the Fight to Islam." *The Observer,* February 4:4.

Anzaldúa, Gloria, and Cherríe Moraga, eds. 1981. *This Bridge Called My Back: Writings by Radical Women of Color.* Watertown, Mass.: Persephone Press.

Appadurai, Arjun. 1992. *Modernity at Large: Cultural Dimensions of Globalization.* Minneapolis: University of Minnesota Press.

Applebaum, Anne. 2007. "The Fight for Muslim Women." *The Washington Post,* February 4. BW05

Arendt, Hannah. 1951. *The Origins of Totalitarianism.* New York: Harcourt.

Arts, Hiske, and Anita Nabha. 2001. "Education in the Netherlands: Segregation in a 'Tolerant' Society." In *Humanity in Action Research Report.* http://humanityinaction.org/docs/Arts__Nabha,_2001.pdf (accessed November 7, 2008).

Ash, Timothy Garton. 2004. *Free World: America, Europe, and the Surprising Future of the West.* New York: Random House.

Assmann, Aleida. 2007. "Europe: A Community of Memory?" *GHI Bulletin* 40:11–25.

Astier, Henri. 2005. "French Muslims Face Job Discrimination." *BBC News,* November 2. http://news.bbc.co.uk/2/hi/europe/4399748.stm (accessed July 28, 2006).

Ates, Seyran. 2008. *Der Multikulti-Irrtum: Wie wir in Deutschland besser zusammen leben können.* Berlin: Ullstein.

Ayim, May. 2002. *Grenzenlos und Unverschämt.* Frankfurt: Fischer.

_____. 2005. *Blues in Black and White.* Trenton, N.J.: Africa World Press.

Baer, Martin. 1999. *Befreien Sie Afrika.* Germany, 83 min.

Baker, Houston A., Jr., Manthia Diawara, and Ruth H. Lindeborg, eds. 1996. *Black British Cultural Studies: A Reader.* Chicago: The University of Chicago Press.

Balibar, Etienne. 2004. *We, the People of Europe? Reflections on Transnational Citizenship*. Princeton, N.J.: Princeton University Press.

Balibar, Etienne, and Emmanuel Wallerstein. 1991. *Race, Nation, Class: Ambiguous Identities*. London: Verso Publications.

Bandini, Paolo. 2009. "Racist Chants Overshadow Juventus's Stirring Comeback against Inter." *The Guardian*, April 20. http://www.guardian.co.uk/sport/blog/2009/apr/20/paolo-bandini-serie-a-juventus-internazionale (accessed July 10, 2009).

Baudrillard, Jean. 2006. "The Pyres of Autumn." *New Left Review* 37 (Jan./Feb.):5–7.

Baumann, Martin. 2001. " . . . That Word 'Diaspora.'" irishdiaspora.net (accessed November 16, 2008).

Bayoumi, Moustafa. 2003. "Moving Beliefs: The Panama Manuscript of Sheikh Sana See and African Diasporic Islam." *Interventions*. 5, no. 1:58–81.

_____. 2006. "Racing Religion." *New Centennial Review*. 6, no. 2:267–93.

_____. 2008. *How Does It Feel to Be a Problem? Being Young and Arab in America*. London: Penguin.

BBC. 2007. "Constitution 'Key for EU Success.'" *BBC News*, Jan. 17. http://news. bbc.co.uk/2/hi/europe/ 6269349.stm (accessed November 7, 2008).

Bechler, Rosemary. 2004. "Reinventing Islam in Europe: A Profile of Tariq Ramadan." *open democracy*, July 5. http://www.opendemocracy.net/faith-europe_islam/article_1996.jsp (accessed February 14, 2009).

_____. 2004. "A Bridge across Fear: An Interview with Tariq Ramadan." *open democracy*, July 13. http://www.opendemocracy.net/faith-europe_islam/article_2006.jsp (accessed February 14, 2009).

_____. 2006. "Democracy, Islam, and the Politics of Belonging." *open democracy*, March 2. http://www.opendemocracy.net/faith-europe_islam/ belonging_3317.jsp (accessed February 14, 2009).

Beck, Ulrich, and Anthony Giddens. 2005. "Europa kann nicht auf den Ruinen der Nationen errichtet werden." *Die Welt Online Edition*, October 1. http://www.welt.de/printwelt/article168315 Europa_ kann_nicht_auf_den_ Ruinen_ der_ Nationen_ errichtet_ werden.html (accessed February 14, 2009).

Beck-Gernsheim, Elisabeth. 2006. "Türkische Bräute und die Migrationsdebatte in Deutschland," *soFid Familienforschung* 2:9–16.

Becker, Jochen. 1998. "BahnCard First?" In *euroland*, www.moneynations.ch/texte (accessed November 30, 2008).

_____. 1999. "Im Gespräch: First Ladies. Sabuha Salaam, Fatma Souad und Edeltraut Plörrenhöfer über den schwulen türkischen Nachtclub 'Salon Orientale.'" *Freitag 40*, October 1. http://www.freitag.de/1999/40/99401801.htm (accessed June 13, 2009).

Benhabib, Seyla. 2002. *The Claims of Culture: Equality and Diversity in the Global Era*. Princeton, N.J.: Princeton University Press.

Benhabib, Seyla, and Nancy Fraser, eds. 2004. *Pragmatism, Critique, Judgment: Essays for Richard J. Bernstein*. Cambridge, Mass.: MIT Press.

Benhabib, Seyla, and Robert Post. 2006. *Another Cosmopolitanism: Hospitality, Sovereignty, and Democratic Iterations*. Oxford: Oxford University Press.

Bentele, Ulrich. 2007. "Die Politik erwacht langsam aus dem Dornröschenschlaf. Interview mit Seyran Ates zum Nationalen Integrationsplan." *Tagesschau.de*, November 8. http://www.tagesschau.de/inland/integration6.html (accessed February 13, 2010).

Bernal, Martin. 1991. "Black Athena: The Afroasiatic Roots of Classical Civilization." In *The Fabrication of Ancient Greece 1785–1985*, Volume 1. New Brunswick, N.J.: Rutgers University Press.

Bhabha, Homi K. 1990. *Nation and Narration*. New York: Routledge.

———. 1996. *Locations of Culture: Discussing Post-Colonial Culture*. London: Routledge.

Blackshire-Belay, Carol A. 1996. *The African-German Experience: Critical Essays*. Westport, Conn.: Praeger Publishers.

Bläser, Fatima, and Heide Oestreich. 2008. "'Lass dein Herz nicht brennen.' Betroffene über Ehrenmorde." *Die Tageszeitung*, June 7. http://www.taz.de/1/politik/ deutschland/artikel/1/lass-dein-herz-nicht-brennen/?type=98 (accessed April 24, 2009).

2006. "'Blonde Opfer' Empörung ueber Schäuble." *SpiegelOnline*, April 20. http://www.spiegel.de/politik/deutschland/0,1518,412195,00.html (accessed July 30, 2008).

Bojadzijev, Manuela. 2001. "Der Kanak Attak-Aha-Effekt und die Überwindung der antirassistischen Arbeitsteilung." *aka 451*, June 7: 14

Bourdieu, Pierre, and Loïc Wacquant. 1999. "On the Cunning of Imperialist Reason." *Theory, Culture & Society*, 16, no. 1:41–58.

Brandzel, Amy. 2005. "Queering Citizenship? Same-Sex Marriage and the State." *GLQ* 11, no. 2:171–204.

Breger, Claudia. 1998. *Ortlosigkeit des Fremden: Zigeunerinnen und Zigeuner in der deutschsprachigen Literatur um 1800*. Vienna: Böhlau.

———. 2000. "'Gekreuzt' und queer. Überlegungen zur Rekonzeptualisierung von Gender, Ethnizität und Sexualität." In *Differenzen in der Geschlechterdifferenz*, eds. Kati Röttger and Heike Paul, 66–85. Berlin: Erich Schmitt Verlag.

Brodkin, Karen. 1998. *How Jews Became White Folks and What That Says about Race in America*. New Brunswick, N.J.: Rutgers University Press.

Bronfen, Elisabeth, and Misha Kavka, eds. 2001. *Feminist Consequences: Theory for the New Century*. New York: Columbia University Press.

Brothers, Caroline. 2008. "EU Passes Tough Migrant Measure." *New York Times*, June 19. http://www.nytimes.com/2008/06/19/world/europe/19migrant.html (accessed July 4, 2008).

Brown, Daniel. 2008. "Rap Musician under Legal Fire for 'Defamation.'" *Radio France International*. June 26. http://www.freemuse.org/sw28748.asp (accessed August 9, 2008).

Browne, Anthony. 2004. "Belgian MP Goes into Hiding after Criticising Muslims." *The Times*, November 19. (accessed November 30, 2008).

Brown, Wendy. 2006. "American Nightmare: Neoliberalism, Neoconservatism, and De-Democratization." *Political Theory* 34, no. 6:690–714.

Brubaker, Rogers. 1992. *Citizenship and Nationhood in France and Germany*. Cambridge, Mass.: Harvard University Press.

_____. 2004. *Ethnicity without Groups*. Cambridge, Mass.: Harvard University Press.

Bruckner, Pascal. 2007. "Enlightenment Fundamentalism or Racism of the Anti-racists?" January 24. www.perlentaucher.de (accessed November 7, 2008).

Brussa, Licia. 2007 "Europe Today: Sex Work from a Female Labour Migration Perspective." In Domenig et al., 1–13.

Buck-Morss, Susan. 2000. "Hegel and Haiti." *Critical Inquiry* 26:821–65.

Buruma, Ian. 2005. "Final Cut: After a Filmmaker's Murder, the Dutch Creed of Tolerance Has Come under Siege." *The New Yorker*. January 3. http://www.newyorker.com/archive/2005/01/03/050103fa_fact1 (accessed January 25, 2009).

_____. 2006. *Murder in Amsterdam*. London: Penguin Books.

_____. 2007. "Tariq Ramadan Has an Identity Issue." *The New York Times*, February 4. http://www.nytimes.com/2007/02/04/magazine/04ramadan.t.html?_r=1&th=&emc=th&pagewanted=print2007 (accessed December 8, 2008).

Büscher, Wolfgang, and Annabel Wahba. 2009. "Es geht nicht um Schwarze. Es geht um Weisse." *zeit online*, December 18. http://www.zeit.de/2009/52/Wallraff-im-Gespraech?page=all (accessed March 9, 2010).

Buschmann, Rainer. 2000. "Exploring Tension in Material Culture: Commercializing Ethnograpy in German New Guinea 1870–1904." In *Hunting the Gatherers*, eds. Michael O'Hanlon and Robert Welsh, 55–80. New York: Berghan Books.

Butler, Judith. 1990. *Gender Trouble: Feminism and the Subversion of Identity*. New York: Routledge.

_____. 1993. "Imitation and Gender Insubordination." In *The Lesbian and Gay Studies Reader*, ed. Henry Abelove et al., 307–20. New York: Routledge.

_____. 1993. *Bodies That Matter: On the Discursive Limits of "Sex."* New York: Routledge.

_____. 1997. *Excitable Speech: A Politics of the Performative*. New York: Routledge.

_____. 1997. "Merely Cultural." *Social Text* 52/53:265–77.

_____. 2001. "The End of Sexual Difference?" In Bronfen and Kavka, 414–34.

Butterwegge, Christoph, et al. 1999. *Medien und multikulturelle Gesellschaft*. Opladen: Leske und Budrich.

Byfield, Judith, ed. 2000. *Special Issue: Rethinking the African Diaspora*, *African Studies Review* 43, no. 1.

Cakir, Naime. 2006. "Emanzipation nur ohne Kopftuch?" *Die Tageszeitung*, April 11: 11.

Campt, Tina. 2003. *Other Germans: Black Germans and the Politics of Race, Gender, and Memory in the Third Reich*. Ann Arbor: University of Michigan Press.

Card, David, and Christoph M. Schmidt, eds. 2003. Symposium on "Second-Generation Immigrants and the Transition to Ethnic Minorities." In *Journal of Population Economics* 16, no. 4:707–849.

Casanova, José. 2004. "Religion, European Secular Identities, and European Integration." *Eurozine*, July 29. http://www.eurozine.com/articles/2004-07-29-casanova-en.html (accessed February 13, 2010).

Case, Sue-Ellen, Philip Brett, and Susan Leigh Foster. 1995. *Cruising the Performative: Interventions into the Representation of Ethnicity, Nationality, and Sexuality*. Bloomington: Indiana University Press.

Çelik, Neco. 2005. "Wir wollten Respekt und natürlich Mädels beeindrucken." In *Interface*, 211–17.

Cervulle, Maxime. 2008. "French Homonormativity and the Commodification of the French Arab Body." *Radical History Review* 100:170–79.

Césaire, Aimé. 1972. *Discourse on Colonialism*. New York: Monthly Review Press.

Charim, Isolde. 2005. "Wirklichkeit wird sichtbar." *Die Tageszeitung*, November 8.

Chasin, Alexandra. 2000. *Selling Out: The Gay and Lesbian Movement Goes to Market*. New York: Palgrave.

Chauke, Prudence. 2009. "Olumide Popoola—More Than Just a Poetess." January 26. http://www.jamati.com/online/books/olumide-popoola-more-than-just-a-poetess/ (accessed June 18, 2009).

Cheesman, Tom. 2002. "Akçam—Zaimoglu—Kanak Attak: Turkish Lives and Letters in German." *German Life and Letters* 55 (April 2):180–95.

Choi, Sun-Ju, and Miltiadid Oulis. 2005. "Kanak TV—der offensive Blick." In *Interface*, 222–28.

Chow, Rey. 1998. *Ethics after Idealism: Theory, Culture, Ethnicity, Reading*. Bloomington: University of Indiana Press.

———. 2002. *The Protestant Ethnic and the Spirit of Capitalism*. New York: Columbia University Press.

Clifford, James. 1994. "Diasporas." *Cultural Anthropology* 9:302–38.

Coleman, Yves. 2006. "The French Riots: Dancing with the Wolves." January 1. www.solidarity-us.org/node/33 (accessed December 2, 2008).

Combahee River Collective. 1981. "Combahee River Collective Statement. A Black Feminist Statement 1977." Reprinted in Anzaldúa and Moraga, 210–18.

Crenshaw, Kimberlé W. 1991. "Mapping the Margins: Intersectionality, Identity Politics, and Violence against Women of Color." *Stanford Law Review*, 43, no. 6:1241–99.

Crul, Maurice, and Hans Vermeulen. 2003. "The Second Generation in Europe." *The International Migration Review* 37, no. 4:965–98.

Crul, Maurice, and Jeroen Doomernik. 2003. "The Turkish and Moroccan Second Generation in the Netherlands: Divergent Trends between and Polarization within the Two Groups." *International Migration Review* 37, no. 4:1039–64.

Cruz-Malavé, Arnaldo, and Martin F. Malansan. 2002. *Queer Globalizations: Citizenship and the Afterlife of Colonialism*. New York: New York University Press.

Cvetkovich, Ann. 2003. *An Archive of Feelings: Trauma, Sexuality, and Lesbian Public Cultures*. Durham, N.C.: Duke University Press.

Davis, Mike. 2004. "Planet of Slums, Urban Involution and the Informal Proletariat." *New Left Review*. March/April, 5–34.

Davis, Vaginal. "Invasion of Privacy: Sneaking a Peek into the Personal Diary of Ms. Davis." http://www.vaginaldavis.com/diary.shtml (accessed June 12, 2009).

Diederichsen, Diedrich, ed. 1998. *Loving the Alien*. Berlin: Id-Verlag.

Doan, Laura, ed. 1994. *The Lesbian Postmodern*. New York: Columbia University Press.

Domenig, Dagmar, Jane Fountain, Eberhard Schatz, and Georg Bröring, eds. 2007. *Overcoming Barriers—Migration, Marginalisation and Access to Health and Social Services*. Amsterdam: Foundation Regenboog AMOC.

Donelly, Paul. 2002. "Tariq Ramadan: The Muslim Martin Luther?" *Salon*, February 15. http://www.nytimes.com/2007/02/04/magazine/04ramadan.t.html?_r=1&th=&emc=th&pagewanted=print (accessed December 8, 2008).

Dougary, Ginny. 2006. "The Voice of Experience. An Interview with Martin Amis." *Times Online*, September 9. http://www.ginnydougary.co.uk/2006/09/17/the-voice-of-experience/ (accessed December 13, 2008).

dpa. 2007 "UNCHR wirft Deutschland in Fluechtlingsfrage Voelkerrechtsbruch vor," *dpa* August 10.

Dregni, Michael. 2004. *Django: The Life and Music of a Gypsy Legend*. Oxford: Oxford University Press.

Dryer, Richard. 1997. *White*. London: Routledge.

Duggan, Lisa. 2002. "The New Homonormativity: The Sexual Politics of Neoliberalism." In *Materializing Democracy*, eds. Russ Castronovo and Dana D. Nelson, 173–94. Durham, N.C.: Duke University Press.

_____. 2005. *The Twilight of Equality? Neoliberalism, Cultural Politics, and the Attack on Democracy*. Boston, Mass.: Beacon Press.

Eder, Angelika. 2006. *'Wir sind auch da!' Über das Leben von und mit Migranten in europäischen Grossstädten*. Hamburg: Dölling und Galitz.

Edwards, Brent Hayes. 2003. *The Practice of Diaspora: Literature, Translation, and the Rise of Black Internationalism*. Boston, Mass.: Harvard University Press.

Elam, Harry Jr., and Kennell Jackson. 2005. *Black Cultural Traffic: Crossroads in Global Performance and Popular Culture*. Ann Arbor: The University of Michigan Press.

El-Tayeb, Fatima. 2001. *Schwarze Deutsche: "Rasse" und nationale Identität 1890–1933*. Frankfurt a. M.: Campus.

_____. 2001. "Germans, Foreigners, and German Foreigners. Constructions of National Identity in Early 20th Century Germany." In *Unpacking Europe: Towards a Critical Reading*, eds. Salah Hassan and Iftikhar Dadi, 72–85. Rotterdam: NAI.

_____. 2005. "The Archive, the Activist, and the Audience, or Black European Studies: A Comparative Interdisciplinary Study of Identities, Positionalities, and Differences." *Transit* 1, no. 1:1–7.

_____. 2006. "Urban Diasporas: Race, Identity, and Popular Culture in a Post-Ethnic Europe." In *Motion in Place/Place in Motion: 21st Century Migration. JCAS Symposium Series 22; Population Movement in the Modern World*. 10.

Eng, David. 1997. "Out Here and Over There: Queerness and Diaspora in Asian American Studies." *Social Text* 52/53:31–52.

_____. 2000. *Racial Castration: Managing Masculinity in Asian America*. Durham, N.C.: Duke University Press.

Eshun, Kodwo. 1998. *More Brilliant Than the Sun: Adventures in Sonic Fiction*. London: Quartet Books.

Essed, Philomena. 1991. *Understanding Everyday Racism: An Interdisciplinary Theory*. London: Sage.

Esteban Muñoz, José. 1999. *Disidentifications: Queers of Color and the Performance of Politics*. Minneapolis: University of Minnesota Press.

European Commission. 2001. *Council Conclusions on the World Conference against Racism, Racial Discrimination, Xenophobia, and Related Intolerance*. July 16. Brussels: General Affairs Council.

European Commission Directorate-General for Employment and Social Affairs. 2004. *The Situation of Roma in an Enlarged European Union*. Luxembourg: Office for Official Publications of the European Communities.

European Roma Rights Center. 2007. *The Glass Box: Exclusion of Roma from Employment*. Budapest.

Evans, Martin. 2006. "Memories, Monuments, Histories: The Re-thinking of the Second World War since 1989." *National Identities*, August 4. 317–48.

Fabian, Johannes. 1983. *Time and the Other: How Anthropology Makes Its Object*. New York: Columbia University Press.

Fanon, Frantz. 1965. "Algeria Unveiled." In *A Dying Colonialism*, 35–64. New York: Monthly Review Press.

Farred, Grant. 2003. *What's My Name? Black Vernacular Intellectuals*. Minneapolis: University of Minnesota Press.

Fehrenbach, Heide. 2005. *Race after Hitler: Black Occupation Children in Postwar Germany and America*. Princeton, N.J.: Princeton University Press.

Feldblum, Miriam. 1997. "'Citizenship Matters': Contemporary Trends in Europe and the United States." *Stanford Electronic Humanities Review*, May 2.

Foreign Policy. 2008. July/August issue, http://www.foreignpolicy.com/story/ cms. php?story_id=4349&page=0 (accessed October 31, 2008).

Ferguson, Roderick A. 2004. *Aberrations in Black: Toward a Queer of Color Critique*. Minneapolis: University of Minnesota Press.

Florida, Richard. 2002. "Bohemia and Economic Geography." *Journal of Economic Geography* 2:55–71.

Forum, Instituut voor Multiculturele Ontwikkeling. 2003. *Homoseksualiteit en gedeeld burgerschap*. Utrecht: Forum.

Frankenberg, Ruth. 1993. *White Women, Race Matters*. London: Routledge.

Fraser, Nancy. 1997. *Justice Interruptus: Critical Reflections on the "Postsocialist" Condition*. New York: Routledge.

Frassanito Network. 2006. "We Didn't Cross the Border, the Border Crossed Us." www.noborder.org/files/060506frassanito_flyer.pdf (accessed July 8, 2009).

"French Police Target Riot Leaders." 2008. *BBC.News*, February 18. http://news. bbc.co.uk/2/hi/europe/7250102.stm (accessed December 2, 2008).

Fröhlich, Margrit, et al., eds. 2004. *Interkulturalität in europäischer Perspektive: Jugendliche aus Migrationsfamilien und ihre Integrationschancen*. Frankfurt a. M.: Brandes & Apsel.

Fuss, Diana. 1994. "Interior Colonies: Frantz Fanon and the Politics of Identification." *Diacritics* 24:2–3, 19–42.

Gallissot, René. 2005. "Mehdi Ben Barka et la Tricontinentale." *Le Monde Diplomatique*, October 21.

Gazic, Sabina, Derya Kaplan, Kore Lampe, and Karina Schaapman. 2006. *Verborgen leed van tienermeiden in Amsterdam*. Amsterdam: Partij van de Arbeid.

Gelbin, Cathy S., Kader Konuk, and Peggy Piesche, eds. 1999. *AufBrüche. Kulturelle Produktionen von Migrantinnen, Schwarzen und jüdischen Frauen in Deutschland*, Königstein: Ulrike Helmer Verlag.

Gheorghe, Nicolae, and Thomas Acton. 1999. "Dealing with Multicultural-ity: Minority, Ethnic, National, and Human Rights." *Patrin Web Journal: Romani Culture and History*, September 3. http://www.geocities.com/~Patrin/ (accessed December 14, 2008).

Ghorashi, Halleh. 2007. "Why Ayaan Hirsi Ali Is Wrong," *signandsight*, March 14. http://www.signandsight.com/features/1250.html (accessed December 8, 2008).

Gilroy, Paul. 1992. *The Black Atlantic: Modernity and Double Consciousness*. Cambridge, Mass.: Harvard University Press.

_____. 1994. *Small Acts: Thoughts on the Politics of Black Cultures*. London: Serpent's Tail.

_____. 1999. "'. . . to Be Real': The Dissident Forms of Black Expressive Culture." In *Let's Get It On: The Politics of Black Performance*, ed. Cathrine Ugwu, 12–33. Seattle, Wash.: Bay Press.

_____. 2000. *Against Race: Imagining Political Culture Beyond the Color Line*. Cambridge, Mass.: Harvard University Press.

_____. 2004. *After Empire: Multiculture or Postcolonial Melancholia*. New York: Routledge.

Glissant, Edouard. 1989. *Caribbean Discourse: Selected Essays*. Charlottesville: University of Virginia Press.

_____. 1997. *Poetics of Relation*. Ann Arbor: University of Michigan Press.

Göktürk, Deniz. 2001. "Turkish Delight—German Fright: Migrant Identities in Transnational Cinema." In *Mediated Identities*, eds. Deniz Derman, Karen Ross, and Nevena Dakovic, 131–49. Istanbul: Bilgi University Press.

Göktürk, Deniz, David Gramling, and Anton Kaes. 2007. *Germany in Transit: Nation and Migration 1955–2005*. Berkeley: University of California Press.

Goldberg, David T., 1993. *Racist Culture: Philosophy and the Politics of Meaning*. Cambridge, Mass.: Blackwell.

_____. 2006. "Racial Europeanization." *Ethnic and Racial Studies* 29:2, 331–64.

Gopinath, Gayatri. 2005. *Impossible Desires: Queer Diasporas and South Asian Public Cultures*. Durham, N.C.: Duke University Press.

Gordon, Avery. 1997. *Ghostly Matters: Haunting and the Sociological Imagination*. Minneapolis: University of Minnesota Press.

Green, Charles, ed. 1997. *Globalization and Survival in the Black Diaspora: The New Urban Challenge*. Albany: State University of New York Press.

Greisalmer, Laurant. 2002. "Maurice Papon une Carrière Française." *Le Monde*, September 19. http://www.lemonde.fr/old-societe/article/2002/09/19/ maurice-papon-une-carriere-francaise_291060_3226.html#ens_id=866527 (accessed August 10, 2008).

Griffin, Gabrielle (with Rosi Braidotti). 2001. "Whiteness and European Situatedness." In *Thinking Differently: A Reader in European Women's Studies*, eds. Gabrielle Griffin and Rosi Braidotti, 221–37. London: Zed Books.

Grigore, Delia. 2003. "The Romanian Right and the 'Strange' Roma." July 28. www.open democracy.org (accessed November 16, 2008).

Guitiérez Rodríguez, Encarnación, and Hito Steyerl. 2002. *Spricht die Subalterne Deutsch? Migration und postkoloniale Kritik*. Münster: Unrast Verlag.

Guitta, Olivier. 2006. "The State Department Was Right to Deny Tariq Ramadan a Visa." *The Weekly Standard*, October 16. http://www.weeklystandard. com/ Content/Public/Articles/000/000/012/800naxnt.asp?pg=2 (accessed December 8, 2008).

Ha, Kien Nghi. 2005. *Ethinizitaet and Migration Reloaded. Kulturelle Identitaet, Differenz und Hybriditaet Impostkolonialen Diskurs*. Berlin: Wissenschaftlicher Verlag.

_____, Nicola Lauré al-Samarai, and Sheila Mysorekar, eds. 2007. *Re/visionen: Postkoloniale Perspektiven von People of Color auf Rassismus, Kulturpolitik und Widerstand in Deutschland*. Münster: Unrast Verlag.

Habermas, Jürgen. 2008. "Die Dialektik der Saekularisierung." *Blaetter fuer deutsche und Internationale Politik*, April. 33–46.

_____. 2006. "Die Erweiterung des Horizonts." *Koelner Stadtanzeiger*, November 8.

_____, and Jacques Derrida. 2003. "Unsere Erneuerung; Nach dem Krieg: Die Wiedergeburt Europas." *Frankfurter Allgemeine Zeitung*, May 31.

Haegler, Max. 2007. "Mit Internetspielen gegen Ausländer." September 17. *Die Tageszeitung*, www.taz.de (accessed January 25, 2009).

Hage, Ghassan. 2003. *Against Paranoid Nationalism: Searching for Hope in a Shrinking Society*. London: Pluto Press.

Halberstam, Judith. 2001. "Telling Tales: Brandon Teena, Billy Tipton, and Transgender Biography." In *Passing: Identity and Interpretation in Sexuality, Race, and Religion*, eds. Maria Carla Sanchez and Linda Schlossberg, 13–37. New York: New York University Press.

_____. 2005. *In a Queer Time and Place: Transgender Bodies, Subcultural Lives*. New York: New York University Press.

Hall, Stuart. 1991. "Europe's Other Self." *Marxism Today*, 18.

_____. 2003. "The White of Their Eyes: Racist Ideologies and the Media." In *Gender, Race, and Class in the Media*, eds. Gail Dines and Jean Humez, 18–22. London: Sage.

Halperin, David. 1995. *Saint Foucault: Toward a Gay Hagiography*. New York: Oxford University Press.

Hamé. 2002. "Insécurité sous la plume d'un barbare." *La Rumeur Magazine*.

Hancock, Ian. 1987. *The Pariah Syndrome: An Account of Gypsy Slavery and Persecution*. Ann Arbor, Mich.: Karoma Press.

Hannerz, Ulf. 1996. *Transnational Connections: Culture, People, Places*. New York: Routledge.

Haraway, Donna. 1991. *Simians, Cyborgs, and Women: The Reinvention of Nature*. New York: Routledge.

Harding, Leonhard, and Brigitte Reinwald, eds. 1990. *Afrika—Mutter und Modell der europäischen Zivilisation? Die Rehabilitierung des Schwarzen Kontinents durch Cheickh Anta Diop*. Berlin: Dietrich Reimer Verlag.

Hargreaves, Alec G., and Mark McKinney, eds. 1997. *Post-colonial Cultures in France*. New York: Routledge.

Harms, Florian. 2006. "Reisewarnung zur WM. 'Ganz Ostdeutschland ist für Dunkelhäutige gefährlich.'" *Spiegel Online*, June 7. http://www.spiegel.de/reise/aktuell/0,1518,419957,00.html (accessed July 10, 2009).

Hass, Amira. 2000. *Drinking the Sea at Gaza: Days and Nights in a Land under Siege*. New York: Picador USA.

Hegel, Georg Friedrich Wilhelm. 1945. *Vorlesungen über die Philosophie der Geschichte*. Stuttgart: Reclam.

Heinrich Böll Stiftung, ed. 2003. *Von Kopftüchern und Grauschleiern. Ein Stück Stoff zwischen Politik, Kultur und Religion*. Berlin: Beauftrage der Bundesregierung für Migration, Flüchtlinge und Integration.

Hermans, Mariette. 2002. "Herinneringen aan Sister Outsider. Zwart, lesbisch en strijdbaar." June. *Lover*, 29, no. 2:16.

Herrmann, Axel. "Menschenrechte für Flüchtlinge und Vertriebene," Berlin: Bundeszentrale fuer politische Bildung. http://www.bpb.de/publikationen/ ET9R43,3,0,Menschenrechte _f%FCr_Fl%FCchtlinge_und_Vertriebene.html (accessed August 13, 2008).

Hieronymous, Andreas. 2003. "'Not at Home and Dangerously Alone?' Gefahr und Sicherheit im Alltagsleben von Jugendlichen. Eine Studie in zwei Hamburger und zwei Londoner Stadtteilen." In *Eder*, 291–312.

Hines, Darlene, Trica Keaton, and Stephen Small, eds. 2009. *Black Europe and the African Diaspora*. Urbana and Chicago: University of Illinois Press.

Hirsi Ali, Aayan. 2006. "Ik heb het land goed wakker geschud," interview with Steffi Louters, *De Volkskrant*, September 23. http://www.volkskrant.nl/ archief_gratis/ article1023548.ece/Ik_heb_het_land_goedwakker _geschud?service=Print (accessed March 28, 2009).

_____. 2007. *Infidel*. New York: Free Press.

_____, and Theo van Gogh. 2004. *Submission I*. The Netherlands, 10 min.

Hisama, Ellie M., and Evan Rapport, eds. 2005. *Critical Minded: New Approaches to Hip-Hop Studies*. Brooklyn, N.Y.: Institute for Studies in American Music.

Holert, Tom, and Mark Terkessidis. 1996. *Mainstream der Minderheiten. Pop in der Kontrollgesellschaft*. Berlin and Amsterdam: Edition ID-Archiv.

Holston, James, ed. 1996. *Cities and Citizenship*. A Special Issue of *Public Culture*.

Hong, Grace. 2006. *The Ruptures of American Capital: Women of Color Feminism and the Culture of Immigrant Labor*. Minneapolis: University of Minnesota Press.

_____. 2008. "'The Future of Our Worlds': Black Feminism and the Politics of Knowledge in the University under Globalization." *Meridians: Feminism, Race, Transnationalism* 8, no. 2:95–115.

Honig, Bonnie. 2001. *Democracy and the Foreigner*. Princeton, N.J.: Princeton University Press.

_____. 2006. "Another Cosmopolitanism? Law and Politics in the New Europe." In Benhabib, 102–27.

Honig, Jan Willem. 2001. "Avoiding War, Inviting Defeat: The Srebrenica Crisis, July 1995." *Journal of Contingencies and Crisis Management* 9, no. 4:200–10.

Hopkins, Leroy T., ed. 1999. *Who Is a German? Historical and Modern Perspectives on Africans in Germany.* Washington, D.C.: The American Institute for Contemporary German Studies.

Horton, James Oliver, and Johanna C. Kardux. 2004. "Slavery and the Contest for National Heritage in the United States and the Netherlands." *American Studies International* 42:51–74.

Hoving, Isabel. 2005. "Circumventing Openness: Creating New Senses of Dutchness." *Transit* 1:1–9.

Huber, Charles M. 2005. *Ein Niederbayer im Senegal. Mein Leben zwischen zwei Welten.* Frankfurt: Fischer.

Hügel-Marshall, Ika. 2001. *Invisible Woman: Growing Up Black in Germany.* New York: Continuum.

_____, May Ayim, and Ilona Bubak, eds. 1993. *Entfernte Verbindungen. Rassismus, Anti-semitismus, Klassenunterdrückung.* Berlin: Orlanda.

Hull, Gloria, Patricia Bell Scott, and Barbara Smith, eds. 1982. *All the Women Are White, All the Blacks Are Men, but Some of Us Are Brave.* New York: Feminist Press.

Huyssen, Andreas. 2005. *Present Pasts: Urban Palimpsests and the Politics of Memory.* Palo Alto, Calif.: Stanford University Press.

_____. 2003. "Diaspora and Nation: Migration into Other Pasts," *New German Critique* 88:147–64.

Interface, eds. 2005. *WiderstandsBewegungen: Antirassismus zwischen Alltag & Aktion.* Berlin, Hamburg: Assoziation.

Ireland, Doug. 2005. "Why Is France Burning?" *The Nation*, November 28. http://www.thenation.com/doc/20051128/ireland (accessed November 16, 2008).

Islamic Human Rights Commission. 2006. "Über-citizens: Briefing on the Recent Naturalisation Tests in Germany." May 11. www.ihrc.org.uk/file/060511uber-citizens.pdf (accessed December 13, 2008).

Ivanov, Andrey, et al., eds. 2006. *At Risk: Roma and the Displaced in Southeast Europe.* Bratislava: United Nations Development Programme.

Jackson, Peter A. 2009. "Capitalism and Global Queering. National Markets, Parallels among Sexual Cultures, and Multiple Queer Modernities." *GLQ* 15, no. 3:357–94.

Jacobson, Matthew Fry. 1998. *Whiteness of a Different Color. European Immigrants and the Alchemy of Race.* Cambridge, Mass.: Harvard University Press.

Jakobs, Hans-Jürgen. 2009. "Minarett-Verbot: Wenn der Staat das Volk nicht mehr versteht." *Süddeutsche Zeitung*, November 30. http://www.sueddeutsche.de/politik/732/496052/text/ (accessed January 30, 2010).

Jam, Afdhere. 2008. *Illegal Citizens: Queer Lives in the Muslim World.* New York: Salaam Press.

James, Harold. 2003. "Aussenpolitik missverstanden: Europa schwelgt in gefährlicher Sehnsucht." *Süddeutsche Zeitung*, June 3.

Johnson, Dominic. 2007. "Sarkozy befremdet Afrika." *Die Tageszeitung*, August 1, 1.

Johnson, E. Patrick. 2003. *Appropriating Blackness: Performance and the Politics of Authenticity*. Durham, N.C.: Duke University Press.

———, and May G. Henderson, eds. 2005. *Black Queer Studies: A Critical Anthology*. Durham, N.C.: Duke University Press.

Johnson, Sara E. 2009. "'You Should Give Them Blacks to Eat': Waging Inter-American Wars of Torture and Terror." *American Quarterly* 61, no. 1:65–92.

Judt, Tony. 2005. "Europe vs. America," *The New York Review of Books* 52, no. 2, February 10. http://www.nybooks.com/articles/17726 (accessed December 13, 2008).

Kagan, Robert. 2002. "Power and Weakness: Why the United States and Europe See the World Differently." *Policy Review* 113, June/July. http://www.hoover.org/publications/policyreview/3460246.html (accessed February 2010).

Kahlcke, Jan. 2006. "Unterschicht aller Nationalitäten," *Die Tageszeitung (taz nord)*, April 18, 24.

el Kaka, Imad, and Hatice Kurşun. 2002. *Mijn geloof en mijn geluk. Islamitische meiden en jongen over hun homoseksuele gevoelens*. Amsterdam: Schorer Boeken.

Kanak Attak. 1998. "Ein Manifest gegen Mültükültüralizm, gegen demokratische und hybride Deutsche sowie konformistische Migranten." www.kanak-attak.de (accessed December 14, 2008).

Kanak Attak and Karawane. 2005. "Für und wider des Konzepts der Autonomie der Migration." In *Interface*, 362–76.

Kanak TV. 2001. *Philharmonie Köln*, 9 min.

———. 2002. *Weisses Ghetto*, 8 min.

———. 2006. *Schland ist das Land*, 11 min.

Kanak TV and Karawane. 2006. *Recolonizing Cologne*, 45 min.

Kania, Magdalena. "'Here Comes the Rest': A Sociological Perspective on Postcolonial Rethinking of the 'Second World'—The Case of Poland." http://postcolonial-europe.eu/index.php?option=com_content&view=article&id=85%3Ahere-comes-the-rest-a-sociological-perspective-on-postcolonial-rethinking-of-the-second-world-the-case-of-poland&catid=45%3Aattitudes&Itemid=65&lang=en (accessed November 7, 2009).

Kantara, Jeanine. 2000. "Schwarz. Und deutsch." *Die Zeit*, September 7. http://www.zeit.de/2000/37/Schwarz_Und_deutsch (accessed November 16, 2008).

Karawane für die Rechte von Flüchtlingen und MigrantInnen. 2003. "Self Description of the Caravan for the Rights of Refugees and Migrants." http://thecaravan.org/about (accessed July 4, 2009).

Karkayali, Serhat, and Uli Spenkoch. 1999. "'Dieser Song gehört uns!' Interview mit Imran Ayata, Laura Mestre Vives, und Vanessa Barth von Kanak Attak." *Diskus: Frankfurter StudentInnen Zeitschrift* 1:48.

Kaya, Ayhan. 2001. *Sicher in Kreuzberg: Constructing Diasporas: Turkish Hip-Hop Youth in Berlin.* Bielefeld: Transcript. Piscataway, N.J.: Distributed in North America by Transaction Publishers.

———. 2006. "The Beur Uprising: Poverty and Muslim Atheists in France." *Eurozine,* May 3. http://www.eurozine.com/articles/2006–05–03-kaya-en. html (accessed February 17, 2010).

Keaton, Trica. 2006. *Muslim Girls and the Other France. Race, Identity Politics, and Social Exclusion.* Bloomington: Indiana University Press.

Kelek, Neçla. 2005. *Die Fremde Braut. Ein Bericht aus dem Innern des türkischen Lebens in Deutschland.* Köln: Kiepenheuer & Witsch.

Kerner, Ina. 2007. "Challenges of Critical Whiteness Studies." Translate.eipcp.net, October 13. http://translate.eipcp.net/strands/03/kerner-strands01en#redir#redir (accessed October 21, 2009).

Khazaleh, Lorenz. 2000. *Sein Ding machen. Eine ethnologische Feldforschung in der Hip-Hop Szene Basels.* Basel: Universität Basel.

Khemiri, Jonas Hassen. 2007. *Das Kamel ohne Höcker.* München: Piper Verlag.

Kjær Jørgensen, Signe. 2008. "Representing Danish Headscarf-Wearing Muslims: A Mapping of Aporias for Identity Formation." Conference Paper, *Representing Islam: Comparative Perspectives, University of Sussex,* September 5. http://www.surrey.ac.uk/politics/conferences/archive/Islam_Conference/SigneKjaer Jorgensen.doc.

Klausen, Jytte. 2006. "Rotten Judgment in the State of Denmark," February 8. www.salon.com (accessed November 7, 2008).

Kleeberg, Michael. 2005. "Apartheid in Europa." *Die Welt,* 12. November. http://www.welt.de/print-welt/article177060/Apartheid_in_Europa.html (accessed December 2, 2008).

Klimt, Andrea. 2003. "Transnationale Zugehörigkeit: Portugiesen in Hamburg." In Eder, 211–32.

Klingst, Martin. 2003. "Feige Richter. Das Kopftuch Urteil." *Die Zeit,* September 25. http://www.zeit.de/2003/40/Kopftuch (accessed April 24, 2009).

Körberling, Gesa. 2005. "Das geht dich an, da draussen—Bevor wir betteln, gehn wir klauen! Ist HipHop eine antirassisitische Praxis?" In *Interface,* 229–38.

Korek, Janusz. "Central and Eastern Europe from a Postcolonial Perspective." http://postcolonial-europe.eu/index.php?option=com_content &view=article & id=60%3A-central-and-eastern-europe-from-a-postcolonial-perspective &cati d=35%3Aessays&Itemid=54&lang=en (accessed November 7, 2009).

Koshy, Susan. 2001. "Morphing Race into Ethnicity: Asian Americans and Critical Transformations of Whiteness." *boundary 2* 28, no.1:153–94.

Kraushaar, Wolfgang. 1973. "Aus der Protest–Chronik. 24.–30. August: 'Die Gastarbeiter, das neue deutsche Proletariat begehrte auf.'" *Eurozine,* July 15, 2004. http://www.eurozine.com/articles/2004–07–15-kraushaar-de.html (accessed July 1, 2009).

Kramer, Julian. 2003. "Living on the Edge: A Roma Clan in Ostrava, Czech Republic." August 1. http://www.opendemocracy.net/people-migrationeurope/article_1404.jsp (accessed November 16, 2008).

Krastev, Ivan. 2003. "Nicht ohne mein Amerika." *Die Zeit*, August 14, 13.

Krekow, Sebastian, and Jens Steiner. 2000. *Bei uns geht einiges: Die deutsche HipHop Szene*. Berlin: Schwarzkopf & Schwarzkopf Verlag.

Kristeva, Julia. 1993. *Nations without Nationalism*. New York: Columbia University Press.

Langfur, Hal. 2006. "Could This Be Heaven or Could This Be Hell? Reconsidering the Myth of Racial Democracy in Brazil." *Ethnohistory* 53:603–13.

Latham, Robert, and Saskia Sassen. 2005. *Digital Formation*. Princeton, N.J.: University of Princeton Press.

Lefkovitz, Mary, ed. 1996. *Black Athena Revisited*. Chapel Hill: The University of North Carolina Press.

Lemke Muniz de Faria, Yara-Colette. 2002. *Zwischen Fürsorge und Ausgrenzung: Afrodeutsche Besatzungskinder im Nachkriegsdeutschland*. Berlin: Metropol.

Leydesdorff, Selma. 2007. "Stories from No Land: The Women of Srebrenica Speak Out." *Human Rights Review*, April-June, 187–198.

Liauzu, Claude. 2005. "Une loi contre l'histoire." *Le Monde Diplomatique*, April, 28.

Linguist. 1993. "'Schwarz' verstehen wir politisch. Die afrodeutsche HipHop-Gruppe Advanced Chemistry über ihre Erfahrungen mit alltäglichem Rassismus." *Die Tageszeitung*, March 25, 16.

Lionnet, Francoise, and Shu-mei Shih, eds. 2005. *Minor Transnationalism*. Durham, N.C.: Duke University Press.

———. 2011. *The Creolization of Theory*. Durham, N.C.: Duke University Press.

Lipsitz, George. 1994. *Dangerous Crossroads: Popular Music, Postmodernism and the Poetics of Place*. New York: Verso.

Loh, Hannes. 2003. "20 Jahre 'Afrodeutsch' Ein Exkurs über Sprache, Hiphop und Verantwortung." March 19. http://www.intro.de/kuenstler/interviews/23013581 (accessed December 14, 2008).

Loh, Hannes, and Murat Güngör. 2002. *Fear of a Kanak Planet, Hip-Hop zwischen Weltkultur und Nazi-Rap*. Wien: Hannibal-Verlag.

Lorde, Audre. 1984. *Sister Outsider*. Freedom, Calif.: The Crossing Press.

Lowe, Lisa. 1996. *Immigrant Acts: On Asian American Cultural Politics*. Durham, N.C.: Duke University Press.

Lucassen, Leo. 2005. *The Immigrant Threat: The Integration of Old and New Migrants in Western Europe since 1850*. Urbana, Ill.: University of Illinois Press.

Luibhéid, Eithne. 2002. *Entry Denied: Controlling Sexuality at the Border*. Minneapolis: University of Minnesota Press.

Luibhéid, Eithne, and Lionel Cantú Jr. 2005. *Queer Migrations: Sexuality, U.S. Citizenship, and Border Crossings*. Minneapolis: University of Minnesota Press.

van der Made, Yan. 2007. "Sarkozy and Chirac Attend Event Marking France's Abolition of Slavery." *Network Europe Radio* Web site, May 11. http://networkeurope.radio.cz/feature/sarkozy-and-chirac-attend-event-marking-frances-abolition-of-slavery (accessed July 28, 2008).

Mahmood, Saba. 2005. *Politics of Piety: The Islamic Revival and the Feminist Subject.* Princeton, N.J.: Princeton University Press.

——. 2006. "Secularism, Hermeneutics, and Empire: The Politics of Islamic Reformation." *Public Culture* 18, no. 2:323–47.

Mak, Geert. 2005."Der Mord and Theo van Gogh." *Geschichte einer moralischen Panik.* Frankfurt, a.M.: Suhrkamp.

Manalansan, Martin. 2003. *Global Divas: Filipino Gay Men in the Diaspora.* Durham, N.C.: Duke University Press.

——. 2005. "Race, Violence, and Neoliberal Spatial Politics in the Global City." *Social Text* 84–85, 23:141–56.

Marlet, George. 2006. "Verbijstering over lintje Dutchbat Srebrenica." *Trouw*, November 4. http://www.trouw.nl/krantenarchief/2006/11/04/2258084/ Verbijstering_over_lintje_Dutchbat_Srebrenica.html (accessed April 24, 2009).

Martens, Daniela. 2006. "Eigentlich bin ich gar nichts." *Der Tagesspiegel*, July 29. http://www.tagesspiegel.de/berlin/;art270,2262052 (accessed December 13, 2008).

Martin, Biddy. 1994. "Sexualities without Genders and Other Queer Utopias." *Diacritics* 24:2–3, 104–21.

Maschino, Maurice T. 2001. "The Hidden History of the Algerian War." *Le Monde diplomatique*, April. http://mondediplo.com/2001/04/04algeriatorture (accessed August 10, 2008).

Mavroudi, Elizabeth. 2007. "Diaspora as Process: (De)Constructing Boundaries." *Geography Compass* 1, no. 3:467–79.

Mazon, Patricia, and Reinhild Steingroever. 2005. "Not So Plain as Black and White." *Afro-German Culture and History, 1890–2000.* Rochester, N.Y.: University of Rochester Press.

Mazrui, Ali A. 2005. "The Re-invention of Africa: Edward Said, V. Y. Mudimbe, and Beyond." *Research in African Literatures* 36, no. 3:68–82.

Mbembe, Achille. 2001. *On the Postcolony.* Berkeley: University of California Press.

——. 2003. "Necropolitics." *Public Culture* 15, no. 1:11–40.

——. 2008. "What Is Postcolonial Thinking?" January 9. http://www.eurozine.com/articles/2008–01–09-mbembe-en.html (accessed November 7, 2009).

McClintock, Anne. 1995. *Imperial Leather: Race, Gender, and Sexuality in the Colonial Contest.* New York: Routledge.

McClintock, Anne, and Mufti Aamir, eds. 1997. *Dangerous Liaisons: Gender, Nation, and Postcolonial Perspectives.* Minneapolis: University of Minnesota Press.

232 BIBLIOGRAPHY

McNevin, Anne. 2006. "Political Belonging in a Neoliberal Era: The Struggle of the Sans-Papiers." *Citizenship Studies* 10, no. 2:135–51.

Meinhof, U. H., and D. Galasinski. 2000. *Border Discourse: Changing Identities, Changing Nations, Changing Stories in European Border Communities—A State of the Art Report*. Brussels: European Commission.

Menrath, Stefanie. 2001. *Represent What . . . Performativität von Identitäten im Hip-Hop*. Hamburg: Argument.

Mercer, Kobena. 1994. *Welcome to the Jungle: New Positions in Black Cultural Studies*. New York: Routledge.

"Migrant Crisis." *BBC News special*, http://news.bbc.co.uk/2/hi/europe/5348192.stm (accessed December 2, 2008).

Ministerie van Defensie. "Toespraak voor de Staatssecretaris van Defensie Cees van der Knaap ter gelegenheid van de uitreiking van een koninklijke onderscheiding aan de heer Van Russel, op 15 augustus 2005, te Paramaribo, Suriname." http://www.nieuwsbank.nl/inp/2005/08/17/L069.htm (accessed September 16, 2010).

de Moor, Margriet. 2007. "Alarm Bells in Muslim Hearts." April 23. www.signandsight.com (accessed November 7, 2008).

Morice, Alain. 2006. "Comprendre avant de juger: à propos des émeutes urbaines en France." January 24. www.samizdat.net (accessed December 2, 2008).

Morisson, Toni. 1992. *Playing in the Dark: Whiteness and the Literary Imagination*. New York: Vintage.

Morsy, Soheir. 1994. "Beyond the Honorary 'White' Classification of Egyptians: Societal Identity in Historical Context." In *Race*, eds. Steven Gregory and Roger Sanjek, 175–98. New Brunswick, N.J.: Rutgers University Press.

Mosse, George L. 1978. *Towards the Final Solution*. Madison: University of Wisconsin Press.

Moten, Fred. 2003. *In the Break: The Aesthetics of the Black Radical Tradition*. Minneapolis: University of Minnesota Press.

Mudure, Michaela. 2005. "The Black Romanians: A Question of Race or a Question of Gypsiness?" Paper presented at "Challenging Europe—Black European Studies in the 21st Century," First International, Interdisciplinary Conference of BEST, Akademie Schmitten, November 10–13.

Muñoz, José Estaban. 1999. *Disidentifications: Queers of Color and the Performance of Politics*. Minneapolis: University of Minnesota Press.

Museum van Europa. 2007. *Dit is Onze Geschiedenis! 50 Jaar Europees Aventuur*. Brussels. http://www.expo europe.be/nl/site/musee/musee-europe-bruxelles.html (accessed February 15, 2010).

Mysorekar, Sheila. 2007. "Guess My Genes: Von Mischlingen, MiMiMis und Multiracials." In Ha, al-Samarai, and Mysorekar, 161–70.

Nadeau, Chantal. 2000. "Between Queer-and-Lesbian: Translated Politics." In *Concerns*, eds. Women's Caucus for the Modern Language Association, 27, nos. 3–4:53–66.

Napoli, James P. 1997. "A 1961 Massacre of Algerians in Paris: When the Media Failed the Test." *Washington Report on Middle Eastern Affairs*, March. 36.

Novick, Peter. 1999. *The Holocaust in American Life*. New York: Houghton Mifflin Co.

———. 2007. "Comments on Aleida Assmann's Lecture." *GHI Bulletin* 40:27–31.

OECD. 2006. Programme for International Student Assessment, Where Immigrant Students Succeed—A Comparative Review of Performance and Engagement in PISA 2003, Paris.

Oguntoye, Katharina. 1997. *Eine Afro-deutsche Geschichte. Zur Lebenssituation von Afrikanern und Afro-Deutschen in Deutschland von 1884 bis 1950*. Berlin: Hoho Verlag Christine Hoffman.

Oguntoye, Katharina, May Opitz, and Dagmar Schultz, eds. 1986. *Farbe bekennen. Afro-deutsche Frauen auf den Spuren ihrer Geschichte*. Berlin: Orlanda Verlag (English transl. 1991. *Showing Our Colors*. Amherst: University of Massachusetts Press).

Open Society Institute. 2007. *Muslims in EU Cities: Background Research Report Denmark*. http://www.soros.org/initiatives/home/articles_publications/publications /museucitiesden_20080101.pdf (accessed March 10, 2010).

———. 2007. *Muslims in EU Cities: Background Research Report Germany*. http://www.soros.org/initiatives/home/articles_publications/publications/museucitiesger_20080101.pdf (accessed March 10, 2010).

———. 2007. *Muslims in EU Cities: Background Research Report Netherlands*. http://www.soros.org/initiatives/home/articles_publications/publications/museucitiesnet_20080101.pdf (accessed March 10, 2010).

———. 2009. *At Home in Europe Project Muslims in Europe—A Report on 11 EU Cities Findings and Recommendation*. December. http://www.soros.org/initiatives/ home/articles_publications/publications/muslims-europe-20091215 (accessed February 17, 2010).

Osman, Ghada, and Camille F. Forbes. 2004. "Representing the West in the Arabic Language: The Slave Narrative of Omar Ibn Said." In *Journal of Islamic Studies* 15, no. 3:331–43.

van Ours, Jan C. and Justus Veenman. 2003. "The Educational Attainment of Second-generation Immigrants in the Netherlands." *Journal of Population Economics* 16, no. 4:739–53.

Owen, Richard. 2008. "Italy Gypsies Find Echoes of Nazism in Fingerprinting Move." *The Times*, July 5. http://www.timesonline.co.uk/tol/news/world/europe/ article4272550.ece (accessed July 30, 2008).

Patterson, Tiffany, and Robin Kelley. 2000. "Unfinished Migrations: Reflections on the African Diaspora and the Making of the Modern World." *African Studies Review* 43:11–50.

Patton, Cindy, and Benigno Sánchez-Eppler. 2000. *Queer Diasporas*. Durham, N.C.: Duke University Press.

People Flow. "Migration in Europe." http://www.opendemocracy.net/globalization-migrationeurope/issue.jsp (accessed November 30, 2008).

Perez, Hiram. 2005. "You Can Have My Brown Body and Eat It, Too!" *Social Text* 23 no. 3–4 (Fall/Winter): 171–92.

Petzen, Jennifer. 2004. "Home or Homelike? Turkish Queers Manage Space in Berlin." *Space & Culture* 7, no. 1:20–32.

Pfaff, William. 2004. "Europe Pays the Price for Its Cultural Naïveté." *International Herald Tribune*, November 25.

Phillips, Caryl. 1987. *The European Tribe.* New York: Random House.

Pilz, Gunter. 2007. "Offener Rassismus und ein ausgeprägtes Feindbild." February 22. http://www.bpb.de/themen/UOUUSY,0,Offener_Rassismus_und_ein_ausgepr%E4gtes_Feindbild.html (accessed July 10, 2009).

PJ. 2006. "La Rumeur devant ses juges." May 14. http://www.acontresens.com/contrepoints/societe/29.html (accessed August 9, 2008).

Poggioli, Sylvia. 2006. "French Rap Musicians Blamed for Violence." *NPR World,* August 6.

Pomrehn, Wolfgang. 2006. "Ausbürgerung der sozialen Probleme." *Telepolis,* April 12. http://www.heise.de/tp/r4/artikel/22/22448/1.html (accessed July 9, 2009).

Popham, Peter. 2008. "Italian Tolerance Goes Up in Smoke as Gypsy Camp Is Burnt to Ground." *The Independent,* May 16. http://www.independent.co.uk/news/world/europe/italian-tolerance-goes-up-in-smoke-as-gypsy-camp-is-burnt-to-ground-829318.html (accessed July 30, 2008).

Popoola, Olumide, and Beldan Sezen, eds. 1999. "Talking Home." *Heimat aus unserer eigenen Feder. Frauen of color in Deutschland.* Amsterdam: Blue Moon Press.

Povoledo, Elisabetta. 2008. "Gypsies in Italy Protest Prejudice." *International Herald Tribune,* June 8. http://www.iht.com/articles/2008/06/08/europe/italy.php (accessed July 30, 2008).

Prashad, Vijay. 2002. *Everybody Was Kung Fu Fighting: Afro-Asian Connections and the Myth of Cultural Purity.* Boston: Beacon Press.

———. 2008. *The Darker Nations: A People's History of the Third World.* New York: New Press.

Preston, Julia. 2006. "Lawsuit Filed in Support of Muslim Scholar Barred from U.S." *The New York Times,* January 26. http://www.nytimes.com/2006/01/26/national/26suit.html (accessed February 14, 2009).

Pronk, Iris. 2007. "Dope Man, om hier rapteksten te spitten." *Trouw,* June 22. (accessed June 26, 2008).

Puar, Jasbir, and Amit Rai. "Monster, Terrorist, Fag: The War on Terrorism and the Production of Docile Patriots." *Social Text* 20, no. 202:117–48.

Puar, Jasbir. 2007. *Terrorist Assemblages: Homonationalism in Queer Times.* Durham, N.C.: Duke University Press.

Puschner, Sebastian. 2008. "Ein deutscher Name ist die halbe Miete." *Die Tageszeitung,* December 9. http://www.taz.de/regional/berlin/aktuell/artikel/

kommentarseite/1/ein-deutscher-name-ist-die-halbe-miete/kommentare/1/1/ (accessed December 14, 2008).

Quaestio, eds. 2000. *Queering Demokratie: Sexuelle Politiken*. Berlin: Querverlag.

Queeley, Andrea. 2003. "Hip-Hop and the Aesthetics of Criminalization." *Souls* 5, no. 1:1–15.

Quist, Pia. 2000. "New Copenhagen 'Multi-ethnolect': Language Use among Adolescents in Linguistic and Culturally Heterogeneous Settings." *Danske Talesprog* 1:143–212. Institut for Dansk Dialektforskning. København: C.A. Reitzels Forlag.

Raatzsch, Jenő André. 2007. "Paradise Lost: The First Roma Pavilion." June 10–November 21. http://www.romapavilion.org/artists/Jeno_Andre_RAATZSCH. htm (accessed December 13, 2008).

Rabaka, Reiland. 2007. "The Souls of White Folk: W. E. B. Du Bois's Critique of White Supremacy and Contributions to Critical White Studies." *Journal of African American Studies* 11:1–15.

Rahmsdorf, Inga. 2006. "Schlechte Chancen für Aussiedlerkids." *Die Tageszeitung*, May 24, 16.

Ramadan, Tariq. 2001. "Existe-t-il un antisémitisme islamique?" *Le Monde*, December 23.

_____. 2003. "Critique des (nouveaux) intellectuels communautaires." *Oumma*, October 3. http://oumma.com/Critique-des-nouveaux (accessed February 14, 2009).

_____. 2006. "The Pope and Islam: The True Debate," www.tariqramadan.com, September 21. http://www.tariqramadan.com/spip.php?article781 (accessed February 14, 2009).

_____. 2007. "What the West Can Learn from Islam." *The Chronicle of Higher Education*, February 16. http://chronicle.com/weekly/v53/i24/24b00601.htm (accessed February 14, 2009).

_____. 2009. *Radical Reform: Islamic Ethics and Liberation*. New York: Oxford University Press.

Raphael-Hernandez, Heike, and Shannon Steen. 2006. *Afroasian Encounters: Culture, History, Politics*. New York: New York University Press.

Rathe, Adam. 2007. "You've Got 'Veil.'" *The Brooklyn Paper*, October 6. http://www.brooklynpaper.com/stories/30/39/30_39youvegotveil.html (accessed April 24, 2009).

Reckwitz, Andreas. 2009. "Die Selbstkulturalisierung der Stadt." *Eurozine*, 1–23, May 20. http://www.eurozine.com/articles/2009–05–20-reckwitz-de.html (accessed June 9, 2009).

Redactie Onderwijs. 2007. "Segregatie op basisschool al ver gevorderd." *Trouw*, November 16. http://www.trouw.nl/onderwijs/article1509551.ece (accessed February 13, 2010).

Reed-Anderson, Paulette. 2000. *Berlin und die afrikanische Diaspora. Rewriting the Footnotes*. Berlin: Die Ausländerbeauftragte des Berliner Senats.

Reeder, Andre. 1996. *Aan Niets Overleden*. The Netherlands, 56 min.

Riegel, Christine. 2003. "Wie junge Migrantinnen mit ethnisiert-vergeschlechtlichten Fremdzuschreibungen umgehen." *Beiträge zur feministischen Theorie und Praxis* 63/64:59–73.

Rifkin, Jeremy. 2004. *The European Dream: How Europe's Vision of the Future Is Quietly Eclipsing the American Dream*. London: Tarcher/Penguin.

Riphahn, Regina T. 2003. "Cohort Effects in the Educational Attainment of Second Generation Immigrants in Germany: An Analysis of Census Data." *Journal of Population Economics* 16, no. 4 (November):711–37.

Roberts, Dorothy. 1997. *Killing the Black Body. Race, Reproduction, and the Meaning of Liberty*. New York: Random House.

Roediger, David. 2006. "The Retreat from Race and Class." *The Monthly Review* 58, no. 3, July–August. http://www.monthlyreview.org/0706roediger.htm (accessed October 19, 2009).

Rommmelspacher, Birgit. 2002. *Anerkennung und Ausgrenzung: Deutschland als multikulturelle Gesellschaft*. Frankfurt: Campus.

Roosen, Adelheid. 2007. "The Veiled Monologues." *Theater* 37, no. 2:23–53.

_____. 2010. "Is.man." In *The Dramaturgy of the Real on the World Stage*, ed. Carol Martin, 109–48. New York: Macmillan.

Rooth, Dan-Olof, and Jan Ekberg. 2003. "Unemployment and Earnings for Second Generation Immigrants in Sweden: Ethnic Background and Parent Composition." *Journal of Population Economics* 16, no. 4 (November):787–814.

Rose, Tricia. 1991. "Never Trust a Big Butt and a Smile." *Camera Obscura* 23:109–31.

_____. 1994. *Black Noise: Rap Music and Black Culture in Contemporary America*. Middleton, Conn.: Wesleyan University Press.

Ross, Marlon. 2005. "Beyond the Closet as Raceless Paradigm." In Henderson and Johnson, 161–89.

Runia, Eelco. 2004. "'Forget About It': 'Parallel Processing' in the Srebrenica Report." *History and Theory* 43:295–320.

Said, Edward. 1979. *Orientalism*. New York: Vintage.

_____. 1997. *Covering Islam: How the Media and the Experts Determine How We See the Rest of the World*. New York: Vintage.

Sanchez, Maria Carla, and Linda Schlossberg, eds. 2001. *Passing: Identity and Interpretation in Sexuality, Race, and Religion*. New York: New York University Press.

Sandford, Alasdair. 2005. "Anger Grips Paris Riot Suburb." *BBC News*, November 1. http://news.bbc.co.uk/2/hi/europe/4397056.stm (accessed January 25, 2009).

Sassen, Saskia. 2005. "Spatialities and Temporalities of the Global: Elements for a Theorization." *Public Culture* 12, no. 1:215–32.

Sassen, Saskia, and Robert Latham. 2005. *Digital Formations: Constructing an Object of Study*. Princeton, N.J.: Princeton University Press.

Sawyer, Lena. 2000. "Routings: 'Race,' African Diaspora, and Swedish Belonging." *Transforming Anthropology* 11, no.1:13–35.

Scheuble, Verena, and Michael Wehner. 2006. "Fussball und nationale Identität." *Der Bürger im Staat*, January. http://www.buergerimstaat.de/1_06/identitaet. htm (accessed July 10, 2009).

Schmidt, Janek. 2008. "Der neue Antisemitismus in Frankreich kommt von unten. Die Historikerin Diana Pinto ueber die Aengste franzoesischer Juden, extemistische Imane und religiöse Bandenkriege in Paris." *Süddeutsche Zeitung*, July 18. 14.

Schofield, Hugh. 2005. "French Rappers' Prophecies Come True." *BBC News*, November 16. http://news.bbc.co.uk/2/hi/europe/4440422.stm (accessed November 30, 2008).

Schramma, Fritz. "Rede des Oberbürgermeisters Fritz Schramma anlässlich des Festakts zum 40.Jahrestag der Migration aus der Türkei am Freitag, 26. Oktober 2001, 10.00 Uhr, Philharmonie." *R20011026 Festakt Migration.* http://74.125.155.132/search?q=cache:ZKZtin3vXiIJ:www.stadt-koeln.de/ mediaasset /content/pdf-ob/reden/2001/10/26-migration-tuerkei-40jahre.pdf+ festakt+ 40+jahre +migration+turkei+koeln+2001&cd=1&hl=en&ct=clnk&g l=us&client=firefox-a (accessed June 29, 2009).

Schultz, Dagmar, ed. 1983. *Macht und Sinnlichkeit. Ausgewählte Texte von Audre Lorde und Adrienne Rich.* Berlin: Orlanda.

Segato, R. L. 1998. "The Color-Blind Subject of Myth; Or, Where to Find Africa in the Nation." *Annual Review of Anthropology*, 27:129–51.

Sellar, Tom. 2007. "World Bodies: Adelheid Roosen and *The Veiled Monologues.*" *Theater* 37, no. 2:7–21.

———. 2007. "Death to the Unchaste: Europe's Muslim Women—and the Men Who Murder Them: Two Islam-Themed Plays at St. Ann's Warehouse," *The Village Voice*, September 25. http://www.villagevoice.com/content/printVersion/ 211433 (accessed April 24, 2009).

Şenoçak, Zafer. 2000. *Atlas of a Tropical Germany: Essays on Politics and Culture, 1990–1998*, trans. and ed. Leslie Adelson. Lincoln: University of Nebraska Press.

Shah, Nayan. 2001. *Contagious Divides: Epidemics and Race in San Francisco's Chinatown.* Berkeley: University of California Press.

Shatz, Adam. 2002. "The Torture of Algiers." *The New York Review of Books* 49, no. 18 (November 21). http://www.nybooks.com/articles/15824 (accessed August 10, 2008).

Shepperson, George. 1993. "African Diaspora: Concept and Context." In *Global Dimensions of the African Diaspora*, 2nd edition, ed. Joseph Harris. Washington, D.C.: Howard University Press.

Sid-Ahmed, Mohamed. 2004. "The Furore over Tariq Ramadan." *Al-Ahram*, January 1–7, No. 671. http://weekly.ahram.org.eg/2004/671/op3.htm (accessed November 22, 2008).

Sieg, Katrin. 2002. *Ethnic Drag: Performing Race, Nation, Sexuality in West Germany*. Ann Arbor: University of Michigan Press.

———. 2008. *Choreographing the Global in European Cinema and Theater*. New York: Palgrave Macmillan.

Smith, Craig. 2005. "France Has an Underclass, but Its Roots Are Still Shallow." *New York Times*, November 6. http://www.nytimes.com/2005/11/06/ week inreview/06smith.html (accessed December 13, 2008).

Skyt Nilsen, Helena, Michael Rosholm, Nina Smith, and Leif Husted. 2003. "The School-to-Work Transition of Second Generation Immigrants in Denmark." *Journal of Population Economics* 16, no. 4 (November):755–86.

Sow, Noah. 2008. *Deutschland Schwarz Weiss*. München: Bertelsmann.

Soysal, Yasemin N. 1994. *Limits of Citizenship: Migrants and Postnational Membership in Europe*. Chicago: The University of Chicago Press.

———. 2000. "Citizenship and Identity: Living in Diasporas in Post-war Europe?" *Ethnic and Racial Studies* 23, no. 1:1–15.

Spivak, Gayatri Chakravorty. 1988. "Can the Subaltern Speak?" In *Marxism and the Interpretation of Culture*, eds. Cary Nelson and Larry Grossberg. 217–313. Urbana: University of Illinois Press.

Stein, Arlene. 1997. "Sisters and Queers: The Decentering of Lesbian Feminism." In *The Gender/Sexuality Reader*, eds. Roger Lancaster and Micaela di Leonardo, 378–91. New York: Routledge.

Stoler, Ann L. 1995. *Race and the Education of Desire: Foucault's History of Sexuality and the Colonial Order of Things*. Durham, N.C.: Duke University Press.

Strange Fruit. 1997. *Strange Fruit Files 1992–1996*. Amsterdam.

Sudbury, Julia. 1997. *"Other Kinds of Dreams": Black Women's Organisations and the Politics of Transformation*. New York: Routledge.

Suleiman, Susan Rubin. 2006. *Crises of Memory and the Second World War*. Cambridge, Mass.: Harvard University Press.

Taiwo, Olufemi. 1998. "Exorcising Hegel's Ghost: Africa's Challenge to Philosophy." *African Studies Quarterly* 1, no. 4. http://web.africa.ufl.edu/asq/v1/4/ 2.htm (accessed November 30, 2008).

Tarrow, Sidney. 2005. *The New Transnational Activism*. Cambridge: Cambridge University Press.

Taylor, Diana. 2003. *The Archive and the Repertoire: Performing Cultural Memory in the Americas*. Durham, N.C.: Duke University Press.

Terkessidis, Mark. 2004. *Die Banalität des Rassismus. Migranten zweiter Generation entwickeln eine neue Perspektive*. Transcript: Bielefeld.

Terkessidis, Mark, and Yasemin Karakasoglu. 2006. "Gerechtigkeit für die Muslime!" *Die Zeit*, February 1. http://www.zeit.de/2006/06/Petition?page=all (accessed February 13, 2010).

Thalhammer, Eva, Vlasta Zucha, Edith Enzenhofer, Brigitte Salfinger, and Günther Ogris. 2001. *Attitudes towards Minority Groups in the European Union: A*

Special Analysis of the Eurobarometer 2000 Survey on Behalf of the European Monitoring Centre on Racism and Xenophobia. Vienna: SORA.

Thiel, Marie-Jo, ed. 2004. *Europa, Religion und Kultur angesichts des Rassismus: Impulse aus der internationalen Konferenz.* (Strassburg August 2003) Münster: Lit.

Torres-Saillant, Silvio. 2000. "The Tribulations of Blackness: Stages in Dominican Racial Identity." *Callaloo,* 23, no. 3:1086–111.

Travis, Alan, and Madeleine Bunting. 2004. "British Muslims Want Islamic Law and Prayers at Work." *The Guardian,* November 30.

Traynor, Ian. 2007. "Feminist, Socialist, Devout Muslim: Woman Who Has Thrown Denmark into Turmoil. Parliamentary Candidate, 25, Finds Herself at Centre of Europe-Wide Controversy." *The Guardian,* May 16. http://www.guardian.co.uk/world/2007/may/16/religion.uk (accessed February 13, 2010).

———. 2008. "Haemorrhaging of Western Influence at UN Wrecks Attempts to Push Human Rights Agenda." *The Guardian,* September 18. http://www.guardian.co.uk/world/2008/sep/18/unitednations.china (accessed February 13, 2010).

Tronti, Mario. 1974. *Arbeiter und Kapital.* Frankfurt a. M.: Verlag Neue Kritik.

Trouillot, Michel-Rolph. 1995. *Silencing the Past: Power and the Production of History.* Boston, Mass.: Beacon Press.

Tzortzis, Andreas. 2006. "In Europe, Quizzes Probe Values of Potential Citizens." *Christian Science Monitor,* April 10. 4. http://www.csmonitor.com/ 2006/0410/p01s04-woeu.html?s =widep (accessed November 30, 2008).

Union of Capitals of the European Union. 2003. "Integration of the Immigrant Population in European Capitals." Report for the XLIII General Assembly of the UCEU, Brussels.

"UNCHR wirft Deutschland in Fluechtlingsfrage Voelkerrechtsbruch vor." 2007. *Deutsche Presse Agentur.* http://www.thevoiceforum.org/node/553 August 10 (accessed August 12, 2008).

United Nations. 1990. "International Convention on the Protection of the Rights of All Migrant Workers and Members of Their Families." December 18. http://www.un.org/documents/ga/res/45/a45r158.htm (accessed February 13, 2010).

Vaterlaus, Anne-Marie. 2006. "Les Minguettes." *Neue Zürcher Zeitung,* December 9. http://www.nzz.ch/2006/12/09/fe/articleEN2G2.html?printview=true (accessed December 2, 2008).

Walcott, Rinaldo. 2003. "Outside in Black Studies: Reading from a Queer Place in the Diaspora." In Johnson and Henderson, 90–105.

Wang, Oliver. 2006. "These Are the Breaks: Hip-Hop and AfroAsian Cultural (Dis)Connections." In Raphael-Hernandez and Steen, 146–64.

Ward, Lucy. 2007. "Where You Live Can Be Crucial to Your Future." *The Guardian online,* September 8. http://society.guardian.co.uk/communities/story/0,,2164822,00.html?gusrc=rss&feed=networkfront (accessed August 12, 2008).

Waterfield, Bruno, Henry Samuel, and Nick Squires. 2009. "European Elections 2009: Far-Right and Fringe Parties Make Gains across Europe amid Low Turnout." *The Telegraph*, June 8. http://www.telegraph.co.uk/news/worldnews/europe/eu/5471893/European-elections-2009-far-Right-and-fringe-parties-make-gains-across-Europe-amid-low-turnout.html (accessed July 24, 2009).

Watkins, S. Craig. 2005. *Hip-Hop Matters: Politics, Pop Culture, and the Struggle for the Soul of a Movement.* Boston: Beacon Press.

Weber, Beverly. 2004. "Cloth on Her Head, Constitution in Hand: Germany's Headscarf Debates and the Cultural Politics of Difference." *German Politics and Society* 22:481–513.

Weheliye, Alexander. 2005. *Phonographies: Grooves in Sonic Afro-modernity.* Durham, N.C.: Duke University Press.

Weigl, Andreas. 2009. *Migration und Integration. Eine widersprüchliche Geschichte.* Wien: Studien Verlag.

Weiss, Moni. 1993. "Profiel van een organisatie. ARGAN. Organisatie Marokkaanse Vrouwen Amsterdam." *ZAMI krant* 3:45–48.

Werman, Marco. 2006. "France: Soundtrack to a Riot. A Rap of Protest from the Ghetto." *Frontline World*, March 28.

West, Tim'm. 2005. "Keepin' It Real: Disidentification and Its Discontents." In Elam and Jackson, 162–84.

Westin, Charles. 2003. "Young People of Migrant Origin in Sweden." *International Migration Review* 37, no. 4:987–1010.

Wheeler, Jacob. 2008. "Caricaturing Danish Muslims." *In These Times*, March 28. http://www.inthesetimes.com/article/3576/caricaturing_danish_muslims (accessed February 13, 2010).

Whitney, Craig. 2007. "Maurice Papon, Convicted Vichy Official, 96, Dies." *The New York Times*, February 18. http://www.nytimes.com/2007/02/18/world/europe/ 18papon .html?_r=1&pagewanted=2 (accessed December 2, 2008).

Wiese, Heike. 2009. "Grammatical Innovation in Multiethnic Urban Europe: New Linguistic Practices among Adolescents." *Lingua* 119:782–806.

Wild, Beate. 2008. "Vor zehn Jahren: Der Fall Mehmet. Der "Schrecken von Neuperlach." *Die Sueddeutsche*, November 14. http://www.sueddeutsche.de/muenchen/652/331511/text/ (accessed June 13, 2009).

Willenbücher, Michael. 2007. *Das Scharnier der Macht. Der Illegalisierte als homo sacer des Postfordismus.* Berlin: b_books.

Wolf, Joachim. 2007. "Fußball und Rechtsextremismus in Europa." February 15. http://www.bpb.de/themen/4IFKR4,0,Fu%DFball_und_Rechtsextremismus_in_Europa.html (accessed July 10, 2009).

Women's Caucus for the Modern Language Association, ed. 2000. *Concerns*, 27:3–4.

Wright, Michelle. 2004. *Becoming Black: Creating Identity in the African Diaspora.* Durham, N.C.: Duke University Press.

Yalcin, Lale. 1998. "Growing Up As a Muslim in Germany." In *Muslim European Youth: Reproducing Ethnicity, Religion, Culture*, eds. Steven Vertovec and Alisdar Rogers. 167–91. Aldershot: Ashgate.

Yoneyama, Lisa. 2003. "Traveling Memories, Contagious Justice." *JAAS* 6, no. 1:57–93.

Young, Marion Iris. 2003. "Europe and the Global South: Towards a Circle of Equality." August 20. http://www.opendemocracy.net/globalization-europefuture/article_1438.jsp (accessed November 30, 2008).

Youssef, Magdi. 2006. "Circles to Be Squared." *Al-Ahram*, 11–17. May. http://weekly.ahram.org.eg/2006/794/cu2.htm (accessed December 2, 2008).

Yue, Ming-Bao. 2000. "On Not Looking German: Ethnicity, Diaspora and the Politics of Vision." *European Journal of Cultural Studies* 3, no. 2:173–94.

Zaimoğlu, Feridun. 1995. *Kanak Sprak: 24 Misstöne vom Rande der Gesellschaft.* Berlin: Rotbuch Verlag.

Zaimoğlu, Feridun, and Guenter Senkel. 2008. *Schwarze Jungfrauen.* Hamburg: Hoffmann und Campe (Audio CD).

ZAMI Krant 3. 1993.

Zemouri, Aziz. 2005. *Faut-il faire taire Tariq Ramadan (suivi d'un entretien avec Tariq Ramadan).* Paris: L'Archipel.

Ziegler, Jean. 2005. *L'empire de la honte.* Paris: Fayard.

Žižek, Slavoj. 2001. "A Leftist Plea for 'Eurocentrism.'" In *Unpacking Europe*, eds. Salah Hassan and Iftikhar Dadi, 112–30. Rotterdam: NAI.

Zucker, Renee. 2005. "Die Macht der Muetter." *Die Tageszeitung*, March 5. 22.

Zumach, Andreas. 2006. "Schweizer Rechte legen nach." *Die Tageszeitung*, September 10.

Mbembe, Achille, xxxvii, 190n26
McClintock, Anne, 83, 92
Meli, 30
memory: crisis, 174; defined, 61; and
    diaspora, 61–62, 77–79, 164; and
    exclusion, 4–5; selecting, 167. *See
    also* amnesia
MIB. *See* Mouvement de l'Immigration
    et des Banlieues (MIB)
Middle Passage, 45, 59, 78, 195n16
migrants/migration: adaptation by, xii;
    and belonging, 53; and citizenship,
    23, 53; containers for, 166; and
    deindustrialization, 20–21; and
    diaspora, 51; as ethnicized, xiv;
    female experience, 154; and
    feminist/queer critique, xvi; and
    homeland, 51, 78; labor, xiv, xxix,
    14, 19, 21–22, 23, 89, 92, 139, 145;
    literature, xxxviii; marginalization
    of, xii; as minoritarian, xxx;
    patterns, xiv; permanent, 146;
    permanent status as, xxxiii; and
    racialized communities, xxi; and
    racism, xxvii–xxviii; second-
    generation, xvii, xxi, xxiii, xxix–
    xxx, xliv, 98, 157; shared history
    of, 4, 78, 165; studies, xxiii, xxvii,
    xxxi, xli, 50–60, 91; survival
    of, xxxvi; third-generation, xxi,
    xxii, xxix; traditions of, 136; and
    transnational ties, xxxv, 47; use
    of term, 179–80n4; worldwide
    movements, 3. *See also* minorities
minorities: and belonging, xxx–
    xxxii, xxxiii, 4–5, 158, 160, 176;
    citizenship rights, 2, 53; cultural
    productions of, xxxviii; and
    European cohesiveness, 159–60;
    identity of, xxi–xxiii, xxx, xxxvii,
    34, 68, 167, 170; as insider/outsider,
    xxx–xxxii, 169; invisibility of,
    xxii, xxiii, xxvii, 158, 168–69;

media representations of, 151;
    multiculturalism in communities,
    xii, 40; and nationalism, xx; as
    permanent migrants, 146; racialized,
    xvii, xix, xxi–xxii, xxviii–xxix,
    xxxix–xl, xlv, 2, 19, 28, 50, 121,
    139, 169, 173–74, 180n4; structural
    violence against, 24; survival of,
    xxxiii, xxxvi; as threat, xxxii;
    traditions of, 136; visible, xv, xxi,
    xxxii. *See also* migrants/migration
minority youth: as agents, xxxvi–xxxvii;
    and belonging, 27, 140; defined as
    migrants, 21; exclusion of, 7, 21;
    homophobia among, 129; mobility
    of, xl, 28; rights, 26; violent, 15, 21,
    24, 28, 139. *See also* hip-hop culture;
    urban youth
Moor, Margriet de, 90, 101, 118
Moraga, Cherríe, xxxiv, 62
motherhood, 68
Mouvement de l'Immigration et des
    Banlieues (MIB), 15–16
Mudure, Michaela, 195n17
multiculturalism: chaos from, 209n11;
    and cross-identifications, xlvi;
    failure of, xxxi–xxxii, 14–19,
    86, 108, 121, 146–47; gaze,
    144–51; and liberalism, 90, 98,
    116, 138, 145–46, 157, 160–61;
    minority communities, xii, 40;
    and neoliberalism, 150; and street
    slang, xi; and WWII, 8
multiethnolects, xii, 183n15
Muñoz, José Esteban, xxxiii–xxxiv,
    xxxvi, 27, 68, 69, 141, 142, 172
Murder in Amsterdam (Buruma), 105–6
Museum of Europe, xlvi, 163–67,
    172–73
Muslims: characteristics, 15; difference,
    80, 81, 83, 93, 95, 101–2, 113,
    116–17, 122; escape narratives,
    100–107; homophobia of, 94,

Fatima El-Tayeb is associate professor of literature and ethnic studies at the University of California, San Diego. She is the author of *Schwarze Deutsche: Rasse und nationale Identität, 1890–1933*.

89194691R00179

Made in the USA
Middletown, DE
14 September 2018